UNITED ISLANDS? THE LANGUAGES OF RESISTANCE

Poetry and Song in the Age of Revolution

Series Editors: Michael Brown
   John Kirk
   Andrew Noble

Forthcoming Titles

Literacy and Orality in Eighteenth-Century Irish Song
Julie Henigan

Cultures of Radicalism in Britain and Ireland
John Kirk, Michael Brown and Andrew Noble (eds)

UNITED ISLANDS? THE LANGUAGES OF RESISTANCE

EDITED BY

John Kirk, Andrew Noble and Michael Brown

Routledge
Taylor & Francis Group
LONDON AND NEW YORK

First published 2012 by Pickering & Chatto (Publishers) Limited

Published 2016 by Routledge
2 Park Square, Milton Park, Abingdon, Oxfordshire OX14 4RN
711 Third Avenue, New York, NY 10017, USA

First issued in paperback 2015

Routledge is an imprint of the Taylor & Francis Group, an informa business

© Taylor & Francis 2012
© John Kirk, Andrew Noble and Michael Brown 2012

To the best of the Publisher's knowledge every effort has been made to contact relevant copyright holders and to clear any relevant copyright issues. Any omissions that come to their attention will be remedied in future editions.

All rights reserved, including those of translation into foreign languages. No part of this book may be reprinted or reproduced or utilised in any form or by any electronic, mechanical, or other means, now known or hereafter invented, including photocopying and recording, or in any information storage or retrieval system, without permission in writing from the publishers.

Notice:
Product or corporate names may be trademarks or registered trademarks, and are used only for identification and explanation without intent to infringe.

BRITISH LIBRARY CATALOGUING IN PUBLICATION DATA

United islands?: the languages of resistance. – (Poetry and song in the age of revolution)
1. Protest literature, English – History and criticism. 2. Politics and literature – Great Britain – History – 18th century. 3. Politics and literature – Great Britain – History – 19th century. 4. English literature – 18th century – History and criticism. 5. English literature – 19th century – History and criticism.
I. Series II. Brown, Michael. III. Kirk, John. IV. Noble, Andrew.
820.9'358-dc23

ISBN-13: 978-1-138-66203-2 (pbk)
ISBN-13: 978-1-8489-3340-8 (hbk)

Typeset by Pickering & Chatto (Publishers) Limited

CONTENTS

Acknowledgements	vii
List of Figures and Tables	ix
List of Contributors	xi
Introduction: The Languages of Resistance: National Particularities, Universal Aspirations – *Andrew Noble*	1
1 Reading the English Political Songs of the 1790s – *Michael Scrivener*	35
2 Why should the Landlords have the Best Songs? Thomas Spence and the Subversion of Popular Song – *Joan Beal*	51
3 'Bard of Liberty': Iolo Morganwg, Wales and Radical Song – *Mary-Ann Constantine and Elizabeth Edwards*	63
4 Canonicity and Radical Evangelicalism: The Case of Thomas Kelly – *Mark S. Sweetnam*	77
5 Charlotte Brooke's *Reliques of Irish Poetry*: Eighteenth-Century 'Irish Song' and the Politics of Remediation – *Leith Davis*	95
6 Homology, Analogy and the Perception of Irish Radicalism – *Vincent Morley*	109
7 Lost Manuscripts and Reactionary Rustling: Was there a Radical Scottish Gaelic Poetry between 1770 and 1820? – *Peter Mackay*	125
8 Virile Vernaculars: Radical Sexuality as Social Subversion in Irish Chapbook Verse, 1780–1820 – *Andrew Carpenter*	141
9 Thomas Moore and the Problem of Colonial Masculinity in Irish Romanticism – *Julia M. Wright*	153
10 Radical Politics and Dialect in the British Archipelago – *R. Stephen Dornan*	167
11 'Theaw Kon Ekspect No Mooar Eawt ov a Pig thin a Grunt': Searching for the Radical Dialect Voice in Industrial Lancashire and the West Riding, 1798–1819 – *Katrina Navickas*	181
Afterword: The Languages of Resistance – *Katie Trumpener*	195
Notes	207
Works Cited	237
Index	255

ACKNOWLEDGEMENTS

The papers in this volume were originally presented at one or other of two symposia entitled *United Islands? Multi-Lingual Radical Poetry and Song in Britain and Ireland, 1770–1820* which were held at Queen's University Belfast from 13–15 November 2008 and 26–29 August 2009 as part of an AHRC Research Networks and Grants Project under the same name. We gratefully acknowledge the financial support of the AHRC for these two symposia. The first symposium doubled-up as the 8th Language and Politics Symposium of the Gaeltacht and Scotstacht within the AHRC Research Institute of Irish and Scottish Studies, University of Aberdeen, to which we are indebted for further substantial funding. Additional funding came from Foras na Gaeilge.

Between the two symposia, there was a total of 120 invited participants – many more participants than are represented in this volume or its companion volume: *United Islands? The Cultures of Radicalism in Britain and Ireland* edited by John Kirk, Michael Brown, and Andrew Noble, in the present series. We wish to acknowledge each of their contributions, especially those who chaired sessions or gave papers in response to our invitations, or acted as rapporteurs. To this last group we are especially indebted: at the first symposium: John Barrell, Claire Connolly, Jon Mee, and Katie Trumpener; at the second symposium: Michael Scrivener, Fred Lock, and Mark Philp. Each of their contributions accumulatively brought together the main inter-connecting strands of this literary and political matrix and greatly sharpened our own thinking. Katie Trumpener's Rapport was written up soon afterwards and is to be read here as an occasional piece. We are deeply obliged to Professor Trumpener for allowing us to reproduce her Rapport here.

At each symposium, there was a multi-lingual concert of song of the types which we are dealing with in these essays, and to which Katie Trumpener refers. There sang, at the first symposium: Ciaran Carson, Maggie MacInnes, accompanied by Brian MacAlpine, Dafydd Idris Edwards, and Terry Moylan; at the second symposium Ciaran Carson, Dafydd Idris Edwards, James Flannery, and Adam McNaughtan. We are deeply indebted to each of them not only for their renditions but also for sharing with us their extraordinary rich knowledge of this song material.

At each symposium, there was a reception at the Linenhall Library, Belfast, founded in 1788 as the Belfast Reading Society. In 2008, the reception coincided with The Thomas Moore 2008 Festival Travelling Exhibition 'My Gentle Harp: Thomas Moore's Irish Melodies, 1808–2008', about which John Gray, the then Librarian, and Siobhan Fitzpatrick of the Royal Irish Academy, spoke. In 2009, John Killen, incoming Librarian, spoke of the 'Hidden Gems of Radical Poetry in the Linen Hall Library Poetry Collection' ahead of a tour of the Linen Hall Library Archives. It is always a pleasure to work with the Linenhall Library and its Librarians, and those present on each happy occasion are indebted for their hospitality as well as their erudition.

For the help of our colleagues, we are grateful especially to Ciaran Carson, Cairns Craig, Donall Ó Baoill, and John Thompson.

We are indebted to Pickering & Chatto for agreeing to publish a new series in the area: *Political Poetry and Song in the Age of Revolution*, of which this volume is to be the first volume, and the companion volume: *United Islands? The Cultures of Radicalism in Britain and Ireland,* the third in the series. See www.pickeringchatto.com/series/poetry_and_song_in_the_age_of_revolution for further details. As our blurb states: 'Titles in this series will appeal to those involved in English literary studies, as well as those working in fields of study that cover Enlightenment, Romanticism and Revolution in the last quarter of the eighteenth century. Scholars working within the disciplines of English, History, Music, Celtic Studies and Politics will find the series of interest, as will researchers whose wider concerns pertain to cultural history, anthropology and the history of philosophy, communications and linguistics.'

John Kirk, Andrew Noble, and Michael Brown
March 2012

LIST OF FIGURES AND TABLES

Figure 5.1: J.C. Walker, 'Provincial Cries' 101
Figure 5.2: William Beauford, 'Caoinan: *or some Account* of the
   ANTIENT IRISH LAMENTATIONS' 102
Figure 5.3: C. Brooke, *Reliques of Irish Poetry* 106

Table 2.1: Spence's songs and their settings 56
Table 2.2: Comparison of the 'Jubilee Hymn' with Isaiah 14
   (King James Bible) 59

LIST OF CONTRIBUTORS

Joan C. Beal is Professor of English Language at the University of Sheffield. She has research interests in the history of Late Modern English (1700–1945) and dialect and identity in northern England. She was a co-investigator on the AHRC-funded Newcastle Electronic Corpus of Tyneside English (NECTE) project. Her *English Pronunciation in the Eighteenth Century: Thomas Spence's 'Grand Repository of the English Language'* (Oxford: Clarendon Press, 1999) was concerned with a pronouncing dictionary written in 1775 by the Newcastle-born radical, Thomas Spence, the subject of her paper in this volume. More recent publications include *English in Modern Times 1700–1945* (London: Arnold, 2004); *Language and Region* (London: Routledge, 2006); *An Introduction to Regional Englishes: Dialect Variation in England* (Edinburgh: Edinburgh University Press, 2010); and (with Lourdes Burbano-Elizondo and Carmen Llamas) *Urban North-Eastern English: Tyneside to Teesside* (Edinburgh: Edinburgh University Press, 2012).

Michael Brown is Senior Lecturer in Irish and Scottish History at the University of Aberdeen and Acting Director of the Research Institute of Irish and Scottish Studies. As well as being a co-director of the AHRC network grant *United Islands? Multi-Lingual Radical Poetry and Song in Britain and Ireland, 1770–1820* in 2008–9 he has directed an AHRC project on Irish and Scottish Diasporas since 1600 (2006–11). His primary research focus is on comparative Enlightenment, and he is the author of *Francis Hutcheson in Dublin* (Dublin: Four Courts Press, 2002) and *A Political Biography of John Toland* (London: Pickering & Chatto, 2011). He is currently finishing a study entitled *The Irish Enlightenment*.

Andrew Carpenter is Emeritus Professor of English at University College Dublin where he taught for nearly forty years. He spent eight years as Dean of Arts and Director of Development, but has otherwise devoted himself to researching the writing – particularly the poetry – of seventeenth- and eighteenth-century Ireland. He has written extensively on the period and edited many texts. His best known publications are the two anthologies *Verse in English from Tudor* *and Stuart Ireland* (Cork: Cork University Press 2003) and *Verse in English from Eighteenth-Century Ireland* (Cork: Cork University Press 1998). He was founding chairman of the Eighteenth-Century Ireland Society and founding editor of the journal *Eighteenth-Century Ireland*.

Mary-Ann Constantine is Senior Research Fellow at the University of Wales Centre for Advanced Welsh and Celtic Studies. She is currently Principal Investigator on a four-year AHRC-funded project, 'Wales and the French Revolution', and (with Dafydd Johnston) General Editor for the resulting series of volumes under the same name (University of Wales Press). Her main research is in the literature and history of Romantic-era Wales; her publications include *Breton Ballads* (Aberystwyth: CMCS publications, 1996); (with Gerald Porter) *Fragments and Meaning in Traditional Song* (Oxford: British Academy/Oxford University Press, 2003) and *"The Truth Against the World": Iolo Morganwg and Romantic Forgery* (Cardiff: University of Wales Press, 2007).

Leith Davis is Professor of English at Simon Fraser University in Greater Vancouver, Canada. She is a co-founder of the Department of English's MA with Specialisation in Print Culture and currently serves as the Director of the Centre for Scottish Studies. She has received numerous awards from the Social Sciences and Humanities Research Council of Canada over her career, including a grant for her current book project on 'Transnational Articulations: Britain, Print Culture and Globalization, 1689–1763'. She is the author of *Acts of Union: Scotland and the Negotiation of the British Nation* (Stanford: Stanford University Press, 1998) and *Music, Postcolonialism and Gender: The Construction of Irish National Identity, 1725–1875* (Notre Dame, IN: Notre Dame University Press, 2005) and co-editor of *Scotland and the Borders of Romanticism* (Cambridge: Cambridge University Press, 2004) and *Robert Burns and Transatlantic Culture* (Farnham: Ashgate, 2012).

R. Stephen Dornan completed his doctoral thesis entitled 'Irish and Scottish Poetry in the Romantic Era' at the Research Institute of Irish and Scottish Studies at the University of Aberdeen in 2006. From 2006–10, he was Post-doctoral Research Fellow for the AHRC-funded project 'The Development of Representations of Dialect in the Novel in Ireland and Scotland in the Nineteenth Century'. His research interests are primarily in eighteenth- and nineteenth-century Irish, Scottish and Ulster Scots poetry, about which he has published several articles in *Scottish Studies Review*, *Irish Studies Review* and the *Journal of Irish and Scottish Studies*.

Elizabeth Edwards is Research Fellow at the University of Wales Centre for Advanced Welsh and Celtic Studies, Aberystwyth, where she works on the AHRC-funded project 'Wales and the French Revolution'. She has written articles on Welsh Gothic, and war poetry from Revolution-era Wales, and recently completed an anthology of poetry, *English-Language Poetry from Wales 1789–1806* (University of Wales Press, forthcoming). She is currently working on an edition of the poetry of Richard Llwyd, 'Bard of Snowdon'.

John Kirk is Senior Lecturer in English and Scottish Language at Queen's University Belfast. During 2008–9, with Michael Brown and Andrew Noble, he held an AHRC Research Networks and Workshops Grant for the project which lies behind the present volume: *United Islands? Multi-Lingual Radical Poetry and Song in Britain and Ireland, 1770–1820*. With primary research interests in dialectology and corpus linguistics, his most recent books are (with Jeffrey L. Kallen) *SPICE-Ireland: A User's Guide* (Belfast: Cló Ollscoil na Banríona, 2012) and (co-edited with Iseabail MacLeod) *Scots: The Language and its Literature: A Festschrift for J. Derrick McClure* (Amsterdam: Rodopi, 2012).

Peter Mackay is Sgrìobhadair, or Writer-in-Residence, at Sabhal Mòr Ostaig. He has worked as a Research Fellow at the Seamus Heaney Centre for Poetry, Queen's University, Belfast, as an Associate Lecturer at Trinity College, Dublin, and as a Broadcast Journalist for BBC Alba. His primary research focus is on contemporary poetry from Scotland and Ireland, Romantic literature and Scottish Gaelic poetry. His monograph *Sorley MacLean* was published in 2010 (Aberdeen: Research Institue of Irish and Scottish Studies), and he is co-editor of *Modern Irish and Scottish Poetry* (Cambridge: Cambridge University Press, 2011). He is currently co-editing a collection of essays on twentieth-century Scottish Gaelic literature and also an anthology of transgressive and erotic Gaelic verse.

Vincent Morley is an independent scholar who works in the public service in Dublin. His main research interest is Irish popular culture from the mid-seventeenth to the mid-nineteenth centuries. He is author of *Irish Opinion and the American Revolution, 1760–1783* (Cambridge: Cambridge University Press, 2002) and *Ó Chéitinn go Raiftearaí: mar a cumadh stair na hÉireann* (Dublin: Coiscéim, 2011). His edition of the selected verse of Aodh Buí Mac Cruitín (*c.*1680–1755) will be published by Field Day Publications in 2012.

Katrina Navickas is Lecturer in History at the University of Hertfordshire. She is Communications Officer of the Social History Society. Her main research interests are popular politics in the eighteenth and nineteenth centuries, and spaces, place and regional identities. Her first monograph is *Loyalism and Radicalism in Lancashire, 1798–1815* (Oxford: Oxford University Press, 2009), and she has published articles on the Luddites, Swing rioters, Chartists and political clothing. She is currently completing a monograph on the spaces and places of popular protest in northern England, 1789–1848.

Andrew Noble is a graduate of Aberdeen and Sussex Universities. He was also a Junior Research Fellow at Peterhouse, Cambridge. His teaching career was entirely at Strathclyde University, where he was for a time Head of the English Literature Section. He specialised in teaching American Literature and Romanticism. Before his retirement, he was the Convenor of the Irish-Scottish Academic Initiative. His published research is mainly in Scottish literature and film. His extensive writings on Burns culminated in the publication of the joint-edition with Patrick Scott Hogg of *The Canongate Burns* (2001, 2003). He has recently been appointed Honorary Visiting Senior Lecturer in the School of English, Queen's University Belfast.

Michael Scrivener, Professor of English at Wayne State University, has published books on Percy Shelley (*Radical Shelley: The Philosophical Anarchism and Utopian Thought of Percy Bysshe Shelley*, Princeton: Princeton University Press, 1982), John Thelwall (*Seditious Allegories: John Thelwall and Jacobin Writing*, Penn State University Press, 2001; 'Incle and Yarico' and 'The Incas': *Two Plays by John Thelwall*, Madison NJ: Fairleigh Dickinson, 2006), Romantic verse in political periodicals (*Poetry and Reform: Periodic Verse from the English Democratic Press, 1792–1824*, Detroit: Wayne State, 1992) and cosmopolitanism (*Cosmopolitan Ideal in the Age of Revolution and Reaction, 1776–1832*, London: Pickering & Chatto, 2007). His new monograph, *Jewish Representation in British Literature, 1780–1840: After Shylock* was published in 2011 by Palgrave Macmillan.

Mark S. Sweetnam is a post-doctoral fellow specializing in Digital Humanities within the School of History and Humanities at Trinity College Dublin, where he gained his PhD in English Literature in 2008 for a thesis entitled 'John Donne and Religious Authority in the Reformed English Church'. His research interests and publications are in the area of literature and theology, with a particular focus on the early-modern period and evangelical writing. He is the editor of a number of volumes, including most recently *Enigma and Revelation in Renaissance English Literature* (2012) and the *Minutes of the Antrim Ministers' Meeting 1654–1658* (2012). As well as a number of scholarly articles and works at popular level, he is the author of *John Donne and Religious Authority in the Reformed English Church* (forthcoming) (each Dublin: Four Courts Press).

Katie Trumpener is Emily Sanford Professor of English and Comparative Literature at Yale University. Her comparative publications on Scottish and Irish literature include *Bardic Nationalism: The Romantic Novel and the British Empire* (Princeton: Princeton University Press, 1997, awarded the British Academy's Rose Mary Crawshay Prize and the MLA Prize for a First Book), her *Cambridge Companion to Fiction in the Romantic Period*, co-edited with Richard Maxwell (Cambridge: Cambridge University Press, 2008) and the articles 'The Peripheral Rise of the Novel: Ireland, Scotland and the politic of form' in Liam McIlvanney and Raymond Ryan (eds), *Ireland and Scotland: Culture and Society* (Dublin: Four Courts Press, 2005) and 'Annals of Ice: Formations of Empire, Place and History in John Galt and Alice Munro' in Michael Gardiner, Graeme MacDonald and Niall O'Gallagher (eds), *Scottish Literature and Postcolonial Literature* (Edinburgh: Edinburgh University Press, 2010). She has also published widely on Central European literature and film.

Julia M. Wright is Canada Research Chair in European Studies at Dalhousie University, and Acting Co-Director of Dalhousie's Centre for European Studies. She has been awarded grants from the Social Sciences and Humanities Research Council of Canada (four since 1997), the Canada Foundation for Innovation (two since 2002) and the Aid to Scholarly Publications Program (2004). Her research focuses on ideas of the nation in Irish and British literature, especially in the Romantic period. Her most recent monograph is *Ireland, India and Nationalism in Nineteenth-Century Literature* (Cambridge: Cambridge University Press, 2007), and her most recent edited books are *Irish Literature, 1750–1900: An Anthology* (Oxford: Wiley-Blackwell, 2008), *Reading the Nation in English Literature: A Critical Reader* (London: Routledge, 2009), *Companion to Irish Literature*, 2 vols (Oxford: Wiley-Blackwell, 2010) and *Handbook to Romanticism Studies* (Oxford: Wiley-Blackwell, 2012). She also co-edits, with Kevin Hutchings, the Ashgate Series in Nineteenth-Century Transatlantic Studies, and recently co-founded the refereed journal, *European Studies: History, Society, and Culture*.

INTRODUCTION
THE LANGUAGES OF RESISTANCE: NATIONAL PARTICULARITIES, UNIVERSAL ASPIRATIONS

Andrew Noble

> Poetical work, Aristotle said, is more philosophical than history. If this is so then it is also more 'historical' than history, as Nietzsche argued, because the 'history' that poems touch and re-present encompasses a far greater scale of possible, and therefore real, human times and events than the most careful and scholarly historical text.
>
> Jerome McGann[1]

In writing this introduction to these two volumes of essays derived from two symposia at Queen's University Belfast on *United Islands? Multilingual Radical Poetry and Folk-Song in Britain and Ireland 1770–1820*,[2] I am perhaps less, but certainly differently, apprehensive than when with my fellow editors we were formulating an AHRC Research Networking application which required for its success high quality, scholarly, interdisciplinary participation from England, Scotland, Wales, Ulster and the Irish Republic and, not least, North America. If we asked them, would they come? The response was, in fact, so positive that, some participants returning, we had to hold a second symposium. Fearing a famine, we actually had a feast.

I will later return as to why there was such a convergence of geographically diverse talents on Queen's University. For the moment my partly-retrospective belief is that Belfast itself, the ghostly historical political and sectarian pressures of the 1790s wholly precursive of the city's still severe contemporary divisions, significantly brought home to the participants, as perhaps no other British city could, the relevance of the 1790s to our present condition. Despite Wordsworth's insistence on the pastoral imagination, song-filled British cities were the key centres not only of conflicting political activity but literary creativity in this period. Belfast, as Ireland, was the site of actual violence. It was here that the American influenced Volunteers were formed initiating a trail of violence that was to lead to Wexford and 30,000 Irish dead in 1798. Consequent of this was the birth of the hyper-loyalist Orange Order which was to be carried back to Scotland by soldiers returning from the Irish killing fields where, as in Ireland, if more insidious and covert, its toxic memories and impulses seem to have a longevity akin to that of radioactive waste. Hopefully what we now see in Belfast after two centuries is closure and not a city, increasingly economically depressed by the self-destructive fiscal tendencies of London and Dublin, in temporary respite care. It has, however, emerged from the last near forty years with sectarian ghettoized streets and a conflict of languages so extreme that Ulster Scots and Irish Gaelic are in a near state of civil war.

If Belfast represented to the symposia participants the British problem *in extremis*, Queen's University with its Seamus Heaney Centre for Poetry offered not so much a consolatory place as an antidotal one. For it is here that English and Irish Gaelic freely mingle in song and poetry. Indeed, as in Seamus Heaney's poetry, there is a spirit of reconciliation about the place, making it the ideal centre for open discussion among the four British nations as to what happened among them two centuries ago. Hugh Kearney provides, in my opinion, a historical context which is altruistically synonymous with both Heaney as poet and translator:

> From this point of view, it is an action of history that several states (nations?) eventually made their appearance in the context of British Isles history. The realities with which historians should deal are the cultures which lay behind the label nation/state. The concept of 'nation' stresses the difference between a particular society and its neighbours. A Britannic approach, in contrast, would emphasize how much these cultures have experienced in common.[3]

The Heaney Centre, in my experience, is also a place which echoes with multilingual song, with its Director, Ciaran Carson, as protean in performance as he is in the mastery of translation and different literary genres. It would surely be a place of celebration dear to Paul Gilroy's heart as described by Marina Warner:

> In eloquent indignation, Gilroy sets out how 'the wholesale privatization of culture' transforms the 'mechanisms of social memory', damaging people's sense of social groups, their history and consequently their identities. Gilroy sees music, and especially live music performed to live audiences as a powerful mode of cultural expression, with the potential to supersede individual interests and political antagonisms.[4]

It was this power of song from singers affiliated to the Heaney Centre combined with new voices which had, I believe, the deepest most lasting impact on the participants. As Katie Trumpener noted at the time:

> Music stirs the body – and song hence has a different, potentially deeper and more transformative effect on auditors than words alone would. Song was thus a crucial weapon in the rhetorical arsenal of political radicals – and of their opponents who on occasion used the singing of traditional religious and political anthems to buttress opposition of change.[5]

Since music does take us to the heart of the most public political conflicts of the period and because we academics, silent readers of the printed page, are generally less secure with that medium, I wish, before turning to the intimately related subject of poetry, to discuss the matter of how it might be resurrected for not only an academic audience. First, what is required is a new alliance between academics and the extraordinary qualities present among the performing and collecting folksong community. As Robert Darnton has recently argued 'we will never have an adequate history of communication until we can reconstruct its most important missing element: orality.'[6] Moreover, putting eighteenth-century dissident French song online, he contends, 'provides a way, however approximate, to know how messages were inflected by music, transmitted through the streets, and carried in the heads of Parisians more than two centuries ago'.[7]

Also, without denying Gilroy's assertion of song as therapy for 'political antagonisms', our study will of necessity reveal these songs as intensely factional. Indeed, it was in Belfast itself that the militia had to be summoned to deal with a riot caused by the singing of that battle hymn of the French Republic, 'Ça Ira'.[8]

Fortunately for evolving scholarship in the area of song as historical evidence, no less a scholar of the French Enlightenment, Darnton, has, as noted, turned his formidable erudite attention to this problem. He defines Paris as a song-saturated city as, indeed, does John Barrell London.[9] Darnton comments:

> The chansonniers make it clear that Parisians improvised new words to old tunes every day and on every possible subject – the love life of actresses, executions of criminals, the birth or death of members of the royal family, battles in times of war, taxes in times of peace, trials, bankruptcies, accidents, plays, comic operas, festivals, and all sorts of occurrences that fit into the capacious French category of *faits divers* (assorted events). A clever verse to a catchy tune spread through the streets with unstoppable force, and new verses frequently followed it, carried from one neighbourhood to another like gusts of wind. In a semiliterate society, songs functioned to a certain extent as newspapers. They provided a running commentary on current events.[10]

Having established this context, Darnton delivers a master class on the text of a poem forged in the vicious internal world of Versailles which, reaching the Paris streets, became musically attached to a popular seventeenth-century tune and took legs as variant songs among the populace. Darnton's account seems to me a template for what we might further hope to do in the world of political song, so I would like to give a brief summary of what he does with it. An attack by Louis XV's seemingly all-powerful, longest-serving minister, the Comte de Maurepas, brought about his own fall when it was finally discovered that he was the agent of a salacious attack on the king's mistress, Madame de Pompadour. A pastoral reference to de Pompadour bearing white flowers was in fact a sexual innuendo for her blanched venereal infected flow. In his initial attempt to locate the author of the song, the enraged king ordered his multitude of spies ('*mouches*') to track him down. This proved utterly impossible, for fourteen versions were traced to fourteen different authors. Such songs, therefore, both modified and added to, were the produce of what Darnton terms 'collective creation'.[11] This multiplicity of authorship can scarcely lead to the courthouse or the jail. As Darnton further remarks concerning regarding the sound of song to power:

> Song and sedition make a formidable combination, at least in the eyes of the police. There is something about words set to music that sets the teeth of the authorities on edge – not always and everywhere, but at certain times and places, particularly in semi-literate societies, where singing in the streets can mobilize passions more effectively than the printed word.[12]

If we move forward to Britain in the mid-1790s, seditious song is no longer merely mocking a degenerate aristocracy but expressive of a desire, albeit strongly French-inspired, to insurrection and the removal of the king. In consequence, loyal voices were raised in defence with singing voices prophesying civil war. Thus it was that the battle hymn of the new French Republic, 'Ça Ira', provoked a riot in Belfast itself which necessitated calling out the militia. Thus, too, it was with a degree of comic irony that Robert Burns, defined by John Thelwall as incomparably the best British songwriter of his age, was in 1792 in the audience of the Theatre Royal Dumfries when a rancorous song contest broke out. As he wrote to Mrs Frances Dunlop, a particularly ill-judged confidante in matters political, of this rammy:

> We, in this country, here have many alarms of the Reform, or rather the Republican spirit, of your part of the kingdom. – Indeed, we are a good deal in commotion ourselves, & in our Theatre here, 'God save the king' was met with some groans & hisses, while *Ça Ira* has been repeatedly called for. – For me, I am a *Placeman*, you know; a very humble one indeed, Heaven knows, but still so much as to gag me from joining in the cry. – What my private sentiments are, you will find out without an Interpreter.[13]

This letter to Mrs Dunlop was written on 6 December 1792, on 31 December 1792 he wrote to his excise supervisor, Robert Graham of Fintry, in markedly different tones:

> I believe, Sir, I may aver it, & and in the sight of Omnipotence, that I would not tell a deliberate Falsehood, no, not thought even worse horrors, if worse can be, than those I have mentioned, hung over my head; & I say, that the allegation, whatever villain has made it, is a Lie! To the British Constitution, on Revolution principles, next after my God, I am most devoutly attached![14]

We are indebted to Bob Harris to revealing the fact that Graham of Fintry was not only a Commissioner of the Scottish Board of Excise but a formidable figure in Robert Dundas' pervasive grasp of Scottish affairs.[15] Burns' hysterical tone in this letter is appropriate to the fact that he was profoundly disloyal both to what he saw as the usurpative Hanoverian king and that Ark of the Covenant of the British state with its belief in its seamless transition from 1689. The pressure on Burns was that he lived in relatively the most loyal of the four nations which, as we shall see, had the most profound consequences of the final disarray of the relationships between radical elements in all four nations on which a successful revolution needed to be based. What we are faced with in Burns' Scotland is a nationalism and language which finds its fullest expression in an assertion in specific universal human values as necessary to a radically reformed British state as opposed to a Scottishness which celebrates Scotland's often material total integration into the British nationalism/imperialism of the Union. Two songs, one by Robert Burns and one by Sir Walter Scott, seem to me to profoundly express the extreme tension present in Scotland in this period. The first song is Burns' 'A Man's a Man for A' That' written in 1795. The second is Walter Scott's 'For A' That and A' That' written in 1814. Everyone knows, or thinks they know, the Burns song. When I read the second one to the first deeply erudite audience at the opening of the first symposium no one recognized the author. I presume, therefore, that contextualizing and analyzing the Scott song will lead to a better understanding of Scottish hyper-loyalism.

Nor should Scottish hyper-loyalism be seen as a little local difficulty prevailing in the northern outposts of the British state. What writing this both comparative and interactive four-nation account of Britain and the Age of Revolution from a Scottish point of view has revealed to me is, as we shall see in later detail, an immoderately reactionary Scotland which, not only in military terms, punched far above its weight in prophet and propagandist against revolutionary France; the intensely Franco-phobic Scottish Literati had also performed a similar role against America. In terms of Britain's internal enemies, Dundas, so singularly important to Pitt, was the master of suppression. He also in his homeland was aided both by family connections and the corruptibility of a Roman-law-based Scottish legal system in exerting near complete control of Scottish dissent. This was the world in which Burns had to financially and creatively survive.

Burns' 'A Man's A Man for A' That' has arguably over two centuries become so shop worn, not least by national sentimentalism bolstered by whisky measured in imperial bumpers, that the song can be heard as a series of received clichés. Recent public performance by Sheena Wellington has caught not only Scotland's mixture of pride and pain that the song evokes in contemporary audiences, but, I believe, an anxious apprehension of the sorry gap between our achievements and Burns' aspirations.[16] The contemporary impact was, however, so potentially explosive that Burns never dared put his name to it. His apparently self-deprecatory remark to George Thomson, as editor whose, at best, genteel censorship was a matter of constant tension between them, that it was 'No song; but will be allowed, I think to be two or three pretty good prose thoughts inverted into rhyme' needs to be severely qualified by the fact that these thoughts derive directly from Thomas Paine's stress that contemporary merit was fundamentally opposed to vested interests and that there had to be a complete redistribution of wealth directed towards the poor. Burns' love for his fellow excise men was consequently one that never dared publicly to speak Paine's name.

As well as following Paine's remedy for healing the nation's socio-economic internal divisions Burns also, and even more treasonably self-endangering, was committed to World-Citizen Paine's cosmopolitanism. Indeed, later in the nineteenth century, a French critic was to describe 'A Man's A Man for A' That' as 'The Marseillaise of Humanity'. In Burns' Scotland such provocative universalist thinking belonged to only a small minority with American and subsequent French affiliations. It was, however, a crucial element in the three conventions held in Edinburgh in 1792 and 1793 as the British delegates sought to integrate the radical elements of the four nations. Thus, in 1793 William Skirving wrote to Thomas Hardy of the London Corresponding Society, a key member of a group of Anglo-Scottish metropolitan radicals, still seriously and sadly mislaid by Scottish historiography, that a British Convention should be held as a prelude to the 'uniting with all affection in *one Assembly of Commissioners* from all the countries of the World'.[17] This was written as a private letter which somewhat not only undermines its global aspirations but reveals Skirving's political anxiety since it was written in the wake of the disarray of the revealingly named 1793 British Convention held in Edinburgh. This convention suffered from not only severe external government intrusion but also increasing tensions between constitutional reformers and Francophile universalizing Republicans and ethnic ones between the Irish, the most persistent advocates of universalism throughout our whole period, and the Reformists Scottish majority.

Despite chronic discords among its multivaried enemies, social and ethnic, the Pitt government viewed universalism, with its consequently associated concepts of anti-national pacifism, socio-economic justice, anti-imperialism and anti-slavery – combined with the reality of French power – as an unholy prelude to Republicanism and, hence, to the highest treason. It was from this point of view that Scott's rebuttal of Burns' poem was written with its violent assertion that things had politically returned to normal. Retrieved from obscurity, here is the poem:

For A' That and A' That[18]
A new Song to an old Tune
Sung at the first Meeting of the Pitt Club of Scotland
Written by Walter Scott Esq

Tho' right be aft put down by strength,
    As mony a day we saw that,
The true and leilfu' cause at length

Shall bear the grie[19] for a' that,
For a' that an a' that,
    Guns, guillotines, and a' that,
The Fleur-de-lis, that lost her right,
    Is queen again for a' that!

We'll twine her in a friendly know
    With England's rose and a' that,
The Shamrock shall not be forgot,
    For Wellington made bra' that.
The Thistle, tho' her leaf be rude,
    Yet faith we'll no misca' that,
She sheltered in her solitude
    The Fleur-de-lis, for a' that!

The Austrian Vine, the Prussian pine.
    (For Blucher's sake, hurra that,)
The Spanish olive too shall join,
    And bloom in peace for a' that.
Stout Russia's hemp, so surely twin'd
    Around our wreath we'll draw that,
And he that would the cord unbind,
    Shall have it for his gra-vat!

Or if to chock saw puir a sot,
    Your pity scorn to thraw that,
The Devil's Elbo' be his lot,
    Where he may sit and claw that.
In spite of slight, in spite of might
    In spite of brags and a' that,
The lads that battled for the right,
    Have won the day, and a' that!

There's ae bit spot I had forgot,
    They ca'd America that!
A coward plot her rats had got
    Their father's flag to gnaw that;
Now see it fly top-gallant high.
    Atlantic winds shall blaw that,
And Yankee loun, beware your croun,
    There's kames in hand to claw that!

For on the land, or on the sea,
    Where'er the breezes blaw that,
The British flag shall bear the grie,
    And win the day for a' that![20]

The Scott who wrote this poem is certainly not the one defined by Thomas Macaulay who, with massive popular success, fused his perception of William of Orange with a similar, archetypal, moderate hero derived from Scott's fiction, creating a staidly progressive, pacific, but all-conquering, British imperial figure.[21] This was a figure capable of combining global democratic justice which was allegedly derived from British culture and notions of free enterprise. Modified versions of Macaulay's Scott have long held sway, at least in academic circles. This poem, then, might superficially be seen as an aberrant, bibulous Edinburgh boys night out at the Pitt Club expressive of manic relief at the apparent defeat of Napoleon in 1814. As opposed to Burns, Scott heard the 'Marseillaise' and 'Ça Ira' as literally the devil's music.

Scott is not the originator of exploiting the power and familiarity of Burns' music by way of inverting the original song's meaning. This was to become something of a cottage industry among Scottish loyalist songwriters. Scott not only knew the Dumfries Loyalist poet, John Mayne, but sought to promote his career, as did perhaps the British government. Thus it is that Mayne's 1799 poem, *English Scots and Irishmen, A Patriotic Address to the Inhabitants of the United Kingdom,* is quite possibly the specific precursor of Scott's poem with its similar version of the meaning of *Scots Wha Hae*:

> English, Scots and Irishmen,
> All that are in Valour's Ken!
> ... Now's the day and now's the hour,
> Frenchmen wou'd the Land devour –
> Will ye watch till they come o'er
> To give ye Chains and Slavery?
> Who wou'd be a Frenchman's slave?
> Who wou'd truckle to the Knave?
> Who wou'd shun a glorious grave?[22]

In actual fact, Burns' Anglophobic poem uses the crucial victory at Bannockburn in 1314 as a template for a similar contemporary act of bravery, itself a prelude of liberation from Hanoverian England into what he and many other British radicals saw as a new Republican world created by revolutionary France. Mayne's poem, its polar opposite, envisages a malign, predatory France, in whose blood-sacrificing defeat we perceive the reintegration of the British nations.

As in Mayne's poem, Scott's version of 'For A' That And A' That' (democratic *man* is missing from the title) is not a parody, that over used, indeed, mutually abused, weapon in the literary conflicts of the period. Its shock tactic is to employ the extraordinary power of Burns' Jacobite-derived tune, to deliver a series of bristlingly violent national, indeed imperial, inversions of Burns' universal democratic aspirations. France is restored to its royal absolute right and she and Hanoverian England reconciled. In this Scotland plays a dominant military role. An irony missed by Scott is that the thistle sheltering the Fleur-de-lis is a historical inversion of Scotland's 'auld alliance' with France, which for centuries had been the strongest anti-English card in its pack.

In stanzas three and four, the organic imagery changing from flower to plan, we find increasingly brutal expression of that which caused the darkest night of the radical soul. Best expressed in the early nineteenth century in Shelley's poetry and Hazlitt's prose, this involved the agonized awareness of Britain's misalliance with the most reactionary elements of what was to become Castlereagh and Metternich's successful international coalition. The pan-European hopes of the Radical Enlightenment were to be choked to death by an atavistic Russia. If the recipient of the song finds this too sadistic, he is advised to send the dissenting radical to hell instead. Conflicting variations of summoning the devil as punishment for or, more frequent, as expressive of alleged posing evil are increasingly present in radical and loyalist poetry as the bitter wrangling over the justification of war against France gave way to the terrible human cost and fluctuating fortunes of that war.

With America, 'There's a bit spot I had forgot' Scott makes a fair attempt at Burns' reductive colloquial genius for cutting nations and men down to size. Ironically, Burns had used this device brilliantly in his passionately pro-American poems to so treat the defeated British politicians and top-brass. Since Burns, however, did not dare publish these poems written in the 1790s, Scott could not have been aware of them when he wrote his song. The American warfare Scott describes was not the American War of Independence, but the more recent fracas of 1812 with its naval conflicts and the British invasion form Canada which led to the burning of The White House. As he could not have known the Burns poems, Scott probably had some sense of the prominence of American in the writings of Paine and Richard Price where their pro-American aspirations are in inverse proportion to what they defined as anti-Hanoverian imperialism. Even worse they shared with Burns the belief that American values would, if not wholly engender, nourish the French Revolution. Thus Burns wrote in 'The Tree of Liberty' (published 1838):

> My blessings aye attend the chief
>   Why pitied Gallia's slaves, man,
> And staw a branch, spite o' the Deil,
>   Frae yont the western waves, man.
> Fair Virtue water'd it wi care, (wi'?)
>   And now she sees wi' pride, man,
> How weel it buds and blossoms here,
>   Its branches spreading wide man.[23]

If we make the generic, formal change from Scott's 1812 song to Coleridge's crucially unamended 1796 version of *Ode on the Departing Year*, we find the reversal of the Scotsman's British triumphalism. Written in the midst of a welter of bad war news, foreign and domestic, this poem prophesies Britain's deserved defeat. It belongs to a tranche of anonymous Coleridge poems of this period which, as we shall see, went, for the Pitt government, well beyond demoralizing defeatism into definably treasonable activity. Coleridge wrote thus:

> O doom'd to fall, enslav'd and vile,
> O ALBION! O my mother Isle!
> Thy valleys, fair as Eden's bowers,
> Glitter green with sunny showers;
> Thy grassy Upland's gentle Swells
> Echo to the Bleat of Flocks;
> (Those grassy Hills, those glitt'ring Dells
> Proudly ramparted with rocks)
> And Ocean 'mid his uproar wild
> Speaks safety to his Island-child,
> Hence for many a fearless age
> Has social Quiet lov'd thy shore;
> Nor ever sworded Foeman's rage
> Or sack'd thy towers, or stain'd thy fields with gore.
> Disclaim'd of Heaven! mad Av'rice at thy side,
> At coward distance, yet with kindling pride –
> Safe 'mid thy herds and corn-fields thou hast stood,
> And join'd the yell of Famine and of Blood.
> All nations curse thee: and with eager wond'ring
> Shall hear DESTRUCTION, like a vulture, scream![24]

This is pastoral, paradise England lost. While that is a conventional enough trope, what is more original is Coleridge's linking the agrarian cupidity of a largely aristocratic land-owning class with the promotion of a terminally self-destructive war-fever. Akin to Burke, he also saw the huge golden wealth streams from corrupt, predatory activities in the East and West Indies as gross stimulants to renewed anti-French aggression.[25]

Given both its historical proximity and its analogous nature as a war for a representational democratic republic, it was predictable that British radicals would refer back to the American War of Independence as the conflict with France deepened. Certainly Wordsworth and Coleridge did, but this time they saw emanating from that victory only dark analogies not a millennial vision of America as precursive of global democratic triumph. As Wordsworth wrote in the advertisement to the aptly titled *Guilt and Sorrow or Incidents upon Salisbury Plain* with its memoir by the Female Vagrant, the soldier's wife who is the witness and victim of all the horrors of that war:

> During the latter part of the summer of 1793, having passed a month in the Isle of Wight, in view of the fleet which was then preparing for sea off Portsmouth at the commencement of the War, I left the place with melancholy forebodings. The American war was still fresh in memory. The struggle which was beginning, and which many thought would be brought to a speedy close by the irresistible arms of Great Britain being added to those of the Allies, I was assured in my own mind would be of a long continuance, and productive of distress and misery beyond all possible calculation. This conviction was pressed upon me by having been a witness, during a long residence in revolutionary France, of the spirit which prevailed in that country.[26]

Wordsworth, remembering the horrors of the American war, was wholly prescient in defining the coming war as 'productive of distress and misery beyond all possible calculation'. If, as Kenneth Johnson has remarked, the great subject of his poetry is 'the extreme suffering of individual human beings at the mercy of economic and political powers far beyond their control', human helplessness is at its most extreme, as typified by the Female Vagrant; not only in the troops' hopes and in actual battle but its manifold terrible consequences.[27] The latter part of the eighteenth century is saturated in blood. Not only for the British the loss of America and the French war but also in keeping control of the remaining empire. The West Indies alone is estimated to have cost the lives of 40,000 soldiers since the plantations were first established.

It was a situation which would have traumatized a far less sensitive spirit than that of S. T. Coleridge. By the mid-1790s his poetry, as is Wordsworth's, is saturated in the terrible violence and consequent suffering of the ongoing war. While Wordsworth tended to a kind of implicit politically critical writing in his intensely physically detailed scrutiny of isolated, bereft casualties of war, Coleridge was discursively explicit. He directly blamed the government for provoking the war, and specifically accused Pitt of the Irish massacres of 1798. Indeed, he saw the British people, certainly its most prosperous elements, implicated in the war:

> Alas! for ages ignorant of all
> Its ghastlier workings, (famine or blue plague,
> Battle, or siege, or flight through wintry snows,)
> We, this whole people, have been clamorous
> For war and bloodshed; animating sports,
> The which we pay for as a thing to talk of,
> Spectators and not combatants![28]

It is in this same poem, 'Fears in Solitude', that Coleridge's characteristic anguished sense of sin and resultant retribution locates itself in a belief that an actual French invasion is appropriate punishment for Britain's predatory imperial assault on what we now term the developing world:

> We have offended, Oh! my countrymen!
> We have offended very grievously,
> And been most tyrannous. From east to west
> A groan of accusation pierces Heaven!
> The wretched plead against us; multitudes
> Countless and vehement, the sons of God,
> Our brethren! Like a cloud that travels on,
> Steamed up from Cairo's swamps of pestilence,
> Even so, my countrymen, have we gone forth
> And borne to distant tribes slavery and pangs,

> And, deadlier far, our vices, whose deep taint
> With slow perdition murders the whole man,
> His body and his soul![29]

For an anxiety-riddled government faced with a possible French invasion, such conscientious objections seemed not so much unpatriotic as treasonable. Coleridge, operating under an, at best, tenuously maintained anonymity, was placing himself at terrible risk. In the midst of his anonymous anti-French poems, however, he gave a public lecture which, dealing with the relatively recent American war, contained the following passage. It is, even by the sustained standards of Coleridge's ever allusive, ever stimulating prose (he is a much more uneven poet), quite extraordinary in both its quality and, even more, in its implications not only for his own work but for a significant change in perspective regarding the relative importance of America in late eighteenth-century four-nations consciousness:

> The principles industriously propagated by the friends of our Government are opposite to the American Constitution – and indeed to Liberty every where; and in order to form a just estimate of our excesses, let us recollect that prominent feature of the late war – *Scalping!*

> The Fiend, whose crime was Ambition, leapt over into this Paradise – Hell-hounds laid it waste, *English Generals* invited the Indians 'to banquet on blood': the savage Indians headed by an Englishman attached it. Universal massacre ensued. The Houses were destroyed: the Corn Fields burnt: and where under the broad Maple trees innocent Children used to play at noontide, there the Drinkers of human Blood, and the Feasters on human Flesh were seen in horrid circles, counting their scalps and anticipating their gains. The English Court bought Scalps at a fixed price! SCALPING this *pious* Court deemed a fit punishment for the crimes of those, whose only crime was, that being Men, and the descendants of Britons, they had refused to be Slaves. Unconditional Submission was the only Terms offered to the Americans – and Death the immediate Menace. Our Brethren (if indeed we may presume to call so exalted a race *our* Brethren,) indignantly rejected the terms, and resolved to hazard the execution of the menace. For this the Horrors of European Warfare afforded not a sufficient Punishment. Inventive in cruelty and undistinguishing in massacre, Savages must be hired against them: human Tygers must be called from their woods, their attacks regulated by Discipline, and their Ferocity increased by Intoxication. But did not this employment of merciless Scalpers rouse the indignation of Britons?[30]

The bulk of this passage is intended to violate the reader with the violation of even the then ongoing 'Horrors of … European Warfare … [by] English Generals'. Coleridge was later to write poetry about what he defined as the demonic suppression by Pitt in 1798 of the Irish. This passage is a precursor of what he saw as the waxing evil of British imperial repression. Along with this, astonishingly compressed, are echoes from the formidable arsenal discoverable in Burke,

Price and Paine of passionate pro-American writing combined with virulent assaults on what they saw as British tyranny. Coleridge's intellectual brilliance was such that the whole passage could be self-created but, as our examples will suggest, it is more likely, given the self-defined book-cormorants omnivorous appetite for print, that this is a brilliant creative synthesis.

What Coleridge was asserting was that it was now the Americans who were the true bearers of the long honourable tradition of English libertarianism. England itself was reduced to ruling by death-threat. Indeed, in the bloody reality of mercenary scalping, to actually killing. Coleridge also believed that he had detected the core essence of the evil force controlling English conduct. Redefining Milton, he saw English imperialism, 'The Fiend, whose crime was Ambition, leapt over into this Paradise', as the death-bringing devil intent on bringing about the fall of America. 'Ambition', also used by Price, needs further investigation as the key term used by British radicals for the insatiable predatory appetite for territorial conquest which they believed defined the imperial project. This was also the view of that most distinguished American Benjamin Franklin in his response to what was the self-destructive motivation mobilizing the English. This is Franklin's analysis as introduced by Gore Vidal, a slightly more skeptical analyst of his mother country than British radical idealists in the late eighteenth century:

> Franklin was often in Europe as an agent for the new American republic. With John Jay and John Adams, he handled the American end of a surprisingly generous-spirited peace treaty with England in November 1782. He also indulged in an interesting diagnosis of what he took to be the British problem that had forced their American colonies into a rebellion that led to a republic more overt than England's. On March 17, 1783 he wrote, in prophetic mode, to his friend Bishop Shipley:

> America will, with God's blessing, become a great and happy country; and England, if she has at length gained wisdom, will have gained something more valuable, and more essential to her prosperity, than all she has lost; and will still be a great and respectable nation. Her great disease at present is the numerous and enormous salaries and emoluments of office. Avarice and ambition are strong passions and, separately, act with great force on the human mind; but when both are united, and may be gratified in the same object, their violence is almost irresistible, and they hurry men headlong into factions and contentions, destructive of all good government. As long, therefore, as these great emoluments subsist, your parliament will be a stormy sea, and your public councils confounded by private interests. But it requires much public spirit and virtue to abolish them; more than perhaps can now be found in a nation so long corrupted.[31]

Franklin, in his combination of the strong passions of avarice and ambition, shares the content, if certainly not the style, of Coleridge's analysis of British imperial corruption. With William Blake the stylistic contrast becomes even more extreme. Hence in Blake's *America: A Prophecy* (1793), we find the revolutionary conflict, in which Blake, like Coleridge, was absolutely committed to the American cause, rendered in Blake's unique mixture of myth-history and psycho-sexual politics.

> The Guardian Prince of Albion burns in his nightly tent:
> Sullen fires across the Atlantic glow to America's shore,
> Piercing the souls of warlike men who rise in silent night.
> Washington, Franklin, Paine & Warren, Gates, Hancock & Green
> Meet on the coast glowing with blood from Albion's fiery Prince.
>   Washington spoke: 'Friends of America! look over the Atlantic sea;
> 'A bended bow is lifted in heaven, & a heavy iron chain
> 'Descends, link by link, from Albion's cliffs across the sea, to bind
> 'Brothers & sons of America till our faces pale and yellow,
> 'Heads deprest, voices weak, eyes downcast, hands work-bruis'd,
> 'Feet bleeding on the sultry sands, and the furrows of the whip
> 'Descend to generations that in future times forget.'
> The strong voice ceas'd, for a terrible blast swept over the heaving sea:
> The eastern cloud rent: on his cliffs stood Albion's wrathful Prince,
> A dragon form, clashing his scales: at midnight he arose,
> And flam'd red meteors round the land of Albion beneath;
> His voice, his locks, his awful shoulders, and his glowing eyes.[32]

In his essay 'The Third World of Criticism', Jerome McGann, linking Aeschylus, Blake and Pound together, argues that creative literature is a constant counterforce to the overwhelming threat of the imperial imagination. Thus he writes:

> To relinquish an imperial imagination is also a difficult if no less urgent task. Empires are maintained by imperial intellects. Cultural studies, and literary work in particular, function either to build or to unbuild such minds. In this respect Blake's work is exactly a prophecy against empire, a model of how the poetic moves against the perpetuation of empires and towards the development of less exploitative societies, less alienated imaginations. Literary work is the art of multiplicities and minute particulars, the science of Unbuildings: One law for the lion and the ox is oppression.[33]

Whether anti-imperialism is, in fact, creative literature's primordial and recurrent theme is obviously not verifiable here. What is certainly arguable, however, is that Romantic or, more appropriately defined, Radical Enlightenment poetry has dynastic anti-imperialism at its dialectical core. What is further arguable is that not only the primary but, indeed, the seminal confirmation for radicals in all four British nations was based on what they conceived of as British anti-imperialism in its conflict with America. American victory in all four nations caused a revivication of their hopes that they, too, might become members of their own modern democratic republic which would either exist in a British federal republic or might merge into a new republican Britain. Of the latter possibility, Linda Colley has recently written that:

As John Belchem and James Epstein have shown, there was also an influential language of rights and constitutionalism that was British wide and British in emphasis. When a radical named Joseph Gerald, on trial for his life, told an Edinburgh jury in 1794, 'You are Britons – you are free men,' he was manifestly not in the business (of employing 'Britons' as an interchangeable term for 'Englishmen'.)[34]

1794 was, unaccidentally, the year in which Burns wrote 'Ode for General Washington's Birthday'. The darkness of that year wrought in Burns, as it had in Wordsworth or Coleridge, a painful, retrospective analysis of the consequences of what he had earlier deemed the universal triumph of the American Revolution. While he still celebrated Washington's success, that success was now utterly detached from a Britain where English self-betrayal of its own libertarian principles had not only destroyed Scotland but doused 'the freeborn Briton's soul of fire'.

> Alfred, on thy starry throne
> Surrounded by the tuneful choir,
> The Bards that erst have struck the patriot lyre,
> And rous'd the freeborn Briton's soul of fire,
> No more thy England own. –
> Dare injured nations form the great design,
> To make detested tyrants bleed?
> Thy England execrates the glorious deed!
> Beneath her hostile banners waving,
> Every pang of honour braving,
> England in thunder calls – 'The Tyrant's cause is mine!'
> That hour accurst, how did the fiends rejoice,
> And Hell thro' all her confines raise th' exulting voice,
> That hour which saw the generous English name
> Link't with such damned deeds of everlasting shame!
> Thee, Caledonia, thy wild heaths among,
> Fam'd for the martial deed, the heaven-taught song,
> To thee, I turn with swimming eyes. –
> Where is that soul of Freedom fled?
> Immingled with the mighty Dead!
> Beneath that hallow'd turf where WALLACE lies!
> Hear it not, Wallace, in thy bed of death!
> Ye babbling winds in silence sweep;
> Disturb not ye the hero's sleep,
> Nor give the coward secret breath.[35]

To understand fully, however, the nature of the British radicals' anti-imperial case in favour of America and against England, we have to revert to their greatest political thinker, Thomas Paine. As early as 1782, Paine, addressing the Abbé Raynal, was presenting a case of complex and, indeed, contentious nature against imperialism in general and English imperialism in particular. Thus he wrote:

> The true idea of a great nation, is that which extends and promotes the principles of universal society; whose mind rises above the atmosphere of local thoughts, and considers mankind, of whatever nation or profession they may be, as the work of one Creator. The rage for conquest has had its fashion, and its day. Why may not the amiable virtues have the same? The Alexander and Caesars of antiquity have left behind them their monuments of destruction, and are remembered with hatred; while those more exalted characters, who first taught society and science, are blessed with the gratitude of every age and country.[36]

It can be certainly argued that Paine's vision, buoyed up by imminent American victory, is grossly over-confident concerning not only America's internal political achievement but the degree of external acceptability for this achievement. It also leads him to underestimate the reactionary power and tenacity of the British state, Rome's atavistic inheritor, to destroy allegedly transformative American republican power both at home and in Europe. This notion of an innovative, transformative republican power is, however, not a personal eccentricity. In 1796 Kant, presumably unaware of Paine, produced in *Perpetual Peace* (1795) a highly similar version of Republican France replicating the role Paine had allocated America. As Allen W. Wood has pertinently noted:

> *Perpetual Peace* may be read as an expression of support for the Republic itself and for the Prussian policy of peace with France. The cause of the Republic is endorsed both in the First Definitive Article, which says that the constitution of every state should be republican, and in Kant's remark in the Second Definitive Article that peace might come about if, through good fortune, 'one powerful and enlightened nation can educate itself up to the form of a republic' and then make itself into the 'focal point for a federative union of other states' The monarchical states, in other words, should not merely tolerate revolutionary France, but even view it as the potential leader of a peaceful cosmopolitan confederation.[37]

Neither Kant nor Paine saw America or France evolving out of a vacuum. Both men detected deep, enlightening change in economics, science, and communications driven by the growth of literacy, and indeed, an increasingly cosmopolitan sense of world community as the underlying force to the new politics. In certain respects both their theories of progress are akin to the stadial theory so beloved of the political and economic theorists of the Scottish Moderate Enlightenment.[38] Rather like them, they believed they had entered the fourth stage of benevolent commercial civilization. Paine himself believed in an elected meritocracy of technocratic entrepreneurs. There is, however, a fundamental political difference between Paine and the Scots. While the latter group were the most loyal section of British society, as their pro-active anti-Americanism during the earlier war had shown, they believed in the stability granted by the hallowed British constitution.[39] Paine did not believe in that constitution any more than the paper it was not written on. In the context of stadial theory he perceived

Britain as belonging in its imperial activities to the predatory hunter/killer stage of the first phase of that theory. He did think, unjustly given the surrounding European imperialisms, it to be exceptional, but in a manner inverse to subsequent Victorian imperial visions. Coleridge's scalping account would not have surprised him.

By far the most serious error present in Paine and Kant, however, is their ingenuousness regarding the fate of a representational republic being born into a world of hierarchical dynasties. Covertly, Britain through European alliances tried to smother France at birth. That failing, she went overtly to war against her. Paine never foresaw any such outcome. Like all optimistic Enlightenment political thinkers, he may not have been the direct cause of violence but he was culpably naïve in not foreseeing the reactive violence his revolutions would provoke. The darkly tragic trouble is that a society so given to belligerence on a global scale as England will not be weaned, good reason or bad, from its lethal practices. Also, it will internalize its violence to the degree necessary to impose conformity to its sovereign will.

With the declaration of war on France in 1793, the need to silence its critics became absolute for Pitt's government. The government were faced with three main problems. First, the constant initial accusations, mainly emanating from Foxite Whig sources, that the government had provoked an unnecessary war. Second, that for a decade the war went extremely badly to the extent that a constant threat of French invasion developed. Third, that, given such a threat, there was a constant fear of both a collapse in national morale, especially as expressed in the Militia Riots and possible mutiny in the fleet. Further, that feared insurrection in England was accompanied albeit unsuccessfully by French landings in Wales and Ireland.[40] Remarkably, given his subsequent career, Coleridge's poetry in the 1790s covers all three categories of government alarm. In his depth of analysis and his longevity as a radical critic of the government he is perhaps unsurpassed.

As late as 1798, when almost all others had been reduced to silence or flight, Coleridge anonymously published *Fire, Famine and Slaughter* specifically identifying Pitt ('Letters four do form his name') as responsible for the terrible bloodshed which ended Irish, with French assistance, military attempts to break with the British state. Unlike much of his political poetry in the 1790s, this is not written in an uneasy stylistic combination of the retro – Miltonic with the, bordering on hysterical, contemporary gothic. The poem's demonic driving rhythm is embodied in the voices of Fire, Famine and Slaughter, intentional echoes of *Macbeth's* three witches. The first part of the poem deals with the French civil war in La Vendée, the second with Ireland:

> *Fire.* Sisters! I from Ireland came!
> Hedge and corn-fields all on flame,
> I triumph'd o'er the setting sun!
> And all the while the work was done,
> On as I strode with my huge strides,
> I flung back my head and I held my sides,
> It was so rare a piece of fun
> To see the sweltered cattle run
> With uncouth gallop through the night,
> Seared by the red and noisy light!
> By the light of his own blazing cot
> Was many a naked rebel shot:
> The house-stream met the flame and hissed,
> While crash! Fell in the roof, I wist,
> On some of those old bed-rid nurses,
> That deal in discontent and curses.
>   *Both.* Who bade you do't?
>   *Fire.* The same! the same!
> Letters four do form his name.
> He let me loose, and cried Halloo!
> To him alone the praise is due.
>   *All.* He let us loose, and cried Halloo!
> How shall we yield him honour due?
>   *Famine.* Wisdom comes with lack of food.
> I'll gnaw, I'll gnaw the multitude,
> Till the cup of rage o'erbrim;
> They shall seize him and his brood –
>   *Slaughter.* The shall tear him limb from limb!
>   *Fire.* O thankless beldames and untrue!
> And is this all that you can do
> For him, who did so much for you?
> Ninety months he, by my troth!
> Hath richly catered for you both;
> And in an hour would you repay
> An eight years' work? – Away! away!
> I alone am faithful! I
> Cling to him everlastingly.[41]

This is both an extraordinary and still underappreciated poem. Released from the customary formal and linguistic bondage of the semi-prophetic monologue, Coleridge, in the voices of the Fire, Famine and Slaughter sees Pitt, the provoker of the violence, as leading the nation into a kind of apocalyptic vortex. Where in the people will take their revenge. It is a country not integrating under foreign threat but at the end of its tether.

While identification of Coleridge's authorship of this poem was contested, his earlier belief that the English had provoked the war had not saved him from government identification.[42] The government sponsored *Anti-Jacobin* was on his case. In his brilliant analysis of Coleridge's confrontation with authority, Paul Magnusson gets to the core of the contest. It is another particularly relevant and brilliant illustration of what this introduction claims to be the essence of radical poetry: its claim to replace restrictive, inherently beleaguered nationalism with a vision of universal humanity. Magnusson puts the matter thus:

> Coleridge's consistent rejection of materialism, atheism, and immorality separates him from Godwin, Thelwall, and the other radicals, but that does not mean that his invocation of the domestic affections places him in Burke's camp. For Burke the domestic affections formed the basis of the British Constitution, a decidedly national allegiance, while Coleridge viewed them in the 1790s as the basis of a universal benevolence and love of all humanity.
>
> The *Anti-Jacobin*, not surprisingly, takes Burke's and not Coleridge's position. 'New Morality' turns Coleridge's image of the sun for the love of humanity against him. The feelings of the 'universal man' run 'through the extended globe'
>
> As broad and general as th'unbounded sun!
> No narrow bigot *he;* – *his* reason'd view
> Thy interests, England, ranks with thine, Peru!
> France at our doors, *he* sees no danger nigh,
> But heaves for Turkey's woes th'impartial sigh;
> A steady Patriot of the World alone,
> The Friend of every Country – but his own.
>
> In the eyes of the defenders of tradition and prejudice, Coleridge then should stand in the ranks with Dr Price and his followers who ask 'What has the love of their country hitherto been among mankind? What has it been but a love of domination; a desire of conquest, and a thirst for grandeur and glory, by extending territory, and enslaving surrounding countries? What had it been but a blind and narrow principle, producing in every country a contempt of other countries, and forming men into combinations and factions against their common rights and liberties ...?'[43]

This admittedly witty assault on universalism does also reveal the government fear of its pacific principles. Magnusson also directs our attention to the sort of war poetry that, in this hour of crisis should be getting written.

Finally in the first of a series on Jacobin poetry (20 November 1797), the *Anti-Jacobin* ticks off the characteristics of the Jacobin poet:

> The Poet of other times has been an enthusiast in the love of his native soil.
> The Jacobin Poet rejects all restriction in his feelings. *His* love is enlarges and expanded so as to comprehend all human kind.
> The old poet was a warrior, at least in imagination; and sung the actions of the heroes of his country, in strains which 'made Ambition Virtue,' and which overwhelmed the horrors of war in its glory. The *Jacobin* Poet would have no objection to sing battles too – but *he* would take a distinction. The prowess of Bonaparte, indeed, he might chant in his loftiest strain of exultation. *There* we should find nothing but

trophies, and triumphs, and branches of laurel and olive, phalanxes of Republicans shouting victory, satellites of despotism biting the ground, and geniuses of Liberty planting standards on mountain-tops.[44]

As Betty K. Bennett's anthology reveals, there was no end of loyalist poetry which attempted to overwhelm 'the horrors of war in its glory'.[45] As soldiers on the Napoleonic battlefield, a disproportionate number of these poets are Scots. Waterloo was seen in Scotland almost as a Scottish away victory. Sir Walter Scott, John Mayne and Hector MacNeill, the latter two quite forgotten, were all best sellers in this genre. The government seems to have subsidized this verse but, as with its truly efficient espionage system, records do not seem to exist and any evidence is largely anecdotal, as in this description of pro-government ballad singing:

> Nor was it only the opposition which used ballads. During the general election of 1784 the *Morning Herald* reported that 'ministers have actually sent down three coach-loads of ballad-singers to Yorkshire'. A covered wagon with their supplies of pamphlets and ballads went with them. Ten years later, according to William Gardiner, 'Ballad-singers were paid, and stationed at the end of streets, to chaunt the downfall of the Jacobins, and the glorious administration of Mr Pitt.'[46]

A similar problem exists with Hannah More's loyalist, evangelical tracks. How much were they financed and how much were they really read? Loyalist authors from all four nations often seemed on warm personal terms. Did the government promote a writerly national network to counteract a radical one?

Whatever successes loyalist literature had either in terms of its own creative merits or in winning its confrontation with the radical enemy were rendered largely superfluous by brutally direct government suppression of oppositional material. Habeas Corpus was suspended in 1794 and the two acts of 1795 extended the definition of High Treason to include acts of speech and writing. These draconian methods were, certainly, war-time acts when treason, defined as giving succour to the king's enemies, had obvious ultimate importance. It is true that a nation at war almost invariably coheres and that there existed a rich ancestral vein of xenophobia towards the French. However, in his recent brilliant *The Spirit of Despotism*, John Barrell narrates from a 1795 book by 'Vicesimus Knox', from which he took his own title, the political/psychological state of the war-time British mind from a radical viewpoint. Thus he writes:

> The war itself, Knox argued, was favourable to the spirit of despotism. It imposed, inevitably, 'a thousand little restraints on liberty', and one reason for its continuance was the aristocratic belief that 'peace ... is productive of plenty, and plenty makes the people saucy', more disposed to claim their rights. The huge increase in the standing army, and the embodiment of thousands of men in the militia, had a 'direct tendency to familiarize the mind to civil despotism', by obliging them to exhibit the unthinking obedience of trained animals. Nothing was more efficient than war in persuading the people to

accept the morality of despotism, the belief that any act of cruelty or revenge was justifiable when undertaken against those supposed to be the enemies of the nation. Wars were waged or avoided on a calculation of the likely expense of money, not of lives, as if the lives of ordinary people were worthless. The spirit of despotism, indeed, was 'totally destitute of feeling for others: It scarcely acknowledges the common tie of humanity', and since the French revolution the contempt of the higher orders for the middle ranks and the poor had become greater than ever. The rich had more and more persuaded themselves that any extension of the franchise would lead to anarchy, a belief that was expressed more stridently the more unfounded it became.[47]

With such terrible, tangible casualties as this war produced, it might seem self-indulgent to complain about writers who were not killed, albeit silenced and frequently self-exiled mainly in America. In his book on Wordsworth, however, Kenneth R. Johnson describes their fate as passing 'into an obscurity almost as deep as death'. He also reminds us that, as Coleridge, Wordsworth's creativity as a poet was synchronous with his radical, even republican political views. Thus Johnston writes:

> If Wordsworth had published the 'Letter to Llandaff', he would, even if he had escaped prosecution and conviction, have set his life on a course very different from the one he took. He would have become a marked man in political discussions throughout the rest of the decade. He would have been noticed in the newspapers far more notoriously than he was as the author of *An Evening Walk* and *Descriptive Sketches*. He would have been damned shrilly by the ministerial press, and hardly praised at all by the opposition papers, since his views were far too radical for establishment Whigs. The name Wordsworth, like those of Burke, Paine, Wollstonecraft, Godwin, Mackintosh, Watson, Thelwall, and others, would have been indelibly fixed (or sunk) in public memory as one of the participants in the great, failed 'Revolution Debate' of 1790–95. Many of these men and women were never heard from again; even if they lived, they passed into an obscurity almost as deep as death. About ten years older than Wordsworth, they formed a generation without a political future. From being the history makers of their era, they found themselves bypassed by history, and have only very recently been rehabilitated. Wordsworth could not have known this would happen, but by not publishing the 'Letter to Llandaff' he saved himself for the future as the history of the 1790s receded into his obscure youthful past. By the end of the decade he had transformed himself into a man of a different era.[48]

In a more recent article 'Whose History? My Place or Yours?: Republican Assumptions and Romantic Traditions', Johnston has evolved a cogent five-stage model demonstrating how Pitt's government eliminated oppositional voices and texts.[49] He has also assembled an extensive list of British radical writers of the period and revealed the different ways in which they were either silenced or chose to conform. Johnston says this list is not exclusive and, from my ongoing Scottish work, I would say this was certainly true. Irish and Welsh scholars would, I am sure, likewise agree. Johnston also in his remark that such writers have 'only very recently been rehabilitated' also puts his finger on two key related questions. Since these writers, certainly within the academy, have only recently and as yet partially surfaced since the 1980s, why were they so long absent? What, after nearly two centuries, caused them to return?

The fundamental reason for this two-century long absence is that, in the wake of their governmental suppression, Victorian historians, with much apparently corroborative evidence, saw the 1689 Glorious Revolution as a seminal act which not only internally integrated the four British nations but laid the basis for the also seamless expansion of British global power. The end of the Second World War brought definitive closure to such external global notions. By the 1980s terrorism exported from Ulster and embryonic devolutionary pressures suggested the internal break-up of Britain. Was the success of Colley's *Britons* (1992) because it was not an account of a critically divided Britain in the 1790s but a retro-Victorian account of an allegedly integrated state, albeit integration created by its predatory belligerence? As Paul Hamilton has written:

> Colley's overwhelming case for concentrating on explaining how the national self-consciousness driving the extraordinary British Imperial successes of the Victorian age was produced understandably tends to leave languishing any radical enlightened dissent.[50]

Paul Hamilton's comment on Colley comes from a book of essays on the period called, wholly appropriately for our purposes, *Repossessing the Romantic Past*. These essays are in honour of Marilyn Butler and, indeed, the book's title is taken from a paradigm-breaking essay of Butler's published in 1989. In that essay Butler called for a democratization of the Victorian-inspired Romantic Canon of six major figures with passion and no little ironic wit. Thus she wrote:

> Together the single line of poets personified the national spirit, separately they were thoughtful, humane men – a little too like the ideal university professor, perhaps, but wisdom and tolerance remain virtues. Wordsworth emerged *primus inter pares* among the other five Romantics – then Coleridge, Scott, Byron, Shelley, Keats – because he taught a stoical, essentially optimistic acceptance of suffering, and because his vision of nature represented England as still a pastoral society, which was comforting in other ways.[51]

In place of this literary Mount Rushmore, Butler suggested a far more extended writerly range:

> Many authors were women, some of the best poets, we might now agree – like Burns and Blake – came from the ranks. Nineteenth-century professionals, journalists and academics, made great writers into an officer class, and imposed restrictions on the entry of women and NCOs. The canon came to look harmonious rather than contentious; learned or polite rather than artless or common; national, rather than provincial or sectarian on the one hand, or dispersed and international on the other. Literature is individualistic or pluralist; words such as 'canon' and 'heritage' impose a uniformity that had some practical advantages, especially at the outset, but was always artificial.[52]

Butler also makes a powerful case for non-canonical writing both for its own sake and for its both literary and historical relevance to the canonical. Literary history or, indeed, arguably history itself becomes impossible to write if literary critics devise an atemporal world populated exclusively by a group of canonical writers whose real connections are not to their time but, allusively backwards, to earlier canonical master texts.

> The questions that can be asked of major figures dwindle in number and importance with the fading of minor ones. The relations between texts are always of crucial significance, but it was left to twentieth-century scholars to claim that only major texts and major authors have meaningful relations. Keats now communes too often with Shakespeare, Wordsworth with St Augustine, everyone with the Bible. However much an artist is indebted to the mighty dead, he or she almost certainly borrows more from the living – that is, from writers no longer available for reading except in the better libraries. In the end, evaluation itself is threatened: how can you operate the techniques for telling who a major writer is, if you don't know what a minor one looks like?[53]

As Paul Hamilton has noted: 'Her work has always been original, critical and self critical, testing disciplinary boundaries, commenting on revising current historical verdicts by attending to neglected literary possibility'.[54]

Whether all the authors of the following essays are aware of Butler's seminal work, they all, in varying degrees, are beneficiaries of its fundamental principles. Indeed, Butler herself, in her extended empathies with writers like Burns and Edgeworth, is our forerunner in taking Romanticism outwith an English border. As she herself wrote:

> Most literature does not speak for the official, London-based 'nation'. It expresses the view of a sect, a province, a gender, a class, bent more often than not on criticism or outright opposition. For literary purposes, the British Isles have always been what the Australian poet Les Murray recently termed them in the present day, 'the Anglo-Celtic archipelago'. As a social institution, literature models an intricate, diverse, stressful community, not a bland monolith.[55]

It has been predicted that the obvious pressures for devolution in contemporary Britain would lead to a break up with each nation evolving a restrictively essentialist nationalism. That we would, indeed, forget that we had so much in common.

Perhaps, then, these Belfast symposia and the consequent essays are an academic aberration, running against the historical grain of what is taking place. Perhaps, however, they should be seen in a more positive light. In one sense, the radical attempt in the 1790s to create a universal basis for nationalism and hence also international relations was certainly terminated by the British state. It may also be the case that Paine's vision of cosmopolitan humanity is a not only political but a psychological impossibility. Nor that, as the more extreme republican thinkers (Paine, Kant, Wordsworth and Coleridge) believed, a new kind of pacific world could be created by a political transformation of the dynastic world into the form of representational republics. However, what the radicals of the 1790s in the four British nations did, by choice and necessity, was, to an unprecedented degree, to attempt to increase their awareness of each other and attempt to enter into a conversation to effect fundamental political change. Certainly, what is true is that nothing increased paranoia in the Pitt government more than the belief from their accurate espionage system that such fraternalization was taking place.[56] What, then, the Belfast symposia represented, albeit not fully consciously, was an honouring of these thwarted attempts. These essays also reflect that honouring. What we also found in Belfast was that the movement towards a four-nation history had already taken root in all four nations, especially in Wales. It is apt, then, to end on a positive Welsh-inspired note as a wholly appropriate introduction to these essays:

> That act of devolution has been proceeding apace in recent years and can now be said to be at the very heart of current debates about the period. A monolithic 'English' Romanticism has been superseded by the plural and culturally complex Romanticisms of the four nations. The process has also involved the salutary 'regionalisation' or 'territorialisation' of Romanticism, resulting not in a narrowing of perspective to parochial ground but rather the very opposite – a more acute awareness of cultural alignments and interconnections in an international context. As one might expect, the complex contours of shire, regional, national and British identities – cultural and political – figure prominently in the academy's reconfigured models of Romanticism, as have debates about internal colonialism and the conflicted investment of writers and nations in the imperial project of the age with its attendant Orientalism.[57]

The following essays from not only international but, even more pleasingly, inter-generational scholars from England, Ireland, Scotland, Wales, Canada and America form an innovative gathering of four-nation voices. Indeed, it should be said singing voices since, not wholly anticipated, the importance of song has emerged as the strongest element in this first symposium derived volume.

II

This, the first of two volumes, provides often comparative studies of texts written by literary scholars with a mutual belief that poetry must *primarily* be understood in its historical context. It is, therefore, a wholly apt prelude to our second volume which, since this is also an interdisciplinary project, will involve historians re-contextualizing the impact of the Radical Enlightenment on the British state and its four national components.

Michael Scrivener is an extremely worthy member of a deeply erudite radically sympathetic American tradition of British Romantic scholarship; the founding father of which was David Erdman. Scrivener has written illuminatingly on both Shelley and, despite his excellent efforts, the still undervalued John

Thelwall. As an editor he has produced *Poetry and Reform: Periodical Verse from the English Democratic Press, 1792–1824* (1992), the singular virtue of which is that he carried out an exploration of reform poetry emanating from the intellectual, technological, theological dynamism of England's mainly provincial urban centres. There is no British edition of this nature. To evoke the enormous power of song in the 1790s, Scrivener begins his essay with a wittily lucid explanation of how in modern America, that most evocative of public spaces, the baseball ground saw in 1942, with the outbreak of the war, the singing of the National Anthem. Post 9/11, 'America the Beautiful', overwhelmingly nationally coercive in the immediate wake of the catastrophe, was also sung. The implicit irony of this, of course, is that, while in the twentieth century the American anthem produced national unanimity, the singing of the British one in the 1790s provoked discord and, from the radicals, innumerable parodic versions. As Scrivener remarks:

> Both sides of the political conflict used the British national anthem to attack their opponents and define themselves. The public singing of songs in this context is a symbolic action to overawe the opposition, strengthen one's own morale and unity, and bring over the audience to one's own side. Songs have to be seen here as weapons, and the difference between physical force and verbal performance is not absolute. (p. 36)

The absolute, minatory nature of the national schism that such opposing singing reveals goes beyond the restraint and compromise of normal politics. As Scrivener notes: 'The rhetorical battle is over nature. Edmund Burke and his numerous opponents fight over ownership of the word'. The conflict, if not the aesthetic level, is that of Shakespeare's *King Lear*. By choosing contesting, conflicting loyalist and radical songs, Scrivener delivers a master class in the explication of such an innately compressed genre. Not the least of his virtues is to reveal how each side saw exclusive evil in the other in variant Gothic terms.

In a book of four-nation essays, which is at least as much about crossing national borders as defining them, **Joan C. Beal** draws our attention to a Scottish propensity to cross the Tweed not to forge an imperial career but to serve, in the late eighteenth century, the opposing cause of political dissent. Two main areas attracted radical Scots: as teachers and pupils in English Dissenting Academies and as part of a highly important, still largely unexamined, Anglo-Scottish community in London. Thomas Spence's father Jeremiah came from Aberdeen to Newcastle where Thomas was born in 1750. In a very influential manner, the family maintained its Scottish roots by its membership of the Scottish minister, Rev. James Murray's Presbyterian chapel. Derived from his interpretation of biblical principle, Murray believed that all men were equal in the sight of God. More dangerously, he further believed that this democratic premise granted them certain natural, inalienable, rights, the most explosive of which was common land ownership. This redistributive notion became Spence's key idea. It was an idea reinforced textually from another Aberdonian source, William Ogilvie

(1736–1813), who, as Professor of Humanity at Aberdeen University, published in 1782 his *Essay on the Right and Property of Land*. Spence's commitment to this most extreme redistributory radical concept led to the most frictive of lives, not only with the Burkean loyalists, to whom sanctity of property was at least as important as the divinity of kings, but with his less economically extreme fellow radicals. A fist-fight with his fellow radical and extraordinary artist, Thomas Bewick, led him to leave Newcastle for London where he could achieve a degree of anonymity. Professor Beal sees him as a seminal figure in creating London's radical underground where, for a plebeian audience, he attempted to devise by a mixed media of subversive song and the minting of his own symbolic coinage a world underneath the government's espionage radar.

There is possibly a point at which the complexities, eccentricities and contradictions, both apparent and real, about Iolo Morganwg cease to surprise. This joint essay by **Mary-Ann Constantine** and **Elizabeth Edwards** is most certainly not that point. It is fertile with stimulating surprise. The most surprising and, given it is a study of song, relevant new fact for me is that between 1802 and his death in 1826, Iolo, in support of the embryonic cause of Welsh Unitarianism, a major home of British dissent, proscribed till 1813, produced around 3,000 three thousand Welsh-language hymns. Our authors further note:

> Iolo's hymns do reveal radical themes, from anti-war and anti-slavery to support those suffering in the cause of rational dissent. Most interestingly, perhaps, they can be read as an attempt to return bardism to its 'original' context, public religious worship. For Iolo, the poet and the priest, the Bard and the Druid, were always one and the same: teachers, explainers, purveyors of truth.

As well as musically purveying in Welsh the truth of Unitarianism, Iolo sought to be the self appointed, or event self-anointed, 'Bard of Liberty' writing in English for a British audience. I do not know if Iolo's Welsh Unitarian hymns were set to Welsh tunes, but in writing for a wider British audience he generally drew on a popular pool of Scottish and English airs. This was not due to the pronounced magpie element in his nature. Like all political song writers in the 1790s he perceived the enhanced communicative value of the popular song. Also, as our authors allege, Wales lacked the strong folk-song element tradition of Ireland, Scotland and Brittany. Predictably Iolo wrote one of the many parodies of the National Anthem: 'that old *War Song of British Savages*'. A strong case is made that he significantly derived his second lyric to that anthem, the Welsh 'Breinian Dyn' (Rights of Man) from Robert Thomson's parodic 'A New Song of 1792', which he would have heard in London at that time. More striking is the fact that the Irish picked up Thomson's song and reprinted it in *Paddy's Resource*. Song, our authors note, gives more substance to the concept of a pan-British radical consciousness than any other genre.

That Welsh and Irish radicals should draw freely on London-based sources for their songs implies, in the first place, a shared language of 'British' (or indeed, since both also adopted and adapted French songs, 'international' radicalism); the songs act as a point of 'cohesion' in Michael Davis' words within a fragmented reform movement. Their subsequent afterlives in the different cultures of Britain (translation into Welsh, appropriation to a particularly Irish 'patriotic' context) provide concrete, that is, datable and locatable, ways of understanding cultural specificity. 'Breinian Dyn', in other words, in ceasing to be a purely 'Welsh' production, gains depth and complexity from its broader British context.

Mark S. Sweetnam, alluding to recent significant advances in English and American scholarship, brings substantial Irish reinforcement to the cause that the textual study of hymns and the socio-political implications of their communal performance is, within the academy, a seriously underused resource. The principal figure in Sweetnam's study is Thomas Kelly, a rich seceder from the Church of Ireland, who, in the first half of the nineteenth century, set up a national network of 'Kellyite' preaching houses. Kelly, a promiscuous hymn composer, from his first publication in 1802, concluded in 1853 with a collected final edition of 765 hymns mostly of his own composition. Sweetnam traces through their multi-editions the evolution of Kelly's theology. This theology became increasingly, in Sweetnam's usage, 'premillennialist'. This foresees the imminent return of Christ when all men will receive their just deserts. This marks the abandonment of enlightened progressive politics for divine salvation on a restrictively sectarian basis. Such visionary thinking is not an Irish innovation. 1790s mainland Britain was replete with secession and millenarian movements created mainly by the vast casualties and manifold economic disturbances of the Napoleonic wars. Sweetnam also notes that Kelly's associate, another Trinity graduate, John Nelson Darby, believed that Christ's return would be preceded by the conversion of the Jews. Darby promulgated this belief in England and on his frequent trips to America where 'it would become an integral part of the Fundamentalist movement, and would go on to have an enormous and pervasive effect on American culture'.

Leith Davis' essay focusing on Irish Gaelic song is a valuable extension of her detailed, earlier work on Charlotte Brooke's *Reliques of Irish Poetry*.

Davis points out that the problems which became manifest in the latter part of the eighteenth century in all cultures of the transmission of oral into print culture is still a matter of considerable scholarly contention. Most pertinently, what are the consequences for remediation if the medium really is the message? Given the problems of translation and, even more, the intense immediate pressure on editors of the terrible historical weight of Irish sectarian and ethnic conflict, how were Anglophone Irish scholars to deal with Gaelic materials? It is all too likely, then, that Brooke evinced a 'marked ambivalence to the attempt to "remediate" Gaelic musical culture through the technology of print'.

Davis reveals how Brooke attempted to provide an aesthetic for Irish song comparable to that prevailing in English and Scottish cultures. She shows, too, how Brooke reacted against the stereotypical comic clownish Paddy song culture of the eighteenth-century mainland Britain musical theatre. She also notes that the dark side of this bibulous, promiscuous stereotyping was that this entailed an Irish incapacity for not only personal but political self-government. Brooke's defining stress in Gaelic song is that of it having from earliest times a seamless lineage composed of serious, even refined, love poetry. Political song is thus bypassed. As Davis concludes:

> Brooke's ambiguous attitude to representing the Gaelic songs reflects her own ambivalent political position. She is, as she notes, concerned to rescue the reputation of the Gaelic people from 'modern prejudice'. Her inclusion of the Gaelic texts in her 'Reliques' suggests her sensitivity to the uniqueness of the Gaelic culture. But she is, after all a member of the elite whose power depended upon the subordination of the majority.

Vincent Morley's essay is an extension of his distinguished publications as both author and editor on Irish Gaelic responses to the American Revolution. This verse, quoted by Morley, gets to the heart of the matter:

> Ciodh fada atá Seoirse brónach feargach
> ag comhrac Washington, Jones is Lee,
> is gur leagadh go leor dá chróntoirc leathana –
> srónach, cealgach, glórach, groí;
> atá Laoiseach fós ag tabhairt gleo dó is anfa,
> Holónt á ghreadadh is an Spáinneach buí,
> is fé thosach an fhómhair atá Fódla dearfa,
> a chómhachta leagtha go deo nó á gcloí.
>
> (While George [III] has long been dejected and furious, fighting Washington, [John Paul] Jones and [General Charles] Lee, and many of his bloated swarthy boars have been felled – big-nosed, treacherous, clamorous, stout; Louis [XVI] is still giving him tumult and terror, Holland is lashing him as is the sallow Spaniard, and by the beginning of autumn Ireland is assured his power will be overthrown forever or vanquished.)

Obviously, this is historically informed Irish Gaelic poetry in that it comprehends the elements of the anti-British alliance of France, Spain and Holland to ensure American victory. It also superficially resembles the violent vilification of the British cause and the exultation in the triumph of the America which we have seen in Blake and Burns' poetry and in Coleridge and Paine's prose. While both such British radical writing and Irish Gaelic poetry display complete disloyalty to the Hanoverian dynasty, they are utterly different in their political anticipations of the consequences of British defeat. For the British radical, it is the vision of transformation into a glorious republican future. For the Irish Gael, it is the millennial return to the true Stuart King and the retrieval of a golden past. Both groups were differently disappointed.

The extended typicality of the abuse heaped on the head of George III is revealed by Morley in eruditely choosing six examples dating from 1728 to 1830 wherein, by not initially identifying the numerical George, he reveals a seamless repetitive stream of often scatological vilification and murderous intent towards the Hanoverian dynasty. Morley sees in this not the revenge fantasies of the politically impotent but an essential lineage of integrated Irish opposition to the British state. This allows him to argue against the contingency thesis of those historians who see Ireland as a non-essential variant of the standard 'ancien régime' state. On another major area of contention, he makes a strong case against the thesis that what we see in this 'aisling' poetry is an apolitical form of 'fossilized' aristocratic verse.

Peter Mackay's account of Gaelic poetry 1770–1820 has the signal virtue of being precisely, factually clear in examining textual evidence which reveals, post-Culloden, no coherent radical programme of resistance in a society undergoing profound, deeply stressful, cultural and political change. It was arguably a society more affected by the Anglophone conservatively evangelical texts of the SPCK than the odd copy of *Rights of Man*. As Mackay cogently notes:

> The temptation is to imagine Gaelic poetry as inherently oppositional and contrary to standard British narratives and ideology; on the contrary, what is often of interest is the extent to which this is only partly true, and to which Gaelic poetry offers a complex negotiation between different identities (Gaelic, Scottish and British). This is not to say that there are no traces of Radicalism in the poetry, but that the political positions espoused (or indeed masked) in Gaelic literature are not simple, but exist in a complex relationship with other social and ideological contexts.

The Scottish Gaelic world Mackay presents us with is, consequently, almost the reverse of the Irish Gaelic world of the same period as presented by Morley with the essential intransigence of its anti-Hanoverian Jacobitism. This should not be surprising. The climactic defeat at Culloden in 1746, immediately followed by execution, destructive repression of clan life and deportation, was rapidly superseded by the Clearances and mass emigration. This was a traumatized society in flux and, as Mackay shows, the poetry is symptomatic of that deeply confused state. Mackay makes revealing use of Homi Bhabba's definition of the malfunctioning nature of colonial hybridity to illustrate the ambivalence surrounding the fusion of the martial spirit of Jacobitism to the British imperial army. With regard to the Clearances, he sees the poets attacking the symptoms, mainly the sheep, but not the root cause, the landlords. There was one great radical poem written about the Clearances, 'Address to Beelzebub', but, published in 1818, it was written in the Lowlands by Robert Burns. Contrary to Bhabba, Burns was a hyper-virile hybrid, his lyric genius often activated by his response to not only Scottish but Irish Gaelic tunes. Mackay ends with a witty note on Gaelic bawdry, where priapic and political risings are tentatively linked. If such a connection can be made, it is apposite to note that the Scottish Gaels seem more anxious about the potency of such risings than those represented in Andrew Carpenter's Irish/English Chapbooks.

The extraordinary longevity and sustained quality of **Andrew Carpenter's** contribution to editing Irish texts is fully exemplified in this exemplary textual and contextual explication of the 1% of chapbooks which he estimates has survived from the period 1780–1820. Written in Hiberno-English, they were designed for a bi-lingual audience unable to read or write Irish Gaelic correctly. As Carpenter notes:

> They are hybrids begot, as it were, by the attempt to communicate in Hiberno-English on Irish-language prosody; they come from a moment when speakers of a sophisticated mother-tongue (Irish) strove to express themselves in a much less sophisticated, half-learned second language.

While, unlike the Victorians, who found such bawdy material anathema, the contemporary reader, Carpenter notes, probably finds the repetitive and 'unrestrained glorification of male sexual power and fantasy of endless, sexually available females distasteful'. Carpenter also identifies, however, several songs of both female revenge, often through the infection of the promiscuously dominating, insatiable male by venereal disease, and poignant female abandonment.

What we perceive in these chapbook poems is the carnivalesque, non-pornographic self-celebration of the common people. While the lyrics are replete with derision for the socially and sexually respectable bourgeois, Carpenter argues that this social tension has no political agenda: 'The world of the suggestive song and the world of genuine political protest do not seem to meet in the chapbooks.'

As a Scotsman reading this, I was made to think of Burns as Scottish song collector, not least of bawdy traditional material. This not only involved his knowledge of specific Irish items such as the infamous 'Una's Lock' but leads one to think that his secretively collected *Merry Muses of Caledonia* probably suggests a mutual exchange of such material between Ireland and the mainland.

Julia M Wright's extensive, consistently explorative Romantic scholarship is marked by its illuminating concentration on the nature of nationalism with particular relevance to the tensions implicit in the creative writer's relation to his or her nation. Significantly, her attention has increasingly focused on Ireland since, arguably, no culture has produced such a sequence of so fertile, complex problems regarding the relation of creative writer to the nation. The main symptom of this disrelation is defined by the concept of exile. This comes in several forms. It can be self-imposed as in Joyce and Beckett who felt their genius incompatible with their native sod. More commonly, given the recurrent colonial catastrophes of Irish history, it was enforced exiles. Ireland, in our period, presents an extreme example of such enforcement. Radical Irish rebels populated Hamburg, the key European city for such men. Irishmen formed a significant part of the radical diaspora to America. Proactively, the United Irishmen set up underground cells in Britain, activating the United Englishmen and Scotsmen, and terrorized the British state. Moore, a quite extraordinary exile himself, was obsessed with the condition of exile. What Wright explores in this essay, however, is not perhaps the more obvious fate of those who fled Ireland, but that of the masculine Catholic leadership, presented in fiction as virtuous, officer-class enlightened civic humanists, who, post-Union, became politically impotent. Their gender was so denied that they were restricted to the private feminine world. As Wright notes:

> While Moore's songs appear to capitulate to a political effeminization traceable in post-1800 fiction's insistence on a nostalgic commitment of radicalism, Moore's larger corpus addresses the problem of colonial masculinity by representing author-figures who, though denied political authority by the colonial regime, still exert some form of power through 'publicity' – or, in Moore's term 'attention'.

Wright's account of 'the disenfranchised' hero in post-Union Irish Romantic fiction and her comparison of this theme with English radical fiction of the 1790s, demonstrates the Irish fiction as a parallel phenomenon with Moore's early song practices is a seminal piece of criticism. Indeed she persuasively argues that the genesis of all Moore's subsequent multi-generic writing is derived from these songs. In them she discerns that both the singer and the male subject of the song are redeemed in performance. These songs then, are not merely the stuff of lachrymose compensatory nostalgia:

> Masculinity emerges in Moore's overall corpus – his songs, his non-fiction prose, his satires in verse and prose – as a complex negotiation with different audiences in which 'attention' can offer an alternative, though not an equivalent, to participation in the nation-state.

R. Stephen Dornan in his cogent, wide-ranging essay brings to our attention two major inter-related problems caused by the ongoing expansion of the Romantic canon. The first problem is the accommodation within the evolving canon of the variety and, indeed, virility of regional English dialects. The second problem is the impact of Scottish, Irish and Welsh vernacular modes of English, especially as this, critically and occasionally creatively, impacted on contemporary English critics/writers and poets. Given the primary democratic impulse implicit in Romanticism, it was wholly undesirable for this new generation to maintain the caricatural verbal and visual strategies by which provincial and non-English voices had been, usually comically, kept in their allegedly inferior station. This could have a darker, phobic side as Dornan reveals in his reading of the pre-Williamite, deeply anti-Catholic Irish song, 'Lilliburlero'. Dornan writes that: 'the rejection of linguistic norms often entails a rejection of mainstream political assumptions. This correlation between dialect and oppositional politics underpins what I call the vernacular aesthetic'. He then illustrates this aesthetical work by a close reading by two early nineteenth-century dialect voices, the Lancastrian Tim Bobbin (John Collier) and, from Cumberland, Robert Anderson.

In his dealing with non-English vernacular writers, Burns is the dominant figure. We cannot overestimate the influence of Burns' songs throughout the British Isles in this period. John Thelwall believed that Burns' lyric genius as a song writer derived from the inherent musicality of the Scottish nation. Sadly, however, he concluded that what the Scots gained in song they lost in poetry. This was *not* Coleridge's view. As he wrote: 'Bowles, the most tender, and, with the exception of Burns, the only *always natural* poet in our Language'. This, albeit cryptic, remark seems to both remove the barrier against vernacular dialect and undermine Wordsworth's anti-dialectical stance in favour of his own purified standards.

Katrina Navickas' very well received 2009 book *Loyalism and Radicalism in Lancashire, 1785–1815* identified the industrializing North-west of England as the new epicentre for the conflict between loyalists as radicals in the first two decades of the nineteenth century. Peterloo, then, was no geographical accident. As the highly literate, independent world of the artisan weaver declined in the face of mass factory production, a new kind of mass-audience, oratorical politics emerged in the form of Chartism. Navickas notes that in the Manchester area in the 1790s United English cells were set ups modelled on those of the United Irishmen. This initial Irish infiltration into the North West seems to have led not only to Irish leadership of Chartism in the area but also appeals to Daniel O'Connell to advise how his Irish dissenting strategies might be applied in an English context. The main focus of Navickas' attention is on authors prior to Chartism but her concluding section does revealingly deal with anonymous chapbooks of the Chartist period.

The most significant author Navickas considers is Robert Walker, the self-styled 'Tim Bobbin, the Second'. Happily Stephen Dornan deals with his predecessor. His main text is *Plebeian Politics or the Principles and Practices of Certain Mole-Eyed Maniacs Vulgarly called Warrites* (1801). The date is significant since 1801 saw the prelude to the ill-fated Peace of Amiens in 1802. It gave Walker a brief, fragile window of opportunity to write a comic dialogue (a form heavily used by both radicals and loyalists) ironically portraying how the Warrites 'just' war had, in *'their* terms', become a 'Bloody, extended and expensive' one. While, as Navickas notes, Walker did not promulgate positive radical values, especially universal suffrage, such pacificism is inherently dangerous. This brings in important generic questions about politically comic dialect use. Does it work by laughter's capacity for disarming insinuation as Dornan suggests? Or, as Navickas suggests, was the educated, standard English-speaking Lancastrian elite's contempt for dialect such that 'out of social and cultural prejudice' they refused to understand them? Also, Navickas does not believe that Walker is writing in the authentic voice of the people which, as his sales suggest, does not mean, that he was ineffective.

Navickas also deals with the dialect of the Wilsons of Manchester. Ironically, Michael Wilson, another Scottish radical émigré, was the son of a Scottish handloom weaver. A more important Scottish influence on dialect was, however, Robert Burns, whose example was omnipresent but whose death in 1796 deprived English dialect writers for almost half a century of the confidence to write in their own tongue.

With a thoughtful 'Afterword', written shortly after the event, **Katie Trumpener** reflects on the place of the volume in recent trends in literary studies, and how it lays out a programme for future research which the series *Poetry and Song in the Age of Revolution* intends to pursue. Subsequent to the extraordinary erudite, innovative Irish/Scottish romantic scholarship in *Bardic Nationalism*, another, more recent potent arrow in Katy Trumpener's comparative bow has been the diffusion of music in our globalized world. We editors, given the pronounced emphasis that was emerging on political song as the principal point of focus for our planned Belfast symposium, were thus delighted when she agreed to act as a Rapporteur for that symposium. What is oriented here, almost verbatim, is the report she read at the conclusion of that first symposium. Densely informative, even more densely suggestive, it is a seminal account of the problems and rewards implicit in bringing the texts and performance of combative political song to the forefront of the study of the romantic period. Her belief that this requires an innovative integration of musicologists, textual analysts and performers is, we hope, one significantly achieved at the two Queen's symposia. It is also a founding principle of the series of books emerging from pour new Pickering & Chatto series, *Poetry and Song in the Age of Revolution*, of which this is the first.

1 READING THE ENGLISH POLITICAL SONGS OF THE 1790s

Michael Scrivener

To say that songs performed in public are complex in terms of meaning and affect is little more than stating the obvious. However, a report in the *New York Times* in the summer of 2009 that the City of New York settled in court for $10,001 with a man who had been arrested in Yankee Stadium for trying to go to the public restroom to urinate during the so-called seventh-inning stretch inadvertently evokes the political atmosphere of the 1790s. The arresting officer informed the man with the full bladder that he could relieve himself only after the song 'America the Beautiful' had been completed. Ever since 11 September 2001, 'America the Beautiful' rather than the traditional and apolitical 'Take Me Out To the Ballgame' had been sung in the seventh inning stretch (a period in a nine-inning game when the fans ritualistically celebrate the moment, usually with a collective song). The practice at Yankee Stadium had been to insist that fans remain standing at their seats during the singing of the song. Astonishingly it took almost a decade before someone finally challenged the practice in court. In the days immediately following 9/11 the singing of 'America the Beautiful' would have been a largely spontaneous act of grief, anger, and special respect for the heroic New York City firefighters. As time passed the song would have become something more like a solemn patriotic duty. Somewhat later the song for most people – but perhaps not the stadium guards and police who enforced the rule – would lose its original anchoring in the events of 9/11. That the situation now is different from 2001 is indicated by the lack of any protests about the court settlement and the new Yankee Stadium policy allowing fans to relieve themselves during the seventh-inning stretch.[1]

Beginning in 1942 all Major League baseball games started with the singing of the National Anthem. This practice, initiated in wartime, has continued up to this day. The hymn-like 'America the Beautiful', much easier to sing than the musically challenging anthem, became a favourite song during the seventh-inning stretch at many baseball stadiums in 2001, but as time passed, most cities returned to the Tin Pan Alley song, 'Take Me Out To the Ballgame', not at all sombre, not remotely hymn-like, but rather fatalistic and unapologetically physical, referring to eating cheap food like peanuts and cracker jacks. If 'America the Beautiful' in fact displaces 'Take Me Out To The Ballgame', it will mark yet another traditional practice initiated because of wartime emotions.

During the 1790s at public theatres British Jacobins and loyalists waged their conflict through songs. In Edinburgh in 1794, for example, during a staging of *Charles the First,* the loyalists' 'God Save the King' was drowned out by the democrats, who also thunderously applauded Cromwell's speeches and laughed and hissed at those of Charles.[2] On other occasions, loyalists singing 'God Save the King' taunted and intimidated the outnumbered Jacobins. John Thelwall complained that 'God Save the King' 'has been made the war-hoop of tumult and civil commotion'.[3] The French had 'Ça Ira' and the 'Marseillaise' but the English democrats, lacking their own iconic song, attached the tune of 'God Save the King' to pointedly Jacobin lyrics, including Thomas Spence's agrarian socialist 'Jubilee Hymn', and numerous London Corresponding Society songs.[4] Edward Williams, the radical poet from Wales, recast 'God Save the King' as 'War Song of British Savages'.[5] Percy Shelley several decades later similarly framed his radical song with the tune of 'God Save the King'.[6] Both sides of the political conflict used the British national anthem to attack their opponents and define themselves. The public singing of songs in this context is a symbolic action to overawe the opposition, strengthen one's own morale and unity, and bring over the audience to one's own side. Songs have to be seen here as weapons, and the difference between physical force and verbal performance is not absolute.

Songs were omnipresent in the political culture of the 1790s. There could not be a political gathering at the Crown and Anchor Tavern in London without songs being sung. At London Corresponding Society meetings and large demonstrations, songs were expected. Thomas Spence's *Songbook* carried propaganda into the taverns and free and easies where labouring-class radicals enjoyed their ale and sang sedition and socialism. On the other side, loyalists disrupted radical lectures with 'God Save the King'. The documentary evidence from the newspapers and pamphlets indicates that both sides were prolific producers and consumers of songs, and that the songs, however different ideologically, were largely identical formally, with rhymed popular diction structured into four-beat and three-beat lines. The symmetry was not complete because the loyalist groups, capable of being mobilized to destroy Joseph Priestley's house in 1791, to burn the effigy of Thomas Paine in 1792–3, or to attempt kidnapping John Thelwall on his lecture tour of 1796–7, depended on government sponsorship and direction. The artful and effective propaganda created by Hannah More's pamphlets of 1793–7 and William Gifford's *Anti-Jacobin* (1797–8) was generously subsidized in contrast with the Jacobins who depended wholly on their own meagre resources and who struggled constantly with libel prosecutions and other forms of repression. In the 1790s the loyalists successfully shadowed and imitated the Jacobins, who did not lack for literary talent and courageous activists but who could not counter the combined weight of traditional Francophobia and a mobilized church and state, all of which produced a popular loyalism at least in England.

Before exploring some 1790s political songs, both loyalist and radical, it is instructive to examine how some writers reflected – and avoided reflecting – on the political song as a subgenre. The form itself of song is in fact a lively topic of discussion in the eighteenth century.

Reflections on Songs and Song-Writing

When Ambrose Philips (1674–1749) wrote about songs in 1713, he considered only certain kinds of songs as truly literary and worth a position in the hierarchy of genres.[7] With Sappho, Anacreon and Horace as the classical models, Philips constructed an aesthetic ideal of the epigrammatic, polished, single thought, 'a little image in enamel'. In his reading of the song genre, Edmund Waller outperformed John Donne and Abraham Cowley, and the French easily overcame the English. His essay has not a single word on the political song, an absence which is explained by the literary historian George Sherburn, who notes that political, drinking and love songs, however popular and commonplace, were viewed as 'non-literary'.[8] Accordingly, the non-literary would not be theorized as literature. With Sappho as a model for the love song, and Anacreon for the drinking song, it would seem plausible to have Horace and Juvenal the classical models for the political song, but in fact those who reflected on songs did not make this fairly obvious connection between satire and political song.

It is surprising that Thomas Percy does not have an extended meditation on the political song in his *Reliques of Ancient English Poetry* (1765), which has so many political songs. Percy notes, for example, how English monarchs coped with Welsh bards supporting rebellion against the English crown, socially disruptive minstrels, and various songs on political and religious conflicts, but he does not devote a section in 'An Essay on the Ancient Minstrels in England' to the political song subgenre. Even more surprising is the neglect of the political song in a later eighteenth-century reflection on the song by John Aikin.

Brother of the poet Anna Barbauld (1743–1825), John Aikin (1747–1822) was the first editor of the influential *Monthly Magazine* in the 1790s, and was a prominent literary intellectual among the middle-class liberal Dissenters. Aikin's *Essays on Song-Writing* (1772) uses Philips's essay as a template upon which he greatly expands and he also develops in the process an anthology of songs to illustrate his analysis. Published by the London Dissenter Joseph Johnson, Aikin's text was reprinted several times in the nineteenth century. Like the neoclassicist

Philips, Aikin reconciles the popularity of songs with the hierarchy of genres, but he also moves in some Romantic directions. To justify the organization of the anthology and its classes of songs he turns not to classical precedent and its synchronic categories but history and its diachronic orientation. Aikin eventually gets to the neoclassical Big Three – Sappho, Anacreon and Horace – but the move to history is decisively unlike Philips. Aikin's literary history is plotted according to standard Enlightenment stadial history, beginning with warlike tribes, followed by pastoralism, farming, and finally cities. This historical narrative provides the structuring logic for his three major groupings of songs: the first group, the oldest and most primitive, is ballads and pastorals; the second group assumes the stability of a settled agricultural society to permit the flourishing of love and descriptive songs; and finally urbane witty songs characterize the most civilized stage of history. Reflecting the impact of Macpherson's *Poems of Ossian* (1765) and Percy's *Reliques* (1765), Aikin assumes the position of civilized man who needs the exotic and primitive intensities he projects onto the literary productions of simpler, more passionate historical epochs. Referring to the old ballads, Aikin writes that the 'language is the language of nature, simple and unadorned; their story is not the wild offspring of fancy, but the probable adventure of the cottage; and their sentiments are the unstudied expressions of passions and emotions common to all mankind'.[9] Anticipating Wordsworth's *Lyrical Ballads* Preface (1800), this passage assumes the ancient ballads are grounded in social actuality and psychological experiences uncorrupted by overly civilized urbane culture. Moreover, the old ballads use an exemplary, natural language the very opposite of the 'artificial prettinesses of language' esteemed by Neoclassicists like Philips.[10] When Aikin finally gets to Sappho it is to praise a model of the love song, while Anacreon provides a model for the drinking song, and Horace for 'sublime' expressions.[11] While Philips preferred the polished 'little image in enamel', Aikin prefers a more naturalistic set of representations. He praises for their realism George Smith's pastoral poetry and engraved images of English landscapes – modelled after Claude (1600–82) and Poussin (1594–1665). Much acclaimed in his day, Smith of Chichester (1714–76), who was from a working-class Baptist background, was admired at the time for the realism and precision of his representations that avoided what was considered the errors of Dutch realism. Aikin's norm of realism was narrow by today's standards, for even when he expresses his distaste for Pope's pastorals as having the quality of 'melodious echoes of an echo', he cannot consider that accurate representations of 'our rural vulgar' would constitute 'pleasing subjects for poetry' but even these unpleasant images have 'infinitely more merit' than those of Pope.[12] Illustrative of his transitional position in literary history, Aikin is backing into Romanticism and away from neoclassicism.

On the issue of political songs, however, Aikin has nothing to say. The omission of the political song requires comment. Because there are no political songs in his anthology and no references to political songs in his essay, one infers that Aikin deemed only the political song – but not the love song or drinking song – as subliterary. Because he himself came from a politically-activist milieu of liberal middle-class Dissenters and London intellectuals, it is not plausible to assign the exclusion of the political song to an oversight. Rather, the exclusion was part of the overall aesthetic system and it was so thoroughly naturalized that he and those who read his text did not even notice the arbitrariness of the omission. Aikin defined a song as 'a poetical composition', which is 'a short piece, divided into returning portions of measure, and formed upon a single incident, thought, or sentiment'.[13] Furthermore, song characteristically produces tender and happy feelings. Aikin is theoretically troubled by the fact that song is universal, existing in both 'uncultivated' and advanced societies, because song thereby calls into question the Enlightenment's stadial history and makes problematic the complacently superior position imagined by the late-eighteenth-century European. The way Aikin discusses music and poetry discloses a high level of affective investment, for he describes the separation of music and poetry as something that was initiated by music, which appeals to the senses only, and the figurative name he gives to poetry is 'heroine', and the name for music is 'harlot'.[14] After the separation poetry survives as the more ideal and spiritual partner. When Aikin complains that most song anthologies have too many 'indecent' selections, one sees that his aesthetic norms entail idealization and sublimation.[15] Not surprisingly, in the huge number of love songs in his anthology there is nothing bawdy or even strongly sensual. Songs about sex and politics deal with the everyday, the common, and the occasional; they seem to be part of the lifeworld – what the phenomenologists call the Lebenswelt, that dimension of the social world of customs and assumptions taken for granted and only partially available to rational conceptualization. Second, the political song does not always produce the 'tender and happy feelings' songs are supposed to create. Third, the topics of political songs are often ephemeral and particularistic, resistant to idealizing interpretations. Fourth, the very style of political songs tends to be extreme, symptomatic of dichotomized conflicts: hyperbolic, demonizing, aggressive, angry, violent, and sadistic. As the category of the beautiful comes to be developed in Romantic aesthetics, it makes the claim of universality, a difficult test for the harshly partisan song to pass. That which is to be understood as the political song is precisely what Aikin's aesthetic idealizations seek to transcend.

The final reflection on the song is by John Thelwall (1764–1834), poet, political and elocutionary lecturer, radical man of letters. Thelwall's brief essay 'On Song Writing' (1822) emphasizes the difficulty of writing good songs, which requires artistry and skills for the exacting demands of the smallness of the work. Only 'minute inspection' and 'polish at every angle' can produce the desired aesthetic object, which is to have a gemlike quality.[16] Although this rhetoric sounds something like the neoclassical preciousness of Philips, Thelwall is actually going in other directions entirely. Practicing a kind of ethnic essentialism, he claims that the English cannot write good songs but the Scots are especially good at it. The two best songwriters are Allan Ramsay (1686–1758) and Robert Burns (1759–96), who by themselves wrote more good songs than all of the English put together. The Scottish superiority in songs entails inferiority in other areas, so that Thelwall is positioning himself – to use Friedrich Schiller's terminology – as a sentimental Englishman envying the spontaneity and energetic imagination of the naïve Scotsman.[17] This heavily ironic essay is richer than I can illustrate here and its ethnic politics are more than a little playful, but the poet who wrote for the London Corresponding Society (1792–9) a number of political songs says nothing about that particular subgenre. It should not be surprising after reading Aikin to find that Thelwall also excluded the political song from consideration because on the aesthetic map, which he inherited and with which he had to work, there was no location for songs of a political nature.

As far as I can tell the first writer in English to discuss extensively the political song as an aesthetic object was Thomas Wright (1810–77), antiquarian and scholar of Anglo-Saxon studies from a Dissenting background. That his *The Political Songs of England, From the Reign of John to that of Edward II*, published in 1838, four years after Thelwall's death and during the founding year of Chartism, was written not by an activist but by a scholar and not on contemporary songs but on French, Provençal, Latin and Anglo-Norman songs, all suggest just how difficult it was to even perceive the aesthetic exclusion of the political. Wright makes no references to the contemporary scene of Chartist songs and the struggle of the unstamped press, but those connections are only too obvious to make today.[18] The double distancing of Wright's angle of perception on the political song – the remote English past in languages other than English – was probably necessary for the breaking of the spell exerted by the category of aesthetic beauty and its idealizing sublimations.

Reading the Political Songs

Reading the English– or any – political song raises the question of approach. Does one read a political song just as one would read any kind of song or poem, or does the specificity of the subgenre require a different methodology? My previous writing on the English political songs of the 1790s in *Poetry and Reform* and *Seditious Allegories* concentrated exclusively on the democratic songs; I identified a recurrent pattern of disguised or muted transgression against established authority. Traditional myths and symbols were reconfigured to support democratic political change; entirely new myths and symbols were rarely deployed to promote the reform agenda. Even the most radical poems and songs, the ones supporting socialism, regicide, and republican violence, sought legitimating authority in a version of tradition.[19] I want here first to examine some of the reformist songs and then look at some loyalist songs.

A song of the 1790s that was composed for a political meeting obscures the actual degree of innovation it advocates by revising a traditional idiom. 'The Genius of France' was published in the *Morning Chronicle* of 30 November 1792, and it was described as the 'best' song sung at the Southwark Friends of the People meeting and public dinner.[20]

> The Genius of France
> While France, full of sense and of spirit, pursues
> The cause of the world, with the noblest of views;
> Where tyranny held her unbounded controul,
> Made nature factitious, and fetter'd the soul.
> Let us fill the gay glass, and with rapture advance,
> The soul and the song, to the Genius of France.
>
> See her swains render'd happy – her cities all shine,
> Her hills 'laugh and sing' with the gen'rous vine;
> Fit emblem of ev'ry true patriot that lives,
> He draws his support, from the embrace that he gives.
> Then hail th' occasion, and boldly advance,
>
> The glass and the song, to the Genius of France.
> See Commerce delighted, extending her arm,
> With virtues, all active, to bless and to charm;
> Where monkery indolent, vicious and blind,
> Laid man all in ruins, and rusted the mind.
> Then lift up the song, and with spirit advance,
> The full-glowing glass to the Genius of France.
>
> See Sages all ardent – see Patriots burn,
> The faith and the moral of nature return;
> While grim superstition retires to her caves,
> And beckons those rebels of nature – the slaves –
> Then Britons join chorus, and nobly advance
> The glass and the song, to the Genius of France. (ll. 1–24)

The four-stress anapaestic lines form a structure whereby each six-line stanza plays against the other stanzas. Moreover, the final two lines of each stanza work as a refrain that provides closure to each stanza and that also cumulatively develops a set of themes. Every stanza but the second contrasts the evils of the old order with the blessings of revolution. In the first, third and fourth stanzas, the first two lines depict revolutionary blessings and the next two the evils of tyranny. The contrast hinges on two key words, nature and soul. Tyranny 'fetter'd the soul' and made it unnaturally indolent, vicious, blind, grim and rusted. Revolution has returned the soul to its natural state of pastoral bliss (st. 2), generous commerce (st. 3) and heroic enlightenment (st. 4). The overall contrast is between pleasure-loving revolution associated with expansive, innocent, pastoral idealism, and a gloomy, inward-looking tyranny associated with Gothic secrets and imprisonment. Each stanza pointedly redefines words with rich political associations. In general, a revolutionary rhetoric undermines a religious rhetoric, principally by redefining soul and nature. Aligned with revolution are sense, spirit, nobility, generosity, love and faith, as the song wrests these emotionally powerful words away from their associations with a feudal structure of feeling. Countering the propaganda that the revolutionaries are godless materialists without morality, the song employs the language that has been used against the revolutionaries. Nature, then, triumphs over the unnatural, as the human soul is now liberated from its unnatural enslavement. The rhetorical battle is over nature. Edmund Burke and his numerous opponents fight over ownership of the word. For Burke, the revolutionaries are unnatural: abstract, speculative and wilful intellectuals who have violated natural law. For Burke's opponents, revolution is an assertion of natural rights, overturning an unnatural old regime.

The song's refrain cleverly involves the audience in a symbolically revolutionary gesture as each of the four refrains commands the singers to lift boldly their glass in tribute to the Genius of France. The word 'advance' here signifies the movement of the hand holding a glass during a toast, and it also has unmistakable military connotations at a time when revolutionary France was at war. In the first stanza, 'rapture' means joy, but the apocalyptic connotations of Revelation's rapture are also present, especially in conjunction with France being identified with the 'cause of the world' (l. 2). In the second stanza, the quoted phrase 'laugh and sing' is another religious echo, this time of Psalm 126. This stanza attaches the Psalm's joy over being liberated from the Babylonian captivity to a pastoral innocence that is reflected even in the shining cities. The bridging of differences – religious/secular, Christian/pagan, rural/urban, English/French – is condensed by evoking *fraternité* with the revolutionary 'embrace' of line 10. In the third stanza, the song urges the singers to 'advance' their glasses, echoing the poem's first line, where revolutionary France is 'full of sense and of spirit'. A jovial Commerce contrasts starkly with a ruined 'Monkery'. The final refrain invites the participants – called more broadly 'Britons' – to 'join chorus', and 'nobly advance' their glasses, as the choral joining and glass-advancing suggest revolutionary imitation: to affirm life, to 'advance' the cause of humanity, one must follow the lead of the French. Indeed, the poem throughout melodramatically represents life-giving action as revolutionary, and immobility and deadly imprisonment as characteristic of the old regime.

This song, then, negates the Gothic gloom of the old regime with the triumphant pastoral cheer of revolution. The song does not reject outright religious words and concepts, but realigns them with a renewed 'nature'. Indeed, the song stresses the visual dimension by beginning three of the four stanzas with 'See'. That which is visible, public, open to inspection is natural; only tyrants hide their secrets in dark 'caves'. The open pastoral plains and the cities of light negate the unilluminated – unenlightened – Gothic enclosures. By redefining nature and spirit/soul, the song recreates symbolically an expansive, cosmopolitan community of which 'Britons' are a part, linked with the revolutionary French, thus discrediting the intellectually narrow and culturally repressive, xenophobic community the democrats were fighting. This song disguises its cultural transgression by portraying revolutionary values not as violent iconoclasm but as nonviolent restoration and return to nature. The old regime is the source of violence; it produces those Gothic images threatening the peace-loving community.

That radical political reform was in effect a nonviolent restoration of and return to a natural condition that had once existed but which had been violently suppressed was an especially compelling idea for the English radical poets who provided myths of validation whereby the origins of the democratic movement were traced to a sacred tradition. Although the French Revolution was the first historic political movement to celebrate rather than conceal its innovative qualities and point proudly to its lack of traditional validation, the English 'Jacobins' rarely embraced and flaunted innovation.[21] Radical politics, according to much 'Jacobin' writing, was not presumptuous innovation but in fact pious fidelity to ancient ideals embodied, for example, in Thomas Spence's Bible or John Thelwall's Saxon democracy.[22]

Another 1792 song, 'The Fire of Liberty' from the *Manchester Herald*, further illustrates this particular quality of the reform movement's ideology.[23] Although this song does not focus on Saxon liberty as such, the first stanza implicitly evokes the Norman yoke ('the Norman Conqu'ror') that stifled a 'heaven-born' freedom. The 'liberty' for which the poet writes is at once divine, ancient, nationalistic, universal, a paternal legacy transmitted from father to son, and a sublime 'fire'. The historical redaction of English history from William the Conqueror to William of Orange is fairly standard Whig mythmaking, except that hurling 'despotic Kings' from their thrones (st. 4) is clearly not something that applies only to the seventeenth-century Stuarts. The figure of fire, a key image in reformist poetry, is at once a source of light, life-sustaining warmth and life-destroying incineration. Fire, an especially apt metaphor for a movement hesitant to declare its allegiance unequivocally for peaceful or insurrectionary change, could serve equally well as a sign of Enlightenment, illuminating the dark spaces of ignorant superstition, or revolution, destroying the old so that the new could be born. In the third stanza the tyrant's blood increases the power of the 'sacred fire' in a revolutionary way. The song's fire also has an expansive effect, bursting the nationalistic boundaries of the 'liberty' to encompass a solidarity with social victims everywhere, 'all the Sons of Earth' (st. 6–7).

Certain features of the song are part of the conventional repertoire for radical poets: the myth of Saxon liberty, liberty as a paternal legacy, and fire as a figure for liberty. A 1795 'Song' by Thomas Best in Daniel Eaton's *The Philanthropist* deploys another convention, the personification of a female Britannia identified with liberty.[24] Indeed, numerous poems, not just songs, depict a feminized Liberty threatened by male tyrants and defended by male reformers. In Best's song Britannia laments how England has deviated so much from its libertarian tradition. I will quote the third stanza:

> Poor country! dear country! – how alter'd and chang'd,
> How harrass'd [sic] and sorely distress'd!
> From your ancestors['] glorious examples estrang'd,
> Whom Providence shielded and bless'd:
> But how shou'd we ever its favours expect,
> Or suppose we shall prosper or thrive,
> When our great men of state, ev'ry duty neglect,
> And at Old England's ruin connive.

The poem, as many other 'Jacobin' poems do, clusters together glorious ancestors, divine blessing, and a venerable tradition ruined by tyrants. In the final stanza Britannia, in despair, plunges herself into the waves. The extreme gesture bespeaks revolutionary desperation and impatience. The poem's rhetoric shifts responsibility for extremism and violence entirely onto the 'great men of state' who have destroyed 'Old England' and forced Britannia to suicide.

Another kind of poem typical of popular Jacobinism was the 'fast' poem. In the 1790s the reformist poets satirized the fast days King George III periodically proclaimed for victory against the French. The Church of England organized these fast days and mobilized British institutions for enthusiastic participation. In *Politics for the People* (1794) there is an especially effective satire, 'An Hymn for the Fast, Day, To Be Sung by The Friends of Mankind'.[25] Beginning with a familiar address to God on the war, the song's speaker notes a level of violent destruction that suggests an apocalypse. The song sets up a triad: the 'we' for whom the song speaks, God, and monarchs. God's responsibility is for letting the kings, the 'scepter'd despots', wreak their havoc on the otherwise peaceful world. The first half of the song identifies 'Monarchs and Princes' as the cause of war which devastates 'us'. The second half of the song, urges God, in pointed biblically prophetic rhetoric, to abolish war by ridding the world of kings; finally, the song concludes with a portrait of what the world would be like without war and tyrants. A Fast Hymn sanctioned by the Church of England would indeed pray for victory and an end to the war, as this 'hymn' does, but this song redefines the terms: kings, not the French, are the enemy; peace is not an insular English patriotism, a 'family' with King George at the top of the hierarchy, but 'one large family of thine, / As brethren knit in bands divine'. The cosmopolitanism of the song is displayed by how it reflects on kings in general, not just George. The song derives its authority to speak in universal terms by revising a religious idiom to accommodate republican ideology. Monarchs are the symbolic equivalent of the Anti-Christ of Revelation or the bloodthirsty Moloch of the Hebrew Bible. Upon the destruction of the kings, however, what follows amounts to a millennial utopia, as bountiful nature once again supplies the economic foundation for a just society. The song figures the tyrants as 'vultures' and biblical locusts, equating war with the plagues of Egypt before the exodus. The song represents a venal royal culture that corrupts society's morality that, after the republican apocalypse, can return to its naturally benevolent sensitivity toward the aged and the poor.

God as king is imaged throughout the poem, to the extent that the song appeals to the monarch over all monarchs to rid the world of kings. Contrasting secular power to the power of God is a common biblical theme, in both the Hebrew prophets and the New Testament. Indeed, radical writers often assume the prophetic stance. The song prophetically redefines 'rights divine' not as royal sovereignty but popular sovereignty; 'nature' does not sanction a narrowly nationalistic allegiance to England and a restrictive social hierarchy, but a universal egalitarianism based on a prolific and generous nature.

Turning now to loyalist songs, one finds similar efforts to lay claim to legitimating traditions and to associate their enemies with darkly Gothic images. Loyalists used the tune and some of the lyrics of another iconic song, 'Rule Britannia', to connect their anti-democratic ideology to popular patriotism, as in 'Church and King. A Song', published in the *Gentleman's Magazine* in 1793:

> While o'er the bleeding corpse of France
>   Wild Anarchy exulting stands,
> And female fiends around her dance,
>   With fatal *Lamp-cords* in their hands,
>
> *Chorus.* – We Britons still united sing,
> Old England's Glory, – Church and King.
>
> Poor France, whom blessings cannot bless,
>   By too much Liberty undone;
> *Defeat* is better than excess,
>   For, having *all* – is having *none*.
>
> *Chorus.* – Let Britons then united sing,
> Old England's Glory, – Church and King.
>
> True Freedom is a temp'rate treat,
>   Not savage mirth, not frantic noise;
> 'Tis the brisk pulse's vital heat;
>   'Tis not the fever that destroys.
>
> *Chorus.* – Let Britons then united sing,
> Old England's Glory, – Church and King.

The Gallic lilies droop and die,
    Profan'd by many a *patriot knave*;
Her clubs command, her Nobles fly,
    Her Church a Martyr – King a Slave.

Chorus. – While Britons still united sing,
Old England's Glory, – Church and King.

Yet – , Faction's darling child,
    Enjoys this sanguinary scene,
And celebrates, with transports wild,
    The *Wrongs*, miscall'd the *Rights*, of Men.

Chorus. – But Britons still united sing,
Old England's Glory, – Church and King.

Thy Puritanic spleen assuage,
    Polemic Priest! restrain thine ire!
Nor with such idle, ideot, rage,
    Against the *Church* thy *Pop-guns* fire!

Chorus. – For, Britons will united sing,
Old England's Glory, – Church and King.

Of *Trains of Powder* preach no more!
Vain is thy force, and vain thy guile!
To GOD and *Kings* their Rights restore,
    Nor HIM blaspheme, nor *them* revile!

Chorus. – For, Britons will united sing,
Old England's Glory, – Church and King.

While, pillow'd on his People's breast,
    Our Sov'reign sleeps secure, serene,
Unhappy *Louis* knows no rest,
    But mourns his more unhappy Queen.

Chorus. – Let Britons then united sing,
Old England's Glory, – Church and King.

He finds his *Palace* a *Bastile*,
    Amidst the shouts of Liberty;
Doom'd ev'ry heart-felt pang to feel,
    For merely striving to be free.

Chorus. – Let Britons then united sing,
Old England's Glory, – Church and King.

Go, democratic Demons, go!
    In France your horrid banquet keep!
Feast on degraded *Prelates'* woe,
    And drink the tears that *Monarchs* weep!

Chorus. – While Britons still united sing,
Old England's Glory, – Church and King.

Our Church is built on Truth's firm Rock,
    And marks each sacrilegious hand,
In spite of each *electric shock*,
    The Heav'n-defended steeples stand.

Chorus. – While Britons true united sing,
Old England's Glory, – Church and King.

Old British sense, and British fire,
    Shall guard that Freedom we possess;
– may write, and *Paine* conspire, –
    We wish no more, and fear no less.

Chorus. – While Britons still united sing,
Old England's Glory, – Church and King.[26]

Drawing upon Francophobia, Burkean tropes, and hyperbolically violent images from political caricature, the song would not have been out of place during a Church and King riot, such as the one in Birmingham in July 1791 that drove Joseph Priestley out of his home and eventually his country. Composed before but published after the king was executed, the song sets the militantly counter-revolutionary tone in the first stanza: 'While o'er the bleeding corpse of France / Wild Anarchy exulting stands, / And female fiends around her dance, / With fatal *Lamp-cords* in their hands'. These allegorical images from Burke and Gothic writing and drama, and from the popular visual culture of prints and caricatures like James Gillray's, mix registers and generic markers to produce fear, alarm and anxiety. The song at the ideological level uniformly and at multiple levels reinforces the anti-Jacobin message. The song contrasts loyalist singing, which unifies the nation, with a violently divided, self-destroying France. France fell into anarchy because of too much freedom and hostility to the Church. Another contrast, drawn from Burke, is between the ancient and venerable traditions of England and the dangerous, untested novelties of the French revolutionaries. 'Rights' is also a contested word, as God and Kings are said to have rights, and revolutionary rights are really 'wrongs'. The song following Burke tries to construct a scenario within which the king and his family are objects of sympathy and concern. The sixth quatrain seems to allude to the French but the signifiers here are England's own sixteenth-century religious war: 'Thy Puritanic spleen assuage, / Polemic Priest! restrain thine ire! / Nor with such idle, ideot, rage, / Against the *Church* thy *Pop-guns* fire!' Calling up the spectre of Britain's own religious conflicts, the song, following Burke, associates the French Revolution and its English supporters with the regicidal 1649 not the Protestant victory of 1689. The harmonious unity and ancient origins of England's glory require wilful affirmation to dispel the doubts generated by religious and civil conflicts. Ideologically the song repels any appeal that the French Revolution might have by using a Whig topos like personal liberty threatened by arbitrary authority to generate legitimacy for the established order. In the ninth quatrain, for example, the song reverses the usual associations of innocent people imprisoned arbitrarily by aristocrats and royalty by focusing on the imprisonment of King Louis: 'He finds his *Palace* a *Bastile*, / Amidst the shouts of Liberty; / Doom'd ev'ry heart-felt pang to feel, / For merely striving to be free'. There was widespread sympathy for the French royal family in the songs and poetry of the 1790s. Even a poet as securely on the left as Mary Robinson (1757–1800) composed several pieces to evoke sympathy for Louis and Marie Antoinette. The English democrats were by no means unanimous on the issue of killing the king and his family. Despite Thomas Paine's well-known objections to executing the royal family, one can readily find approving regicidal statements in the English radical songs and poems. Inferring from the newspapers and journals, however, it seems that on the issue of regicide middle-class opinion was with Paine and Robinson rather than Thomas Spence and the physical force republicans. Playing up the suffering of the royal family, however cynically deployed, was shrewd propaganda for an English audience.

I will conclude with a loyalist song of 1798 that thematizes the ideological use of songs themselves. This degree of self-reflexiveness is not typical but it suggests how overdetermined, ritualistic, and highly conventional the battle between right and left had become by the end of the 1790s.

Song
'H. D. B.'
The Gentleman's Magazine, LXVIII (October 1798), p. 883
The Anti-Gallican (1804), 66–7. Tune, 'To Anacreon in Heav'n'.

To learn Johnny Bull a la mode de Paris,
Some half-starv'd Republicans made declaration,
That they would instruct him like them to be free;
When this answer return'd from our loyal Old Nation;
  'Ye ragged banditti
  'Your freedom we pity,
'And mean to live happy, while frantic you sing
  'Your fav'rite Ca ira,
  'And hymn Marseillois,
'For the true Briton's song shall be 'God save the King.'

Our forefathers bled on the scaffold and plain
T'establish a government, wise, just, and pure:
We'll defend it till death, and reject with disdain
One that scarce for a day or an hour can endure.
    Shall your fam'd Guillotine
    In Old England be seen?
No! – we mean to live happy, while frantic you sing
    Your fav'rite Ca ira,
    And hymn Marseillois,
For the true Briton's song shall be 'God save the King.'

This answer of England to Gaul swiftly flew,
The Frenchmen pretended to give themselves airs;
'Soon, soon, they exclaim'd, shall that proud island rue,
'A New Carthage be humbled, defend it who dares:
    'They Freedom abuse,
    And our kindness refuse,
'We'll enlighten them quickly, with us shall they sing
    'Our fav'rite Ca ira,
    And the hymn Marseillois,
'Shall re-echo instead of their 'God save the King.'

But shall resolute Britons at threats be dismay'd?
No! – we're ready to meet them though twenty to one,
From our scabbards leap forth ev'ry sword, who's afraid?
Though they're joined by the cowardly, blust'ring Don.
    In battle we'll shew,
    To our sans-culotte foe,
That, in spite of their efforts, we never will sing
    Their fav'rite Ca ira,
    Or Hymn Marseillois,
For the true Briton's song shall be 'God save the King.'

If we fall in conflict, how noble the cause;
The stone will record it that stands on our grave;
'Here lies one who defended his country and laws;
And died, his religion and monarch to save.
    This and more shall be said;
    But, thank Heav'n, we're not dead,
We can all of us yet, with one heart and voice, sing
    Not the Frenchman's Ca ira,
    Or Hymn Marseillois,
But the true Briton's song, huzza, 'God save the King'.[27]

By 1798 repression and propaganda in England had thoroughly defeated the English 'Jacobins' but there was widespread fear of invasion, anxiety about the Irish rebellion and massive losses of troops in the West Indies, and general disillusionment with the war. The song attempts to invigorate the declining morale of a weary and apprehensive public by drawing upon yet again traditional Francophobia and appealing to national pride by evoking the forefathers and Old England. Expressing contempt for the French revolutionaries, hardly fearful of the unpopular ideology, the loyalist song is confidently nationalistic, but also suggests that dying for one's country is not a remote possibility and requires justification. More about national identity during wartime than repelling the threat of an English Jacobin insurgency, the song appeals to the example of the forefathers who sacrificed for the nation. The final stanza is an anticipatory elegy for those who will indeed lose their lives. It is striking that the song-writer, who knew the ideological magnitude of the political song subgenre, deploys the political song as a metonym for the two warring nations.

Conclusion

Songs of any kind had little cultural status despite their importance in every social stratum. When ambitious claims for the song and ballad began to be made in the eighteenth century, the political song was left out of consideration because even the most expansive conceptions of the aesthetic field did not take account of something so wholly material and commonplace. To recognize the political song as a legitimate subgenre would have required a sociological awareness that was not developed until much later in the nineteenth century. Although it did not receive intellectual attention as a cultural object in the 1790s, the political song was everywhere and served various ideological and communitarian functions. The song performed in public is a socially symbolic action that intervenes forcefully in political conflicts, especially the deployment of iconic songs like national anthems. To say the least, a political song is a speech act with illocutionary and perlocutionary force. Precisely because the meaningful context of political songs is so broad and deep, reading political songs requires a focus beyond formalism and Kantian aesthetic norms.

2 WHY SHOULD THE LANDLORDS HAVE THE BEST SONGS? THOMAS SPENCE AND THE SUBVERSION OF POPULAR SONG

Joan C. Beal

Introduction

This chapter is devoted to the English Radical Thomas Spence and his use of popular song as a medium for the dissemination of his ideas. After an account of Spence's early life in Newcastle upon Tyne and his activities in London, it goes on to discuss the importance of his 'free and easy' gatherings in taverns as a forum for radical debate at a time when political meetings were outlawed. A number of Spence's songs are discussed, demonstrating how he parodied popular and/or patriotic songs. Although Spence used other media, including graffiti and coins, to propagate his message in ways that would evade sanctions, I argue that song was particularly important to him because, as a popular medium, it created a convivial atmosphere that helped to bond his followers.

Spence's Early Life and Influences

Thomas Spence was born on 21 June 1750 on the Quayside, which was then one of the poorest areas of Newcastle upon Tyne. His father Jeremiah was a native of Aberdeen who had settled in Newcastle some eleven years previously, working as a netmaker and shoemaker and later becoming a hardware dealer. Although this places him in the artisan/small business rather than the labouring class, the family could not have been wealthy, since Thomas was one of nineteen children. All that we know about Thomas Spence's formal education is that, according to P. M. Ashraf, he 'began his working life at his father's trade of netmaking at the age of ten after some schooling'.[1] However, by Spence's own account in *The Important Trial of Thomas Spence* Jeremiah Spence took an active part in his sons' education:

> My father used to make my brothers and me read the Bible to him while working in his business, and at the end of every chapter, encouraged us to give our opinions on what we had just read. By these means I acquired an early habit of reflecting on every occurrence which passed before me, as well as on what I read.[2]

Spence had a radical and dissenting upbringing. His family belonged to the High Bridge Chapel congregation of the Reverend James Murray, who is described by Ashraf as 'well to the left of Whig tradition ... an egalitarian democrat'.[3] Murray's sermons were well attended and advertised in the local press. His ideas on political and religious freedom and his use of animal imagery in publications such as *Sermons to Asses* were to prove an important influence on Spence.[4] Spence's brother Jeremiah was later to join the Glasites and became an elder in the congregation which met in Forster Street. According to D. B. Murray, 'members were expected to care for their own poor, and to hold their material possessions at the disposal of the church, to create a potential community of goods'.[5] Although there is no evidence that Thomas Spence joined this congregation, the Glasites' adherence to the apostolic principle of holding goods in common was certainly compatible with his ideas, and Ashraf states that Jeremiah junior 'accepted Spence's Plan as compatible with Glassite precepts'.[6]

We know little else about Spence's early life, but the title page of *The Grand Repository of the English Language* refers to the author's 'School in the Keyside', so by then he must have become a schoolteacher.[7] Spence was a friend of the engraver Thomas Bewick, who, in his memoirs quoted in Robert Robinson's *Thomas Bewick: His Life and Times* (1887), tells us that Spence had 'got a number of young men together and formed into a debating society, which was held in the evenings in his schoolroom in the Broad Garth'. This practice of gathering like-minded companions together for political discussion was to continue throughout Spence's life. The debates seem to have been lively and impassioned, for Bewick goes on to provide an anecdote about how he and Spence came to blows over a political disagreement. Bewick took the more moderate view that Spence's plan for common ownership of land could only work in a new colony, but not even a severe beating with cudgels could dissuade Spence from his core belief that 'property in land is everyone's right'.[8]

Newcastle in the eighteenth century was a radical city with a lively intellectual life. Bookshops and the circulating library in the Bigg Market were open for twelve hours a day and, according to P. M. Horsley, were 'the regular meeting place of the prominent citizens of the town'.[9] As well as Spence's gathering, there were several clubs, such as the Constitutional Club and the Independent Club, where political debates took place and the prevailing views were reformist or even republican. In 1775, the Newcastle Philosophical Society was formed as a club for intellectual debate in which members took turns to deliver lectures.

Spence was a founder member of this society, along with his friend Thomas Bewick and the Reverend James Murray.

1775 was also the year in which Spence's two first, foundational works were published: the *Grand Repository of the English Language* and his lecture to the Newcastle Philosophical Society. The *Grand Repository* is a pronouncing dictionary, with all words re-spelt in a phonetic alphabet of Spence's own devising.[10] This was intended as the first step towards a spelling reform which would make it easy for what Spence called 'the labouring part of the people' to learn to read and therefore become enlightened.[11] The lecture to the Philosophical Society, which set out the agenda for what became known as 'Spence's Plan', was reprinted several times under different titles, but the original title appears to have been *Property in Land is Every One's Right*. Soon after delivering this lecture on 8 November 1775, Spence was expelled from the Philosophical Society. The reason given by the Society was that, contrary to the Society's rules, Spence had published the lecture as a pamphlet and sold it on the streets of Newcastle. However, a report in the *Newcastle Chronicle* hints that the 'levelling tendencies' displayed in the lecture and pamphlet were the real reason for Spence's dismissal. In Spence's account of his life in *The Important Trial of Thomas Spence,* he asserted that both these publications were equally important and that with these, he had cured all society's ills (at the age of twenty-five): 'When I first began to study, I found every art and science a perfect whole. Nothing was in anarchy but language and politics. But both of these I reduced to order, the one by a new alphabet, the other by a new Constitution'.[12]

Spence was never to change or compromise his ideas despite facing considerable opposition and hardship. Other publications from Spence's time in Newcastle are *The Real Reading Made Easy* (1782), *A Supplement to the History of Robinson Crusoe* (1782) and *The Rights of Man in Verse* (1783). The last of these was set to the tune of the popular border ballad 'Chevy Chase', thus setting the pattern for his later song compositions.

There are no extant publications from Spence between 1783 and 1792. In December 1787 he was dismissed from his post at St Anne's School in Newcastle, and seems to have moved to London soon after this. According to the memoir of Spence in *The Newcastle Magazine*, Spence:

> became discontented with Newcastle, and resolved to seek the Metropolis. He was often heard to say that there was no scope for ability in a provincial town, and that London was the only place where a man of talent could display his powers.[13]

Little is known about Spence's life between 1787 and 1792. Harold Dickinson writes in the *Oxford Dictionary of National Biography* 'there is some evidence that he was settled there [i.e. in London] by early 1788, but that he was unknown as he eked out a living in a series of casual labouring jobs'.[14] By 1792 Spence was certainly known to the authorities in London, for his first publication in the capital was *The Case of Thomas Spence, Bookseller* which relates how he was imprisoned for selling Thomas Paine's *Rights of Man*.[15]

Spence had arrived in the capital at a time when fear of popular uprising inspired by the French Revolution of 1789 had led to draconian actions against anyone espousing radical doctrines. Habeas Corpus was suspended in 1794 and the Two Acts of 1795 extended the definition of High Treason to include acts of speech or writing. Far from being deterred by this repressive legislation, Spence found ingenious and inventive ways of spreading the word: as we shall see, song played an important part in this. Spence became a member of the London Corresponding Society, but his views were too extreme for many of his fellow members. David Bindman tells us that Spence 'was on the radical wing of the LCS; a 'violent democrat', in the words of an informer, with 'levelling' tendencies that worried the more moderate executive'.[16] Much of what we know about Spence's life in London comes from the reports of government informers. Spence was arrested three times between 1792 and 1794, when he was arrested under the Suspension Act, imprisoned for seven months, charged with High Treason, and acquitted in December 1794. The publication of *The Restorer of Society to its Natural State* led to a charge of seditious libel, for which Spence was sentenced to a year's imprisonment and a fine of £20.[17] Spence insisted on presenting his own defence, because this would lead to it being recorded for posterity. He published a full account of the trial both in his reformed spelling as T. Spence *Dhĕ Impörtănt Triăl ov Tŏmĭs Spĕns* and in conventional orthography as T. Spence *The Important Trial of Thomas Spence*.[18]

Spence's 'Free and Easy' Meetings

After his release from Shrewsbury Jail Spence was careful to promote his ideas in ways which could elude sanctions against political meetings. Ashraf tells us that the Combination Acts of 1799 and 1800 prohibited 'all corresponding societies or such as were organized in branches, administered oaths, had secret committees, did not keep lists of members. There were penalties for allowing "unlawful meetings" in public or private houses, lecture rooms charging admission were classed as disorderly houses'.[19] In order to avoid falling foul of this legislation, Spence kept his meetings informal. A handbill of 1801 advertised these meetings as follows:

> Resolved – therefore. That it be recommended to all the well-wishers to that System, to meet frequently, though in ever so small Numbers, in their respective Neighbourhoods, after a free and easy Manner, without incumbering themselves with Rules, to converse on the Subject, provoke investigation, and answer such Objections as may be stated, and to promote the circulation of Citizen Spence's pamphlets.[20]

Iain McCalman considers Spence's establishment of the 'tavern free-and-easies' as marking the beginning of the 'London political underworld' which is the subject of his monograph.[21] Although McCalman here argues that the 'roots' of this London underworld need to be traced back to metropolitan tavern debating clubs of the 1790s, Spence had, clearly, been acquainted with such clubs as a young man in Newcastle in the 1770s. Although these Newcastle clubs had been venues for debate rather than song, the atmosphere was often informal and many met in taverns. Indeed, Kathleen Wilson states that 'at least sixteen distinct political clubs supported the causes of radical politics in Newcastle between 1769 and 1784' and that 'all of these clubs met in inns or taverns'.[22] Jenny Uglow relates how in 1778 'Bewick joined Swarley's Club, which met at the Black Boy Inn run by Richard Swarley in the Groat Market'. Here members paid an entry fee of fourpence 'to be spent on beer only' and engaged in debates.[23]

When Spence instituted the free-and-easies in London, he was thus responding to the exigencies of the times by adapting a format with which he was familiar from his Newcastle days. Ashraf gives the following account of the free-and-easy meetings:

> Spence would reserve a room in the pub for a social evening with friends like any other convivial club and take care to give tickets outside the regular circle only to individuals whom he trusted ... It is possible that the Spencean Free and Easy had a continuous if muted existence the whole time from 1801 to 1814. It shows a remarkable tenacity. There was no conspiracy – just bread and cheese and porter and cheerful songs.[24]

Spence's strategy of disguising his political meetings as convivial social gatherings seems to have succeeded. According to McCalman, 'Spence's free-and-easy organization was intended to be elusive. Government intelligence did not take notice of his small informal tavern meetings until around 1812–13, and even then ... the spy Arthur Kidder did not take them seriously'.[25] In *An Address to all Mankind* in *Spence's Songs, Part the Second,* Spence explicitly acknowledged this strategy:

> What could hinder small Companies from meeting, in a free and easy Manner, and singing their Rights and instructing each other in Songs? Can Tyrants hinder People from singing at their Work, or in their Families? If not despair no longer but begin immediately, too much time has already been lost. Sing and meet and meet and sing, and your Chains will drop off like burnt Thread.[26]

However, Spence here gave the impression that, as well as being a relatively 'safe' form of gathering, the free-and-easy meetings had a genuine social purpose: the act of singing itself would cause the singers' 'chains to drop off'. Michael Scrivener suggests that song played a particularly important role at this time:

Political songs and satirical allegories could be more symbolically defiant than ordinary political prose. Moreover, at meetings, celebratory dinners, and demonstrations, songs played a ritual role, inviting mass participation and gleeful defiance and maintaining morale. Such poetry was designed not to change political perspectives but rather to perform symbolically the ideology already taken for granted.[27]

Song and conviviality were clearly important to Spence. I noted above that he had begun composing political songs and poetry in Newcastle, and Uglow's *Nature's Engraver: A Life of Thomas Bewick* provides a glimpse of his convivial character when she cites a letter of John Bewick (Thomas Bewick's brother, who lived in London) relating that Spence 'called in for a meal and after a drink or two was 'as hearty as a Cracket[28] & as full of his Coally Tyne Poetry as ever'.[29] The role of political song as described by Scrivener in the extract cited above is similar to that of congregational hymn singing and also the more secular forms of community singing at sporting occasions.

Ashraf points out that radical songs such as Spence's were in effect secular hymns, and that the Glasites, the millenialist sect to which Spence's brother Jeremiah belonged, 'were the pioneers of congregational hymn singing' and had 'introduced a variety of popular verse forms and the more lively metres of secular songs and set them to traditional tunes rather than ecclesiastical music'.[30] The phrase 'Why should the Devil have all the best tunes?' is often attributed to the founder of the Salvation Army, William Booth, but the practice of using popular music for hymns predated Booth: as well as the Glasites, Charles Wesley set some of his hymns to secular tunes and the evangelical preacher Rowland Hill (1772–1842) has also been credited with the phrase. Spence's use of popular song as a political instrument should be viewed against this background of communal hymn singing, which, together with his use of biblical references, testifies to the importance of his dissenting upbringing.

The Subversion of Popular Song

Table 2.1: Spence's songs and their settings.

Song	Tune
The Rights of Man in Verse	Chevy Chase
The Rights of Man in Verse	Babes in the Wood
Burke's Address to the Swinish Multitude	Derry Down, Down
The Year Ninety-three	Derry Down, Down
God Save 'The Rights of Man'	God Save the King
Hark how the Trumpet's Sound	God Save the King
An Old British Song	God Save the King
The Progress of Liberty	Britannia Rules the Waves
A Song to be sung a hundred years hence	Hearts of Oak

Spence's songs were often sold as broadsides, but also appeared in his other publications. Many of them can be found in his periodical *Pigs' Meat* (1793), named in a conscious rebuttal of Edmund Burke's denunciation of the populace as a 'swinish multitude'.[31] The illustration on the title page of the periodical shows a pig trampling the symbols of royalty, with the verse:

> This is that matchless Pigs meat
> So famous far and near
> Oppressors' hearts it fills with Dread
> But poor Mens [sic] hearts with cheer

The subversion of Burke's metaphor in the title of *Pigs' Meat* demonstrates Spence's eye for the topical and popular. In Newcastle, he had exploited the popularity of *Robinson Crusoe* to present his utopian vision of Crusonea and had set 'The Rights of Man in Verse' to the tune of 'Chevy Chase'. Although this ballad, which tells the tale of a battle between Percy of Northumberland and Douglas of Scotland, would have had local resonance in Newcastle, Joseph Addison in *The Spectator* (1711), testified to its nationwide popularity:

> The old song of 'Chevy-Chase' is the favourite ballad of the common people of England, and Ben Jonson used to say he had rather have been the author of it than of all his works. Sir Philip Sidney, in his discourse of Poetry, speaks of it in the following words: 'I never heard the old song of Percy and Douglas that I found not my heart more moved than with a trumpet'.[32]

Both 'Chevy Chase' and the ballad to whose tune it was later set, 'Babes in the Wood', were included in Thomas Percy's *Reliques of Ancient English Poetry* (1765). The tune 'Derry Down, Down', to which both 'Burke's Address to the Swinish Multitude' and 'The Year Ninety-three' were set, could have been one of a number of ballads with this chorus. The most likely contender is 'The World Turned Upside Down', published in the *Gentleman's Magazine* in 1767 and itself a political parody of an older song. Many of Spence's songs were set to patriotic songs, such as 'Hearts of Oak', 'Britannia Rules the Waves' and, most of all, 'God Save the King'. At least two of Spence's songs, 'God Save the Rights of Man' and 'An Old British Song', are direct parodies of the national anthem, whilst 'Hark How the Trumpet Sounds', otherwise known as the 'Jubilee Hymn' and the most frequently published of all Spence's songs, includes the clearly antimonarchical line 'The Sceptre now is Broke'. Referring to 'Hark how the Trumpet's Sound', Malcom Chase suggests that, with the royal Jubilee of 1809, the biblical and radical meaning of jubilee, used by Spence, was being challenged by this new, patriotic usage:[33] 'Effectively the idea of jubilee had become contested territory, appositely illustrated in the Spenceans' use of the tune "God Save the King" for their "Jubilee Hymn"'. Chase may be right about the Spenceans who continued to sing this song after 1809, but Spence had set this and other songs to the National Anthem long before the royal Jubilee. Spence's choice of tunes was certainly subversive, but it was also practical: there was no need for his followers to learn new tunes, newcomers could join in without embarrassment, and, given that Spence was constantly watched by spies, the tunes could well have acted as a cloak for his activities: anybody passing by the pub would just hear patriotic songs being sung.

To illustrate both the practicality and the subversive quality of Spence's songs, I will turn to 'Hark how the Trumpet's Sound'. We can see in the content of this song the influence of Spence's early religious upbringing. His minister in Newcastle, James Murray, had defended Spence after his expulsion from the Newcastle Philosophical Society by pointing out: 'Was not the Jewish Jubilee a Levelling Scheme'?[34] Spence provided footnotes and biblical references to invoke this precedent.

> Hark, how the trumpet's sound
> Proclaims the land around
> The Jubilee!
> Tells all the poor oppress'd
> No more they shall be cess'd
> Nor landlords more molest
> Their property.   [See Leviticus. Chap. 25]
>
> Rents t'ourselves now we pay,
> Dreading no quarter day,
> Fraught with distress.
> Welcome the day draws near,
> For then our rents we share,[35]
> Earth's rightful lords we are
> Ordain'd for this
> How hath the oppressor ceas'd   [See Isaiah, Chap. 14.]
>
> And all the world released
> From misery!
> The fir-trees all rejoice,
> And cedars lift their voice,
> Ceas'd now the FELLER'S noise
> Long rais'd by thee.
>
> The sceptre now is broke,
> Which with continual stroke,
> The nations smote!
> Hell from beneath does rise,
> To meet thy lofty eyes,
> From the most pompous size,
> How brought to nought!
>
> Since then this Jubilee
> Sets all at Liberty,

Let us be glad.
Behold each man return
To his possession
No more like doves to mourn
By landlords sad!

The wording of the song is also biblical and hymn-like, which is why it is often referred to as the *Jubilee Hymn*. Spence draws attention in a footnote to chapter 14 of the book of Isaiah, in which God promises to set Israel free from the oppression of Babylon, and much of Spence's 'hymn' paraphrases this chapter, as Table 2.2 demonstrates.

Table 2.2: Comparison of the 'Jubilee Hymn' with Isaiah 14 (King James Bible).

'Jubilee Hymn'	Isaiah 14 (King James Bible)
How hath the oppressor ceased	How hath the oppressor ceased! (14: 4)
The sceptre now is broke	The Lord hath broken the staff of the wicked, and the sceptre of the rulers. (14: 5)
Which with continual stroke, The nations smote	He who smote the people in wrath with a continual stroke (14: 6)
Hell from beneath does rise, To meet thy lofty eyes	Hell from beneath is moved for thee to meet thee at thy coming (14: 9)
The fir-trees all rejoice, And cedars lift their voice, Ceas'd now the FELLER'S noise Long rais'd by thee	Yea, the fir trees rejoice at thee, and the cedars of Lebanon, saying, Since thou art laid down, no feller is come up against us (14: 8)

Spence reordered the Bible verses and fitted the wording to the metre of 'God Save the King', presenting the monarchy and landlords as Babylon and the 'the people' as God's chosen. At the Free and Easy, this would be a rousing hymn invoking the promise of a 'world turned upside down'.

The song 'to be sung an hundred years hence' provides an alternative form of patriotism to that of *Hearts of Oak*, to whose tune it is set. The original words were written by David Garrick in 1759 to celebrate British naval victories against the French, and contains the lines 'We never see the French but we wish them to stay / They always see us and they wish us away'.[36] In Spence's vision of the future, 'Britain's brave sons' will not fight against the French, but will join with them to overthrow tyrants. The British standard, with emblems of Scotland, Ireland and France, is evoked. The flag will no longer fly nor Britain's mighty navy sail in 'a cause that's not right'. In this case, Spence subverted not only the patriotic song, but patriotism itself. It is also possible that Spence was influenced by an earlier American parody 'The Liberty Song', written by John Dickinson, one of the leaders of the American Revolution, and published in *The Boston Chronicle* in 1768. Dickinson's version includes the line 'In so righteous a cause let us hope to succeed', which is perhaps reflected in Spence's 'in a cause that's not right'.

A SONG
To be Sung an Hundred Years Hence.
To the Tune of 'Hearts of Oak'

Come cheer up my lads, lo! The day draweth Near
When Britain's brave sons Freedom's standard will rear;
And joining with Frenchmen, all tyrants o'erthrow,
Th'oppressed world releasing, wherever they go.

Then mankind rejoice,
France and Britain agree;
Their faiths they have plighted,
Fleets and armies united
To drive tyrants from you.

Britain's standard bears emblems prophetic of this,
Caledonia's wild horse, England's lion fearless,
The lilies of France in their quarter behold,
And Hibernia's sweet harp makes the union quite Bold.

Then mankind, &c.

None but tyrants hereafter this flag shall e'er fright,
No more shall't be spread in a cause that's not right;
These ensigns of freedom all nations shall hail,
Where'er the sea flows or a ship spreads her sail.

Then mankind, &c.[37]

'Burke's Address to the Swinish Multitude' is more directly satirical. In this song, Spence put words into Burke's mouth, developing the conceit of the 'swinish multitude' cited in the footnote. This is a long song, but a few verses should be enough to convey its vigour.

BURKE'S ADDRESS
TO THE
'SWINISH MULTITUDE!'
Tune, 'Derry, down, down,' *&c.*

YE vile SWINISH HERDS, in the Sty of Taxation,
What would you be after? – disturbing the Nation?
Give over your grunting – Be off – To your Sty!
Nor dare to look out, if a KING passes by:
Get ye down! Down! Down! – Keep ye down!

Do ye know what a KING is? By *Patrick* I'll tell You;
He has Power in his Pocket, to buy you and sell you:
To make you all Soldiers, or keep you at work?
To hang you, and cure you for Ham or Salt Pork!
    Get ye down! &c.

Do ye think that a KING is no more than a Man?
Ye Brutish, ye Swinish, irrational Clan?

I swear by his Office, his Right is divine,
To flog you, and feed you, and treat you like Swine!
    Get ye down! &c.
To conclude: Then, no more about MAN and his RIGHTS,
Tom Paine, and a Rabble of *Liberty Wights*:
That you are but our 'SWINE,' if ye ever forget,
We'll throw you alive to the HORRIBLE PIT!
Get ye down! down! down!- Keep ye down![38]

Spence substituted the traditional merry chorus of 'derry down, down, down' with Burke's imperative 'Get ye down!', intended to keep the lower classes 'down' in their place: the pigsty of the 'swinish multitude'. Spence created a brutally imperious persona for Burke here through his use of peremptory questions and imperatives: 'what would you be after?' ... 'Be off! To your sty!'

The 'Multimedia Propagandist'

Why did Spence use these songs set to popular tunes as a means of propagating his ideas? One reason is that the 'free and easy', with its emphasis on convivial drinking and singing, was the only safe way for Spenceans to meet. However, Spence had always used popular genres and idioms: his writings made use of figures such as Robinson Crusoe from popular literature, and Jack the Giant Killer from folklore, as well as from biblical material. His intention was always to reach what he termed 'the labouring part of the people'. As Ashraf comments, 'Goliath was slain with a common pebble. Spence turned to the crudest, simplest methods'.[39] These methods included a range of practices all designed to transmit his message in ways that would reach the lower classes and evade the law. James Epstein sums this up perfectly:

> Above all others, Thomas Spence strove to convert the minds of 'the lower class of people', working as a multi-media propagandist in the republican cause ... Alive to the culture of the street and plebeian tavern, he stretched representational conventions, using proverbs, aphorisms, songs, chalking slogans on walls and striking his own token coinage.[40]

John Barrell cites Spence's coins as 'one obvious exception to the claim that the reform societies ... did not seek to disseminate the reform agenda by visual means'.[41] Spence's coins were a particularly effective medium: there had been a fashion for collecting coins and Spence even produced a catalogue of collectible coins, *The Coin Collector's Companion* (1795). The iconography of Spence's coins was influenced by his early mentor James Murray: several bear the image of an ass with panniers, representing the common man bearing the double burden of rent and taxation. Murray's *Sermons to Asses* has a similar illustration of an ass bearing panniers marked 'politics' and 'religion'. Animal iconography is also employed on Spence's favourite coin, which was buried with him. On one side is a cat and the legend 'I among slaves enjoy my freedom' and on the other a dog and 'much gratitude brings servitude'. There is a copy of this coin in the Fitzwilliam Museum, Cambridge, and an image can be viewed at http://www-cm.fitzmuseum.cam.ac.uk/dept/coins/exhibitions/spence/index2.html. These coins are still collected by numismatists, so Spence's message continues to be spread.

3 'BARD OF LIBERTY': IOLO MORGANWG, WALES AND RADICAL SONG

Mary-Ann Constantine and Elizabeth Edwards

On 4 February 1795 the Welsh stonemason Edward Williams, better known as Iolo Morganwg ('Iolo from Glamorgan'), celebrated the acquittals of Thomas Hardy, John Horne Tooke and John Thelwall at the Crown and Anchor Tavern with a song. *Trial by Jury*, subsequently printed as a broadside, comprises four heady stanzas of 'Triumph's exulting excess': mountains of innocence standing firm against the raging storms, spies and informers helplessly gnashing their fangs. In the final stanza, as homage is paid to the defendants' lawyers, the glorious institution of Trial by Jury is claimed for Britain.

> Boast, BRITAIN, thy JURIES! thy glory! thy plan!
> They treat the stern Tyrant with scorn!
> O! bid them descend, the best Guardians of Man,
> To millions of ages unborn,
> Far and wide as the light, of true FREEDOM the soul
> Be thy BLEST INSTITUTION proclaim'd;
> With ERSKINE, with GIBBS, on Eternity's roll
> In the language of Glory be nam'd.[1]

This is not untypical. On the printed page, all brash capital letters, italics and exclamations, Iolo does tend to assert more than he persuades. But a good voice can work magic, even on bombast, and this is, or rather was, a performance. In front of an audience of some 900 people, Iolo Morganwg became at this point most fully, and most publicly, the character for which he was best known in radical and literary circles in 1790s London, 'Bard Williams', or, as he put it himself in the rather wittier 'Newgate Stanzas', the 'Bard of Liberty':

> Of late, as at the close of day
> To Newgate cells I bent my way
> Where Truth is held in thrall.
> I, 'twas to scorn a Tyrant's claim,
> Wrote *Bard of Liberty* my name
> And terror seized them all.[2]

What, though, did it mean to be a 'bard', and a Welsh bard at that, in 1790s London? This was, as Jon Mee has shown, a period of exceptional potential for 'self-fashioning': the character of the bard was reinvigorated at this time not only by Iolo, but simultaneously, and perhaps not coincidentally, by William Blake.[3] Yet Iolo's 'Bard of Liberty' persona was fraught with all manner of contradictions, not the least of which was the act of channeling a radical, oppositional voice through a role traditionally supportive of authority and power. Focusing on a group of songs and poems produced (but not always published) during the 1790s, this chapter will discuss some of the tensions inherent in Iolo Morganwg's idiosyncratic yoking of 'Jacobin ideology to august bardic – that is, public – duty'.[4]

It should be emphasized that the poems and songs which circulated within a small circle of radically-minded Welsh writers, many of them based in London, cannot be taken as representative of the political hue or temperature of the country as a whole.[5] Wales at this period remained, by and large, loyal to the crown; men 'of the people' as they were, the squibs and effusions, and indeed the more heavy-weight political pieces, of the stonemason Iolo Morganwg or the weaver Thomas Evans (Tomos Glyn Cothi) are not representative of popular singing in Welsh – at least as far as we know. Ephemeral genres are vulnerable to historical misreadings, of course: we can only work with what has survived in print or manuscript, and 'dangerous' material is damned twice over by being suppressed or never committed to paper in the first place. But printed Welsh ballads from the period are, like their counterparts in England, overwhelmingly conservative and loyalist: a few anti-slavery pieces apart, responses to the events of the 1790s crowd to the reactionary end of the political spectrum.[6] As there is no significant surviving body of orally-transmitted folk-song in Welsh to match, say, that of Ireland or Brittany, it would be unwise to place much faith in a lost tradition of radical songs.

What survives of radical Welsh poetry and song from this period, in both Welsh and English, was born of the energy created by a few intersecting groups of writers and idealists in Wales and London. Recent and ongoing work is revealing, in increasingly precise detail, how and where the lines of communication between Wales, London and the wider world operated, whether through individuals stopping at each others' houses to copy manuscripts and exchange books, through the webs of information spun by letters shuttled back and forth, or through the sharing and copying and translating of items from published periodicals.[7] Not all of it is radical, certainly, but then the historical record does not capture the half of it: the conversations over dinner, in taverns and bookshops and coffee-houses, the subversive snippets of doggerel, the political songs. In London the societies of the Cymreigyddion, the Gwyneddigion and the Carado-gion all formed sociable hubs, encouraging writers to celebrate Wales by reviving its traditional poetic forms and recovering early manuscripts.[8] Of these, the two latter, though hardly hotbeds of radicalism, had a more liberal attitude to the early stages of the French Revolution, and nurtured attitudes to Welsh language and literature which would, in the course of the nineteenth century, grow into an oppositional nationalism resistant to Anglocentrism.[9] Enthusiasm for the Welsh past and a passion for its language and history did not determine political affiliation, however; neither did the assumption of the title 'bard'. Edward Jones, 'Bardd y Brenin' (the 'King's Bard'), was Iolo Morganwg's conservative alter ego and, by the 1790s, his sworn enemy; a high Tory employed as official harpist to George III, he produced the landmark *Musical and Poetical Relicks of the Welsh Bards* (1784, substantially revised and augmented in 1794), a collection containing both medieval poetry and traditional songs.[10] Richard Llwyd, 'Bard of Snowdon' (1752–1835) was no Jacobin either, but his work is politically complex, reflecting the conflicted positions of the Welsh writer in English essentially loyal to the crown and to a notion of a unified Georgian Britain but disturbed by dark episodes from the Welsh past.[11] There are, in short, models of Welsh Bardism in 1790s Britain to suit most political stances. It is nonetheless the case that perceptions of Wales and Welsh identity in the late eighteenth and early nineteenth centuries were significantly affected by a relatively small number of radically-minded thinkers and writers. Iolo Morganwg, creator of the most enduring form of Welsh bardism, was undeniably the most vocal of these.

Bards are thick on the ground in late eighteenth-century Britain: the literary creations of James Macpherson and Thomas Gray in the 1760s continued to inspire and obsess a new generation of readers and writers in the altered political context of the 1790s. But Iolo's version of the prevailingly melancholy 'last bard' topos is strikingly different.[12] For a start, Iolo's native oral poet is not a literary construct, whether drawn from tradition like the figure of Ossian, or imagined anew as in Gray's Bard: he does not, for example, take on the persona or voice of the most obvious Welsh candidate, the legendary sixth-century poet Taliesin, used as a mouthpiece for prophecy and political propaganda throughout the middle ages (although he did name his son after him). Nor, on the other hand – and in spite of the reams of manuscript he would later devote to the subject in his unfinished 'History of the Bards' – is Iolo's 'last bard' at this point a scholarly reconstruction like Thomas Percy's medieval minstrel.[13] Rather, in the 1790s, his version of the figure is performative, and surprisingly upbeat: Iolo is his own last bard, the sole living embodiment of the line in Britain. The oral nature of the inheritance is emphasized in an often-cited letter published in the *Gentleman's Magazine* in 1789 in which the busy society of reading, book-borrowing and manuscript-copying described elsewhere in his autobiographical writings is transformed into a more arcane world of word-of-mouth customs and 'Mysteries, as they are pleased to call them'.[14]

Iolo's 'lastness', then, is a way of claiming authority; refuting Gray, it rejects the notion of the death of a tradition and looks forward. Performance is central.

Iolo's most visibly enduring legacy to Wales is the *Gorsedd* or ceremony of bardic initiation, first held on Primrose Hill in London in September 1792. Part of the ritual, still played out every year during the National Eisteddfod, involves the conferring of various ranks of poet (ovate, bard and druid) on those deemed to have contributed significantly to Welsh culture; it is an intensely theatrical affair of gestures and proclamations, with great emphasis placed on the spoken word. In theory, claimed Iolo, it is possible for bardism itself to be rescued from periods of historical hibernation simply by speaking it into being: 'the officiating agents of those principles are rather dormant than extinct; and to be called into action by proclamation'.[15] In this way centuries of knowledge could be contained in a single mind, and re-launched into futurity by a single voice.

Between 1792 and 1795 Iolo spent much of his time in London. His friends and acquaintances came from a number of overlapping circles – literary/Welsh (David Samwell, Owen Jones 'Myfyr', William Owen Pughe) radical (Joseph Johnson, William Godwin) and Unitarian (John Aiken, John Disney, George Dyer). Periods of frenzied activity – organizing the Gorsedd ceremony or planning expeditions to discover the 'Welsh' American Indians – alternated with paralysing spells of depression. Letters to his wife Peggy in Glamorgan are bleak, often barely coherent, cursing London and referring darkly to the fate of Thomas Chatterton, who had lived and died 'within a door or two' of Iolo's miserable lodgings in Holborn.[16] Iolo's principal, and most arduous, task during this period was the completion and publication of his two-volume *Poems, Lyric and Pastoral*, which finally came out early in 1794. The book's difficult and lengthy genesis explains many of its idiosyncrasies. Its gentler lyrics, written in the 1780s and evoking a pastoral Glamorgan of shepherd boys and bright-eyed lasses, are laced with the angry footnotes of an increasingly radicalized poet struggling to keep himself and his family alive.[17] Encouraged, it seems, by the response he received from Joseph Johnson, a more strident 'bardic' voice comes increasingly to the fore in the second volume.

Several titles in *Poems* are explicitly designated as songs, and it is clear from the manuscripts that Iolo often composed with popular tunes in mind. The majority of these are drawn from a general pool of popular Scottish and English airs: Iolo thus did not make a point of using Welsh melodies, such as those already published by Edward Jones, or collected some years later in North Wales by the Scottish publisher George Thomson, to inflect his English poetry with 'national' characteristics.[18] It may be, as Daniel Huws has suggested, that his real interest in Welsh folksong developed after his period in London; visits to 'prick down' songs for Joseph Ritson date from 1802, and there is talk of collecting songs in letters to William Owen [Pughe] around this time.[19]

Since, unlike another of his bardic role models, Robert Burns, Iolo did not have the option of a regional language like Scots through which to perform his Welshness, his productions in English can seem on the page less obviously 'national' than those of other four nations.[20] Writing in the Welsh language itself, of course, does away with the need to signal cultural allegiance, and, although the political aspects of his work have been played down (indeed, arguably, suppressed) in Wales, many strands of Iolo's work in Welsh can be read as radical.[21] Among these can be included a largely forgotten aspect of Iolo's song-making in Welsh – his hymns. After his return from London, between 1802 and his death in 1826 Iolo produced an extraordinary corpus of around 3,000 Welsh-language hymns, specifically written to further the fledgling cause of the Unitarians in Wales; he also helped draw up the rules and regulations of the first society and later translated a catechism.[22] Proscribed until 1813, Unitarianism was a natural home for various names in radical dissent – Joseph Priestley, Gilbert Wakefield, John Disney, George Dyer – many of whom gave moral and financial support to the nascent Welsh branch through their links with both Iolo and Tomos Glyn Cothi (who became the first ordained Unitarian minister in Wales). In spite of their rather dry abstraction (which Cathryn Charnell-White reads as a deliberate distancing from the perceived emotional 'madness' of the Methodist hymn-writer William Williams, Pantycelyn),[23] Iolo's hymns do reveal radical themes, from anti-war and anti-slavery to support for those suffering in the cause of rational dissent. Most interestingly, perhaps, they can be read as an attempt to return bardism to its 'original' context, public religious worship. For Iolo, the poet and the priest, the Bard and the Druid, were always one and the same: teachers, explainers, purveyors of truth.

The public role of the bard is, however, compromised when the 'truth' becomes unpalatable to the powers he should technically be serving. The complicated positioning and repositioning demanded by the political events of the 1790s is nicely exemplified by Iolo's English and Welsh transformations of 'God Save the King', the text and tune of which led a fecund double existence at this period as both loyalist rallying cry and as an oppositional piece.[24] Iolo's English version, which appeared in *Poems, Lyric and Pastoral,* is an anti-war rewriting 'intended, till a better appears, as a substitute ... for that old *War Song of British Savages*'.[25] Its distance from the original would not, one suspects, have disturbed his majesty overmuch:

> Peace like an Angel smiles,
> And all the British Isles,
> Joyfully sing;
> Hailing the blissful day,
> Reason's new-dawning ray,
> GEORGE, and his lenient sway,
> GOD save the King.[26]

The Welsh bard here publicly maintains his traditional role of support and praise for his lord (we know, from numerous poison-spitting drafts, what he privately felt), but pointedly shifts the mode from the martial to the pacific. It is a tactful, but not ineffective, form of protest.

Writing in Welsh – possibly at around the same time, though more likely some years later[27] – 'God Save the King' became a mould into which he poured far more inflammatory material. *Breiniau Dyn* ('Rights of Man') is eighteen verses in pure 'Bard of Liberty' style:

> Rhyddyd y sydd yn awr
> Fal Llew rhuadgar mawr,
> Pob Tîr a'i clyw
> Ar gwir sydd ar ei daith
> Dros yr holl ddaear faith
> Yn senio peraidd Iaith
>   I ddynol rhyw.

> (Liberty is here now
> Like a huge roaring lion
> For every land to hear
> And the truth is on the move
> Across the whole world
> Proclaiming its pure tongue
> To all mankind)

The piece, circulated in manuscript and declaimed in 1798 at the spring Gorsedd, met with approval from like-minded radical bards, and seems, indeed, to have had a rare afterlife as part of Iolo's otherwise neglected radical legacy, being reprinted as a broadsheet during the Chartist uprisings of the 1840s.[28] It is, in places, quite explicit enough to be a dangerous offspring to acknowledge in public:

> Clyw'r Brenin balch di râs!
> A thi'r offeiriad bras;
> Dau ddiawl yng nglyn!
> Hîr buoch fal dau gawr
> I'r Byd yn felldith mawr
> Gann drochi'n llaid y llawr
> Holl Freiniau Dŷn.

> (Hear, O proud and graceless King
> And you the fattened priest
> Two devils together!
> You have long been like two giants
> A great curse on the world
> Soiling in the earth's mud
> All the Rights of Man)

The happy coincidence of vowel sounds between the Welsh *Holl Freiniau Dyn* (All the Rights of Man) and the English *God Save the King* may have been enough to inspire Iolo's spirited transposition, but it is worth noting that in 1792–3 a rather similar version, to the same tune, was doing the rounds in London. 'A New Song', which can be tentatively attributed to Robert Thomson, first appeared, not entirely legitimately, under the auspices of the London Corresponding Society in 1792; it was reprinted the following year in Thomson's *Tribute to Liberty: or, A New Collection of Patriotic Songs*.

> GOD save – "THE RIGHTS OF MAN!"
> Give him a heart to scan
> Blessings so dear!
> Let them be spread around
> Wherever Man is found
> And with the welcome sound
> Ravish his ear![29]

Iolo's eighteen stanzas can hardly be called a 'translation' of the eight-stanza English piece, but there are a number of striking points of contact. The Lion of Liberty, cited above, is perhaps the most obvious of these: ('But now the Lion roars / And a loud note he pours / Spreading to distant shores / Liberty's name'). Images of subjugation are also similar in both songs:

> Sore have we felt the stroke
> Long have we bore the yoke
> Sluggish and tame
> Hir buom dan yr Iau
> Pob calon yn llesghâu
> Pob braich yn wann
>
> (Long have we been under the yoke
> Each heart fainting
> Each arm made weak)

In both poems, more generally, darkness gives way to light: 'See, from the universe / Darkness and clouds disperse' – ('Ffoi mae'r cymmylau'n wir / Mae'r nos yn gado'n Tîr'); while monarchs 'with terror hear – See how they quake!' (Iolo's, more amusingly, knock their knees together: 'Gorthrymwyr yr holl fyd / Yn curo'u gliniau ynghyd / Mawr yw eu crŷn'). France figures in both pieces, somewhat indirectly in Iolo's, with 'all countries now, like France' giving the throne to the Rights of Man; in Thomson's poem, more brashly, 'FRENCHMEN are FREE!'). Iolo's piece, also, undoubtedly, develops its religious imagery in ways that feel typically Welsh: persecution and suffering are presented in biblical mode, while the 'true' God is on our side, though he can only be named in secret ('Ni chawn ond yn y cudd / Iawn enwi'n Duw'). In spite of these differences, and although both pieces most likely draw from a common pool of radical imagery, it is hard to believe that Iolo did not have 'God Save the Rights of Man' very much in his mind when he composed his 'Breiniau Dyn'. The fact that the song was discussed during the trial of Thomas Hardy, which he attended, strengthens this supposition.[30]

It is also noteworthy that Thomson's version was reprised verbatim in *The Irish Harp*, one of the various collections of radical songs known as *Paddy's Resource* produced by the United Irishmen in the 1790s.[31] Although Iolo and his fellow radicals never organized sufficiently to form a group of 'United Welshmen' (and would doubtless never have had much popular support had they done so), this pooling of radical texts and imagery across the very different political and cultural contexts of the British Isles is suggestive. That Welsh and Irish radicals should draw freely on a London-based source for their songs implies, in the first place, a shared language of 'British' (or indeed, since both also adopted and adapted French songs, 'international') radicalism; the songs act as a point of 'cohesion', in Michael Davis' words, within a fragmented reform movement.[32] Their subsequent afterlives in the different cultures of Britain (translation into Welsh, appropriation to a particularly Irish 'patriotic' context) provide concrete, that is datable and locatable, ways of understanding cultural specificity. 'Breiniau Dyn', in other words, in ceasing to be a purely 'Welsh' production, gains depth and complexity from its broader British context.

Iolo's postscript to his English anti-war version of 'God Save the King' is a timely reminder of the fickleness of songs, and of how subversive they can be, bounced back and forth across political boundaries, their meanings twisted and turned with the loss or addition of a few lines:

> Copies of the first hasty draught of this trifle, consisting then of three stanzas, were given to a few friends, by which means it found its way into some of the daily papers. — GOULDING, the *ballad* and *fiddle-monger*, of *James-street, Covent garden*, claimed the *Welsh Bard's* little fugitive for *his own*, and set it to very *dull* music, after having mangled it to his mind. — At OXFORD, *a bedoctored Song-wright*, divesting it of its original pacific sentiments, pinned an additional stanza (like a dish-clout) to its tail, full of, doubtless very proper, severity against poor TOM PAINE. — *Alas! poor Song!*[33]

Iolo's account of the song's 'escape' from his control amongst a private circle of friends into the wider world of the newspapers nicely summons up the nervous, unstable atmosphere of the 1790s, in which a political song could, by crossing the private/public interface at an inopportune moment, affect the outcome of a trial, could lead, indeed, to a hanging, a prison sentence or an acquittal.

As we have seen, in the early to mid-1790s Iolo was not the only writer playing games with 'God Save the King'. The meanings of the song continued to be manipulated, and were fought over in and out of court. It appeared in the treason trials when the spy John Groves was questioned about songs that John Horne Tooke may have sung at meetings of the LCS – Tooke had, Groves replied, added a verse to 'God Save the King', 'which he said had been forgot'.[34] The trial of Thomas Hardy included a long exchange on song, as the prosecution tried to establish that 'God save the Rights of Man', the republican song 'Plant, Plant the Tree' and songs by Thelwall had gone the rounds at LCS meetings. 'You know more of ['Plant, Plant the Tree'] than me', countered Florimand Goddard, the LCS member under examination, when the prosecution quoted the following lines at him:

> Plant, plant the tree, fair freedom's tree,
> 'Midst dangers, wounds and slaughter,
> Each Patriot's breast its soil shall be,
> And Tyrant's blood its water.[35]

In 1801, Iolo's friend the Unitarian minister Thomas Evans, 'Tomos Glyn Cothi', found himself in a similar situation, facing charges of sedition for allegedly singing an English version of 'La Carmagnole' at a Carmarthenshire bid-ale in March 1801. 'La Carmagnole' was a song that had, along with other revolutionary anthems such as 'Ça Ira' and 'La Marseillaise', provided the treason trials with a soundtrack.[36] Like Thelwall, Iolo and Evans were, Geraint Jenkins has argued, 'marked men' long before 1801; their 'clandestine meetings, coded messages and druidic moots' were conducted in Welsh, and they were closely watched.[37] Evans had gained a reputation for his revolutionary sympathies in the 1790s,[38] and by the turn of the nineteenth century, local magistrates and orthodox Trinitarians seemed no longer willing to tolerate his activities.[39] He was convicted on slim and suspect evidence, in which personal grudges and informers seem to have played a large part. Iolo, clearly furious about the outcome of the trial, poured scorn on those who had testified against Evans: 'Informers are *state lights* who when they've burnt themselves down to the snuff Stink and are thrown away'.[40]

Iolo railed against 'God Save the King' in manuscript as well as print, calling it a 'vile murdering bloodthirsty song' in footnotes to 'John Bull's Litany', unpublished verses (discussed below) dating from late 1793 to early 1794. The song was, he felt, being 'used as a kind of charm to lay the spirit of the times which is that of rational enquiry'.[41] But when this spell of quietism did not work, when the ministry could not (as Iolo saw it) mesmerize people into submission, it turned to other means. Iolo belongs to what Alan Liu (following Kenneth Johnston) has called 'the disappeared', a casualty of the Pitt ministry's sustained efforts to silence oppositional voices.[42] It is possible to see Iolo as a silenced figure since he published little (and nothing in English, 'Trial by Jury' aside) after his English-language collection *Poems, Lyric and Pastoral* appeared in 1794. In another context, Iolo was not at all lost or gagged, since he was, in the 1790s and beyond, at the forefront of a cultural revival that created a modern sense of nationhood for nineteenth-century Wales.[43] But he *was* lost after 1795 or so to the causes of radicalism and reform in England that centred on London, in which he had earlier so strongly wished to participate.[44] Yet he continued to write; there are manuscripts, fragments and finished pieces in poetry and prose that have rarely, if ever, seen the light of day. If they had – and here perhaps we see the suppression or self-censorship at work – Iolo may have been even more of a 'usual' suspect (an officially persecuted one, on trial like Thelwall) than he claimed to be, as well as an 'unusual' one who suffered the informal hegemonic persecutions of the 1790s.

If it was, generally speaking, not that easy to be a 'Bard of Liberty' in the 1790s, then it was particularly difficult in 1794. The publication of *Poems, Lyric and Pastoral* in January 1794 was followed by a period in which, freed from the constraints of the collection, he was full of new writing plans. 'I am not Tom Paine yet,' Iolo wrote just after the appearance of *Poems*, 'And for the sake of my little children ... I will not endeavour to be so till I am in America'.[45] Iolo never did reach America, but in 1794 he was increasingly drawn towards, and yet, one senses, also constantly backing away from composing works that directly attacked king, church and state.

Amongst the manuscript pieces – which, as we have seen above, may have circulated orally, amongst friends – appears 'Church and King rampant', replying to 'a blasphemous Song that appeared lately (1794) in a newspaper, its chorus, Church & King'.[46] Or, inspired perhaps by earlier Welsh political poetry in mock-religious mode, there is 'John Bull's Litany', an imitation prayer text intended 'to be said or sung in all churches and chapels in England and Wales and the Town of Berwick upon Tweed'.[47] This sixteen-stanza assault on monarchy, war, oppression, Reevesite loyalism and religious and political placemen is one of Iolo's most ambitious political pieces. The text exists in at least three broadly similar drafts, with spiky footnotes that more than double the length of the poem. Although it looks as though it was being prepared for publication, 'John Bull's Litany' remained unprinted:

1.
Thou, truly Majestic, on heaven's high throne,
Our oppressors are strong, a fierce multitude grown,
For mercy we call and to thee make our moan.
    Have mercy upon us.

2.
Oh! spare us a while from the vultures of Law,
That feed on man's blood with insatiable maw,
Till to some foreign desart [sic] we in safety withdraw,
    Spare us good Lord.

3.
Deliver us all from the Tygers of Pow'r
That seek ev'ry moment our souls to devour
Oh! guard us from these in this dangerous ^{Perilous} hour,
    Good Lord deliver us.

4.
From Falshood [sic] canine, that runs, madden'd, around,
Who ^{that} strives to give Truth an incurable wound,
And _{Joys} exults to see Liberty bleed on the ground,
    Good Lord deliver us.

5.
From blood-thirsty K-gs, ^{blockheads enthroned} who make slaughter their sport,
And, shameless, to lies for pretences resort
From the ravings, the Pride and punctilio's [sic] of Court,
    Good Lord deliver us.

6.
From Edmund O Paddy, that bull-making dolt,
Who cannot ^{ne'er could} distinguish a Pig from a colt,
From all Fools of his cast that shoot rashly the bolt,
    Good Lord deliver us.

7.
From conspirating Courts, and their infamous work,
The Russian she Bear, the Pope, Emp'ror, and Turk,
The scandal of Reeves, and the daggers of Burke,
    Good Lord deliver us.[48]

Iolo signs himself a member of the 'Swinish Multitude' in the heading to the poem, but this heading also spuriously claims that 'John Bull's Litany' is a translation 'from the Ancient British of Iolo Morganwg, a Mad Welsh Bard'. To a far greater extent than anything published in *Poems*, 'John Bull's Litany' develops a Welsh radical perspective through wordplay and deliberate mistranslation. Its double-tongued energy can particularly be found in the poem's footnotes, where, for instance, Iolo glosses the 'Archy MacBlunder' of stanza eleven – in reality the ex-Attorney General, Sir Archibald Macdonald – as, 'according to our Welsh Bard, a Fellow that lived about three hundred years ago, in the time of Owen Glendower. He was an Atheist, and made very light of morality and Religion.'[49]

Iolo's paratexts sometimes appear to follow a sort of radical-inflected associationism or stream of consciousness. The reference to Macdonald as an imagined historical figure segues, Iolo pretends ('it puts me in mind of the following'), into a passage from the published trial of Thomas Paine for seditious libel in December 1792, in which Macdonald was, as Attorney General, head of the prosecution. Macdonald had alleged at Paine's trial that Part Two of *Rights of Man* (1792) represented hereditary monarchy as an 'oppressive and abominable tyranny', and that it claimed that the British people 'had no law to defend our lives, our property, or our reputations; but were reduced back to a state of Nature.'[50] '[W]hat horrid falshood [sic]', Iolo counters, 'to assert that Tom Paine had said any such thing! – what horrid Atheism, that makes light of morality and religion!'[51] In his criticism of Macdonald Iolo transports the legal controversies of 1792 to 'three hundred years ago', and to (or so he claims) the rebellious age of Owain Glyndŵr, a real historical figure who led the last Welsh uprising against the English in 1400.[52] The maths, however, fail to reach as far back as Glyndŵr's late fourteenth-century Wales; they take us, instead, to a period of history that does not exist in quite the way that Iolo suggests it does. In this way Iolo carefully displaced his attack on Macdonald. As they are shaded by the medieval Welsh past, so it becomes more difficult to see Iolo's criticisms of the Attorney General as clear and unambiguous – and, perhaps, more difficult to construe his comments as libellous.

This sort of ludic Welsh radicalism takes a linguistic turn in the footnote to stanza thirteen:

> 13.
> From the broods of self-interest with dagger in hand,
> That drive humble Reason away from the Land,
> From these Journey-men K—s, a detestable band,
>   Good Lord deliver us.[53]

Pretending to enlarge on this passage, Iolo notes,

> it is not very clear what the Welsh Bard means by K—s, it may possibly be Knaves, the word in the original welsh is Brenin, which anciently signified K—g, synonymous to Knave. In its modern acceptation it signifies any Officer that executes the Law, from the Monarch up to the Hangman, this may be wrong, tho' it does not yet appear to be so, for the Welsh Bards and their language are very barbarous things. I asked the old Celtic Rhymer what he meant by the word Brenin, Why said he, I mean a Journey-man K—, that is a Bumbailiff, Hangman, Informer, Attorney general, or, in short a place-man of any description whatever.[54]

Iolo's joke here is a simple one that relies only on knowing the real meaning of the word *brenin*, Welsh for 'king'. But it offers an example of what using the Welsh language permits in an English-language context, in an unstable and litigious moment. As Iolo conjures with the word *brenin*, playing off the terms *king* and *knave*, he is also careful not to leave much at his door. The joke is cautiously blurred or distorted by the distancing effect of a hypothetical translation, and the final abbreviation – 'a Journey-man K—' leaves the *reader* to fill in either the word *king* or the word *knave*. Balanced on only one word, Iolo's joke is, we feel, easily understood, unlike his more complex wordplay elsewhere in the poem. Yet using Welsh at all raises questions about intelligibility. Welsh enables the inclusion of edgy comments, but also risks obscurity; risks failing to make the point at all.

Even aside from Iolo's play on kings and knaves, 'John Bull's Litany' is an exceptionally layered poem. There is, for example, first the unnamed member of the 'Swinish Multitude' who claims authorship of the poem. Then there is the poem's invented Iolo Morganwg, the 'Mad Welsh Bard'. Finally, in contrast to Iolo the 'old Celtic Rhymer', there is the 'real' Iolo Morganwg somewhere behind the poem, the flesh and blood figure who would later sing his stanzas at the Crown and Anchor. 'John Bull's Litany' clearly draws on the urban radicalism of 1793–4, especially its poems and songs, but, perhaps more uneasily, it is also located nowhere (sold at a non-existent bookshop, in a made-up street), and set in no-time: 'Pandæmonium, printed by Edmund and Teague, and sold by Paddy Macdonald, at the sign of Burke's Head, in Quibble Court, All-fools Alley, in the year one thousand seven hundred and nine o' clock'.[55]

These fake, satirical printer's details may hint at the fugitive and disoriented mood of some opposition writers around 1794, but Iolo's sense of the absurd here also ridicules the repressive forces increasingly acting on radicals in this period. Being unclear and non-committal came to seem necessary for radical sympathizers, particularly after 1792. In 1794, Thomas Spence noted how it was necessary 'to publish every thing relating to Tyranny and Oppression, though only among brutes, in the most guarded manner'.[56] Poems featuring tigers (Spence's example) and other beasts were likely, Spence warns, to be understood as seditious comments on kings and governments 'in these prosecuting times' (and that they were commenting on these subjects is beside the point). In 1794 Daniel Isaac Eaton was acquitted of seditious libel for publishing Thelwall's 'King Chaunticlere' fable, yet despite this turn of events – or perhaps because of it – allegorical writing remained an unsafe activity in this year.[57] 'John Bull's Litany', with its 'vultures of Law' and 'Tygers of Pow'r' is, just a little, playing with fire.

Iolo's stage-managed complaints about the obscurity of the poem apparently translated as 'John Bull's Litany' – 'it is not very clear what the Welsh Bard means' – flag up something that is a problem for readers and interpreters, but also a problem (as well as an opportunity) for *writers*. Blurring his references, Iolo fashions a 'catch me if you can' response to attempts to suppress subversive or seditious voices. However, Iolo's interest in vague, ambiguous methods of representation had a particular relevance in late 1793 to early 1794 since he had his own brush with Sir Archibald Macdonald in this period. In a letter of January 1794 Iolo claimed that his writings had recently been reviewed by the Middlesex Grand Jury – that is, they had been examined for evidence on which to base a prosecution. '[T]hough [the jury] strove with might and main', Iolo remarked, 'they could find neither personality nor any particular and direct application. It was of course dismissed'.[58] 'It would have been good for Archy Mac blunder and his bear-leaders' Iolo continued,

> if he had not been the means of acquainting daring writers that any one might write for the kingdom of Eutopia [sic], whatever he pleased, provided he applied nothing to the government of England. This is very good and I shall soon avail myself of the information.[59]

The 'Litany' is an intensely cynical and oppositional piece, still aching over Burke and Paine, John Reeves and 'Archy MacBlunder', yet, more seriously, it also repeatedly calls for divine intervention in the current scene of war and political tyranny. The work of the prayer, the hopes and pleas of the speaker or singer, are not at all lost in the satire. The 'Litany' represents Iolo's attempts to move on, move away from *Poems, Lyric and Pastoral*, but it also remains a deeply occasional poem. In this, it is typical of Iolo's political songs, both Welsh and English, closely meshed as they are into the particular language and imagery of other songs born of 1790s radicalism. It is appropriate, perhaps, that his most ostentatiously bardic production for this period, *Trial by Jury*, is itself a song about proceedings in which song had played a minor but significant role. Unlike *Trial by Jury*, 'John Bull's Litany' has no known performance context, yet it does have a public aspect in its aspirations – however satirical these may be – 'to be sung or said in all chapels and churches in England and Wales and the Town of Berwick upon Tweed'. The silencing of this piece, forgotten in manuscript, is thus perhaps oddly incomplete. It now seems to speak out from within Iolo's manuscript volumes, articulating the reflections and protests Iolo could not complete, or dared not publish, as a Bard of Liberty in 1794.

4 CANONICITY AND RADICAL EVANGELICALISM: THE CASE OF THOMAS KELLY

Mark S. Sweetnam

The Early Printed Books collection of the Library of Trinity College Dublin holds copies of some of the many versions and editions of hymnbooks produced by Dublin evangelical clergyman and secessionist Thomas Kelly (1769–1854).[1] Among its holdings is a copy of the sixth edition (1826) of Kelly's *Hymns on Various Passages of Scripture* which is inscribed 'For Lady Powerscourt'. Theodosia Wingfield, Lady Powerscourt was the widow of the fifth Viscount Powerscourt, the *chatelaine* of the great Powerscourt estate in County Wicklow, and a person of definite significance in Irish society.[2] At first glance, such a personage might seem an unlikely recipient for the gift of a small volume of hymns, written by an enthusiastic evangelical who had seceded from the established church, and established a denomination of his own. The fact that the gift was perfectly chosen, and eminently suitable is an indication of the extent of the impact that radical evangelicalism was having on the shape of Irish society. This chapter will outline this impact by examining the contents of this and other volumes, considering the significance of the hymns written and published by Kelly.

That the close of the eighteenth century was a time of unprecedented social upheaval is an historical truism. Revolutions in France and America, armed uprising in Ireland and increased social unrest in England seemed to be the harbingers of a cataclysmic reordering of established society. The world, it appeared, was changing, violently and irrevocably. And this social transformation was echoed in a far-reaching religious transformation. As evangelicalism began to prosper, the assumptions that had underpinned generations of religious life were vigorously questioned. The hegemony of an established church that embodied and perpetuated the existing social order came increasingly under attack. Seceders – both laity and clergy – left the church behind in a conscious – though not concerted – bid to rediscover the pristine purity of Christian life outside the camp. These primitivist endeavours were always implicitly – though seldom explicitly – radical in their theology. And this theology tended – as theology does – to have significant social implications. The precise nature of those implications remains the subject of heated historiographical debate, but their existence is difficult to deny.[3] Much of the debate has centred on Methodism, and thus, arguably, on the more conservative end of the evangelical spectrum. Other secessionists were far more willing to abandon the structures of an ordained ministry and a set liturgy in favour of egalitarian Christian communities where education and social class conveyed no special status.

In fact, as David Bebbington has argued, evangelicalism is invariably activist in nature.[4] While that activism may, at various points in the history of the movement, have taken different forms, it has always existed, both as a theological and a social force. Socially, the evangelicalism of the eighteenth and nineteenth centuries had a decidedly radical orientation. The implications of a thorough-going application of evangelical verities demanded a reappraisal of the institutions of society, and of the role of the individual in relation to that society. The recent efflorescence of scholarship on evangelicalism has done much to highlight the importance of evangelical theology as a socially radical force.[5]

The theological radicalism of late eighteenth-century evangelicalism is, perhaps, most clearly expressed in its understanding of prophetic Scripture. The period covered by this volume was marked by a dramatic increase in prophetic speculation, and a paradigm shift in the way in which Biblical prophecy was understood.[6] The prevailing optimistic postmillennialism, which anticipated the gradual improvement of society until millennial bliss was achieved, was difficult to sustain in the light of the events on the continent and across the Atlantic.[7] Increasingly, individuals within and without the established church were turning instead to a premillennialism that expressed deep pessimism about the eventual fate of society and that anticipated its violent demolition prior to the return of Christ.[8] Though premillennialism expectation was in general quietist, tending not to express itself in political activism, it nonetheless indicated a radical rethinking of the assumptions of the Enlightenment. As Timothy Stunt's account reveals, varieties of premillennial expectation abounded, and the details of contesting schema were hotly debated. But these debates were of a more enduring significance than we might, at first, imagine. Ireland's most significant theological export in this, or arguably in any period, was the dispensationalism that developed in parallel with the emergence of the Open Brethren in Dublin.[9] From Dublin, this distinctive premillennialism spread to England, and, with the help of numerous visits from John Nelson Darby, to America. There it would become an integral part of the Fundamentalist movement, and would go on to have an enormous and pervasive effect on American culture.[10] Kelly provides a useful perspective here. The background to the emergence of dispensational premillennialism in the thought of the Irish clergyman John Nelson Darby is both unclear and contested.[11] F. F. Bruce's conclusion that Darby's ideas emerged from the prophetic speculation that 'was in the air in the 1820s and 1830s among eager students of unfulfilled prophecy' is not terribly satisfactory.[12] Intellectual historians may struggle to define what influence is, and how it may operate, but, in general, they seek for origins somewhat more concrete than the æther. Unsatisfactory though it may be, it remains the best explanation that we have to hand. By considering the eschatology embodied in Kelly's hymns we gain an important insight concerning the nature of radical Irish evangelicalism at the turn of the nineteenth century. We can also understand more about the origins and development of an interpretation of Scripture that had social and cultural, as well as theological reverberations far beyond the time and the place in which Kelly ministered.

It is vital that we correctly estimate the importance of evangelical literature in creating and propagating this social impact. Too often, the literature produced and consumed by evangelical Christians has remained below the scholarly radar, because it has not been recognized as part of the canon of literary studies. Since the days of Matthew Arnold and the Leavises, that canon has grown in scope and diminished in determinative power. Nonetheless, it continues to influence the focus of scholarly enquiry, and continues, therefore, to discriminate against the popular literary culture of radical evangelicalism. Hymns are an especially illuminating way of thinking about issues of canonicity. While individual works have, at times, been revered as great literary accomplishments, hymns as a whole have never really formed part of the mainstream canon. And, even as the notion of a single and totalizing canon has disintegrated, and as non-canonical texts have been 'discovered' and recovered by all sorts of sectional interests within the discipline of English, hymns have remained largely unchampioned. This is a particularly unfortunate fact for studies of the Romantic period, given both the sheer number of hymns produced during the period, and the significance of those hymns for our understanding of the movement. A similar argument can, and will, be made for the relevance of hymnody to the study of radical poetry. As the channel, *par excellence*, for the dissemination of the ideas of radical evangelicalism, there are very considerable benefits to be gleaned from paying attention to the content of these works. And it is equally important that we pay attention to the way in which hymns work. The way in which hymns are experienced and consumed gives them a unique cultural power. They had all the advantages that give poetry its peculiar power to form opinion. Like ballads, they added to this the further advantage of being singable and sung. And, uniquely, they drew authority from their association with religious observance and their use of the tropes and language of Scripture. The importance of the hymn as a cultural force is difficult to overstate.

However, scholars have managed to overlook this importance. It is easy to recognize the truth of S. T. Kimbrough's complaint that 'hymnody as a branch of study in theological and Christian education has enjoyed little integrity, due to approaches to the subject which have not taken hymns themselves seriously as theology'.[13] Richard Mouw further suggests that 'historians have only just begun to describe the profound connections that hymnody sustains to other spheres of existence'.[14] Nor has sociology been kinder, failing, as it has, to appreciate the significance of a community's hymns to the creation of their identity and the forging of their thought. Indeed, with some honourable exceptions, there has been a notable lack of engagement with the texts of hymns, or with their value as literature and as commentary on society.[15] Particularly valuable amongst these exceptions is J. R. Watson's *The English Hymn* (1999). Watson is trenchant in his defence of the literary value of hymns. In them, he contends, we find 'traces of the great contradictions and confusions of our fallen and redeemed nature'.[16] Hymns, he argues, 'are not Christian Dogmatics, or Systematic Theology, but the expression of human religious experience, the dark places of the soul, the exaltation, the sense of penitence, and the sense of joy'.[17] Mouw stresses their role as 'an important means of theological pedagogy' and as 'an important record of the past spiritual experiences of the believing community'.[18] Stephen Marini has made similar point in relation to the importance of the hymn for the formation of American evangelicalism, and his analysis generalizes admirably to evangelicalism on the eastern side of the Atlantic.

> Hymns have performed vital functions in evangelical religious culture. The experience of singing is central to revivalism, the characteristic evangelical ritual mode, and hearing or meditating upon hymns often mediates the new birth, the movement's classic form of spiritual experience. For all evangelicals, hymn-singing has been a primary vehicle of transcendence, the very wind of the Spirit itself. Hymns have also served as educational media for children, aids to prayer for adults, homiletic devices for preachers, and literary material for poets and novelists. They played a crucial role in the transmission of Christianity to African Americans and Native Americans. Above all, hymns have articulated the everyday beliefs and practices of generations of American evangelicals. In all these ways hymnody has played a crucial role in creating the evangelical movement in America.[19]

It is important, however, that we do not underestimate the complexity of hymns as texts. One of the key factors complicating the canonical assimilation of hymnody is the textual instability of hymns. The route that hymns take to their place in our consciousness is far from simple, and at no point on that route can we assume that meaning has been fixed. As David Stowe has pointed out, in an American context:

> Sacred songs are densely layered artifacts, gathering additional meanings over time. Hymns are at once intensely personal yet eminently social documents ... Hymns can be remarkable linguistic and musical palimpsests. They are revised formally by hymnbook editors, compilers, translators, and ecclesiastical authorities. Informally they are

altered by worship leaders, music directors, organists, soloists, and congregations who adapt them over time ... Words are often created independently of music, producing an even more complexly determined artifact.[20]

In attempting to trace and understand the cultural power of the hymn, it is important to allow for the complex layers of mediation that stand between authorial intent and the end product received by congregations or individuals. In particular, it is worth remembering that hymns are most commonly experienced not in single author works, but in hymnbooks. This is an important point, given the perennial willingness of the editors of these collections to reshape these texts in small but significant ways, in the interests of maintaining doctrinal probity.

Editorial intervention is only one means of transforming the meaning of hymns, and instability in meaning often goes beyond the words on the page. Different presuppositions on the part of an audience can radically alter the perceived meaning of the text of a hymn. This transformation is possible because of the tendency to use the language of Scripture – language that will have specific meaning for some of those who sing the hymn. Edith Blumhofer remarks on this process at work in Fanny Crosby's use of the rhetoric of the Methodist 'holiness' movement. The 'language [used is] often simply familiar Christian terminology invested with particular meaning. One could employ its general sense without intending its particular connotations'. This shared body of language is a result of the fact that evangelical Christians 'tapped a common heritage, though all who sang the words did not endorse the same theological detail'.[21] Furthermore, meaning in hymns is often underdetermined. The compression and ellipsis vital to effective hymn writing introduce theological ambiguities, allowing the meaning of the hymn to be renegotiated by an audience whose presuppositions are different from those of the writer. Thus, a hymn that is, let us say, post-millennial in its intent may well be performed, and appreciated, as a pre-millennial work, with its imagery transposed to a different matrix of reference.

Hymns, then, do present challenges; they also promise rewards for the scholar prepared to address these challenges. And, indeed, it would be impossible to attempt to understand the history of evangelicalism without understanding the role and power of the evangelical hymn. The record of Methodism would be incomplete without Charles Wesley's hymns, or the story of American revivalism only partially told without the contributions of Ira Sanky, P. P. Bliss and Fanny Crosby being included. So, too, will the history of radical Irish evangelicalism fall short unless it includes the hymns that expressed and formed new doctrinal emphases. Nor can we neatly confine the sociological importance of the hymn to the study of evangelical history. To do so would be to underestimate the influence of evangelicalism and the extent to which its key texts were disseminated through society. Hymns were widely consumed and, as well as functioning as theological vehicles perpetuating the central tenets of evangelical doctrine, they served to spread the key assumptions of the evangelical world view well beyond the walls of church or chapel. Often simple in their language, and plain in their metrical form and musical setting, the hymns of the evangelical movement were ideally placed to appeal across a wide social spectrum. In the stratified and confessionally fractured context of society at the turn of the nineteenth century, hymns provided a sort of ideological *lingua franca*. As such, hymns have the potential to serve as valuable historical resources.

Hymns, then, are illuminating cultural artefacts from a theological, a literary, and an historical perspective. Their importance, in each of these contexts, is substantial. And that importance is often entirely independent of literary merit. Great hymns need not be great poems, and too elevated a literary tone could just as easily serve as an impediment to the impact of the hymn. Indeed, hymns have a particular value in the study of verse, for they embody for us the form in which it was encountered by most people, most of the time. Quite simply, no other poetic genre has anything like the social reach of the hymn. Accompanied by their musical settings hymns, regularly sung in ecclesiastical and domestic contexts, were uniquely equipped to form an integral part of the social consciousness, as well as the theological formation, of generations.

The history of radical evangelicalism in Ireland is an important one. Thomas Kelly was only one figure in the increasing growth of evangelical dissent that centred on Dublin. Indeed, it was in Ireland that what Grayson Carter has termed the 'unacceptable face of evangelicalism' was most clearly on display:

> While a few examples of outré clergy could still be found in England, during the first decade of the nineteenth century they became noticeable in and around Dublin. Here, a revival of so-called 'apostolic' practices occurred around 1803, accompanied by determined separatism, anti-Erastianism, anti-clericism, and high Calvinism. This movement quickly led to the secessions of two of the most prominent Irish Evangelicals from the Church of Ireland, as well as to the creation of two new religious 'connexions' which rivalled – and often vehemently opposed – both the Anglican Establishment and one another.[22]

Kelly was not the most colourful of these secessionists – that honour falls to John Walker. Nonetheless, his influence on Anglicanism in Ireland and beyond was to be deeply significant.

Thomas Kelly's biography is typical, in many ways, of the Ascendency Protestants who were the main secessionists from the Anglican via media over the next half decade or so. Born in 1769, the son of Thomas Kelly a prominent and wealthy Dublin lawyer, Kelly enjoyed a privileged upbringing. He seemed destined to follow his father in a legal career, and entered Trinity College Dublin to read Law in 1795. While at Trinity, he came into contact with John Walker, and began a spiritual journey that culminated in his abandoning law – to the dismay of his family – and taking orders in the Church of Ireland in 1792. On taking orders, he rapidly b ame identified with the radical evangelical fringe of the Established Church, attracting the disapproval and censure of his superiors for 'irregulaity' and 'preaching strange and pernicious doctrines'.[23] Inhibited by Dublin's archbishop, Robert Fowler, Kelly took to preaching in the open air, and in dissenting chapels. Over time, he moved towards his eventual secession from the established church, and set up his own connexion of chapels, partly in collaboration with the countess of Huntington. Drawing on his very considerable private fortune (which had been usefully augmented by his marriage) Kelly soon established a national network of preaching houses, and his followers soon came to be known as Kellyites. It was with these congregations in mind that Kelly engaged in a programme of anthologizing the hymns of others, and writing individual compositions of his own. He was nothing if not prolific. His first collection, *A Collection of Psalms and Hymns extracted from Various Authors, by Thomas Kelly* (1802) contained, in addition to 247 hymns by various authors, an appendix of thirty-three hymns written by Kelly himself. In 1804, he produced *Hymns on Various Passages of Scripture* a collection of ninety eight of his own hymns, which was updated in 1806, 1809 and 1812. The 1812 edition was divided into two parts, the second of which was entitled *Hymns for Social Worship*. An 1815 collection entitled *Hymns by Thomas Kelly: Not before Published* was incorporated into a new edition of *Hymns on Various Passages of Scripture* in 1820, and this was enlarged later in 1820, in 1826, 1836, 1840, 1846 and 1853. By the time the collection had reached its final edition it included no less than 765 hymns, mostly written by Kelly himself.

In addition to the general usefulness and importance of hymns as sources, Kelly's hymns have a relevance to assessments of his theological views. In his prose writings, Kelly avoided doctrinal specifics, stressing the 'one thing necessary' of the gospel, and emphasizing a broadly inclusive ecclesiology, in keeping with that adopted by other secessionists throughout the nineteenth century. It is only in his hymns that we really get an insight into those issues and concepts that Kelly regarded as essential for the formation of evangelical believers in Ireland in the first half of the nineteenth century. In this context, Kimbrough's contention that 'hymns are theology and hymns are liturgy' gains considerable force.[24] As in many evangelical communions, hymns and scripture provided the only set text for worship and for witness. So, in the iterations of his hymnbooks we can see Kelly providing a congregational resource for the guidance and edification of his fledgling denomination. It is more difficult to recover the way in which Kellyite members might have viewed these hymns but, by virtue of their authorship and their oft repetition it seems likely that they would have attached no small significance to the content of their lyrics, insofar as they thought about them as something more than lines to be sung. The example of other congregations where set liturgy is abandoned and extemporary worship espoused suggests that these hymns would have quickly come to form an important part of the texture of worship.[25] It is also important to note that Kelly, then, is an outstanding exemplar of why we ought to give careful consideration to hymns as sources. However, he also illustrates some of the difficulties associated with using these highly compressed texts designed to edify and exhort as well as to educate the faithful. The chief of these difficulties is illustrated very clearly in the list of hymnbook editions outlined above. The key point here is that each revision is larger than the preceding edition. Kelly added hymns, but he did not excise them. So, even as his comprehension of Scripture developed, he was happy to retain those texts that had been informed by an earlier understanding. Thus, as we consider Kelly's intellectual and spiritual development through the lens of his hymns what we are doing is closer to examining the growth of a tortoise by examining the rings on his shell than a snake's by looking at a series of discarded skins.

In this context too, Kelly's hymns offer commentary on his views of the whole gamut of Christian doctrine. The subject index to the 1853 volume that collected all his hymns lists a wide range of areas, beginning the events of Christ's life, from nativity to exaltation. These sections are followed by others on the offices of Christ as king, priest, prophet and shepherd, which in turn are followed by sections on the whole range of Christian experience. Within the scope of this chapter it will, manifestly, be impossible to look at these in any very comprehensive way. Nonetheless, it is illuminating to look at the content of a number of key sections that relate most directly to the most immediately pressing debates within contemporary evangelicalism. For, while evangelicals largely agreed on many areas of Christian doctrine, fascinating differences of opinion were beginning to assume a new prominence and importance. The issues of prophecy and the place of Israel in God's purposes are, therefore, two important markers that allows us to locate Kelly's thought in relation to contemporary currents within evangelicalism.

Kelly's views on prophetic teaching are a logical point of commencement for a number of reasons. First, as we shall see, these views have fundamentally important implications for his understanding of both missionary work and the status of Israel. Second, even a cursory glance at the subject index amply indicates the importance of this issue. One of the largest sections within that index is entitled 'The Day of Christ', a section gathering hymns covering the range of prophetic Scripture. Nor, as we shall see, is the treatment of prophetic themes limited to this section alone. Clearly, the interpretation and application of prophecy was an issue of particular concern to Kelly. Third, as we have seen, prophetic interpretation was also an issue of general concern in the wider context of radical evangelicalism in Ireland. This source is therefore especially useful given how little we know about the way in which social issues shaped the development of premillennialism in this period. Kelly's hymns provide us with concrete information about the exact mix of ingredients in the air of Dublin in the first half of the nineteenth century. Furthermore, the parallels between Kelly's background and that of John Nelson Darby throw the focus firmly on the role played by Trinity College Dublin in the formation of radical evangelicalism in Dublin and Ireland.

It is worthy of note, therefore, that Kelly's interest in the prophetic seems to have increased. The subject index of his 1802 hymnal subsumes all prophetic material to the rather vague 'latter days', and this section contains only four hymns. The second edition of *Hymns on Various Passages of Scripture*, published in 1806, and itself a rather larger collection, contains only one section of prophetic hymns, a section that occupied nine pages of the collection. This section was entitled 'The day of Chist', and embraced hymns dealing with a wide range of more-or-less prophetic subjects. Subsequent editions enlarged this section until, as we have seen, it became one of the largest single sections of the final 1853 edition. As the hymnbook as a whole grew, individual sections were enlarged as well, but the marked increase in the number of hymns dealing with prophetic issues is telling.

The layout of Kelly's collections, then, provides us with clear evidence of his interest in millennial themes. We must, however, look to the hymns themselves to understand the nature of that interest. In light of the groundswell of interest in premillennial theology emerging in radical Irish evangelicalism at this time, and in light of the longer tradition of postmillennialism that had been taught as part of the divinity course in Trinity College Dublin, it is difficult to avoid coming to Kelly's hymns looking only for indications of a commitment to pre- or postmillennialism. But many of Kelly's hymns complicate this sort of binary analysis, because he often seems closer to the third major eschatological position, namely amillennialism, which denies the literal fulfilment of millennial prophecy, generally spiritualizing these and seeing them as fulfilled in the history of the church.

Thus, while the hymns collected in the section on the day of Christ appear to reiterate classical themes of premillennial expectation – Christ is coming, His return in imminent, it will take the unbelieving world by surprise and, while the moment of His arrival will be the apotheosis of blessing for Christians, it will be deeply unpleasant for everyone else – they do so without allowing for a millennial rule on earth. So, for example, one of the hymns in Kelly's 1806 collection appears to anticipate the sort of display of Christ's majesty usually connected with millennial reign:

> From far I see the glorious day,
> When he who bore our sins away,
> Will all his majesty display.[26]

This majesty, Kelly goes on to point out, contrasts totally with Christ's humiliation while on earth. And, he suggests the majesty that will be displayed in 'the glorious day' is presently the portion of Christ in Heaven:

> But now he reigns with glory crown'd
> While angel hosts his throne surround,
> And still His lofty praises sound.

But, just as we are cued up to expect the manifestation of that kingly glory on Earth, the millennial rug is jerked away:

> But yet there is a day to come,
> When he will seal the sinner's doom,
> And take his people home.

Thus, Christ's reign is a present and spiritual one. His glory will be briefly manifest on Earth, but only as he acts 'to seal the sinner's doom and take his people home'.

Another hymn in the 1806 edition of his hymnbook, replicates the same sequence promising, with a less than happy choice of metre:

> The Saviour with crowds
> Shall come in the clouds;
> His glory to all shall appear:
> All power is giv'n,
> In earth and in heav'n,
> To him who was crucified here.
> Then joy to the saints;
> Whatever complaints
> Attend on their state here below,
> They all in that day
> Shall vanish away;
> No more shall their tears ever flow.[27]

Strikingly, all the hymns in this section anticipate a compressed version of Christ's return, figuring His manifestation, the last judgement, and the dissolution of the heavens and earth as virtually simultaneous events. This schema leaves little room for a millennium, and, while it does share some of the features of premillennial expectation – most strikingly societal pessimism and an evangelical emphasis – it ultimately figures an amillennial future for Christ and his people.

All this notwithstanding, the moment of Christ's return remains a hugely important one for Kelly. He seems particularly interested in the contrast between the significance of Christ's return for His chosen people, and for the mass of humanity. So, in a hymn that appears in his first hymnbook, he differentiates very clearly between the fates of the believer and unbeliever at Christ's return.

> With Him they shall sit down and feast
> On heav'n's unbounded store;
> Enjoy an everlasting rest,
> And never hunger more.

> When once the chamber door shall close,
> Be sure beyond a doubt,
> No further hope remains for those
> Who then are found without.[28]

There is an explicit contrast here between those who enter heaven, and those who remain without, a contrast succinctly stated in a hymn that appears in a later edition:

> Now the world's duration ends
> Now the Lord will meet his foes;
> These shall perish, but his friends
> Shall in heav'n obtain repose.[29]

What is striking here is the juxtaposition between heavenly reward and earthly punishment, and the correspondence between Christ's return and the ending of the world's duration. Again, it is clear that there is little room in this scheme for a millennium to take place.

As we have seen, however, one of the advantages of Kelly's prolific hymn publishing career is the way in which the successive editions of his work allow us to reconstruct the development of his thought. And, it is telling to observe that it is precisely in the direction of a more normative premillennialism that Kelly's thought appears to have developed. *Seems* is appropriate here – we should note once again that Kelly did not excise hymns as he went along. We should also notice that the clearest anticipations of a millennial reign is found not in the section entitled 'the day of Christ', but in one headed 'the exaltation of Christ'. It is in this section of the 1826 edition that we find one of Kelly's best-known hymns. 'Who is this that comes from Eden' allows for the conquering of Christ's enemies and the adjustment of social and religious wrongs in a way that anticipates a period in which Christ can reign, implicitly if not explicitly a millennium:

> Who is this that comes from Edom,
> All His garments stained with blood;
> To the slave proclaiming freedom;
> Bringing and bestowing good;
> Glorious in the garb He wears,
> Glorious in the spoils He bears?
> 'Tis the Saviour, now victorious
> Travelling onward in His might;
> 'Tis the Saviour, O how glorious
> To His people is the sight!
> Jesus now is strong to save,
> Mighty to redeem the slave.
> This the Saviour has effected
> By His mighty arm alone;

> See the throne for Him erected;
> 'Tis an everlasting throne:
> 'Tis the great reward He gains,
> Glorious fruit of all His pains.
> Mighty Victor, reign forever,
> Wear the crown so dearly won;
> Never shall thy people, never
> Cease to sing what Thou hast done;
> Thou hast fought Thy people's foes;
> Thou wilt heal Thy people's woes.[30]

That there is a social context here is clear – Christ is 'mighty to redeem the slave', a concept with enormous contemporary resonance. In contrast to the amillennial focus of the hymns in the earlier editions, Christ's reign on Earth is now seen as the period when pressing social concerns will be addressed as Christ comes 'bringing and bestowing good'. But in addition to the freeing of the slave, there will be spiritual blessings – the returning and reigning Christ will address his 'people's woes'.

It is tempting to see a straightforward trajectory here – from amillennialism to a premillennial expectation. It is the more tempting to trace such a trajectory given the emergence of premillennialism within Irish evangelicalism at this point. That the evidence should seem to organize itself so obligingly is appealing. Unsurprisingly, perhaps, the data reveal a picture that is less straightforward in that. The 1806 edition of Kelly's hymnbook already included another of his best known hymns, which already hints at a premillennial mode of prophetic understanding. 'Zion's King shall reign victorious' anticipates a temporal and earthly reign of Christ, establishing dominion over the nations of Earth:

> Zion's King shall reign victorious,
>   All the earth shall own His sway;
>   He will make His kingdom glorious,
>   He will reign through endless day.
> What though none on earth assist Him,
>   God requires not help from man;
>   What though all the world resist Him,
>   God will realize His plan.[31]

There is a great deal in this stanza that calls for our attention. For instance, Kelly's statement that, in the establishment of His kingdom 'God desires not help from man' explicitly contradicts the prevailing postmillennial optimism which suggested that, while God may not precisely have needed the help of man to inaugurate His kingdom, those efforts were still of value in that regard. The establishment of the millennial kingdom is inexorable and irresistible. The second stanza, likewise, stresses a distinctively premillennial orthodoxy:

> Nations now from God estrangèd,
> Then shall see a glorious light,
> Night to day shall then be changèd,
> Heaven shall triumph in the sight;
> See the ancient idols falling!
> Worshipped once, but now abhorred;
> Men on Zion's King are calling,
> Zion's King by all adored.[32]

Whereas Kelly's other hymns in this edition of his hymnbook anticipate the immediate judgement and destruction of the unbelieving nations, he now foresees their recovery. And the timeframe of this discovery stresses the now and the then in a way that makes it clear that, once again, it is not a global Christianization preparatory to Christ's return that is in view here, but a future enlightenment and illumination to be obtained 'then' when 'Zion's King' is established.

Thus, Kelly's hymns provide a complex and suggestive view of the development of a theological perspective. That development was not straightforwardly linear – it involved palimpsest, contradiction, and renegotiation. Kelly's understanding of prophecy generally steers clear of a postmillennial position that tended to call for direct social activism, producing radical social change and inaugurating the conditions in which Christ could return. Both the a- and the premillennial orientations of his thought tended to privilege a pessimistic view of society and a concentration of the heavenly aspects of Christ's reign that lead to a distinctly quietist engagement – or lack of engagement – with contemporary politics. For all that, however, the social as well as the theological implications of evangelicalism can be seen in his hymnody and would have shaped the thought and the actions of those who, week by week, gave expression to their faith in the words of Kelly's hymns.

However, we have not yet exhausted the evidentiary value of 'Zion's King shall reign victorious'. In the context of contemporary evangelical thought, the third of the hymn's three stanzas demands our attention:

> Then shall Israel, long dispersèd,
> Mourning seek the Lord their God,
> Look on Him whom once they piercèd,
> Own and kiss the chastening rod;
> Then all Israel shall be savèd,
> War and tumult then shall cease,
> While the greater Son of David
> Rules a conquered world in peace.[33]

This stanza is particularly interesting in terms of locating Kelly within contemporary evangelicalism. Throughout the eighteenth century, the prophetic importance of Israel had been increasingly highlighted.[34] In particular, many prominent premillennialist theologians confidently expected the conversion of the Jews to Christianity before Christ's return. It was this belief, in part, that gave impetus to such groups as the London Society for the Promotion of Christianity among the Jews, and that increased the profile of missionary efforts to the Jews immeasurably. In the second half of the nineteenth century, evangelical philo-semitism was to find its apotheosis in the dispensationalist theology developed by John Nelson Darby. Darby, indeed, has been accused by not a few of his detractors of having a more glorious hope for Israel than for the Church. Such claims are mistaken, but that they are specious in any degree does underscore the depth of Darby's affection for the Jews. Kelly's views as outlined in this hymn are significant in this context. But they are also suggestive because, unlike many of his premillennial peers, but like Darby and his dispensationalist followers, Kelly does not appear to anticipate that the conversion of the Jews will precede Christ's return. Rather, it seems, the manifestation of Christ will effect this sea change as they simultaneously recognize their mistake and their Messiah, and mournfully acknowledge both.

It is important to stress that this stanza of this hymn is not an isolated instance of philo-semitism in Kelly's writings. In fact, his 1853 collection includes sections entitled 'Israel in Exile', 'Israel Victorious', 'Israel Forgetful' and 'Israel Encouraged'. In line with the sort of progression we have already noted, there is a slippage in these hymns, both fascinating and frustrating between Israel as Israel, and Israel as a type of the Church. This is further complicated by the existence, earlier in the volume of a five-part poem of thirty verses, entitled 'Israel as a type' tracing the early history of the nation of Israel out of Egypt, through the wilderness, and into the promised land. The typological treatment of this material was classical. But in the later sections, laments about present scattering and promises of future blessing leave the precise application of Kelly's words very unclear.

In some of these later sections, Kelly's intention seems to be the straightforward encouragement of the nineteenth-century Christian by reference to their Israelite forebears. So, for instance, in a section of the 1853 collection entitled 'a state of joyful hope', he conflates Jewish history and Christian present in a hymn also contained in the 1826 edition:

> Methinks I stand upon the rock
> Where Balaam stood, and wond'r
> Upon the scene below:
> The tents of Jacob goodly seem,
> The people happy I esteem,
> Whom God has favoured so.
> The sons of Isra'l stand alone,
> Jehovah claims them for his own,
> His cause and theirs the same:
> He sav'd them from the tyrant's hand

Allots to them a pleasant land,
And calls them by his name.
Their toils have almost reach'd a close
And soon in peace they shall repose
Within the promised land.[35]

The hymn contains a fairly unremarkable use of Old Testament imagery and terminology. More striking is a hymn found in a section of the 1853 hymnal entitled 'Israel encouraged', in which he issues another summons of contemporary exhortation:

Sons of Zion, haste away,
'Tis the acceptable day,
'Tis the day expected long,
Burden of prophetic song;
Thus the mighty God has spoken,
Haste away, your chains are broken.
From the willows, where they've hung,
Long neglected and unstrung,
Take your harps again, and sing,
Sound the praise of Zion's King;
Sing, for Zion's sons have reason,
'Tis a joyful, glorious season.[36]

Two things are noteworthy in these verses. First, Kelly is clearly addressing contemporary Christians as 'sons of Zion', and is applying to them the imagery of harps hung upon willows used of Israel in her Babylonian captivity in Psalm 137. But what is also striking is Kelly's depiction of the present as 'the day expected long, burden of prophetic song'. In both these aspects, this must be seen as an amillennial hymn.

But Israel is not always so uncomplicated a signifier, and the hymns contained in a section entitled 'Israel victorious' seem to envisage an imminent restoration for Israel. So, for example, Kelly avers:

Isra'l shall obtain a pardon,
(Thus the Lord proclaims his love),
He shall be a water'd garden,
Israel shall no more remove;
He shall come from distant lands,
Thus my sovereign purpose stands.
O my servant Jacob fear not,
I have called thee, thou art mine;
Though thy glory yet appear not,
It will come, thy light shall shine;
Object of my love and care,
I will save thee from afar.
…

> Yet thou shalt not be unpunish'd,
> Thou shalt know that I am God;
> Though belov'd, yet still admonished,
> Thou shalt feel the chastening rod;
> But thy night shall soon be past,
> And the day shall dawn at last.[37]

This appears to envisage a geographical as well as a spiritual restoration – it contemplates the blessing of the nation. And the physical and geo-political orientation of this expectation emerges with equal clarity in a later hymn in the section:

> 'Tis the time of Isra'ls trouble,
> Lo! The enemy is chief;
> Yet shall Isra'l have the double,
> Double joy for all his grief:
> Isra'ls Saviour
> Will appear and bring relief.
> Isra'l's foes rejoice to see him
> Forc'd to bow to their command;
> Who, they say, shall ever free him?
> Can Jehovah
> Now restore them to their land?
> Yes, though Isra'l were removed
> To the world's remotest end;
> Know ye, Isra'l is beloved,
> Isra'l has a faithful friend;
> He will save him,
> And with pow'r his cause defend.
> ...
> Isra'l then shall fear no dangers,
> Sav'd from ev'ry hostile hand;
> Dwelling far from foes and strangers,
> And increasing as the sand;
> Joys abounding
> Through his peaceful happy land.[38]

It seems very clear that this hymn is focusing upon a physical regathering of Israel. This regathering was increasingly expected by pre-millennial evangelicals, who saw the restoration of Israel as a vital step in the fulfilment of Divine prophecy. In this context, it is significant to note that Kelly identified the present with 'the time of Jacob's trouble' spoken of in Jeremiah 30:7, and understood by many evangelicals, and especially by dispensationalists, as a key eschatological moment.

These are all major issues in understanding Kelly's thought, and in understanding the emergence of premillennial concerns in Irish evangelicalism. Beyond that, these issues are of immense importance for our understanding of the intellectual history of global evangelicalism, and of all the socio-political trends and movements that have been energized by evangelical belief. Within the scope of this chapter, we cannot do more than gesture tentatively towards the concerns that must inform this long overdue study. But we need not be at all tentative about the importance of hymnology for the unfolding and development of this sort of work. Hymns have too great a potential for us to collude any longer in their canonical marginalization. As we have seen, Kelly is an excellent example of the way in which hymnology can both facilitate and complicate our study of evangelicalism. The latter contribution is at least as important as the former. More than any other cultural artefact, hymns, and the hymnals in which they were collected, allow us to trace the formation and dissemination of religious and social identity within and beyond the radical evangelicalism of the nineteenth century. This chapter has highlighted complex and important areas for future study, but, more importantly, it has attempted to make the case that these areas are most accessible to us when we enlarge our concept of the radical canon to embrace the hymnody of radical evangelicalism.

5 CHARLOTTE BROOKE'S *RELIQUES OF IRISH POETRY*: EIGHTEENTH-CENTURY 'IRISH SONG' AND THE POLITICS OF REMEDIATION

Leith Davis

Charlotte Brooke's *Reliques of Irish Poetry* (1789) has long been recognized as the first printed collection of Gaelic poetry translated into English. In *Mere Irish and Fíor-Ghael: Studies in the Idea of Irish Nationality, Its Development and Literary Expression Prior to the Nineteenth Century*, Joep Leerson calls her 'the first mediator of importance between the Irish-Gaelic and the Anglo-Irish literary traditions'.[1] Critical discussion of the *Reliques* has centred exclusively on the work's poetry, however, ignoring Brooke's interventions in another medium of Irish-Gaelic culture: music. In fact, Brooke's first published work was a translation of a song by Turlough Carolan that she supplied to Joseph Cooper Walker for his *Historical Memoirs of the Irish Bards* (1786).[2] Brooke included this and other songs in her *Reliques of Irish Poetry*, along with an extensive commentary entitled 'Thoughts on Irish Song'. This essay examines how the *Reliques* negotiates with perceptions of 'Irish song' that appeared in popular and antiquarian discourses in late eighteenth-century British and Irish venues. It will suggest that Brooke's reconfiguration of the lyrical productions of her nation offered a new perspective on the subject of 'Irish song' to contemporary readers, while, at the same time, constituting an important comment on the media culture of the eighteenth century. For unlike contemporary works supposedly representing 'Irish song', Brooke registered what I will identify as a marked ambivalence to the attempt to 'remediate' Gaelic musical culture through the technology of print.[3]

The use of the term 'media' in an eighteenth-century context is a matter of some contention. On one extreme, Jay Bolter and Richard Grusin trace continuities in the ideas of media 'throughout the last several hundred years'.[4] Wendy Hui Kyong Chun and Thomas Keenan, however, counter that an investigation of the history of media must 'grapple with the ways that mediums have changed, rather than concentrating on the remarkable yet overdetermined similarities between entities now considered media'.[5] Maureen McLane, Steve Newman and Janet Sorensen have recently undertaken that 'grappling' for the eighteenth century, focusing their critical attention on what McLane calls '"mediality" – the condition of existing in media'.[6] For the most part, however, their investigations focus on the Scottish/English nexus. McLane argues, for example, that, 'for eighteenth-century Scots, the introduction of orality into print form often functioned as a form of cultural resistance to the domination of English and a London-based Britain'.[7] But because of its complicated colonial history involving a triangulation of Gaelic, Anglo-Irish and English interests, issues of mediality were more complex in Ireland, often manifesting themselves in ways which trouble models operative in other geopolitical locations.[8] In *Reading Ireland: Print, Reading and Social Change in Early Modern Ireland* (2005), for example, Raymond Gillespie suggests that the conclusions that Elizabeth Eisenstein draws in *The Printing Press as an Agent of Change* (1979) must be modified in an Irish situation: 'the revolution which print engendered is a more complex affair [in Ireland], operating over a longer time-scale and as much concerned with the reception of the printed word as about its production'.[9] Similarly, Toby Barnard points out the ways in which political resistance in eighteenth-century Ireland was expressed not by introducing 'orality into print form', but by employing standard English.[10] The ambivalence that I am identifying in Brooke's attitude to the printing of Gaelic poems and songs which had appeared before only in Gaelic and in oral or manuscript form both reflects and calls attention to the 'anomalous' relationship between politics and mediality in Ireland.[11]

In the Preface to the *Reliques of Irish Poetry*, Brooke draws attention to the fact that her work is designed to introduce 'the British muse' to her 'elder sister in this isle' in order to make Britain and Ireland 'better acquainted' and also to present 'the productions of our Irish Bards' to Irish readers in order to make them 'gratified, at the lustre reflected on them by ancestors so very different from what modern prejudice has been studious to represent them [sic]'.[12] In 'Thoughts on Irish Song', she elaborates on these concerns, justifying the remarks she makes by suggesting that, even though 'the subject of song, in general, has been already so well, and copiously treated of' by John Aikin and Joseph Ritson, Irish song 'seemed to demand some notice, and had never before received it'.[13] In fact, the works to which Brooke refers, Aikin's *Essays on Song-writing: With a Collection of such English Songs as are most Eminent for Poetical Merit* (1772) and Ritson's *A Select Collection of English Songs* (1783), focus exclusively on English songs.[14] And while the collections of Allan Ramsay (*The Tea-Table Miscellany* (1724)) and David Herd (*Ancient Scottish Songs* (1769)),[15] whom Brooke does not mention, introduced Scottish vocal productions to eighteenth-century audiences, and commentators like William Tytler discussed the particular characteristics of Scottish music,[16] Brooke is correct to suggest that Irish song had not been similarly considered. However, numerous works referring to themselves self-consciously as 'Irish songs' had been in circulation in the popular press and theatrical venues since the end of the seventeenth century. In her remarks on Irish song in the *Reliques*, then, Brooke was not only filling a gap in eighteenth-century musical commentary, but also providing an alternative to popular perceptions of 'Irish song'.

The varied appearance of 'Irish song' in the eighteenth century reflects the complicated colonial politics of Ireland. Songs deriving from the Gaelic tradition began to appear in highly mediated forms in Anglo-Irish and British contexts in the early part of the century.[17] Lyrics were divorced from the music, and the tunes were turned into 'instrumental melodies and song airs'.[18] The first collection of Gaelic tunes to be published, John and William Neale's *Colection [sic] of the most Celebrated Irish Tunes*, printed in Dublin in 1724, features a number of tunes with Gaelic names, but no words.[19] Gaelic tunes derived from songs were also grouped with airs from other British national locations in collections like Daniel Wright's *Aria di Camera* (1730), Burke Thumoth's *Twelve Scotch and Twelve Irish Airs with Variations* (1750) and James Oswald's *Caledonian Pocket Companion* (1743–64). (The latter, along with later collections like James Aird's *A Selection of Scotch, English, Irish and Foreign Airs* of 1782, would inspire the songs of Robert Burns.)[20]

As well as being published as instrumental works, Gaelic songs were frequently repackaged with new lyrics in new contexts. John Gay's 1727 *The Beggar's Opera* features English words to the 'Irish Howl' and the 'Irish Trot', while Charles Coffey's 1729 *The Beggar's Wedding* utilized fifteen Irish tunes out of a total of fifty-six musical pieces. Brooke's father, Henry Brooke, employed Irish tunes for his *Jack the Giant Queller*.[21] Helen Burke discusses the hybridity of the Gaelic Irish tunes in the context of the Dublin musical scene, suggesting that:

> Even after the political catastrophe of the seventeenth century, traditional Irish music survived in the underground culture of Dublin's displaced Catholic community. And by appropriating the music of the dispossessed ... Irish Protestant Patriots created an opportunity for members of this community to remember and restore their nation's dreams and aspirations.[22]

Burke pays particular attention to how the re-presentation of Irish tunes in ballad operas created a voice, albeit disguised, for Gaelic Ireland. While the performance of Irish tunes in Ireland may have served as a marker of political resistance, however, their presentation in other venues throughout the British archipelago resulted in various decodings. In the English metropolitan context in which many of the ballad operas were performed, for example, the resistant voices would have remained primarily uncontextualized and silent. At the same time that Gaelic tunes were working their way into the musical culture and theatrical spaces throughout Britain, other kinds of song identified as 'Irish' began appearing in less positive contexts: political ballads, broadsheets and early song collections printed in Dublin and London and designed to appeal to Anglo-Irish or English consumers. The most famous of these early political ballads, 'Lillibulero', for example, satirizes Irish political aspirations under James II by presenting a dialogue between two Irishmen discussing the arrival of the new lord deputy of Ireland, Richard Talbot, earl of Tyrconnel. Dianne Dugaw comments on the 'complex matrix of eighteenth-century song culture' that involved both 'cheap ballads sold on the streets' from 'a longstanding substratum of lower-class culture' and more 'fashionable' song collections.[23] 'Lilliburlero' made its way from broadsheets circulated in taverns to collections designed primarily for entertainment rather than political propaganda. The 'Irish Hallaloo', a song which, like 'Lillibulero', mocks the fall of the Irish aristocracy, appeared in *Wit and Mirth: Pills to Purge Melancholy* by Henry Playford (1707–9).[24] *Songs Compleat, Pleasant and Divertive; Set to Musick by Dr John Blow, Mr Henry Purcell, and Other Excellent Masters* (1719) also includes an anti-Irish Catholic selection with its 'A Dialogue between Teague an Irish Priest and the Arch-bishop of Paris, on the Taking of Tournay and the State of French Affairs'.[25] Other so-called Irish songs printed in songbooks find their thematic affiliation not with Williamite propaganda, but with theatrical representations of the comic stage Irishman introduced by George Farquhar and exploited by numerous subsequent playwrights.[26] 'An Irish Wooing' and 'An Irish Jigg', for example, also published in *Wit and Mirth*, focus on Irish sexual appetite rather than on Irish Jacobitism.

Later eighteenth-century 'Irish songs' identify the Irish with drinking, 'Irish bulls' and economic aspirations in England rather than rebellion. In common with their Williamite predecessors, however, they derive part of their political power from the fact that they claim to offer a direct representation of Irish speech and thought, relying on what Andrew Carpenter calls 'Hiberno-English' for their comic effect.[27] 'Darby M'Hone's Lamentation. An IRISH SONG', published in Henry Howard's *Fun a la Mode, or, Sing, and Be Jolly* (1763), a later eighteenth-century equivalent of *Wit and Mirth*, represents a comic Irish speaker who is eager to benefit from the advantages in London. His fellow Irishmen who came to England earlier managed to marry 'rich dames', but Darby is unable to catch the eye of 'some lady' because '*Scotsmen* are now all the fashion' since Lord Bute has come to power.[28] 'Darby M'Hone's Lamentation' concludes with a nod to the earlier-mentioned bawdy song, 'The Irish Jigg', as it regretfully comments that 'the fam'd *Irish* jigg is no more, sir'.[29]

Even works that aimed at a more refined audience borrowed the linguistic comic effects of their more bawdy contemporaries. *Parsley's Lyric Repository, for 1789, Containing a selection of all the favorite songs, duets, trios, &c. now singing at the Theatres-Royal* (1789), for example, contains 'A New Irish Comic Song' which mocks the economic aspirations and the logic of an Irishman who comes to the English capital, much like Darby M'Hone, to find his fortune:

> O! London, he says, is a very strange town,
> Where you scarcely can walk if you chance to lie down;
> There all things may be had he declares, me dear honey,
> For nothing at all, if you've plenty of money.
>   Derry down, &c.[30]

The Banquet of Thalia, or the Fashionable Songsters Pocket Memorial (c. 1788), a publication which made explicit its attempt to avoid 'all those obscene and trifling compositions with which many publications of this nature are indelicately crowded', features 'A Favorite Irish Song' in its section on 'Bacchanalian, Convivial Songs, &c.', associating Irish song with the enjoyment of liquor, women and song: 'Your glass to your lips, and your lass on your knee./ Sing away, honeys, and cast off all sorrow'.[31] The author of 'A Favorite Irish Song' cannot resist the chance to include an Irish bull, although it is rendered suitable to the gentility of the publication: 'Tho' we all die today, let's be merry tomorrow'.[32] In 1789, the same year that Brooke's *Reliques* was published, Charles Dibden enjoyed steady success on the London stage in performing 'The Oddities', an 'Entertainment' that featured 'an Irish Drinking Song' which employed 'Hiberno-English' to suggest the drinking habits of classical authors and heroes:

> Wid your smalliliow nonsense, and all your queer bodders,
> Since whisky's a liquor divine,
> Do be sure the old ancients, as well as the moderns,
> Did not love a sly sup of good wine.[33]

In a late eighteenth-century variant of the matrix of song culture which Dugaw describes, Dibden's 'Irish Drinking Song' was also published as a cheap broadsheet and included in his five-volume edition of collected songs.[34] Although they had little to do with any traditional song culture in Ireland, such productions nevertheless worked to establish in the minds of metropolitan consumers certain expectations of the subject of 'Irish song'.

The mid-century also witnessed the evolution of another attitude to Irish song, however, as the interest in both sensibility and popular culture brought the geographic margins of Britain into focus.[35] This shift in taste is reflected in an article concerning Irish song which appeared initially in the *London Public Advertiser and Literary Gazette* for Thursday, 12 September 1751 and which was republished in the *Gentleman's Magazine* a month later. The article, a letter sent 'To the Inspector' from one 'M. N. M.' describes the latter's observations 'during a Residency of a whole Summer in the remote Country Parts of Ireland, where the lower Rank have as yet received scarce any Tincture of the Manners, Habit, Customs, or Language of *Britain*'.[36] M. N. M. remarks on the 'universal Passion that prevails among [the lower ranks of the Irish] for Poetry, Music, and Dancing, after their own Rustic Fashion', and adds that 'in the Wildness of their

Notes, I have often found something irregularly charming'. Struck by the fact that the songs they sing must be indicative of their original 'Thought and Manner', as the composers are illiterate and know no other language from which they might import their ideas, M. N. M. employs the help of 'a very agreeable Young Lady, who understood the Irish Tongue perfectly well' and obtains 'several literal Prose-Translations of Irish Songs done by that Lady, which have many beautiful Touches of Nature in them'. He concludes that the Irish songs are always about 'Love': 'they seem to understand Poetry to be designed for no other Purpose than to stir up that Passion in the Mind'. The writer expresses his interest in the original Irish words of the song, even though he does not understand Gaelic himself. He includes '*A Translation of an* IRISH SONG, *beginning*, Ma ville slane g'un oughth chegh khune, &c.', but begs 'all possible Indulgence for a Version done by a Person who does not understand a single Syllable of the original Language.'

In fact the article points out one of the important differences between the interest in national culture in Ireland and that in the other 'remote Country Parts' of Britain. While such works as Thomas Percy's *Reliques of Ancient English Poetry* (1765) and David Herd's *Ancient Scottish Songs* represented the 'first efforts of ancient genius', frequently using language that stretched the comfort level of readers of standard English, the songs and poems were ultimately intelligible.[37] In Ireland, however, the language issue proved a barrier to the discovery and publication of national songs. With the important exception of Charles O'Conor, most scholars discussing the 'first efforts of ancient genius' in Ireland did not have an understanding of Gaelic. Moreover, rather than printing collections of popular Irish songs or ballads, these Irish antiquarians focused their efforts on describing the importance of music and song in ancient Irish society in an effort to refute judgments of it as barbaric. Taking much of his information from O'Conor's *Dissertations on the History of Ireland* (1753), for example, Joseph Cooper Walker argues in his *Historical Memoirs of the Irish Bards* (1786) that music and song constituted an important medium through which Irish politics was conducted.[38] Song was an important part of the education of bards, asserts Walker, citing the fact that at the 'university at Teamor, called MUR-OLLA-VAN', bards were taught 'verse and song, by being initiated in the mysteries of metrical cadence, vocal harmony, and graceful action'.[39] Walker follows O'Conor in suggesting the political importance of Irish song: 'you find that our ancients in Ireland were far from being strangers to the powers of harmonized sound, in directing, as well as exciting, the human passions. Sounds were therefore cultivated and modified, so as to produce extraordinary civil and political effects'.[40]

Walker and O'Conor confine their researches to the productions of ancient bards. Walker indicates that 'the Irish language abounds in lyric compositions that would do honour to the most polished nation of ancient or modern times' and suggests that 'did the nature of my plan admit of it, several of them should find a place in this work', but it is clear that 'the nature of [his] plan' admits no such liberty.[41] His concentration, like that of other members of the Royal Irish Academy, is on ancient Ireland, as he designs his work exclusively for the 'Speculative and Refined'. Moreover, Walker and other scholars seeking to promote the cause of Ireland represent its music in terms of Western European musical standards in order to make it more widely acceptable. Walker's *Memoirs* focuses on analogies between Irish and other European music, as he uses the article contributed to the *London Public Advertiser* and the *Gentleman's Magazine* in order to 'corroborate' his own points about the nature of Irish music. He draws an affinity, for example, between what he calls the 'Irish pastoral sonnet' and the work of the English poet, William Shenstone, suggesting that the 'sonnet' is 'not unworthy the muse of Shenstone'.[42] Walker also includes fifteen tunes in the *Historical Memoirs*, notating each of them, even the 'Provincial Cries' which are drawn from 'remote antiquity', in standard Western European notation, as exemplified in Figure 5.1.

Figure 5.1: J.C. Walker, 'Provincial Cries', *Historical Memoirs of the Irish Bards. Interspersed with anecdotes of, and occasional observations on the music of Ireland* (London: 1786), p. 128.

[46]

C A O I N A N,

Or IRISH FUNERAL SONG.

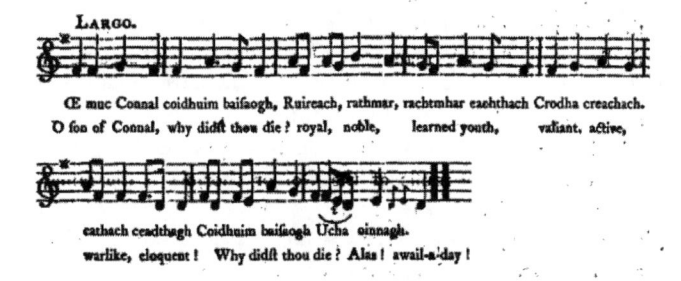

Largo.

Œ muc Connal coidhuim baifaogh, Ruireach, rathmar, rachtmhar eachthach Crodha creachach.
O fon of Connal, why didst thou die? royal, noble, learned youth, valiant, active,

cathach ceadthagh Coidhuim baifaogh Ucha cinnagh.
warlike, eloquent! Why didst thou die? Alas! awail-a-day!

First Semi-Chorus.

Termante.

Ulla-lulla-lulla-lulla lù lù ucht o ong.

Second Semi-Chorus.

O ong ulla lulla lulla lulla lulla lulla lulla lu ucht o ong.

Figure 5.2: William Beauford, 'Caoinan: *or some Account* of the ANTIENT IRISH LAMENTATIONS', *The Transactions of the Royal Irish Academy* (Dublin: [1787]-1800), vol. 4, p. 45.

Following in Walker's footsteps, William Beauford published an article in the *Transactions of the Royal Irish Academy* entitled 'Caoinan: *or some Account* of the ANTIENT IRISH LAMENTATIONS' that attempted to transform the caoinan into Western European notation (see Figure 5.2). Beauford notes that the caoinan 'bears evident marks of bardic origin both in its versification and language'.[43] His description of the practice of the caoinan suggests its affinities with Greek tragedy, however: 'The chief bard of the head chorus began, by singing the first stanza in a low doleful tone, which was softly accompanied by the harp; at the conclusion, the foot semi-chorus began the lamentation or Ullaloo, from the final note of the preceding stanza, in which they were answered by the head semi-chorus; then both united in one general chorus'.[44] Beauford walks a middle line, however, presenting the caoinan as exotic, but also not too exotic. While there are clearly some unconventional intervals and complicated timing at work in the piece, each sound in the 'Full Chorus of Sighs and Groans' is represented on the staff, and the song is fitted into ¼ time. Beauford also supplies directions regarding the dynamics of the song in Italian: the first stanza is to be sung 'Largo' with the answering semi-chorus 'Termante'.[45] He attempts to render the caoinan understandable, approachable and immediate to those familiar with Western music.

It is in response to these variant representations of Irish song circulating in the late 1780s – the comic and the antiquarian – that I wish to situate Brooke's representation of Irish song in the *Reliques of Irish Poetry*. Brooke's comments significantly contest the identification of Irish song with the negative presentations that were appearing in songbooks and on the stage, but she also corrects the representations of scholars like Walker and Beauford. In contrast to images of Irish song as comic, Brooke argues for 'the almost total absence of humour' found in Irish poetry and song.[46] In fact, she asserts, 'a strain of tender pensiveness is discernible throughout, in most of the musick of this nation'.[47] Brooke's denial of humour reconfigures the politics involved in the representation of Irish song. Songs like 'The Irish Wooing' and Dibden's 'Irish Drinking Song' reinforced the political subordination of the Irish by suggesting that they were motivated less by rational thought than by physical desires. How could people who could not govern their own bodies be expected to govern their nation properly? As if in answer to this, Brooke entertains the possibility that political subordination is not the logical extension but the root cause of the character of Irish song; far from being sources of comedy, the Irish people may have simply been too unhappy under the oppression of the English to write songs 'of a sprightlier strain'.[48] She quotes Walker at length here, who suggests that either the subordination of their country affected the bards 'with heaviest sadness' or that they were driven to live in such gloomy situations that 'their voices, thus weakened by struggling against heavy mental depression' rose only by minor thirds.[49] But Walker also backtracks from his position, as he cites the opinion of the writer of the *Gentleman's Magazine* that the Irish were too susceptible to 'the passion of love'.[50]

Brooke revises Walker's variant theses, however, as she asserts that 'it does not seem to me that the antient [sic] poetry of Ireland was *ever* composed in a very lively strain'[51] and she suggests that 'another reason [for the lack of humour in Irish songs] still occurs, which I will give to the reader's indulgence'.[52] She argues that Irish composers were too full of the 'vital spirit of poetry' to be able to practice the superficialities of wit. While English composers may have been more 'in earnest' than the French, the Irish were even more sincere: 'In Ireland, this fascinating art was still more universally in practice, and still more enthusiastically admired. The music was here the goddess of unbounded idolatry, and her worship was the business of life'.[53] For Brooke, Walker's suggestions that the Irish bards were either too sad or too overcome by their gloomy surroundings to write happy songs constitute a re-subordination of the Irish, presenting English oppression as responsible for Irish song production. She also rejects the notion offered by the *Gentleman's Magazine* writer about the amorous nature of the Irish. Brooke chooses to represent Irish song in its own positive terms rather than in relation to past English activity or present English opinion.

While Brooke's comments correct the negative views of Irishness found in comic Irish song in metropolitan centres, then, they also negotiate her place among the male antiquarians in Ireland.[54] In the Preface to her work, Brooke indicates her diffidence about embarking upon 'so important a task' as the translation of 'the productions of our Irish Bards'.[55] She anticipates that the reader will expect to see 'the subject elucidated and enlarged upon, with the pen of learning and antiquity', and regrets the fact that she lacks 'the learning requisite for such an undertaking'. However, she also suggests that even if she did write such a discourse, 'it would only have qualified me for an unnecessary foil to the names of [Charles] O'CONOR, [Sylvester] O'HALLORAN and [Charles] VALLANCEY'.[56] What she chooses to do is not another antiquarian dissertation, but an effort at imaginative re-creation, as she revises the bardic material for a contemporary audience. She also differs from her antiquarian peers in extending her concerns from the ancient past to the near present. She presents her work in a roughly chronological ordering from the 'Poem of Conloch' (written in '*a very early period*')[57] to songs by Carolan, Cormac Common and Patrick Linden composed in the early part of the eighteenth century.

It is clear that in Brooke's work the bardic poetry and the later songs are intimately connected. In his *Historical Memoirs*, Walker laments the death of Irish music at the time of Carolan, whom he presented as the last of the bards: 'Our musical taste became refined, and our sweet melodies and native Musicians fell into disrepute'.[58] In contrast, Brooke suggests that the songs constitute the continuing legacy of bardic poetry. She notes that she has chosen the songs of Carolan along with '*some other songs of modern date, to shew of what the native genius and language of this country, even now, are capable; labouring, as they do, under every disadvantage*'.[59] Brooke represents the continuity between the bardic poetry and the songs composed in modern times. She also indicates the way in which modern composers are influenced by material from the past. In 'The Maid of the Valley', the poet compares the beloved to Deirdre, already mentioned in Brooke's translation of 'Conloch', and Blanaide, who is discussed in Walker's *Historical Memoirs*.[60] Similarly, Brooke notes Cormac Common was inspired by listening to the work of the ancient bards: 'poetry was the muse of whom he was most enamoured. This made him listen eagerly to the Irish songs, and metrical tales, which he heard sung and recited around the 'crackling faggots' of his father, and his neighbours'.[61] Cormac himself was able to recite '*any of* Oisin's *poems*'.[62] Unlike O'Conor, Walker and the other antiquarians, Brooke makes a seamless connection between the poetry of the past and near contemporary songs.

Brooke also parts ways with her antiquarian peers in the way in which she shows herself attuned to the cultural issues of remediation. Walker indicates little concern with the effects of media transfer. He acknowledges the 'sympathetic' power of songs conveyed orally in bardic culture,[63] but he also wants to assure his readers that the bards were also fully able to write. The songs he includes in the *Historical Memoirs* are taken from manuscripts of fellow antiquarians. Walker himself did not know Gaelic, and as such was less invested in the original lyrics of songs.[64] Brooke, however, draws attention to the fact that she is the first to translate the Gaelic poetry into English. She also indicates her awareness that she is transferring texts from an oral medium into a 'new medium', print, observing, for example, that one of the elegies was '*taken down from the dictation of a young woman, in the county of* Mayo, *by* Mr. O'Flanagan, *who was struck with the tender and beautiful simplicity which it breathes.*'[65] Tellingly, the songs that Brooke selects to include in the *Reliques* emphasize the importance of the voice, particularly the singing voice. In 'The Maid of the Valley', the speaker likens himself to the bards of old, singing the praises not just of heroes, but of his beloved:

> My muse her harp shall at thy bidding bring,
> And role th' heroic tide of verse along;
> And Finian Chiefs, and arms shall wake the string,
> And Love and War divide the lofty song![66]

In 'Song for Mable Kelly', Carolan specifically indicates that Mabel inspires not just poetry, but song: 'To thee harmonious powers belong, / That add to verse the charms of song'. Without her to inspire his 'soft melody', the poet has mere 'numbers' at his disposal.[67] Mable's own voice is so powerful that it ultimately controls the speaker and works against the forces of nature:

> Thy voice, that binds the list'ning soul, –
> That can the wildest rage controul;
> Bid the fierce Crane its powers obey,
> And charm him from his finney prey.[68]

'Song for Gracey Nugent' also highlights Gracey's voice: 'Her's is the voice – tun'd by harmonious Love, / Soft as the Songs that warble through the grove'.[69]

While the songs she translates promote the power of the singing voice, Brooke's own commentary in 'Thoughts on Irish Song' reveals an ambiguous attitude to the process of transforming the 'charms of song' into print, however. On the one hand, she expresses herself eager to engage in remediation so that she can share the 'exquisitely charming' Irish songs with the English reader.[70] She goes to great pains to try to describe the acoustics of her subject, drawing the reader's attention to the fact that 'the poetry of many of our Songs is indeed already Musick, without the aid of a tune; so great is the smoothness, and harmony of its cadences'. She attributes this musical effect to the fact that Irish contains more vowels in relation to consonants because 'many of the consonants are aspirated': the Irish has an 'advantage ... beyond every other language, of flowing off, in vowels, upon the ear'.[71] Whereas in English 'and ... in most other languages, the Italian excepted', she notes, most of the poetry is 'composed on consonants', Irish is 'singular in the happy art of cutting off, by aspirates, every sound that could injure the melody of its cadence'.[72] 'Thoughts on Irish Song' also contains one of the only sections in the *Reliques* in which Brooke offers a direct prose translation, as she presents two stanzas of a song in Gaelic, the second of which 'struck me, as being so particularly beautiful, that I was tempted to translate them both for its sake.'[73]

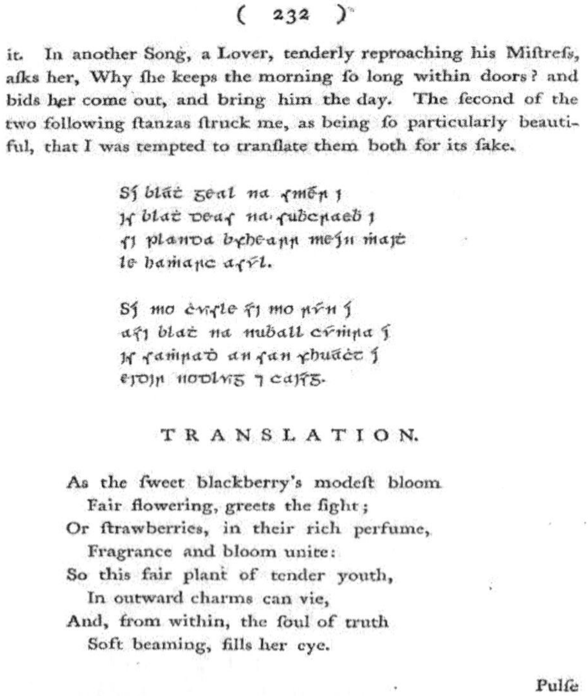

(232)

it. In another Song, a Lover, tenderly reproaching his Mistress, asks her, Why she keeps the morning so long within doors? and bids her come out, and bring him the day. The second of the two following stanzas struck me, as being so particularly beautiful, that I was tempted to translate them both for its sake.

Sí blát geal na ṡméṅ ṡ
Is blát ḋeaṡ na ṡubcṙaeḋ ṡ
ṡí planḋa byḃeaṅṅ meṡn maṡṫ
le haṁaṅc aṡíl.

Sí mo ċuiṡle ṡí mo ṗṙún ṡ
aṡí blát na nuball cṁṡṅa ṡ
Is ṡaṁpaḋ an ṡan ṡbuaċṫ ṡ
eṡoṡṅ noḋlṡg ṡ caṡṡṡ.

TRANSLATION.

As the sweet blackberry's modest bloom
  Fair flowering, greets the sight;
Or strawberries, in their rich perfume,
  Fragrance and bloom unite:
So this fair plant of tender youth,
  In outward charms can vie,
And, from within, the soul of truth
  Soft beaming, fills her eye.

Pulse

Figure 5.3: C. Brooke, *Reliques of Irish Poetry: Consisting of heroic poems, odes, elegies, and songs, translated into English verse: with notes explanatory and historical; and the originals in the Irish character. To which is subjoined an Irish tale* (Dublin: George Bonham, 1789), p. 232.

On the other hand, however, Brooke refuses the possibility of remediation, arguing that 'the beauty of many of [the passages to which she draws attention] is considerably impaired by translation; indeed, so sensible was I of this, that it influenced me to give up, in despair, many a sweet stanza to which I found myself quite unequal'.[74] As well as containing the direct translation noted above, one of a very few that Brooke includes in the *Reliques*, 'Thoughts on Irish Song' also contains one of the only passages which Brooke indicates that she is unable to translate: 'I wished ... to have translated the following lines of a favourite song; but it presented ideas, of which my pen could draw no resemblance that pleased me.' After including four lines from the song 'Cean Dubh Deelish' in Gaelic, she writes, 'I need not give any comment upon these lines; the English reader would not understand it, and the Irish reader could not want it, for it is impossible to peruse them without being sensible of their beauty'.[75] The attempt to translate songs brings Brooke to an impasse in which the 'English' are ultimately unable to gain access to an 'Irish' perspective. The Gaelic words – and typeface – in this case present an impenetrable walls that the English reader cannot scale. Although Brooke suggests that 'there is no other music in the world so calculated to make its way directly to the heart' as Irish music, she also indicates that a complete knowledge of Irish song in unavailable to English readers.[76] Unlike Beauford and others of his ilk, she refuses to try to render the Irish sounds comprehensible and consumable for a non-Gaelic audience.

Brooke's ambiguous attitude to representing the Gaelic songs reflects her own ambivalent political position. She is, as she notes, concerned to rescue the reputation of the Gaelic people from 'modern prejudice'.[77] Her inclusion of the Gaelic texts in her *Reliques* suggests her sensitivity to the uniqueness of the Gaelic culture.[78] But she is, after all, a member of the elite whose power depended upon the subordination of the majority. Moreover, as a woman without means, she was economically dependent on the good will of the Anglo-Irish community, many of whom were themselves practitioners of 'modern prejudice' toward the Gaelic community. Dominick Trant, for example, the dedicatee of Brooke's original poem, the 'Tale of Maon', and the purchaser along with his wife, of twelve copies of the *Reliques*, was the author of *Considerations on the Present Disturbances in the Province of Munster* (1787), an anti-Catholic pamphlet which fulminated against the Rightboy protests in Munster.

Faced with the task of both representing a positive Gaelic Ireland and appealing to readers and supporters like Trant, Brooke adopts a mediating perspective. Although she asserts the political importance of song in Ireland's past and encourages her readers to regard Irish song as possessing its own aesthetic concerns independent of the influence of England, she also downplays the politics of individual songs. In her commentary on the 'Elegy' by Edmond Ryan, a piece which is actually a song but which she includes in the sections on 'Elegies', she notes Ryan's history as a 'rapparee', one of those who, '*after the defeat of the* Boyne, *were obliged to abandon their dwellings and possessions*.'[79] However, instead of representing the song, a lamentation for a woman, as a reflection of his political situation, she concludes: '*From passages in this* Elegy, *we may infer, that, to the misfortunes of its author alone, the desertion of his mistress was owing; but I have not been able to discover the name of this fair inconstant*.'[80] Ryan, or Éamonn An Cnuic as he was also called, is not represented as suffering from his political situation; rather, he is just unlucky in love. Similarly, although Brooke suggests that Carolan's songs indicate '*of what the native genius and language of this country, even now, are capable; labouring, as they do, under every disadvantage*',[81] the songs she selects to bring to the English-speaking readers' attention are love songs: 'Song for Gracey Nugent', the cousin of one of Carolan's early patrons, George Reynolds of Letterfyan, and 'Song for Mable Kelly', the daughter of another one of Carolan's patrons. The other selections in the section on songs, 'Song by Patrick Linden' and 'The Maid of the Valley', are also love songs. In choosing to focus on love songs, Brooke may have also been trying to avoid calling attention to more politically questionable kinds of Irish song in circulation at the time: Jacobite or radical pieces, many of which were distributed by means of an oral rather than a print culture network.

What Brooke presents in her selection of Irish songs, then, is a politically ambiguous stance; she contests comic versions of Irish songs as well as antiquarian perspectives on Irish culture, but she is also careful not to fan the flames that would later blaze into a bloody and ultimately doomed revolution. In the *Reliques*, what Brooke ultimately succeeds in highlighting is the process of mediation involved in the transfer of Gaelic songs into print networks. In contrast to the 'Lillibuleros', the 'Irish Hullabaloos' or even the *Historical Memoirs of the Irish Bards*, Brooke's renditions of Irish song deny the possibility of obtaining an immediate perspective on Irish culture. Rather, they cast light on the difficult business of cultural transmission. In a nation consisting of such deep divisions as Ireland in 1789, the safest way to communicate, Brooke suggests, is to focus on the medium rather than the message.

6 HOMOLOGY, ANALOGY AND THE PERCEPTION OF IRISH RADICALISM

Vincent Morley

'But he who would not be found tripping, ought to be very careful in this matter of comparisons, for they are most slippery things.'

Plato, *The Sophist*.

If comparisons are slippery things, words are more treacherous still. Before I venture to discuss the presence or absence of radicalism in the Irish verse of the revolutionary era, it would be prudent to outline my understanding of the term. 'Radicalism' is a concept of English origin and the word entered the language in the early nineteenth century: the earliest citation in the *Oxford English Dictionary* dates from 1820, at which time it signified the political principles of those who advocated a 'radical' – that is to say, a root and branch – reform of the Westminster parliament. The use of the adjective in this context can be traced as far back as the 1780s when Christopher Wyvill proposed a 'radical reform in the representation' and John Jebb envisaged a 'radical reformation'.[1] Not unreasonably, if somewhat anachronistically, historians commonly describe those who campaigned for an extensive reform of parliament in the later decades of the eighteenth century as 'radicals' – from John Wilkes and the Society for the Defence of the Bill of Rights in the 1760s and 1770s, to John Cartwright and the Society for Constitutional Information in the 1780s, to Thomas Paine and the various Corresponding Societies of the 1790s.[2] Aside from their core demand for parliamentary reform – encompassing such measures as frequent elections, more equal constituencies and a broader franchise – radicals also became identified with opposition to the royal prerogative, with support for religious toleration and repeal of the Test and Corporation Acts, and with sympathy for the American and French Revolutions. In terms of its political antecedents, radicalism can be seen as an outgrowth of the 'real Whig' ideas espoused by sections of the Country opposition during the early decades of the eighteenth century; traditional Whig shibboleths concerning the ancient constitution and the historic liberties of Englishmen continued to form an important part of the radicals' rhetorical armoury.

With the above background in mind, I was somewhat perplexed on receiving an invitation to the first United Islands? symposium to read a paper on the subject of 'radical poetry and folk song' *in Irish*. While I would be quite content to pin the 'radical' label on various anglophone bodies situated on the margins of a Patriot opposition that itself drew heavily on Whig ideas – bodies such as Dublin's Society of Free Citizens in the 1770s, the reform congress of 1785, or the Dublin and Belfast societies of United Irishmen during their legal phase in the early 1790s – it would not have occurred to me to use the term with reference to the vernacular literature of the period.[3] Nonetheless, a short period of reflection led me to conclude that the task I had been asked to undertake was neither impractical nor entirely without merit – given the obvious parallels that can be drawn between the political literature composed in Irish during the revolutionary era and English texts from the same period that are conventionally described as radical. The features I have in mind are far from trivial and include the following: hostility to the monarch, the ministry, the established church, and Britain's war efforts, as well as sympathy for the American colonists, revolutionary France, and domestic opponents of government. But comparisons, as Plato warned us, are slippery, and we need to be on our guard against the temptation to interpret external similarities as evidence of an underlying relationship. Thoughts such as these persuaded me that it would be a useful exercise to place the apparently radical sentiments found in the literature of the late eighteenth century in context and to show that they owed little or nothing to radicalism but were, in reality, expressions of an indigenous political culture which existed long before 1770 and persisted well into the nineteenth century.

I propose to demonstrate this proposition by reviewing the evidence of political verse in Irish both synchronically and diachronically. In the first place, I will consider two songs from the revolutionary period – songs that could, by a judicious use of selective quotation, be plausibly presented as radical works. I will argue that such a conclusion would be wide of the mark and that the political outlook expressed by the songs was completely at variance with any English concept of radicalism. In the second place, I will show that the superficially radical outlook displayed in the Irish song and verse of the revolutionary period is also to be found in compositions which are considerably earlier and later in date. Finally, I will briefly discuss the implications of these observations.

I

I have previously edited the first of my chosen songs in *Washington i gCeannas a Ríochta*, an anthology of political verse from the period of the American war. The work was composed by Ceallachán Mac Cárthaigh, an author about whom little is known; the first verse is as follows:

Ciodh fada atá Seoirse brónach feargach
 ag comhrac Washington, Jones is Lee,
is gur leagadh go leor dá chróntoirc leathana –
 srónach, cealgach, glórach, groí;
atá Laoiseach fós ag tabhairt gleo dó is anfa,
 Holónt á ghreadadh is an Spáinneach buí,
is fé thosach an fhómhair atá Fódla dearfa,
 a chómhachta leagtha go deo nó á gcloí.[4]

(While George [III] has long been dejected and furious, fighting Washington, [John Paul] Jones and [General Charles] Lee, and many of his bloated swarthy boars have been felled – big-nosed, treacherous, clamorous, stout; Louis [XVI] is still giving him tumult and terror, Holland is lashing him as is the sallow Spaniard, and by the beginning of autumn Ireland is assured his power will be overthrown forever or vanquished.)

The song survives in an autograph manuscript which records that its author was a resident of *Ard na Pailise*, which may be the townland of Pallas in the parish of Ardfield, not far from Clonakilty in west Cork.[5] Certainly, the other contents of the manuscript, as well as the scribe's name, are consistent with a Cork provenance. But whatever doubt attaches to the place of composition, there is none at all in relation to the date of composition as the song contains unambiguous references to conventions of Volunteer delegates from the provinces of Ulster and Connacht that were held at Dungannon and Ballinsaloe in the months of February and March 1782 respectively:

Ag Baile na Slógh atá na slóite fearchoin –
 beoga, calma, óga, groí,
is tuilleadh dá sórt atá ag pórt Dún Geanainn –
 mórga, macánta, cróga a ngíomh;
beidh fearaibh na Mumhan go clúmhail eatarthu
 i dtosach na dtrúp nach dúchas eagla,
cuirfidh siad Lúndain úd ar ball-chrith
 is búraibh Sacsan go brách gan bhrí.[6]

(At Ballinasloe are the heroic hosts – vigorous, valiant, youthful, spirited, and there are more of their kind in the fort of Dungannon – noble, honest, brave their deed; the men of Munster will be famously among them, at the head of the troops to whom fear is alien, they'll make yon London tremble and leave the English boors forever enfeebled.)

Clearly, some elements in the above quotations are consistent with the outlook of English radicals during the American war: most obviously, the Americans were lauded and the reigning monarch was abused. Furthermore, the success of the Patriot opposition in mobilizing significant sections of the Volunteer movement to demand legislative independence had enthused the author. But already a note of caution must be sounded: would an author influenced by radical ideas have applauded the military successes of the Bourbon monarchies or looked forward to a permanent eclipse of English power? The final verse (and the essential message of Irish political songs is often relegated to the end of the composition) provides the answer and leaves us in no doubt that the worldview of Ceallachán (Callaghan) Mac Cárthaigh had little in common with that of English radicals:

> Beidh *free trade* ag Gaeil gan mearbhall
>   taoscadh an bhairille is ól na dí,
> *Carolus Rex* mar Caesar calma
>   in Éirinn geallaimse fós 'na rí;
> beidh gairm is réim gan bhréag ag Callaghan;
>   tréada, fearainn is fáil ar chíos
> is ag cantain *Te Deum* beidh cléir na heaglaise
>   naofa beannaithe d'ordaigh Críost.[7]

(The Gaels will have free trade without mistake, draining the barrel and imbibing drink, I pledge that *Carolus Rex* [Charles Edward Stuart] like a valiant Caesar will yet be king in Ireland; Callaghan will truly have honour and power – herds, lands and access to rent, while the clergy of the holy blessed church ordained by Christ will be chanting *Te Deum*.)

Mac Cárthaigh anticipated an invasion by the Catholic powers which would lead to the restoration of the Stuart pretender, re-establish Catholicism, and install the native Irish as the dominant group in Irish society – a reordering of the social structure from which he expected to benefit. This was certainly political disaffection with a vengeance, but it was political disaffection of a very traditional type – a type that can be found in the literature of every decade from the Williamite Revolution onwards.

Let us next consider a song from a slightly later period, one associated with the French rather than the American Revolution. The song in question was composed by Fínín Ó Scannail, a cooper from Killarney whose works were still current in the Sliabh Luachra area of County Kerry during the youth of the lexicographer Patrick Dinneen (1860–1934).[8] The song can be precisely dated as it celebrates the failure of a British expedition to Flanders commanded by the Duke of York. The duke returned home in defeat in December 1794 but Ó Scannail also mentions the defection of the Dutch to the republican cause, an event which occurred in January 1795, and his song can therefore be assigned to the early months of that year. As far as I am aware, only the first of the verses has previously been published.[9] Ó Scannail's composition contains twelve verses and the radical-like tone is evident from the opening:

> Táid maithe na Breataine in anbhroid péine
>   gan taise le tréimhse dá ngreadadh tar fóir,

ag beartú le hainbhios mearbhaill céille
   tré mhachnamh drochmhéine do theagmhaigh don chóip;
a n-airm do tharraing gan ábhar gan éirim
   ar ghasra chéasta ba fada faoi *yoke*,
is gan acu dá ghairm ach lagsaine faosaimh
   'na mbailte poirt féinig dá mb'áil ligean dóibh.[10]

(The worthies of Britain are in dire distress, having been mercilessly pummelled to excess of late, they're plotting in ignorant disorder of mind with the mischievous scheming that afflicts the crew; their arms they drew without cause or skill against a tormented group who were long under a yoke, and who asked for nothing but a spell of respite in their own strongholds if they'd been left alone.)

Already we can see in the first verse a frank delight at the reverse suffered by British arms, as well as hostility directed at British ruling circles, who were portrayed as malicious warmongers. The French, on the other hand, were represented as a long-oppressed people who desired only to be left in peace. Ó Scannail's francophile sympathies are again displayed in the sixth verse, along with a hint of fashionable anti-clericalism:

Níl tairbhe in eascaine sagairt don réir sin –
   tá an fharraige in éineacht 's an machaire leo,
is beidh startha á n-aithris i leabharaibh léannach
   tré chaitheamh na saoghal ar ghaisce na leon;
ag freastalamh catha in aghaidh scata de réxaibh
   gan caraid le héileamh gur athraigh Holónt,
acmhainn nár measadh d'aon aicme ar bith daonna
   cé chaitheadar géilleadh go mb'fhearr ligean dóibh.[11]

(A priest's curse is worthless for that purpose – they [the French] command the sea and battlefield together, and tales will be told in learned books through the ages about the feats of the lions; giving battle against a pack of kings, without an ally to call on until Holland defected, an ability that wouldn't have been attributed to any human group, though they had to concede it would have been better if they'd been left alone.)

In defiance of general expectations, and contrary to the hopes of the Catholic clergy, the French republic had single-handedly repulsed a coalition of the crowned heads of Europe in an unparalleled display of revolutionary élan, and one member of the counter-revolutionary alliance had just gone over to the republican camp.

The opening verses of Ó Scannail's song reflect the republican climate of the decade in which it was composed. Many of its sentiments would not have been out of place in English radical literature of the same period. Again, however, this song expresses ideas that would never have been shared by English radicals: hostility to England and to Protestantism, loyalty to Catholicism (notwithstanding the expression of a certain anti-clerical sentiment that is not uncommon in the literature of the later eighteenth century), and the hope that a French invasion would sweep away the Anglo-Irish ruling class. The penultimate verse reads as follows:

> Gach draga duairc danardha damanta daoldubh
>   cas cealgach craoschuthaigh caismirteach crón,
> ná seachanadh aitheanta an Athar do réabadh
>   is do dhear bhaigh claon in aghaidh mhaitheas na hÓighe,
> caithfid a mbeatha is a rachmas do thréigean
>   is gan comairce caomhnaithe ar talamh 'na gcomhair –
> sin fala do tharraing a n-ainbhios féin é,
>   de dheascaibh gan géilleadh go mb'fhearr ligean dóibh.[12]

(All the gloomy, barbarous, damned, beetle-black, devious, treacherous, violently-angry, quarrelsome swarthy dragons who never failed to break the Father's commandments and who swore falsely against the Virgin's virtue, they'll have to abandon their livelihoods and wealth and there'll be no protection left for them on land – that's a retribution brought on by their own ignorance, for not conceding it would have been better if they'd been left alone.)

The explicitly religious nature of Ó Scannail's invective is notable: the Anglo-Irish gentry were condemned, not merely for their treachery and violence, but for their irreligion and their repudiation of the Virgin Mary. Their sins would, however, be punished; in the all-important final verse the author anticipated that he would shortly be able to compose new songs to celebrate the burning of the stately homes of ascendancy 'fanatics':

> Stadfad is geallaim nach bagartha baotha
>   le machnamh na mbréithre so beartaithe im dheoidh,
> is a dhearbh bíodh agaibhse ar thaisteal na laochra
>   ag creachadh is ag tréanbhriseadh caladh is póirt;
> beidh feannadh agus fealladh ar na *fanatics* claona
>   is a mbailte, cé aerach, 'na lasrach smóil,
> ar amharc do bhreacfainnse meamram dréachta
>   is i gceangal gach véarsa 'go mb'fhearr ligean dóibh'.[13]

(I'll conclude and promise that the following words are no idle threats to consider, but be assured of the heroes' expedition, plundering and devastating harbours and fortresses; the crooked fanatics will be flailed and deceived, and their homes, though airy, will be in scorching flames, at the sight I'll jot down a verse on parchment – and as the reprise of every verse, 'it would have been better if they'd been left alone'.)

If the outlook expressed in Ó Scannail's composition were an innovation associated with the 1790s it might be possible to view it as a 'radical' work: although clearly not an expression of the radicalism one would associate with the London

Corresponding Society, the song might still be seen as a product of a distinctively Irish radicalism, a radicalism coloured by the course of the country's history – by the conquests, plantations and expropriations of the seventeenth century, by Penal legislation, and by continuing British control of the Irish executive.

Such a reading *would* be possible if the superficially 'radical' features of the literature of the 1790s were characteristic of that decade – or, at least, of the revolutionary era as a whole – but this is not the case. While it is true that compositions from the 1790s employ an explicitly republican rhetoric which is not found in earlier or later decades, the other putatively radical features from that period were common in Irish political literature before the French or, indeed, the American Revolutions began, and they persisted even after the old order had been restored throughout Europe.

II

A survey of the political verse of the eighteenth and early nineteenth centuries would show that many of the sentiments it expressed varied little throughout the entire period: these included hatred of the reigning monarch; hatred of England and the English; hatred of the established church and of the Anglo-Irish gentry; support for France and the other Catholic powers of Europe; anticipation of a French invasion and the resulting liberation of Ireland from English and Protestant rule.[14] This much was constant, irrespective of whether France was ruled by a Bourbon, by republicans, or by the emperor of the French.

I could not hope to demonstrate the continuity and persistence of all the above themes in the space available for this essay and I therefore propose to illustrate the continuity of attitudes which existed in relation to the single issue of greatest political significance: namely, the hostility with which the British monarch was consistently viewed in Irish political literature. To this end, I have selected brief quotations from six works composed over a period of 100 years. The examples were chosen to illustrate the continuity of attitudes towards the reigning monarch in the first half of the eighteenth century, again during the revolutionary era, and finally in the post-Waterloo period when political reaction was triumphant throughout Europe.

Example 1

> Is dóigh má ghabhaimse an cóta dearg so
>   leo go rachad tar sáile,
> a scóda leathan, a seolta scartha,
>   is an sról 'na mbratachaibh arda;
> cóir ná ceannach ní gheobhaid ó Ghallaibh
>   go dtógaid sealbh a n-áitreabh,

> is Seoirse a thachtadh le córda casta
> is is ceolmhar screadfas an chláirseach.[15]

(I suppose if I put on this red coat I will go with them overseas, their sheets spread, their sails deployed, and silk in their tall banners; no justice or recompense will they receive from the *Gaill* until they take possession of their dwellings, and strangle George with a twisted rope and musically the harp will cry out.)

The author of the first example anticipated the execution of his Britannic Majesty – not by a guillotine, it must be admitted, but by the less revolutionary means of a gallows. He imagined that the happy event would be celebrated by a spontaneous outpouring of music from a harp – the heraldic symbol of Ireland. Can we perhaps detect in this combination of images the influence of the 1790s? Does the predicted execution of King George recall the fate of Louis XVI? Could the reference to the harp be an echo of the United Irish motto 'it is new strung and shall be heard'?

Such speculation would be unfounded. The monarch threatened with execution was George II and the verse occurs in a poem composed by Aodh Buí Mac Cruitín, a County Clare author, in 1728 when he was an enlisted man in the *Régiment de Clare*, one of the Irish regiments in the French service. His comrades-in-arms constituted the intended audience and it is significant that the work was composed at a time when a diplomatic alliance existed between France and Great Britain. Mac Cruitín's composition indicates that the rank and file of the Irish regiments had an agenda of their own: they looked forward to a renewal of hostilities, to an invasion of Great Britain, and to the execution of George II. I have discussed the background to this revealing composition in some detail elsewhere.[16]

Example 2

> An eol díbhse a dhaoine i bhFonn Fáil
> Seoirse go cloíte is i lomghá?
>   Aiteas mo chroí istigh
>   mar theagmhaigh a bhríste,
> is ná glanfadh an taoide a thiompán![17]

(Do you know O people in the land of Fál [Ireland] that George is crushed and in dire need? It's a joy to my heart within, what happened to his breeches – and the tide wouldn't clean his fundament!)

The second example expresses the author's delight – a delight he assumed would be shared by his audience – at a recent military setback suffered by Great Britain. There is nothing in the quotation to indicate a date of composition, unless the scatological nature of the abuse directed at King George might suggest that it was composed at a time when the institution of monarchy had already fallen into some disrepute.

Yet this example also belongs to the pre-revolutionary era: the king who soiled his breeches was George II and the verse is from a song composed in 1757 by William English, a member of the Augustinian community in Cork city, to celebrate Austrian victories over Britain's ally, Frederick II of Prussia. English was a highly politicized author, and his song reminds modern readers that much of the Irish verse of the eighteenth century was originally intended to be sung rather than recited.[18]

Historians who are concerned to achieve an understanding of opinion in eighteenth-century Ireland *wie es eigentlich war* will value English's corpus as a primary source of great importance. The case is otherwise with those who have a teleological focus on the growth of the British state. In 2006, for example, Stephen Conway published what he described as a 'view from the grassroots' of Cork city during the War of Austrian Succession and the Seven Years' War. He failed to use any Irish-language sources, however, and instead relied on municipal and other official records to portray Cork as a town in which 'almost every British success, by sea or land, was marked by celebrations'.[19] This is part of the story and it deserves to be told, but the majority community in Ireland's second city was left entirely voiceless in Conway's 'grassroots' account. If the 'New British History' sometimes casts 'Paddy' in walk-on parts, it reserves the speaking roles for Anglo-Saxons; inevitably, the anglocentric agenda and anglophone methodology of its practitioners produces a seriously distorted image of the Irish past.

Example 3

Thall ins an Fhrainc a chuala mé an chaint,
agus abraimse mo cheol le réasún,
go geal shoilsigh sí fríd dorchadas na hoích',
is bheir solas in iomadaí réagún.
Nár thé an choinneal seo a choíche as
ach coinneáilt i gcónaí i mbladhair' é,
nó go gcuiridh sí críocha le clannaibh Gall
agus ar lorg Sheoirse.[20]

(It was over in France I heard the talk, and let me sing my song with reason, it shone brightly through the darkness of night and carried a light into many regions. May this candle never expire but always be kept alight, until it puts an end to the offspring of the *Gaill* and to George's progeny.)

The author of the third example expressed the wish that a certain flame of French origin would continue to burn until it had consumed, not just the Hanoverian dynasty, but the entire English race. A reference to the French Revolution seems likely, but the quotation leaves open the possibility that the flame may represent one of the several Anglo-French wars fought during the *ancien régime*.

For once, appearances do not deceive and the king in question was indeed George III. The quotation is taken from an anonymous song of the 1790s collected from the oral tradition near Convoy, County Donegal, and edited by the pioneering folklorist Énrí Ó Muirgheasa in one of his anthologies of Ulster verse. In Ó Muirgheasa's edition the song is a macaronic composition in which each verse is expressed alternately in English and Irish – a format that became increasingly common with the spread of bilingualism from the late eighteenth century onwards. The English text was clearly the original in the current example and a version was included in a Dublin edition of *Paddy's Resource*, an anthology of republican songs from the 1790s, although it did not appear in the original Belfast edition of 1795.[21] The verse quoted above is not found in the text as published: whether this discrepancy reflects an excision by the publisher or an addition by a local author is uncertain, although the latter possibility may be more likely. The verse is included in an alternative English-language version of the song collected by R. R. Madden, an early historian of the United Irishmen.[22] I will give Ó Muirgheasa's text here:

> It was in France our first advance,
>   as I may sing with reason;
> it shone so bright on a dark, dark night,
>   and enlightened many nations.
> And may this torch be never quenched,
>   but kept in constant blazing,
> till it consumes all Luther's seed
>   and George's generation.[23]

As can be seen, the texts in the two languages do not correspond exactly: while the Irish version stressed ethnicity (*'clannaibh Gall'*) the English version placed the emphasis on religion ('Luther's seed').

Example 4

> Do fhreagair an ógh mé go deorach lag,
>   do b'eol di a ceasaí a lé' dhom:
> 'Is í m'ainmse Fódhla fheochta, chaite,
>   bhrónach, chathach, chéasta.
> Gurb é Gaige na mBó is a fhorsaí a chreach mé,
>   do stróic mo chneas gan éadach,
> Oliver crón agus Seoirse dearg
>   do chaith coróin mo mharcaigh Ghaelaigh.'[24]

(The maiden replied tearfully and feebly that she could list her sorrows for me: 'My name is Ireland, withered, worn, sad, grieving, tormented. It was *Gaige na mBó* and his forces who plundered me, tearing at my naked skin; swarthy Oliver and bloody George wore the crown of my Gaelic cavalier.')

The fourth quotation is placed in the mouth of Fódhla, just one among many personifications of Ireland in the literature. She had been abused by a succession of historical villains: by '*Gaige na mBó*', apparently a reference to Diarmait Mac Murchadha, the Leinster king who solicited the Anglo-Norman invasion in the twelfth century; by Oliver Cromwell; and by the present sanguinary occupant of the throne. The latter two personages are described as having usurped the crown of the woman's "*marcach Gaelach*" (Gaelic cavalier) – undoubtedly a reference to the Stuart pretender. The inclusion of a Jacobite reference will surely suggest an early data of composition to those historians who discern a lack of continuity between Jacobitism and later manifestations of Irish disaffection.[25]

In reality, the quoted verse is taken from an *aisling* collected from the oral tradition in Drimoleague, County Cork, which is attributed to Donncha Ó Súilleabháin, a local author of the early nineteenth century. L. M. Cullen has characterized the *aisling* genre as 'a literary form, not a message for the people' – arguing that it was 'aristocratic in inspiration' and reproduced the outlook of the 'landed class uprooted in the social and political upheavals of the seventeenth century'.[26] To appreciate how misconceived this thesis is we need look no further than the present composition. Far from being an imitative pastiche based on a century-old model, Ó Súilleabháin's *aisling* was innovative in both form and content. In relation to form, his song – like the previous example – is a macaronic composition in which each verse in Irish (which appears to be the original in this case) is followed by a loose translation. Interestingly, the quoted verse omits the Jacobite reference in its English dress:

> Then answered me with flattering voice,
>   her cruel case could state well:
> 'My name is Éire forlorn in anguish,
>   trampled, torn and breached now.
> Those cruel men of *Gaige na mBó*
>   and their forces tore my raiment;
> Oliver Cromwell and George the Third
>   my royal crown are wearing'.[27]

Furthermore, the message of Ó Súilleabháin's *aisling* is as innovative as its form. As there is little difference between the Irish and English versions of the crucial final verse, I will give it here in English:

> In Dingle Bay our troops will land
>   to fight for *Gráinne Mhaol bhocht*,

>   so let the bowls of royal punch
>   be here brought on the table.
>   A toast give round and merrily drink,
>   and then we will repeat it,
>   that in triumph brave young Bonaparte
>   we'll soon see here in Erin.[28]

Readers may judge for themselves whether this prediction of an imminent descent by 'brave young Bonaparte' on the Irish coast can be more reasonably interpreted as a fossilized 'literary form' or as a contemporary 'message for the people'.

Example 5

>   Sa bhfómhar so chugainn 'sea dhófam púirt
>   le glór an údair naofa,
>   beidh Seoirse dubhach gan choróin, gan chlú,
>   gan sólás boird, gan féasta;
>   ólfam lionn is beoir le fonn,
>   is comhsheinnfeam tiúin den Ghaeilge,
>   beidh bróga dubha ar gach ógfhear chlúil
>   cé gur rófhada dúinn á n-éagmais.[29]

> (In the coming autumn we'll burn fortresses by the word of the holy author, George will be despondent, without a crown or reputation, without the consolation of a table or a feast; we'll drink beer eagerly and together warble an air in Irish, each reputable young man will wear black shoes – although we've been without them for too long.)

This example would appear to date from a time of international conflict or perhaps of revolution: within a year, the author predicted, fortresses would be destroyed and the reigning monarch would be deposed. Surely, therefore, this text cannot have been composed any later than 1815?

But appearances are again misleading. The monarch threatened with deposition on this occasion was George IV and the quotation is taken from a song by Tomás Rua Ó Súilleabháin, a County Kerry schoolmaster, which was composed to celebrate Daniel O'Connell's historic victory in the Clare by-election of 1828.[30] The '*údar naofa*' ('holy author') mentioned in the second line of the quotation was 'Pastorini', pseudonym of the Catholic controversialist Charles Walmsley, who had interpreted the Apocalypse of St John as prophesying the downfall of Protestantism in 1825.[31] As far as Tomás Rua was concerned, Pastorini's prediction was essentially correct, albeit some three years premature. His song gave voice to millennial hopes that were widespread among lower-class Catholics earlier in the 1820s and were given a fresh stimulus by O'Connell's electoral success.

Example 6

    Táid crónbhodaigh cnaíte gan feolta gan fíonta
       gan sóchas gan saoirse gan séadaíbh,
    is Seoirse ba rí acu re fórchur i ndaoirse
    fá chomhrainn dá ghríobhadh re daolaíbh.[32]

(The swarthy churls are wasting away without meats or wines, without freedom or treasure, and George who was their king is to be consigned to captivity – in a coffin being attacked by beetles.)

The final example evidently alludes to the recent demise of one of the Hanoverian monarchs but the passage contains nothing to indicate which of the four Georges has died. Nonetheless, the ghoulish imagery of beetles feasting on the royal cadaver may suggest a certain scepticism on the author's part concerning the divinely ordained nature of kingship.

This quotation is taken from a composition by Eoghan Ó Comhraí, a County Clare author, that was apparently intended as a campaign song for James O'Gorman Mahon, the O'Connellite candidate who stood in the same county in the general election of August 1830, George IV having died in June of the same year. The song has been edited by Pádraig Ó Fiannachta together with several other pieces by the same author – who is better known in English-speaking circles under the anglicized form of his name: Eugene O'Curry. Some five years after he composed the present song he was employed by the Ordnance Survey and later obtained a position with the Royal Irish Academy; in 1854 he was appointed the first professor of Irish history in the Catholic University.[33] One suspects that the university's rector, the very English Henry Cardinal Newman, may not have been fully apprized of the nature of his professor's writings in the vernacular.

III

The above examples are representative of the hostile attitude expressed towards the reigning monarch in Irish political literature throughout the eighteenth and early nineteenth centuries. Indeed, I am unaware of even a single contemporary poem or song in Irish that praised any of the following: William III, Anne, George I, George II, George III, George IV or William IV. Neil Buttimer recently speculated that he might have identified a poem in praise of George I, but inclined to the view that the piece was probably ironic in intent.[34] His caution was justified and it is in fact an acephalous fragment of a longer work by the well known Jacobite author Seán Ó Neachtain.[35] The numerous puns in the opening verse of the complete version put the poet's intention beyond doubt:

> Ar feadh na hEorpa fál te
> go raibh roimh Sheoirse cátach;
>   is andúil liom
>   anfhlaith nár chrom
> fo smacht neamhchumtha an Phápa.[36]

(Throughout Europe may there be a 'lively resentment' (*fál te*) / 'welcome' (*fáilte*) for 'twisted' (*catach*) / 'esteemed' (*cátach*) George; an 'evil being' / 'passion' (*andúil*) for me is the 'tyrant' / 'great prince' (*anfhlaith*) who didn't bow to the 'heaven-formed' / 'uncreated' (*neamhchumtha*) authority of the Pope.)

If the Irish literature of the eighteenth and early nineteenth centuries contains any poems or songs in which a British monarch is praised, they are exceedingly rare – a remarkable lack of deference on the part of the native population that is impossible to reconcile with the *'ancien régime'* model of Irish society.[37] In this respect, Ireland's political culture stands in sharp contrast to that of Highland Scotland. There, the voice of Jacobite disaffection was answered from within the Gaelic-speaking community by the voice of Hanoverian loyalism: for every Alasdair Mac Mhaighstir Alasdair who excoriated the reigning dynasty, a Donnchadh Bàn Mac an t-Saoir could be found to extol it.[38] In Irish-speaking Ireland, on the other hand, the voice of disaffection was effectively unchallenged throughout the long eighteenth century.

In purely formal terms, the two earliest examples in the series of quotations above can be categorized as Jacobite texts, the third as republican, the fourth as Bonapartist and the last two as O'Connellite. In substance, however, the elements of continuity are more significant than the distinctions between them. The two songs from the revolutionary era form part of an evolving yet unbroken political tradition that began long before the 'shot heard round the world' and continued long after Bonaparte had been consigned to St Helena: an unbroken political tradition extending from Jacobitism, through Defenderism, to Ribbonism and beyond. The political ideas expounded in the Irish verse of the late eighteenth and early nineteenth centuries owed little or nothing to English radicalism – to myths of an ancient Saxon constitution or contract theory, to schemes for parliamentary reform or for social improvement. Literary influences and historical myths were present, certainly, but to identify them we must look to the native tradition: to Geoffrey Keating rather than to Algernon Sidney, to Seán Ó Conaill rather than to John Bunyan.[39]

In short, the application of the 'radical' label to the political verse of the revolutionary era would not help us to '"understand or explain the process by which Ireland's distinctive political culture was formed. On the contrary, it would simultaneously obscure fundamental continuities between popular attitudes at different periods while exaggerating the importance of superficial similarities between the very different ideologies articulated by Irish versifiers and by English radicals. Their common features were real enough but (to borrow from the language of evolutionary biology) they were analogous rather than homologous. That is to say, the similarities between Irish political verse and English radicalism were not the result of an organic relationship – of a common origin or of a shared body of thought. Instead, like bats and birds or dolphins and fish, they evolved independently from different antecedents and acquired similar features in response to similar environmental pressures – represented in this case by the overlapping political and religious establishments in Ireland and England. Given the profound differences between the popular cultures of the two countries, this conclusion should occasion little surprise.

7 LOST MANUSCRIPTS AND REACTIONARY RUSTLING: WAS THERE A RADICAL SCOTTISH GAELIC POETRY BETWEEN 1770 AND 1820?

Peter Mackay

This chapter discusses how Scottish Gaelic poetry engages with political Radicalism between 1770 and 1820, and also whether Gaelic poetry can be considered oppositional or contrary, both within the Gaelic community itself, and in terms of the relationship between the Gaelic community and the ideological narratives of the rest of Britain during the period. A cautionary note to begin: what might appear radical in British terms frequently turns out to be a reaffirmation of a conservative position in Gaelic terms, and vice versa; therefore, when looking for 'Radicalism', you often discover (small r) radicalism: opposition to change; a desire to return to *radices*, 'roots'. The temptation is to imagine Gaelic poetry as inherently oppositional and contrary to standard British narratives and ideology; on the contrary, what is often of interest is the extent to which this is only partly true, and to which Gaelic poetry offers a complex negotiation between different identities (Gaelic, Scottish and British). This is not to say that there are no traces of Radicalism in the poetry, but that the political positions espoused (or indeed masked) in Gaelic literature are not simple, but exist in a complex relationship with other social and ideological contexts.

The fifty-year period under discussion can be seen, in Gaelic terms, as an interregnum, falling between the clan system (the decline of which is associated in part with the failure of Jacobitism) and the crofting community. The death of Alexander MacDonald (Alastair Mac Mhaighstir Alastair) around 1770 marks the end of one era in Gaelic poetry. MacDonald, as poet and propagandist of the Jacobite cause, was participant in and representative of many of the political events of the preceding fifty years. His death suggests the end of Gaelic cultural Jacobitism, although the imagery and motifs of Jacobitism continue in mutated ways, as we shall see, beyond 1770. In truth, during the last twenty years of MacDonald's life, Gaelic culture had become more assimilated into the fabric of Scottish (and especially Edinburgh) life as a whole, partly following MacDonald's inauguration of a Scottish secular publishing industry – his *Aiseirigh na Seann Chànain*

Albannaich (The Resurrection of the Old Scottish Language) was published in Edinburgh in 1751 – and the Ossian phenomenon of the 1760s. As a result the cultural importance of Jacobitism is very much open to debate.

Also immediately pre-dating this period was the poet Rob Donn Mackay, who was famous for critiquing the behaviour of the landlords in his native Sutherland. Though he did not die until 1778, Mackay in effect stopped writing in 1768, and his extant poetry does not comment on the social upheaval that Sutherland underwent after 1769, following the death of the fifth Lord Reay. Mackay was first and foremost a poet of his own social milieu and was willing to publically rebuke the misdeeds of landowners and aristocracy. It may be no coincidence that the two main instances of violent opposition to clearance and the creation of sheep-runs came in Sutherland – around Kildonan, Kildermorie and Strathnaver – where Mackay's songs critical of landlords were passed down in oral tradition.

Despite the lack of a poeto-political commentator or activist such as MacDonald or Mackay, there is not an absence of political poetry in the period 1770–1820. Instead, there is a nuanced and complex 'political' poetry. Instead of a single, dominant cultural narrative within the Gaelic communities (although Jacobitism itself was never universally dominant), there are different narratives which meet and undermine one other. On one level what occurs between 1770 and 1820 in Scottish Gaelic poetry is a meeting of a late, metamorphosed Jacobite strain of poetry and early and rather unfocussed satirical and violent verse attacks on the forces and manifestations of clearance within the Scottish Highlands. Both of these, however, interact with and undermine a strong and pervasive identification with British imperialism and militarism. The combination of these narratives suggests a hybrid, multifaceted and – in many ways – self-contradictory Gaelic identity. The remainder of this essay focuses on three things in particular with regard to this multifaceted identity: the passage from Jacobitism to an engagement with British military imperialism; the response and reaction to clearance and forced emigration; and a strain of radical sexual poetry. The chapter does not mention, except in passing, Gaelic responses to the invasion of Scotland by Dr Johnson and his army of Boswell, the Ossianic controversy or religious writing (though this last accounts for most of the Gaelic literature of this period).

The Jacobite Metamorphosis

One of the most remarkable military-political achievements of the eighteenth century in Britain is the manner in which over thirty to forty years the martial prowess and organization of Scottish Highlanders was channelled from Jacobitism to a British Imperial cause. This is in part because, following the 1746

Disclothing Acts, British Army regiments provided the only social space or grouping in which wearing full Highland dress – a crucial part of Highland identity – was permitted.[1] The poetry of the period celebrates and fortifies the Highlanders' acquiescence of this metamorphosis; it also, however, shows the stresses and strains of the meeting of these two identities.

The work of Kenneth Mackenzie (Coinneach MacCoinnich), for example, shows how the meeting of explicitly Jacobite poetry and the support for British military Imperialism can be unsettling. Mackenzie's *Òrain Ghaidhealach* was published in Edinburgh in the turbulent year of 1792, and his songs feature a strange mix of Jacobite iconography and British Imperialist gusto. His 'Oran do na Chath-Bhuithinn Cheudna' (Song to the same regiment (the 42nd Royal Highlanders)) is written to the tune of 'I'll Follow the Lad with the White Cockade', and in the first verse the ideologically loaded word *èirigh* (to rise) is repeated twice:

> Mo rùn do na gillean, a philleadh an tòir,
> Gun churam 'an cunnart, cruaidh currant gu leoir,
> Tha 'n aigne'ein dìleas 's iad rìoghail gun leoin,
> 'S cha biodh iad air dèireadh 'an aireachdas slòigh
> Tha cridheachan èatrom fo' sgè nam fear òg,
> Mar eoin o na slèibhtean a g-èiridh 's na neoil,
> Tha misneach a g-èiridh, o na dh'eug 's tha bèo,
> Gun di-chuimhn air *Brènnus* chuir sèid ris a'n Ròimh.[2]

(My love to the boys, who'd return the chase, | with no thought of the danger, hard heroic enough | Their spirits are faithful and they are royal without wounds, | And they won't be tardy in guarding the people. | Their hearts are light under the shield of young men | Like birds of the slopes rising in the clouds | Confidence is rising, from those who died and are alive, | Not forgetting Brennus who set fire to Rome.)

The reference to Brennus, the General of the Gauls who burnt Rome, is ominous in a song to a regiment of the army of an Empire to compare to that of Rome. The song, however, then both celebrates and laments the role of the regiment as defenders of the country. The third stanza runs

> Na fir a tha tàpaidh, 's na gaisgich tha treun,
> Ann an ònair an dùcha' cha diulta iad feum,
> Bithidh pioban ga'n spealadh le calanail rèidh,
> 'S bith meoiren ri gearradh cruaidh charan nan leum
> 'Nuair shìneadh iad cùmnant air builleachas streup,
> Cruaidh-bheumnach deagh mhùlad gach buille gu feum.
> Bithidh naimhdean nan càiteis gan strachdadh gu feur,
> 'S gur còimeas dhoibh nise fir-chlis ann san speur.

(The men who are hardy, the heroes who are brave | For the honour of the country they wouldn't refuse to be used | Their pipes will mow them down with ready 'calanail', | And fingers for cutting hard twists will be jumping | when they extend a covenant for strife and striking, | each blow's hard-cutting good-sadness of use. | Their enemies will be rubbish thrashed to grass, | their like now the northern lights in the sky.)[3]

By context, the *dùcha* (country) here must be Great Britain. The song that precedes this one is the 'Oran do'n Chath-Bhuithinn Rioghail Ghai'leach air dhoibh teachd dhachaidh a America, 42nd Regt. Royal Highlanders' (Song to the Royal Highland regiment on their return home from America, 42nd Regt. Royal Highlanders), which identifies the Scottish Gaels as British, claiming

> Co fad sa mhaireas Breatanach,
> Bi'dh clìu orr ann a 'n èachdraidhachd,
> O lìnn gu lìnn le raitneachas,
> A' cuir 'an feill a 'n tapachais,
> A 'n *Tiganderoga* b' acuinneach.'[4]

(as long as there's a Briton. | They will be renowned in history-telling, | from generation to generation through recitation, | Throwing feasts to their manliness, | Expert at *Tiganderoga*).

The song also mentions fighting in 'Gadalup, Havannadh, Spàinn' and America where 'Le luaigh is fùdar gràineanach' (with lead and grainy powder) they 'Cuir Innseinich air àireachas' (put Indians on guard).[5]

How, though, to read these songs? Is the 'Oran do na Chath-Bhuithinn Cheudna' an example of the channelling of Jacobite militarism to a British cause? Does it use Jacobite imagery – and the explicitly Jacobite tune – to undermine and unsettle the avowals of loyalty to the country (it is notable that in this song the regiment's exploits abroad are not mentioned; the only place named is Glasgow, where the soldiers are gathered)? Or is there confusion in the song which means that it is both of these at once, as two ideological constructions meet and are both undermined and troubled?

The 'Oran do'n Chath-Bhuithinn Rioghail Ghai'leach', if one takes the risk of overreading it, presents such an unsettling of any notion of the loyalty of the Highland Regiments. It celebrates the exploits of 'Na Gaidheil rioghail Albannach' (The Royal Scottish Gaels) who stood

> dìl as ainmeineach,
> Gu sgairteil, sgaiteach, feara-bhuilleach,
> Cuir as doibh pailt gun leanabaidheachd,
> Le lanna glasa ceanna-bheartach,
> 'S bha cuirp gun uchdach feanachais![6]

(loyal and proud | bold, sharp and manly | destroying many without childishness, | with grey swords, heraldic, | bodies without heraldic breastplates!)

The line 'dìl as ainmeineach' is ambiguous. *Ainmeineach* can mean not only 'proud' but also 'froward' or 'contrary': the Highland soldiers are at one and the same time both 'loyal and proud' and 'loyal and contrary'. This is the dual, ambiguous relationship of the Highlanders in the British Army. These songs are both a channeling of Jacobitism into British militarism and a Jacobite undermining of British militarism. They are an unsettling of both, a 'hybrid' unsettling of any power relation based on recognition and dominance: this unsettling is the troubled meeting of Jacobitism and British militarism.[7]

However, even if the rhetoric and symbolism of Jacobitism provides a movement in opposition to the dominant political ideology of the day, it would be very hard to label this 'Radical'. Jacobitism was essentially a conservative ideology, based on the return of a Catholic monarchy and a feudal or quasi-feudal society. Jacobites certainly cannot be said to be in tune with the ideological radicalism of Paine or the French or American Revolution; their Radical potential occurs, if at all, in the way that Jacobite imagery unsettles the rhetoric of British militarism.

Clearance and Emigration

Gaelic cultural manifestations of British militarism are also undermined when considered alongside responses to emigration and clearance. The range of such responses was wide, from fatalism to identification with the plight (and hopes) of the Israelites to violent resistance; they also included, as Donald Meek has commented, the traditional genres of reflection, debate, incitement, praise, satire and elegy.[8] It is the violent end of the spectrum, however, that is of most interest in terms of a possible Radical response. Throughout the period from 1770 to 1820 there were clearances, forced emigration and the creation of sheep runs; perhaps the two most famous and most instances come in 1792 and 1812–13. The first of these, 'Bliadhna nan Caorach' (the year of the sheep), centred on Kildermorie, the second, around Kildonan in Sutherland, following the clearances orchestrated by Patrick Sellar and William Young respectively. Such clearances were met with direct-action and passive resistance. The responses in song, meanwhile, commonly featured criticism and condemnation of the policies of the landlords, though they were rarely simply or coherently critical of the dominant social order.

Iain MacCodrum's 'Òran do na Fògarraich' (Song to the Exiles) is typical in this respect. Written in response to large scale emigration from North Uist to South Carolina between 1771 and 1775 (following a large increase in the rents in 1769 by the landlord Sir Alexander MacDonald), MacCodrum's poem has various functions: to encourage the Uist people to emigrate optimistically; to give them his blessing; to rebuke the landlords for not caring about their tenants; and explicitly to compare them with the *ceannardan mìleant* (warrior chiefs) of old who respect their tenantry:

> Ciod am fàth dhomh bhith 'g innse
> Gun d' fhàs sibh cho mìodhar
> 'S gun spothadh sibh frìghde
>   Far an dìreadh i fàrdan?
> Dh'fhalbh na ceannardan mìleant'
> Dh'an robh sannt air an fhìrinn,
> Dh'an robh geall air an dìlsean
>   Agus cuing air an nàmhaid,
> Air an tuath bha iad cuimhneach
> (Cha b'ann gus an sgrìobadh),
> Bhiodh bantraichean 's dìlleachdain
>   Dìolta gu saidhbhir;
> Gach truaghan gun dìth air
> Mun cuairt air na suinn sin
> Nach sealladh gu h-ìseal –
>   Bha 'n inntinn ro stàtail.

(What's the point of my telling | That you've grown so mean | That you'd geld even a louse | If it gained a farthing in value? | Gone are the warrior chiefs | Who yearned for the truth, | Who respected their followers | And held back their enemies, | Ever mindful of their tenants | (But not to fleece them), | Widows and orphans | Liberally provided for; | Each pauper looked after | All around those heroes | Who would never look low – | Their minds were too stately.)[9]

MacCodrum proceeds to criticize the landlords for breaking the tie between the people and the land (the people being seen as belonging to the land, and not vice versa):

> Seallaibh mun cuairt duibh
> Is faicibh na h-uaislean
> Gun iochd annt' ri truaghain,
>   Gun suairceas ri dàimhich;
> Sann a tha iad am barail
> Nach buin sibh don talamh,
> 'S ged dh'fhàg iad sibh falamh
>   Chan fhaic iad mar chall e:
> Chaill iad an sealladh
> Air gach reachd agus gealladh
> Bha eadar na fearaibh
>   Thug am fearann s' on nàmhaid –
> Ach innseadh iad dhòmhsa
> Nuair théid sibh air fògradh
> Mur caill iad an còir air
>   Gun dòigh air a theàrnadh.

(Look all around you | And behold the nobility | With no pity for unfortunates | And no decency to kinsfolk; | They are convinced | That you don't belong to the land, | And though they've left you with nothing | They don't see it as loss: | They have lost sight | Of each law and commitment | Binding the men | Who took this land from the foe – | But let them just tell me | When you go into exile | If they won't lose their right to it | With no way of saving it.)[10]

As this stanza suggests, however, the poem also warns the landlords and the king about the risk that they run in encouraging the young men to emigrate (or indeed *letting* them emigrate). The threat here is not revolution, but invasion; and it does not come from a rebellious evicted populace, but through the absence of that populace. MacCodrum warns that men are needed to defend the Highlands – in effect to feed the British army – and that if they all emigrate their absence will leave the country with a huge undefended border:

> Ma thig cogadh is creachan
> (Mar as minig a thachair)
> Sann a bhios sibh 'nur starsaich
>   Fo chasaibh ur nàmhaid;
> Tha sibh soirbh ri bhur casgairt
> 'S gun neach ann gu'm bacadh,
> Tha bhur guaillean gun tacsa
>   'S na gaisgich gur fàgail.

(If war and plundering come | (As has frequently happened) | You'll be a threshold | Under enemy feet; | You are easy to slaughter | When there's no one to stop them, | No support at your shoulders | As the heroes are leaving you.)[11]

The refrain thus accords with the policies of Henry Dundas (though whether it actually derives from Dundas' policies is unclear). Dundas, as Alexander Murdoch comments, 'had long campaigned to limit emigration from the Scottish Highlands to North America on the grounds that it affected Scotland's ability to contribute to British defence, and indeed reduced the supply of labour necessary for economic improvement'.[12]

Though the song criticizes the policy of the landlords, and warns them of the disastrous consequences of this policy, it is still tied intimately to a notion of the Highland role in the military of the British state. Following a tendency to celebrate Highland dress that had been common since the Disclothing Act, the song almost fetishes the uniform of the Highland regiments:

> Rìgh, gur sgiolta ri'm faicinn.
> 'Nan seasamh air faithche
> Le'n aodaichean gasta
>   De bhreacanan càrnaid
> Na tha falbh uaibh an ceartuair
> De dh'òganaich dhreachmhor –

> Gun truailleadh, gun ghaiseadh,
>   Gun taise gun tàire.

(O King, how trim to be seen | Standing on greensward | With their splendid attire | Of red tartan plaids | Are those handsome young men | Who are leaving you soon – | Uncorrupted, unblemished, | Without fear or reproach.)[13]

By the time MacCodrum was writing celebrating the plaid was a standard way of celebrating Highland identity. Although the military was the only social space in which many of the traditions of the Highlands soldiers – and the 'warrior chiefs' of MacCodrum's song – could be maintained, it provided a significantly different context and form to these traditions.

Just as it was possible for there to be a co-existence – however uneasy – of Jacobitism and British militarism, so too was it possible for a sense of partnership in the British military adventure to coexist alongside anti-landlordism. This might partly explain – along with the desire to make the song humorous – the fact that although MacCodrum does criticize the landlords his most vehement and violent condemnation is directed at the sheep themselves:

> 'S ged a chruinnicheadh sibh caogad
> Mholt is reitheachan maola
> S beag a thogadh a h-aon diubh
>   Claidheamh faobharach stàilinn.

(And if you mustered fifty | Hornless rams and wedders | Not one of them would lift | A bladed sword of steel.)[14]

The criticism of sheep does suggest that the anger of the song is to some degree misdirected; the effect or symptom of the changes – the sheep – are of more concern in the song than the landlords, the causes or agents of change. This, as we shall see, is a mis-focussing that continues for some decades.

How far this is proto-radical poetry is difficult to gauge. Indeed, highlighting any engagement with a broader Radical movement in the poetry and songs in response to the clearances is relatively difficult. This might be to do with the nature of the riots in the Highlands, especially in 1792. Within recent historical analysis there is a desire to downplay the radical or even political extent of these riots. Bob Harris stresses that in the case of riots in Ross-shire in July to August 1792, although 'some contemporaries were quick to discern political motives behind these protests ... the causes were primarily social and economic. In Ross, the source of grievances amongst the protestors was the removal of tenants to create sheep runs'.[15]

Alexander Murdoch goes further, suggesting that if there is a Radical or revolutionary grouping in the Highlands in this period, it is the landlord class:

When economic and social change were introduced by the landowners in this area, it was 'not, primarily, to make money', but to compete on equal terms with an expanded British elite. In this the gentry in Easter Ross and their agents did not act in conjunction with their tenantry, nor in opposition to them, but independently of them. They acted as a class and they had no doubts about the efficacy or propriety of the economic changes they brought to their region. Their behaviour might be termed 'revolutionary', in reference to 'a small, highly motivated group of people' who carried out substantial economic change because they wanted to increase their own standard of living and because they had come to believe, such was the impact of Enlightenment ideology, that in the modern world of the eighteenth century all things were possible.[16]

It was certainly the gentry, of all the people in the Highlands, who followed the teaching of the Scottish Enlightenment most assiduously, in their attempts to 'improve' and rationalize the land use of the Highlands. In this formulation, the common population of the Highlands at large is not a Radical or revolutionary grouping, but a force of conservatism or backwardness which needed to be opposed in the name of progress and change; and it is true that the Gaelic speaking population (landlords aside) was reactionary, if only because they were struggling to maintain their rights to the land and their homes, as well as their culture.

It is such local battles that are reflected in the songs of the period in rebukes to landlords and to those mistreating emigrants. Although these motifs are rarely linked to wider political movements, there are some traces of Radical political currents in the popular culture of the Highlands during this period. Iain Fraser Grigor, in his *Highland Resistance: The Radical Tradition in the Scottish North*, describes how Sir Hector Munro's leasing of land in Easter Ross in or around 1790 to two farmers had led to alarm

> among the natives of the district. As Sir George Steuart MacKenzie noted, 'strong symptoms of opposition began to appear about this time, among the lower order of the people.' Nor was this opposition entirely isolated in nature, events far beyond the Highlands having induced 'the lower classes inhabiting the low country to make common cause with the dispossessed Highlanders'.[17]

The fear that events beyond the Highlands would spark revolt in the locality is reflected in the concerns about the possible existence of a copy of Thomas Paine's *Rights of Man* translated into Gaelic. Grigor describes how the rumour of such a publication was almost as powerful as the presence of the pamphlet itself:

> It was rumoured ... [in the early 1790s] that a Gaelic-language edition of Paine's *Rights of Man* was spreading rapidly through the Highlands. In public affairs a well-rooted rumour can command amazing strength, and sedition in an unknown language must surely be counted by any propertied elite as a danger most doubly poisonous.[18]

If a Gaelic *Rights of Man* existed – and if it did it quite possibly no longer does – it is far from clear how widely it would have been circulated. Donald MacLean in his 1912 *Literature of the Scottish Gael* rejected the possibility that the book was ever published since 'If it were published it is not at all likely that a book which caused such commotion in the English-speaking world would have been unknown in the Highlands'.[19] MacLean did, however, give the strongest evidence of the existence of at least a pamphlet version of another Radical text having been disseminated. He quoted a letter from Thomas Hardy, formerly Secretary of the London Corresponding Society, who wrote to the reformer Francis Place on 16 October 1824:

> At the same time you will receive a copy of the Declarations of Rights of Men and Citizens adopted by the National Convention of France, 23rd June 1793, translated into Gaelic by the Rev. Dr. Shaw, and printed at my expense. Some of the copies have lain beside me for many years. It has now become a curiosity.[20]

This would most likely have been more than a 'curiosity' had it been circulated in the Highlands in the 1790s. However, without an extant copy of the Gaelic *Rights of Man*, or contemporary accounts of its circulation, it is impossible to know how or if it influenced Gaelic culture in the 1790s (and there does not appear to be a contemporary discussion of 'rights' in the extant Gaelic material of the time). There may well also have been English Radical texts in the Highlands, as MacLean claimed that 'Copies of the English edition [of Paine's *Rights of Man*] ... circulated as far north as Stornoway'; certainly, by the end of the decade, there was awareness of contemporary events in France.[21]

'Oran do na Cìobairibh Gallda' (Song to the Lowland Shepherds) by Allan MacDougall (Ailean Dùghallach) probably dates from between 1798 and 1802. In a song which once more suggests different and confused levels of identity and attachment, MacDougall called for a French invasion of the Highlands:

> Mar gun tuiteadh iad fon chraoibh,
> Cnothan caoch dol aog sa bharrach;
> 'S ann mar siud a tha seann daoine,
> 'S clann bheag a h-aogais bainne;
> Thilgeadh iad gu iomall cùirte
> Bhon dùthchas a bh' aig an seanair;
> B' fheàrr leinn gun tigeadh na Frangaich
> A thoirt nan ceann de na Gallaibh.

(As if they had fallen from the tree, | blasted nuts are dying in brushwood; | that too is how old folk are, | And little children for lack of milk; | they have been flung to the fringe of privilege, | away from the patrimony of their grandfathers; | We would love the French to come | and chop the heads off the Lowlanders.)[22]

MacDougall's song thus goes beyond the immediate local context of the relationship between the landlord and the tenantry to seek a solution derived from political movements outside the Highlands. It does not look for a return to the previous way of life of Highland society (as was the case with Jacobitism and post-Jacobite ideology), but instead seeks an alternative engagement with and alignment of the contemporary international political order (even if the French are invoked very much as a solution to a local problem, rather than an example to follow in their own right).

However, as with MacCodrum's poetry of the 1770s, this is not a straightforward oppositional or Radical poetry. The call for a French invasion exists alongside an unwillingness to condemn the landlords for the changes in the Highland way of life and – most confusingly – strong support (once more) for Highland involvement in the British military. Like MacCodrum, MacDougall primarily targets the sheep and the shepherds, not the Highland landlords:

> Nuair dhìreas fear dhiubh ri beinn,
> An àm dha èirigh gu moch,
> Bidh sgread Ghallda 'm beul a chlèibh,
> 'G èigheachd an dèidh a chuid chon;
> Ceòl nach b' èibhinn linn, a sgairt;
> Bracsaidh, 'na shac air a chorp;
> E suainte 'na bhreacan glas;
> Uaimh-mheulan 'na fhalt 's 'na dhos.

(When one of them climbs up a mountain | after he has risen early, | a Lowland screech will come from his chest, | calling for his pack of dogs; | his yell would be no sweet music to us – | there is a load of braxy on his body, | wrapped in his grey plaid; | lice are in his hair and forelock).[23]

MacCodrum compared the current chiefs unfavourably to their predecessors (a trope that was common in centuries of panegyric poetry),[24] with the effect of praising benevolent feudalism. MacDougall, on the other hand, as Donald Meek points out, avoids criticizing Alexander MacDonell (of Glengarry), or debating

> the role of the MacDonell chiefs in fostering new economic practices, but (condemns) in the strongest terms the effect that the coming of the shepherds ... is having on traditional Gaelic society ... He does not attack the new economic system; he hits out at the symptoms rather than the cause, but he recognises, with an intensity equalled by few Gaelic poets, the power of these economic forces to displace the earlier Gaelic characteristics of Highland society.[25]

Even less Radical is MacDougall's approval of the raising of Highland Fencible regiments. In the final stanza he celebrates the 79th Regiment of Foot, *Rèisimeid an Earrachd* (later known as the Cameron Highlanders), created by Alan Cameron of Erracht in 1793 as a way of keeping the Highlanders on the land:

> Dèanaibh gloineachan a lìonadh,
> 'S gun dìochuimhn air Fear an Earrachd,
> Bhon as math leis maireann beò sinn,

> 'S gun am pòr ud a thighinn tharainn;
> Nan seasadh uaislean na rìoghachd
> Cho dìleas ri càirdeas Ailein,
> Cha bhiodh an tuath air a sgaoileadh,
> Gan cur gu aoidheachd a dh' aindeoin.

> (Fill up the glasses | and do not forget the Laird of Erracht | since he wishes us to survive | without that bad lot crossing our path; | if all the nobles of the kingdom | maintained kinship as faithfully as Allan, | the people would not be dispersed, | and made to live on charity, regardless.)[26]

Although MacDougall was celebrating Alan Cameron (and others in the song) for opposing the introduction of sheep to the Highlands, he did not see that the raising of the Highland regiments and the introduction of the sheep are 'not mutually exclusive', in Meek's terms; nor did he see the contradiction between celebrating Cameron and wishing for a French invasion – unless the reference is, and this is unlikely, a version of the old Polish joke.[27] As with Kenneth MacKenzie's songs earlier in the 1790s, distinct and opposed ideologies combine in MacDougall's song. The viewpoint is both one at the same time 'loyal and proud' and 'loyal and contrary', the identity expressed here is hybrid, both Gaelic and British, with each undermining or confusing the other.

One final response to clearance comes from the after the trial of Patrick Sellar in 1816 (Sellar having been acquitted). There is none of the ambiguity of MacCodrum, MacKenzie or MacDougall's poems in 'Aoir air Pàdraig Sellar' (Satire on Patrick Sellar), by Donald Baillie (Dòmhnall Bàillidh):

> Chunnaic mise bruadar,
> 'S cha b' fhuathach leam fhaicinn fhathast,
> 'S nam faicinn e 'nam dhùsgadh,
> Bu shùgradh dhomh e rim latha.
> Teine mòr an òrdagh
> Is Roy 'na theis-meadhoin,
> Young bhith ann am prìosan,
> 'S an t-iarann mu chnàmhan Shellair.

> (I saw a dream | and I would not mind seeing it again; | If were to see it while awake, | it would make me merry all day. | A big fire was ready | and Roy was right in its middle, | Young was incarcerated, | and there was iron about Sellar's bones.)[28]

This is a vehement, violent denunciation of the clearers of Sutherland, without the wavering ideological positions of MacCodrum, MacKenzie or MacDougall; as such it may seem to represent a less riven or confused Gaelic identity, in which there is the freedom to criticize the landlord class without at the same time expressing loyalty to the British state. However, the targets of the satire – Sellar, Young and Roy – were all incomers, fulfilling the role of the lowland shepherds (or the sheep) in the other poems. There is no condemnation of the landlords that Sellar and Young worked under, unlike, for example, Ewen Robertson's 'Dùthaich MhicAoidh' ('Mackay Country', or Sutherland), which dates from after Sellar's death in 1851, and which accuses the duke and duchess of Sutherland directly.[29] Between these songs you can see the development of a 'crofting community', which would be recognized in the legislation of the 1880s. The agitation following Sellar's clearances and trial – and the poetic responses – could perhaps be seen as the beginnings of this phase of Highland radicalism; it is chastening to note, however, that Baillie's satire on Sellar survived only among emigrants in Canada, and not in the Highlands of Scotland.

The Light-Blue Book

There is one further possible Radical strain from the early 1800s. Ronald Black describes how a 'duodecimo volume of eight pages' was printed in Glasgow in 1845 entitled *An Leabhar Liath*, with the following ante-dated front-cover (in Black's translation):

> **THE**
> **LIGHT-BLUE BOOK;**
> IN WHICH ARE
> **Four Excellent Songs:**
> THAT IS: – HECTOR THE RASCAL –
> THE OOBIE NOOGIE
> – MY HANDSOME LITTLE TINY HERO –
> AND LITTLE BLACK DONNIE.
> COMPOSED
> *BY LEARNED GENTLEMEN:*
> Now published at the request of,
> and at the expense of many lovers
> of true poetry.
> PRINTED IN PAISLEY;
> AND TO BE SOLD PRIVATELY BY
> ITINERANT BOOKSELLERS. 1801[30]

Black suggests as editor of this collection John MacKenzie, the editor of *Sar-Obair nam Bard Gaelach; or the Beauties of Gaelic Poetry, and Lives of the Highland Bards* (Glasgow: 1841). The songs contained in it are all sexually explicit. Two of them, 'Dòmhnallan Dubh' (Little Black Donnie) and 'An Seudagan' (My Handsome Little Tiny Hero), focus on the male member (most likely from a first-person perspective), and the excitement or difficulties involved in its 'rising'. Poems about penises had been common currency at least since Iseabal Ní Mheic Cailéin's 'Éistibh, a Luchd an Tighe-se' (Listen, People of this House) from the late sixteenth or early seventeenth century, a poem about the family priest's penis.[31] In the late eighteenth century, then, such poems do not necessarily offer a challenge to the dominant moral order within the Gaelic tradition. They do, however, suggest a possible Radical comment on the relationship between the Gaelic community and the rest of Scotland / Britain.

'Dòmhnallan Dubh' concerns the narrator's desire to find a means to prolong the life of his 'Dòmhnallan Dubh', so he can continue entertaining the 'iomadh caileag bhòidheach bheusach / A tha nochd air sràid Dhùn Éideann' (the many beautiful well-behaved lassies / That's tonight on an Edinburgh street).[32] In a narrative at least in part commenting on Catholic licentiousness he approaches first of all a priest and then a wise old woman, who encourages him to eat milky porridge; finally – angrily rejecting the advice of the old woman – he settles on whisky, the milk of a farrow cow and pepper from the Lowlands, and resolves to continue rampaging through Kilaulay in South Uist until All Hallows' eve. 'An Seudagan', meanwhile, puns on the notion of rising: the speaker asks why it (the little jewel that is the literal translation of the title) will not rise; he comments 'Ged dh'éireadh tu cha b'fhuathach leam' (I wouldn't hate it if you rose); and finally states, in the penultimate verse:

> Cha bhi mi fhìn fo ghruaimean ris
> Ged dh'éireadh e air uaireannan,
> Ach dearbh is adhbhar buairidh dhomh
>   Nuair ghluaiseas e do m' anntoil!

(I don't get annoyed at him | Though he might arise now and then, | But it's truly irritating | When he moves against my will!)[33]

The repeated imagery of rising, and the desire to control this 'rising' suggests – on a light-hearted level – a reading of this song as representing the relationship between the Gaels and the rest of Scotland / Britain; the desire of the Gaels to keep rising, and the desire of the British to bend this rising to their imperial will.

The final two songs, 'An Oba Nodha' (The Oobie Noogie)[34] and 'Eachainn an Slaoightear' (Hector the Rascal), on the other hand, give voice to female sexual desire or fear, though 'An Oba Nodha' was written by a George MacKenzie (Seòras MacCoinnich). A 'Radical' context is also possibly suggested in 'An Oba Nodha' ('Eachainn an Slaoightear' is more concerned with the maltreatment of the narrator by the eponymous Hector, who took her maidenhead). In the last of the 'sexual case-studies' in the poem Ewen's daughter describes her boyfriend, and in doing so gives the only place name in the song:

Ach seo mar thuirt nigh'n Eóghainn.
"O bhóu! Mar tha mi fodham,
   Triallaidh mi do Chromba
A shealltainn air m' oba nodha.
   Tha mo ghiullan òg ann
'S bha eòlas agam air roimhe
   'S gheibh mi na seachd òirlich –
'S an còrr, ma bhios e fon tomhas!"

(But here's what Ewen's daughter said. | "*O bhòu!* The way I feel beneath, | I'll travel to Cromarty | To see my oobie noogie. | My boyfriend is there | And I knew him once before | And I'll get the seven inches – | And more, if that's an underestimate!")[35]

'An Oba Nodha' was composed before 1735, but included in this collection for publication in 1801. This is in the recent aftermath of the land raids and riots; the location of male sexual prowess and virility in the North Highlands (even if it be Cromarty rather than Ross-shire of the 1792 riots) hints at and mildly celebrates the riotous, 'uprising' potential of the Highlands (a potential of at least seven inches, if not more). One of the possible reasons for the delay in publication of the volume to 1845 – and there are obvious others – may have been the radical undertones of this imagery of rising and virility, which would have been far from welcome in Great Britain in 1801. However, one should remember that, just as it is possible to be 'loyal and proud' and 'loyal and contrary' at the same time, not every rising was a rebellion. Also, although there may be Radical undertones in the volume, it was not published during the period we are looking at. Indeed, of the texts we were looking at, one volume remained unpublished, one survived only in Canada and the others tended to waver towards one or other form of loyalism: these texts, in other words, provide a very uncertain basis for a Gaelic Radicalism.

8 VIRILE VERNACULARS: RADICAL SEXUALITY AS SOCIAL SUBVERSION IN IRISH CHAPBOOK VERSE, 1780–1820

Andrew Carpenter

One of the least explored and potentially most interesting areas of late eighteenth- and early nineteenth-century Irish writing is the vernacular poetry found in its printed verse chapbooks. These chapbooks are fragile items – folded half sheets, poorly printed on cheap paper by Irish jobbing printers (mostly in provincial towns like Monaghan, Limerick and Strabane) and sold by chapmen throughout the countryside; most (probably over 99 per cent) of them have long since disappeared, several hundred of them have, somehow, survived and they give us, between them, a fascinating glimpse of what was sung and recited to Irish town and country audiences between about 1780 and about 1820.[1] The song chapbooks are particularly unusual in that their contents were not copied from one printed text to another but taken down, at dictation, by compositors for whom the singer would recite the words. Thus what we have is the unedited, unabridged, uncensored, unadulterated texts of what was actually sung in rural Ireland during a period of social (as well as political) upheaval.[2]

This material is in English – or rather in Hiberno-English – though some songs contain passages in a phonetically rendered form of Irish. Though everyone concerned with these songs would have been functionally bilingual – that is, able to understand and to speak both English and Irish – few (if any) of them, poets, compositors, printers, chapmen or eventual purchasers, would have been able to read or write the Irish language correctly or with any facility, despite the fact that material in Irish was widely disseminated orally throughout Ireland.[3] These printed chapbooks contain songs sung in the English that was used in rural Ireland in the latter part of the eighteenth century, and were designed for this functionally bilingual audience.

What makes these texts particularly significant is their linguistic and textual freshness; neither their authors nor their audience seem to have been tainted by the bourgeois sense of propriety which was beginning to assert itself in Irish town society in the latter decades of the eighteenth century – and which is so prevalent in the hundreds of conventional poems collected in such Irish anthologies as those by Samuel Whyte and Joshua Edkins.[4] Whyte (who was a schoolmaster) and Edkins (who was librarian to the Dublin Library Society) aimed their anthologies at a readership able to afford their well-printed, well-bound volumes – English-speaking, governess-educated, piano-playing young Church of Ireland ladies and their Trinity College-educated lawyer brothers, all of whom had been taught to hear the cadences of classical English poetry; those who bought the chapbook songs, on the other hand, had only pennies to spend on reading matter and would have had the cadences of Irish rather than English poetry in their heads. They were working people – servants, artisans, carmen, fisherman, farm labourers, cowherds, cotters, broguemakers, beggars and weavers. If the men among them could read and write, they would have learned these skills in hedge schools where men such as Eoghan Rua Ó Súilleabháin taught English reading and writing, mathematics, book-keeping, the Catechism and stories from the classics.[5] Since many of the hedge-schoolmasters had learned their English from books rather than from native speakers, the English they taught their pupils was often quaintly divorced from the language of Dr Johnson's definitions or the rules laid down by the Irish elocution-teacher Thomas Sheridan; the chapbooks contain many examples of nouns and adjectives used in ways that would have sounded at the time – as they do today – unusual to middle-class, metropolitan English ears. When a girl describes herself as a 'rural female' or a poet asserts that he is 'recruiting his sensations' and 'condoling his situation', we are aware that book-learning rather than experience of educated speech lies behind the choice of words.[6]

The influence of Irish-language prosody is also strongly discernible in the metrical patterns of many of these songs: the metres are Irish *amhrán* or song metres and the poems are held together (like songs in the Irish language) by internal assonance and echo rather than by end rhyme. Those who composed these texts were working within the poetic tradition of their culture – that of verse in Irish – and adapting it to the new language: they also expected many of their songs to be sung to traditional Irish or Scottish (rather than English) airs, and so were consciously differentiating themselves from the equivalent song tradition in the centre of the archipelago.

In addition to the eccentric vocabulary and unorthodox grammar emanating from the hedge schools or based on echoes from the Irish language, the printed texts often exhibit spellings based on Hiberno-English pronunciation of the time. These poems and songs are, in fact, literary rarities: they contain material roughly but enthusiastically transposed from one culture into another, and never edited or 'corrected'. They are hybrids begot, as it were, by the attempt to communicate in Hiberno-English on Irish-language prosody; they come from a moment when speakers of a sophisticated mother-tongue (Irish) strove to express themselves in a much less sophisticated, half-learned second language (English).

Although the chapbook verses cover many topics – political and social events, violent death, soldiering, shipwrecks, merry-making in the shadow of the gallows and travel, for instance – a good proportion of the material that has survived from the period 1780–1820 or so is indecent or sexually explicit. These poems are full of double meanings and witticisms, more designed to delight and entertain than to arouse. They are earthy and outspoken – the product of a society very different from the puritanical, repressed one that which was to develop in nineteenth-century Ireland. Four-letter words are widely used and multiple levels of meaning gleefully exploited. To add spice and suggestiveness there are many (often otherwise unrecorded) euphemisms for the genitals and for sexual activity. A song called 'The Gobbio', for instance, celebrates a girl who 'engages her gobbio' with an impressive number of the inhabitants of the local barracks, including the piper, the drummer, the Captain, the Lieutenant, the engineer and 'the Champion' – the last of whom is, it seems, too much for her. Names given to the human genitals are often witty adaptations into English of Irish words – 'peas' from Ir. *pis* (the pudenda), for instance. Everyday activities, such as those of the weaver, the carpenter, the smith or the piper, are given multiple double meanings and when the musical piper and his damsel meet in a meadow, 'Her heels on my back they beat time to my tune'.[7] *Double-entrendres* are particularly appreciated. At the end of another song, an energetic lass named Kitty remarks to Robin that: 'If that all the Generals were like unto you, / The Volunteers surely would dread a Review'.[8] And one should perhaps be alarmed at the tale of Paddy O'Rafferty who, after visiting the fair in Drogheda and spending time with 'Dolly-come-straddle-me', falls in with a fair maid who is digging parsnips: 'My darling young Paddy', she asks, 'Have you the length of my Parsnip?'[9]

Modern sensibilities tend to shy away from this type of verse – not because modern readers are shocked by its outspokenness so much as because they find its unrestrained glorification of male sexual power and the fantasy of endless satisfied, sexually available females distasteful. However, these eighteenth-century demotic songs are too witty and self-mocking to be classed as pornography and they are certainly not intended to arouse or excite their listeners. On the contrary, some of them – 'The Coughing Old Man' for instance – arouse more sympathy and pity than laughter.[10]

But even as the crowd around the street singer laughed at the anarchic fantasies that make up the subject matter of these songs, they were laughing also to hear the values of the rising middle class so thoroughly ridiculed. It is the storyline – of the apparently docile farmwife enjoying wild sex with the travelling weaver, or the respectable widow who (in a comic reversal of roles) is willing to pay for sex with the well-hung passing labourer – that subvert the values of settled society. If the content of these songs makes fun of the normative pattern of an ordered society, it is social rather than political order that is under attack;

a group listening to a politically subversive song is potentially a mob and then a rebellion whereas a group listening to bawdy verses is laughing at the overturning of ideas of respectability, marital fidelity and chastity before marriage. Though a local priest or magistrate might personally disapprove of these songs, there was no effective means of censoring popular culture in late eighteenth-century rural Ireland. As James Kelly puts it:

> The absence in eighteenth-century Ireland of a formal system of censorship, such as existed in eighteenth-century France, meant that the vast majority of what was printed in Ireland was produced and disseminated without ever coming to the notice of the political or religious authorities who conceived themselves as the guardians of public behaviour.[11]

'Despite the shrill voices raised periodically in respect of the threat posed to public morality by blasphemy and obscenity,' Kelly continues, 'the priority of the authorities, municipal as well as national, was to curb expression of heterodox political opinion.'[12] From time to time – particularly in late eighteenth-century Dublin – material mocking the political establishment or advocating radical change was seized and suppressed, but naughty chapbooks printed in Monaghan or Limerick and circulating in the countryside did not warrant any action – even if action could have been taken. In any case, political sedition did not normally appear first in provincially-printed chapbooks. When loyalist, nationalist and revolutionary songs appeared in them during and after the 1790s, or when they included verses praising revolution in America or France, the chapbooks were, on the whole, repeating what was in circulation rather than creating it.[13] The naval and military songs they contained assumed sailors and soldiers loyal to the crown – just as they assumed milkmaids always ready for a tumble in the hay and young men of prodigious sexual prowess. The world of the suggestive song and the world of genuine political protest do not seem to meet in the chapbooks. There is a similar use of stock material in both types of song at this period, as well, and what Georges-Denis Zimmermann says of the writers of political ballads can also be said of those writing suggestive songs: they 'devoted little time to the composition of their texts. To fill up the lines, they had at their disposal a stock of tags, of recurring phrases frequently employed to express similar ideas'.[14] There are only so many ways of describing sexual activity.

For its part, the established church did not attempt to suppress immoral material but rather to counter it by printing and circulating very large quantities of improving tracts. This was the aim of the 'Association for the Discountenancing Vice and Promoting the Knowledge and Practice of the Christian Religion' founded in 1792 within the Church of Ireland and, a generation later, 'The Irish Society for the Promotion of the Education of the Native Irish through the Medium of their own Language' (1818–27). Though both these associations

– and several others – flooded the market with tracts, the printing of obscene songs in chapbooks continued into the nineteenth century. Surprisingly, perhaps, the Presbyterian church seems does not seem to have been troubled and John Moulden has recently written on an interesting cache of chapbooks from a poor early-eighteenth century Presbyterian farmhouse in County Down.[15] In that house were bawdy songbooks as well as less *risqué* material. Meanwhile the Catholic church was going through a period of change: the arrival of clerical dress for priests in the latter part of the eighteenth century effectively distanced them from their flock, inserting what S. J. Connolly has called 'the new social distance between the pastor and his flock'.[16] Priests no longer went to patterns, wakes or social gatherings – at which gatherings, all accounts agree, there was much drinking, much merry-making and much sexual activity.[17] But events like these – where bawdy songs were certainly sung – were not policed by church or state and the evidence overall is that such songs were a living part of the rich cultural life in rural Ireland. They could be sung in public or in private, copied by hand or in print; they were, in short, embedded in a flourishing demotic society which was generally left alone by church and state.

Though most of these 'indecent' songs are unashamedly enthusiastic about the sexual prowess of the protagonist and his overpowering male attractiveness, there are several songs that undermine this dominant male position. For though the women involved in these sexual bouts invariably express themselves delighted and satisfied during the action, they are no fools and several of them vow revenge on their seducers. One way of doing this is to inflict real pain on the men who have used them by deliberately infecting their lovers with venereal disease. The wandering philanderer who leaves a string of ruined women in his train may be seen (from one point of view) as a lovable rogue, but from another point of view, he is a brute and a villain who needs to be taught a lesson. This happens in many of the surviving songs. In one, the roving lad has been given 'a smoking hot pip', in another his 'quill' has been 'scorch'd' and in yet another he has been lent some coals 'to keep fire in his chamber'. In the macaronic song 'Stauka an Varaga', the 'market idler' complains: 'My flail she fractured, I'm teased with doctor's fee.'[18] At least these particular songs introduce a sense of realism into the fantasies. In addition, there are scores of chapbook poems, from England and Scotland as well as from Ireland, which adopt the female voice and bewail the departure of a faithless lover – some of which songs are truly poignant.[19] One can surmise that a street or country-house-kitchen performer would need to balance songs about bold hammermen and their slithery seductions with tales of the pathetic consequences of girls left without their lovers – lovers taken from them by desertion, press-gangs, death in the armed forces, emigration or hanging.

However in performance, many of these 'bawdy' poems would be expected to provoke laughter through the use of outrageous puns, comic comparisons, strongly visualized images and, perhaps most of all, the use of forbidden words. The chorus of 'The Boys of Stoneybatter', for example, is: 'Is your wife at home, Is she ripe for fucking', and there is the notoriously sordid song 'The lock which scatter'd Oonagh's piss' which ends with the deeply unpoetic line: 'With showers of sperm they jointly oiled the lock'.[20] One wonders whether those who heard the song in Strabane (where the poem was printed early in the nineteenth century) or Dublin (where it appeared in 1789) would have greeted the word 'sperm', in this context, with a shout of laughter or the shock of silence. The word is an old and honourable one, but rare in the eighteenth century outside medical or quasi-medical treatises.

There is no hard evidence of how a song such as 'Oonagh's Lock' or a word such as 'sperm' was received in rural Ireland in the late eighteenth century; however, the fact that this song, and many others like it, was reprinted in different parts of Ireland over a considerable period of time suggests regular and repeated performance and a degree of tolerance for the public performance of such material. Francis Place described the performance of such material in late eighteenth-century London.

> Servant maids used to stop in the markets to hear (the ballads) sung and used to purchase them. Two women used to sing a song opposite to public house at the back of St Clement's church in the Strand ... The song was a description of a married man who had a lecherous wife. It described his being a hale fellow reduced by her to a skeleton. I can only remember the last two lines:
>
> And for which I am sure she'll go to hell
> For she makes me fuck her in church time.
>
> I always remember those words in consequence of the shout which was always set up as the song closed.[21]

Given the extent to which members of the upper and middle classes of late eighteenth-century Ireland used euphemism and innuendo to protect their sensibilities when describing sexual activity (as in Edkins, Whyte and in all bound volumes of poetry of the age, even those containing the work of Allan Ramsay), four-letter words in print indicated that the speaker was meant to be seen as from the working class. Jonathan Swift, who was fascinated by coarse language and the way it challenges polished, polite language, once wrote:

> Great folks are of a finer mold:
> Lord, How politely they can scold!
> While a coarse English tongue will itch
> For whore and rogue, and dog and bitch.[22]

The bawdy songs we have been considering came nowhere near 'great folks of a finer mold'; they were dictated by itinerant singers to minimally-educated compositors working in small printing sheds in provincial towns, printed by printers who were very likely illiterate, and never proofread or corrected by anyone.[23] Thus the four-letter words survived onto the printed page as did the descriptions of vigorous love-making: what Francis Place saw and heard in the streets of London was probably seen and heard in every town and settlement in late eighteenth-century Ireland.

Turning to the songs themselves, the first two printed below belong to a tradition of bantering exchange in which, in a comic conflation of terms, the rake and his penis share a suggestive name and each song in the series strives to prove its hero more virile than his predecessors. The first song below answers one called 'Morgan Rattler', a well-known version of which is graced with the refrain 'I lathered her up with my Morgan Rattler'.[24]

Darby O'Gallager, or the Answer to Morgan Rattler[25]

Great boasting of late we have heard of the fates,[26]
Of the comical rake called Morgan Rattler,
But now we have found one will cut him down
Well known by the name of young Darby O'Gallagher.
He is a brisk blade and a black-smith by trade,
Well known by the ladies to be a gay frolicker;
As he passes by the ladies replies,
There goes the bold hammerman Darby O'Gallagher.
His music excels all carillon bells,
His stroke's more sweet than the warbling chorister.
No flute or guitar can ever compare
To the musical hammer of Darby O'Gallagher.
At Mullingar fair young Dermot was there,
With Nancy Adair that well noted smaliker;[27]
Her gown she did pledge for the triangle wedge,
That was drove by the sledge of Darby O'Gallagher.
If you would see him dandle that yellow sledge handle,
As stiff as the leg of a stool in a wallet,[28] sir,
Each maid with surprize does twinkle their eyes,
At the wonderful size of his D. O'Gallagher.
His excellent musick is good for the tisick,[29]
It works the fair maids like a dose of jallip,[30]
No Doctor of skill can cure it so well,
As the two smacking hammers of Darby O'Gallagher.
A maid most rare with a languishing air,
Whose skin was fair and locks were black sir,
She being distrest did beg the request
Of a blast of the bellows from D. O'Gallagher.
So now to conclude girls don't think it rude

For singing the praise of this sporting frolicker;
Now Morgan may sleep, he's the boy that can sweep
Twelve shillings away with his Darby O'Gallagher.

Despite its outrageous celebration of male domination, the poem is enjoyable for its energy, for its witty conceits, for its clever use of alliterative and semi-alliterative effects, and for its ingenious playing with multiple layers of meaning. A modern editor of the poem has noted that a shilling piece measured an inch in diameter[31] – a fact that would have ensured that this particular song was greeted – as were the songs in Francis Place's story – with a shout of laughter.

It is interesting that the 'come-ye-all' routine that begins the second song I have selected deliberately targets a female audience and suggests that a smile is the appropriate feminine response to tales of debauchery. The poet also suggests, at the end of the song, that girls will happily sing the song in private. The verse complies with the standard accentual syllabic prosodic pattern of English verse, with end rhyme, except in the first line, which is clearly corrupt.[32]

The New Dhooraling[33]

You maidens pretty attend this ditty
And 'twill make you smile,
'Tis of a rattling roving blade
That's well beloved by each fair maid,
The sporting girls take great delight
In his sweet company day and night.
On his bagpipes he plays them a tuneful spring,
While he muffles the tune on his Dhooraling.
Too long the Doodeen[34] was the toast
Altho' no more than an empty boast,
Sweet Dhoora now is the pleasing toy
Diverts the girls tho' ever so coy,
The Piper's fees they never dispute
When he plays them a lilt on his German flute,
Then away with M'Teague and his Doodeen Pin
And left room for M'Lean and his Dhooraling.
In Patron,[35] Market, Town or Fair,
The girls do treat him every where,
His chanter[36] is of the largest size,
And for it they'd freely part their eyes,
When to M'Lean they do repair,
For money or liquor they never spare,
The price of the yarn they to him bring
For a musical lilt on his Dhooraling.
Of all other music that ever was known,
They give the degree to the Piper's drone,
With a blast of his bellows he fills the bag,

Then his triangle Chanter begins to wag,
Each bar on the Gamot[37] he plays so true,
[*line missing*]
No harpsichord, fiddle or tuneful spring
Can equal M'Lean and his Dhooraling.
A buxom widow below Coleraine
Heard several talk of young Dan M'Lean
Resolved she was no time to waste
But sent for the Piper to come in haste.
He squeezed up his pipes without delay,
With his bags and his drones he leathered away,
Five guineas in gold and a diamond ring
She gave for a trust[38] of his Dhooraling.
He met an old woman in Portadown,
Who had not a tooth in her jaw but one,
Tho' she mumbled her meat with a horn spoon,
Yet this merry going heiffer she liked the tune,
Altho decripid, blind and lame
She longed for a touch of the sporting game,
Her pipe and tobacco away she did fling,
And beat time with her crutch to his Dhooraling.
One night dancing at a ball,
A youthful Lady chanced to fall,
Young Dan to her assistance went
Which filled this fair one with content,
She slipped him into a private room,
Where he blew up his bags like an air balloon,
In raptures round him she did cling,
Whilst he played her the humours of Dhooraling.
But least[39] I should detain you long
I'll here conclude my merry song.
In hopes I have offended none
By praising of the Piper's drone,
The prudent maids that seem so shy
Are willing the game to try,
And when alone they'll merrily sing
Concerning the fate of Dhooraling.

Light-hearted and determinedly 'merry', this poet certainly assumes that no one will choose to take offence at this particular song.

The third text is a selection of stanzas from a classic 'rambling' poem in which the protagonist – an itinerant weaver in this case – works his way around Ireland bedding damsels as he does so. The droll double meanings in stanzas 2–4 assume that the audience has an intimate knowledge of the technical terms of hand weaving.

from: Shales's Rambles, or the Lurgan Weaver[40]

You ladies free of each degree, now hear my invitation,
I am a lad tho' trade is bad, that's known by reputation,
If you comply and wont deny, and wants your work done neatly,
Your looms I'll square to half a hair, and wave[41] your webs completely.
So now you maids that love the trade, and now has took the notion,
Apply to me we'll soon agree, I'll put your loom in motion,
If your geers be struck to fit the work, I'll do my best endeavour
To raise a twill with art and skill, for I'm the Lurgan weaver.
I your beams will streatch in the broad reach, I'll pick and dress your yarn,
Your sliders raise will cloath with ease, in cellers shops or barns,
One I have to graze and stave, [I] use no comb or sheers,
My pullies hings your yarn springs, when e'er I touch your geers.
My slays will play without a stay, my headless falls a working,
Both right and left throws in the weft, without the temples bursting,
My bore staff's long, both stiff and strong, my shuttle still in order,
With open shades I'll fall to trade, and selvage neat your border ...
... Then to Clonmell and through Cashel, I wetted up their sheeting
On Youghall shore I drank galore, I use no thumbs or bating,
To Cork and Cove I there did rove, Bandon, Tralee and Dingle,
In Limerick I staid a week, and made their looms to jingle.
To Iniss and Clare I did repair, I decently was used,
In Banagher I was Journeyman, my shuttle ne'er refused;
In Athlone when I was known, the men they strove to slay me,
Unto Loughreagh without delay, the females did convey me ...
... In Monaghan the ladies ran, I kindly was received,
And from Glastlough unto Armagh, both night and day I weaved,
And round Richhill I showed my skill, I thought no crime to flatter,
I crossed the Bann to Ligoland, and spent the winter quarter.
I am roving Sheales that never fails, though Misers do envy me,
They need not fret their gold I'll get, their daughters still employ me;
In Lurgan town I will set down, in back lane I'll tarry,
And with young maids I'll always trade, but hang me if I marry.

This popular poem is, again, in *amhrán* metre, the assonance within individual lines in this case. Travelling weavers, like other labourers and artisans, often appear in these poems, the details of their craft offering the poet opportunities for many ingenious comparisons. The sheer verbal ingenuity of this poem gives it its charm and it is notable that in both the second poem and this one (though the actual passage is omitted from this selection) there is a comic reversal of situations when it is the female rather than the male who finds herself paying for the service offered.

A point worth noting is that these naughty songs were in no way hidden from view. On the contrary, several chapbook collections place a well-known obscene song at the head of the list of songs in a particular chapbook and so use it to advertise the collection and, presumably, to increase sales.[42] Censorious voices in the newspapers inveighed against 'the evil tendency of those obscene ballads hourly chaunted in our crowded streets, to the subversion of morality, and the wounding of every delicate ear that hears such grossness and licentiousness',[43] and some 'infamous and obscene books' were publicly burned in Dublin in 1795; but no-one thought it worth while taking action against obscene ballads on a country-wide scale – particularly given the lack of appropriate legislation.

In sum then, it was no more than respectability and the idea of a decent, upright and decorous society that was subverted by these Irish-printed bawdy songs. The relentlessly cheery jolliness of their descriptions of illicit sex and the provocatively anarchic voices of their witty narrators may have threatened the values that sustained the increasingly prosperous planters of late eighteenth-century Ulster, the substantial tenant farmers of Munster and the respectable shopkeepers of Monaghan; but, in the real world, the tales of Morgan Rattler or D. O'Gallagher were no more likely to lead to an outbreak of sexual or social anarchy in Strabane, Cork or Coleraine than films about murders lead to street anarchy today. As long as they stay in their place, virile rogues like D. O'Gallagher are no more of a threat to world order or family life than James Bond.

9 THOMAS MOORE AND THE PROBLEM OF COLONIAL MASCULINITY IN IRISH ROMANTICISM

Julia M. Wright

Discussions of Irish Romanticism and gender have to date largely focussed on femininity, especially, for instance, in the recovery and canonization of such women writers as Maria Edgeworth and Lady Morgan, but also in discussions of Thomas Moore's depiction of women and orientalist representations of feminized men.[1] But this focus on one pole of the binary construction of gender has occluded the problem of colonial masculinity in the decades after the Act of Union (1800) abolished the Irish parliament and with it the vestiges of official Irish sovereignty. Ireland was instead to be ruled from the British parliament with a newly added block of Irish seats, no longer to be governed (even nominally) through a native institution that might be reformed to include Catholic men — and decisively alienating the men of the Irish ruling class from the nation-state. This political sea-change is contemporary with a broad shift in literary writing about the nation that generally follows generic lines. In the 1790s, there was an ongoing radical project, led largely by the United Irishmen, to educate and involve the lower classes in political life, particularly through songbooks and affordable newspapers with political content; the United Irishmen also argued for an end to the Penal Laws which disadvantaged Catholics and Dissenters, and some of their materials were pitched at breaking down the linguistic divide in Ireland. The nationalist songs of the radical 1790s, disseminated particularly through the songbooks known as *Paddy's Resource* (published from 1795 to about 1803), invoked Thomas Paine and condemned Edmund Burke, generally featured lower-class (often bilingual) speakers, and circulated popularly through print and oral culture. Many of these songs were republished or adapted in the early 1800s, but new radical songs are thin on the ground after 1800. Instead, the loss of the Irish parliament contributed to an increasing focus in narrative fiction on Catholic Emancipation and specifically ending the prohibition against Catholics sitting in the new Irish seats in London, a problem focussed on the full enfranchisement of wealthy men of some rank. Numerous novels and other prose narratives after 1800 feature protagonists who are Catholic, educated and upper-class, but unable to contribute to Ireland as citizens because of the Penal Laws. In a number of these narratives, nationalist song is included to mark the passage of Irish heroism and civic leadership into the past, suggesting that such public forms of masculinity can now be known only through nostalgia. The radical implications of nationalist song — both because of song-production in the 1790s and because of the genre's recognizablity and accessibility across class lines — are thus simultaneously resurrected and contained, confined to the private moments of elite figures who have become resigned to political failure.

Moore's *Irish Melodies* (1808–34) in key respects belong to this post-1800 swerve away from the radical underpinnings of song, offering nostalgia about past heroism in place of a call to populist action in the present. Moore, after all, famously insisted that the *Melodies* were intended for 'the piano-fortes of the rich and educated'.[2] But Moore also imagined commemorating the Irish leaders of the past — in song and in other public literary forms – as a masculine activity that undermines political disempowerment, turning this nostalgic containment of radicalism to liberalizing political effect. In doing so, Moore anticipates, at least in broad terms, Jürgen Habermas's distinction between political authority and a bourgeois public sphere that functions partly through 'publicity' — in that sphere, private individuals (generally men in this era, and middle-class), through public debate, print culture and so forth, develop public opinion which pressures the state, decentering pre-Enlightenment structures of power and mediating between individuals and government.[3] In a colonial context where male subjects are largely excluded from participation in the state and the state exercises its authority to repress dissent, this Habermasian model, already at work in Britain and other parts of Europe, cannot function properly — and yet Irish print culture began to thrive in the Romantic period, especially in the development of periodical culture. While Moore's songs appear to capitulate to a political effeminization traceable in post-1800 fiction's insistence on the nostalgic containment of radicalism, Moore's larger corpus addresses the problem of colonial masculinity by representing author-figures who, though denied political authority by the colonial regime, still exert some form of power through 'publicity' – or, in Moore's term, 'attention'.[4] Here, after briefly elaborating on these trends in post-1800 fiction and their depiction of song, I shall turn to Moore's search for 'attention' through his largely apolitical song output and, more suggestively, through his commemoration of Irish leaders from the *Melodies* to his late-career biographies.

Irish Romantic Fiction and the Disenfranchised Hero

In Irish Romanticism, which Claire Connolly dates between 1800 and 1830,[5] the depiction of masculinity in texts critical of the colonial regime often focuses on the disempowerment of those men who would, if they were English and/or Church of Ireland, wield political and social power, as represented widely in canonical British novels of the period. Jane Austen's heroes, for instance, regularly hold the power that they deserve in narratives in which an unchallenged moral order is happily restored by the conclusion. But Irish fiction of the first third of the century often refuses such assurances that merit will be rewarded, resisting the integration of ideology and plot that gives such assurances their credibility – Maria Edgeworth's novels being the leading exception to this trend. Instead, the heroes of many Irish Romantic novels speak for the moral high ground while, in the plot, they are imprisoned, dispossessed, exiled or killed. In this respect, Irish Romantic fiction has a great deal in common with 1790s radical English fiction, both bodies of work often depicting an ethical protagonist in an unethical political sphere who is, despite considerable promise, hounded into catastrophe by 'Things as They Are', in William Godwin's phrase. But there is a key difference in that Irish Romantic fiction centres not on the thwarted potential of the lower-class man or patriarchally oppressed woman, like the protagonists in such radical novels as Godwin's *Things as They Are; Or, the Adventures of Caleb Williams* (1794), Eliza Fenwick's *Secresy; Or, the Ruin on the Rock* (1795) and Mary Hays' *Victim of Prejudice* (1799), but on that of the upper-class hero who, despite maleness, wealth, birth and education, is shut out from power by the ruling regime because of his religion.

As Tim Fulford has suggested, in the Romantic era, 'power was accepted to be masculine and its exercise to be a prerequisite for true manliness in politics and letters'.[6] Fulford focuses on the earlier part of the British Romantic period and hence on the culture of sensibility and of chivalry — the man of feeling and the man of duty as the two modes of masculine virtue, both coming out of Enlightenment thought (and tacitly an Irish Enlightenment, since Fulford traces these ideas to Burke).[7] Each of these modes was used to legitimate the claims of the middle classes to the power previously the preserve of the aristocracy, part of the transformation discussed by Habermas.[8] Hence, 'In the Romantic period, modern nationalism imagined a synergetic relationship between well-educated, civic-minded men and a nation-state through which they expressed collective sovereignty. The loss of the Irish nation-state through the formal abolition of the Irish parliament produced a nationalist crisis to which much of the literature of the early nineteenth century responds'.[9] The Act of Union also, as a corollary, produced a crisis of masculinity: with no nation-state, such men could neither assert their sovereignty (as sovereign subjects, in the full Enlightenment sense of the term) nor participate in public political life as civic models required. They could claim merit – under chivalry or sensibility or aristocratic birth or Enlightenment rationality — but could not claim power, and hence were excluded from, in Fulford's phrase, 'true manliness'.[10]

This crisis is readily apparent in a wide range of early nineteenth-century Irish texts in which elite male protagonists have no purpose because they are disqualified from participating in politics: the hero of Alicia Sheridan Lefanu's play, *Sons of Erin* (1812), lost his position as an Irish M.P. because of the Act of Union; the title character of Adelaide O'Keeffe's poem, 'The Irish Officer' (1818), was destined for the Irish parliament as well but had to join the British military instead because of the Union; and a number of heroes in various Irish national tales are men of ability and rank who have no public place in their homeland.[11] In national tales, a striking number of these characters are military men, including the protagonists of Charles Robert Maturin's *The Milesian Chief: A Romance* (1812), Robert Torrens' *Victim of Intolerance: Or, the Hermit of Killarney, A Catholic Tale* (1814) and Lady Morgan's *O'Donnel: A National Tale* (1814) and *The O'Briens and the O'Flahertys: A National Tale* (1827). These are men who should, in the dominant ideology of the time, have power and, without it, are tragically all potential and no effect. (They also clearly belong to the tradition of the 'wild geese'; a number of these characters are at their most successful when they are working, like the seventeenth-century 'wild geese', as Continental mercenaries.)

Torrens' hero, O'Connor, is an exemplary instance. He repeatedly decries the Penal Laws, offering various versions of the same lament: 'every effort that I made to escape the annihilation of mediocrity, the laws of my country have rendered abortive. Without a place in society, without an object to pursue, I floated listless on the stream of time'.[12] Discussing the 'capitulation of Limeric [sic]', his friend notes, 'the weight of these oppressive statutes has fallen principally on those, who, born to affluence, and gifted with genius, are ... calculated to conduct the affairs of the community'.[13] O'Connor is clearly one of those 'born to affluence, and gifted with genius', and his political acumen is repeatedly praised in the novel even as its exercise is confined to the drawing room and other private spaces. However, Russel, his would-be father-in-law, as a 'lineal descendant' of one of Strongbow's force who is unencumbered by religious disabilities, epitomizes 'true manliness': 'adhering to the religion of the state, he was subject to none of those exclusions which affected his fellow subjects of other persuasions, and was permitted to exercise his genius uncontrolled. At an early age he entered upon public life'.[14] Even he, however, finds his will occasionally frustrated by Ireland's colonial status. The novel not only juxtaposes the brilliant O'Connor who cannot enter 'public life' with the nearly-as-brilliant Russel who freely inhabits that sphere, but also tacitly feminizes O'Connor by comparing his disenfranchisement to that of women. Russel refuses to allow O'Connor to marry his daughter only because, as a Catholic, O'Connor is 'excluded from political influence', and we are earlier told that Russel did not bother to educate his daughter because 'she was a female' and so 'could never become of any political importance'.[15] The novel defines its characters according to political power: women and even high-ranking, well-qualified male Catholics cannot have power; aristocratic Church of Ireland men have considerable power though it is curtailed by the British parliament; and the absent centre of power, represented primarily through complaints about its interference in Irish affairs, is that London-based parliament. This, however, is just the domain of politics and legislation. *Victim*, like much of Morgan's work, also represents the domestic as a countervailing space, where religious differences do not divide, women can educate themselves, and Catholic men of the middling ranks can find happiness outside of the public sphere. This private sphere, however, is decisively separated from political action, and O'Connor is expelled from both — he cannot inhabit the domestic realm (that is, marry Russel's daughter) because he cannot participate in the state, and there is no bourgeois public sphere to mediate between the two domains.

In *O'Donnel*, Morgan's hero, a Colonel who 'served six years in the Austrian service', laments, 'the O'Donnel family is but too much distributed: they are at this moment leaders in the armies of almost every great state but their own'.[16] This depiction of the O'Donnels as excluded, like O'Connor, from the Irish state includes a footnote: 'The fate of many branches of this ancient Irish family is alluded to in Mr Moore's beautiful and characteristic poetry in the Irish Melodies'.[17] This is an important gesture not only as a rare reference between the two friends in their literary work, but also as part of a larger tradition of prose works which use songs to add a sentimental gracenote to moments of national failure. Alicia Lefanu's *The Outlaw* (1823), for instance, represents a United Irish leader returning from nearly twenty years of exile in the United States. He is a broken man who wends his way home and there insists that his daughter sing him Moore's 'When He Who Adores Thee' from the *Irish Melodies* – later that day, he is killed by the same man who caused his flight from Ireland in 1798.[18] The sensationalist pamphlet, *Exile of Ireland!*, published in the early 1800s, ends its account of the Exile's participation in the 1798 Uprising with a similar scene. Arrested during the Uprising, the Exile turns to a fellow prisoner:

> Having heard him, on the preceding evening, sing a most pathetic song, which had made considerable impression on my mind, I requested him once more to sing those delightful verses; he complied with my request, and before we parted presented me with a copy of them, which I here insert for the perusal of the reader.[19]

The lines are 'The Exile of Erin', widely attributed to Thomas Campbell but also loudly claimed for George Nugent Reynolds in the early nineteenth century and later.[20] As in Lefanu's novel, the song's performance is a sign of retreat and resignation: Lefanu's hero retires to the domestic sphere, and the Exile is about to leave Ireland. All that is left for these United Irish leaders is passively listening to 'a most pathetic song'. Both of these lyrics recount the impossibility of further action: the exile of Erin can only leave, as the protagonist of the pamphlet soon does; the adoring 'He' only anticipates his death, foreshadowing the auditor's death within hours of his daughter's performance of Moore's song. These songs reinforce the narratives' emphasis on the protagonists' political paralysis even as the men's reaction to song registers, at a sentimental level, both a profound commitment to the nation and the morality of that commitment. In these texts, nationalist song does not rally the general populace, as United Irish songs were intended to do, but marks a break between the nation's leaders and the public realm in which they might have acted for the nation (as it does in Morgan's footnote as well) — the political problem, then, for these texts, lies in the organization of power at the upper levels of society rather than the monopolizing of power by those upper levels, markedly distinguishing the Irish political novel from the British radical novel.

Performing for the Public: Pseudonymist Satirist and Celebrity Songster

Thomas Moore, as a Catholic man of talent, education and civic commitment, was himself implicated in the crisis of colonial masculinity, and his organization of his work under various names echoes the fiction's division between public action and the private performance of song. Moore was, to stretch a metaphor, an Irish-Romantic Superman, a 'mild-mannered' lyricist under his real name, and a rights-defending satirist and polemicist behind pseudonymous masks, especially 'Thomas Brown the Younger'. As Byron famously quipped,

> Oh you, who in all names can tickle the town,
> Anacreon, Tom Little, Tom Moore, or Tom Brown,
> For hang me if I know of which you may most brag,
> Your Quarto two-pounds, or your Twopenny Post Bag.[21]

Jane Moody has suggestively argued that the persona of Brown emerges in *Intercepted Letters: Or, the Twopenny Post-Bag* (1813) in response to rising censorship during the Regency.[22] But Brown's true identity was known by the time of Moore's later satires under that name: in *The Fudge Family* (1818), 'Thomas Brown' contests the attribution of his work to 'Thomas Moore' and the 1819 anti-Moore satire *Fudger Fudged* refers directly to Moore's pseudonyms Little and Brown.[23] Across Moore's poetic corpus, pseudonyms function less as defences against censorship than as organizational tropes through which Moore established the particular position from which the poems proceed (recalling Jonathan Swift's extensive use of pseudonyms as well). Brown produced his satires of the English and Ascendancy elite, for instance, while 'an Irishman' or 'an Irish Gentleman' usually appeared on the title pages of his works centrally concerned with anti-Catholic bias, from *Corruption and Intolerance* (1808) to *Travels of an Irish Gentleman in Search of a Religion* (1833).

The work that Moore published under his own name similarly suggests the crafting of a particular 'Tom Moore' for public consumption (and sale). As Leith Davis has argued, Moore's invitation to participate in the *Melodies* project was based on Moore's marketability to English audiences because of early volumes under his name and his connections to the English ruling elite.[24] Significant as well was Moore's early success as a song-writer with 'A Canadian Boat-Song', included as a poem in Moore's 1806 *Epistles, Odes, and Other Poems* but earlier available as a published song. Between his *Epistles* and his *Poetical Works* (1840), Moore published poetry under his own name only in his songbooks and his 'romances', *Lalla Rookh: An Oriental Romance* (1817) and *Loves of the Angels: An Eastern Romance* (1823) (he did, however, occasionally publish prose under his own name, most notably his pamphlet on the Veto Controversy). Largely apolitical, despite the well-established influence of the United Irishmen's radical songs on Moore's *Irish Melodies*, his songbooks were heavy volumes which sold for fifteen shillings or more, and the first edition of *Lalla Rookh* cost forty-two shillings.[25] Conversely, his satire *Intercepted Letters* sold for just six shillings. From early in his career, Moore separated his public persona from his politics, using his own name only to market very specific, and very expensive, sorts of publications that echo the fiction's project of neutralizing the radical uses of song. But in so doing, Moore established a public position for himself.

Even though the *Irish Melodies* are so strongly identified with Moore, the series began as the project of James Power and Sir John Stevenson, as the first number indicates, with Moore just one of 'several' writers to assist in the 'Collection'.[26] Stevenson's musical settings were at the centre of the first number, with the first pages devoted to four melodies presented without lyrics. But the rising importance of Moore can be traced in the advertisements for 'New Music' placed at the end of each number. The first number lists work by a number of authors, about half by Moore, and at the price of 1s6d or 2s for each song; the second number advertises 'New Music, by Thomas Moore Esq. and Sir John Stevenson', giving Moore top billing for the first time, and increases the prices to as high as 3s per song.[27] In the third number, Power added to the list of work by Moore and Stevenson the announcement that he had 'purchased of Mr. Carpenter', Moore's early publisher, 'the copyright of the following much-admired Works, by Mr Moore, new Editions of which are now ready for delivery', a list that begins with 'A Canadian Boat-Song' for 3s. With the third number in 1810, the printer's advertisement changed, no longer mentioning Stevenson and assuring the audience, 'there is still in reserve an abundance of beautiful Airs, which call upon Mr. MOORE ... to save them from the oblivion to which they are hastening'.[28] Later numbers have advertisements signed by Moore himself, placing him clearly at the head of the project. By 1810, in other words, Moore was a highly marketable, and marketed, song-writer, presented as the driving force behind the *Melodies* — a reputation on which a number of other songbook projects proceeded.

While the lyrics in *Irish Melodies* collectively argued for a wronged Ireland but referred rarely, and then only obliquely, to contemporary politics, Moore's other songbooks were concertedly inoffensive and catered to elite tastes. *Sacred Songs* (1st number, 1816; 2nd number, 1824), which first appeared soon after Moore (prematurely) announced the end of the *Melodies* in 1815, consists of largely conventional religious poems with footnotes identifying relevant passages in the King James Bible, locating them in an Anglican tradition for a well-to-do English audience who could afford a piano and pay over a pound for a songbook. The music for *Sacred Songs* is not taken from popular tunes, like the *Melodies*, but the work of elite continental composers such as Beethoven, Haydn and Mozart. *National Airs* (1818–27) builds on Moore's early success with national ballads, from 'A Canadian Boat-Song' to the *Melodies*, while *Legendary Ballads* (1828) appeals to interest in classical and northern European antiquity. For *Evenings in Greece* (1825, 1832), each 'evening' constituted its own songbook with a main narrative line and embedded songs, echoing the form of *Lalla Rookh*. *Summer Fête* (1831) follows the same structure, embedding short melodies within a larger poetic narrative. It commemorates 'a memorable Fête' attended by R. B. Sheridan's granddaughter, the author Caroline Norton, to whom the volume is dedicated, locating it firmly within an aristocratic world described idyllically and at length in the framing poem. From the Anglicanism of *Sacred Songs* to the positive depiction of the wealthy in *Summer Fête*, from the folkloric *National Airs* to the orientalist *Evenings in Greece*, Moore's songbooks effectively targeted popular trends among the well-to-do and left hegemonic views unchallenged if not actively reinforced.

The songbooks not only capitalized on Moore's early success with aristocratic audiences but also perpetuated it; the volumes were a significant source of income, though he continued to struggle financially, and gave him, as a performer, access to the homes of the powerful. I note this not to resurrect the old and dubious slur, 'Tommy *loves* a Lord', but rather to point out that songwriting gave Moore a kind of economic and social power — it gave him 'attention'.[29] However, his songs, including those of the *Melodies*, focus on foreign, historically remote, or private spaces, staying well clear of the Romantic-era state that was the target of his cheap, anonymous and pseudonymous satires. 'Thomas Moore' was packaged and sold as a singer and romance-writer, addressing the British state neither through 'politics' nor 'letters' and so excluded from 'true manliness' as well as working in the 'feminine' genres of light song and romance.[30] In some of his *Melodies* and his prose, however, Moore complicated this feminization by developing an author-figure who, though proscribed from political action, exerts power through writing.

Witnessing Past Heroism: Moore's Political Sage

Moore was publishing satires and songs while his contemporaries — including Torrens, the Lefanus, Morgan and O'Keeffe — were returning again and again to the well-educated, civic-minded, upper-class hero who cannot act in the public sphere because of legal disabilities. Torrens' protagonist, successful in the British army and day-dreaming of being 'at the head of armies leading on the British troops to victory', cannot achieve promotion in the army: 'An official note was transmitted to him, stating, that as information had been received that he professed the Roman Catholic religion, before his commission as major could be laid before the king, he must read his recantation, and take the oaths prescribed by law'.[31] Instead of lacking motivation or self-discipline or talent, these characters lack only achievable goals. Moreover, this lack is, as noted above, sometimes represented through a scene in which they listen passively (and privately) to nationalist song, indicating that nationalist emotion is still in place to motivate action even though action is not possible in the public sphere — and so describing a masculine subject who is in crisis because he cannot act according to his will and beliefs. He is thus no longer a sovereign subject, in Enlightenment terms, precisely because there is no sovereign nation in which he can find a place.

This lyrical scene finds a compelling echo in one of Moore's best-known *Melodies*, 'Oh! Blame Not the Bard' (1810), 'both an *apologia* and a statement of artistic credo'.[32] The poem encourages a reading of Moore-the-songster as fearful of political engagement under his own name at the very beginning of his career as a satirist. As Gregory Schirmer has noted, the poem offers the past-ness of Ireland's heroic times as 'justification' for the bard's passivity and yet insists on the poet's function 'to keep alive the transcendent spirit of Ireland'.[33] In the poem, Moore also distinguished two kinds of nationalist masculinity, the 'warrior' of the past and the 'bard' of the present:

> He was born for much more, and in happier hours
>   His soul might have burn'd with a holier flame.
> The string that now languishes loose o'er the lyre,
>   Might have bent a proud bow to the warrior's dart;
> And the lip, which now breathes but the song of desire,
>   Might have pour'd the full tide of a patriot's heart.[34]

The gendering here is heavy-handed. The bard is feminized and sexualized – he 'languishes loose' and 'breathes but the song of desire'.[35] But 'happier hours' would have produced a more conventionally masculine subject – soul rather than sense, a 'bent ... bow' rather than a 'loose' 'lyre'. But Moore represents masculinity here specifically in relation to publicity. The poem continues, 'Unpriz'd are her sons, till they've learned to betray; / Undistinguish'd they live, if they shame not their sires'.[36] Masculinity is being shaped by public recognition; if the bourgeois public sphere is corrupt, sanctioning 'betrayal' and 'shame[ful]' behaviour, the only space for the would-be warrior is the feminine one of the private sphere, 'in pleasure's soft dream'.[37]

The performances of nationalist song in *The Outlaw* and *The Exile of Ireland!* take place in private – only the singer and an auditor in an enclosed space, recalling Moore's line, 'O'er the ruin her children in secret must sigh'.[38] But Moore's poem ends by announcing the very public distribution of the bard's song: 'The stranger shall hear thy lament on his plains; / The sigh of thy harp shall be sent o'er the deep', even causing Ireland's 'masters' to 'weep'.[39] This performance of nationalist song is very different from that in *The Outlaw* and *The Exile*: the song is insistently public, and through it the bard can act, on new terms, in the bourgeois public sphere. These two kinds of masculinity – warrior and commemorative voice, one active in the state and the other in the developing public sphere – recur throughout Moore's larger corpus, and constitute what James Eli Adams has termed 'style[s] of masculinity'.[40]

Adams argues that the sage is one of 'the various ways in which male Victorian writers represent intellectual vocations as affirmations of masculine identity'.[41] The Victorian sage is removed from the public sphere except insofar as his writing has 'an imagined audience', and 'embod[ies] masculinity as a virtuoso asceticism', through 'self-discipline', a construction of masculinity that Adams traces in the work of such disparate writers as Thomas Carlyle and John Henry Newman.[42] Moore's construction of the author-figure in 'Oh! Blame not the Bard' and in other works anticipates key aspects of this 'sage': Moore's bard is, like Adams' sage, public only through print and able to affirm a masculine position through that medium; suggestively, instead of 'self-discipline' or 'asceticism', evident in Adams' sages, Moore offers the nationalist variant of self-sacrifice.[43] Alternatively, like the Young Ireland martyr discussed by David Lloyd and more recently explored as a masculinist figure by Marjorie Howes, Moore's nationalist public leaders (warriors, politicians) exemplify the 'spirit of the nation', particularly in bearing 'the full tide of the patriot's heart' – and, like Moore's version of the sage, the principle of self-sacrifice inherent in the martyr.[44] The sage occupies the present, while the leader is always in the past (either the remote past or the turbulent days of 1782–1803); through the act of commemoration in writing, the two are allied and together re-enter the public sphere. The bard's 'cultivation of remembrance' is, as Joep Leerssen argues, crucial to the *Melodies*.[45] Yet it is also central to the biographical prose works that consumed the latter part of Moore's career. Moore's author-figures offer a provocative variation on the disabled nationalists of the fiction and poetry produced by Moore's contemporaries inasmuch as they are able to benefit the nation through writing and, moreover, act in the public sphere of print if not of politics proper by commemorating the very form of (national) public masculinity that is no longer possible in the present.

In the first paragraph of his *Letter to the Roman Catholics of Dublin*, published the same year as 'Oh! Blame Not the Bard', Moore takes the position of the untried speaker of truth:

> Inadequate as I am to this undertaking, and entering the lists, like David, in armour 'which I have not proved', I am yet conscious of bringing an honesty of feeling to the task, a zeal for my country's honour, and an ardent wish for her liberties, which entitle me to attention at least, though they should fail in producing conviction.[46]

Drawing on images of the warrior-hero who risks all – fighting for his country's honour, 'like David' against Goliath – he argues that he deserves *attention*. As with Adams' sage, writing puts Moore in the public eye, and Moore contends that he merited that publicity because of his 'patriot's heart'. The patriot-warrior and the writer are paralleled, both motivated by nationalist sentiment and both acting in public — one literally martial and the other figuratively so, rendered masculine by his 'entering the lists', with its attendant risks, as an author.

In his *Memoirs of the Life of the Right Honorable Richard Brinsley Sheridan* (1825), Moore returned to these two figures. Sheridan's speeches on the Hastings impeachment 'throw around him an interest, like that which encircles a hero of romance' and, at the end, Moore, after detailing Sheridan's financial difficulties, declares,

> Let it never too be forgotten in estimating this part of his character that had he been less consistent and disinterested in his public conduct, he might have commanded the means of being independent and respectable in private. He might have died a rich apostate, instead of closing a life of patriotism in beggary ... While, therefore, we admire the great sacrifice that he made, let us be tolerant to the errors and imprudences which it entailed upon him; and ... rest satisfied with the Martyr without requiring also the Saint.[47]

This representation of Sheridan the author – particularly as speech-maker in the British parliament – insists on Sheridan's power to act through voice, and as a national martyr. His 'public conduct' is allied to 'a life of patriotism' and 'great sacrifice'. Like Moore in the *Letter*, he 'enter[s] the lists' for his country. Sheridan, however, could engage in 'public conduct' in the state because he was Anglican and so (like Burke) able to take political office and fully access, through both 'politics and letters', the 'true manliness' that Fulford discusses.

The Catholic Moore, however, could sing but could not enter the political arena of the state. In his Preface to the fifth edition (1827), Moore aligns himself with Sheridan as a writer but carefully separates himself from the political world. Moore insists that he intentionally took a non-partisan approach to the material and hence drew the ire of all political factions. He claims that he only wished to be a 'speaker of truth' – a martyr to the cause of objectivity.[48] This objectivity is yoked to his role as sage: 'Conscious, however, as I was of approaching my task, with that fairness of spirit which should characterize such a work, in my other qualifications for the undertaking I was far from having the same confidence. My only hope was, that I should be able, by research and care, to make up for my deficiency in political knowledge.'[49] The Preface thus separates Moore on two levels from political authority: he is both objective, unlike 'the partisans on all sides' who attacked him, and ignorant of politics, as he must be in 1827, two years before Catholic Emancipation. Like the Catholic heroes of Torrens' and Morgan's novels, Moore could read about politics but not participate in the state's functioning, as Sheridan and Moore's other major biographical subject, Lord Edward Fitzgerald, could – but he could write and so participate in the bourgeois public sphere that was emerging to mediate between individuals and the state.

Moore's varied constructions of masculinity in relation to the twin poles of political action and scholarly or poetic redaction constitute an important pre-history of (and offer alternatives to) the figure of the national martyr central to Young Ireland. While much of the scholarship on this figure focuses on the Young Ireland poets of the early Victorian era, the figure's origins lie in such United Irish ballads as William Drennan's 'Wake' (1797) for William Orr and the anonymous 'Edward' on the death of Lord Edward Fitzgerald. Moore clearly built on this radical tradition in his *Irish Melodies*, as Mary Helen Thuente has detailed,[50] but carried it through much of his non-satirical work, from *Lalla Rookh*, where Hafed, grounded in allusions to Fitzgerald and Emmet,[51] conforms precisely to Lloyd's definition of 'The figure of the martyr', to his biography of Fitzgerald in 1831. But Moore's gendered vision is more complicated than establishing 'the spirit of the nation' through a hyper-masculine martyr or accepting feminization in the softly dreaming bard or retired hero who sits and listens. Moore's historical martyr-figures are both counterweighted and reinforced by author-figures in the present who remain apart from the world of public leadership – from the poet in 'Oh! Blame Not the Bard' to the protagonist of *Travels of an Irish Gentleman*, who concludes, after a long interrogation of the history of Christianity, that 'repose' and 'forebear[ance]' constitute the proper posture, to the eponymous hero of *Memoirs of Captain Rock*[52] whose narrative effects political change when his rebellion cannot. Although inactive on conventional masculine terms (as warriors, politicians, leaders, and so forth), these author-figures *speak*, laying a claim to public 'attention' that partially undoes their own political disenfranchisement and resurrects past leaders as public martyrs who can, through the author's writing, claim renewed 'attention' in the present. Moore thus identified a range of masculine 'styles' and so responded to the problem of masculinity under a colonial regime not simply in terms of disenfranchisement or feminization. Masculinity emerges in Moore's overall corpus – his songs, his non-fiction prose, his satires in verse and prose – as a complex negotiation with different audiences in which 'attention' can offer an alternative, though not an equivalent, to participation in the nation-state.

10 RADICAL POLITICS AND DIALECT IN THE BRITISH ARCHIPELAGO

R. Stephen Dornan

It has long been established that many writers in the Romantic period were concerned with revising and refreshing traditional literary language.[1] Furthermore, scholars of the literature of the period have often posited connections between changing linguistic choices and the dynamic political and historical context. This is particularly true of those writers traditionally configured as 'Romantic'. Richard Marggraf Turley succinctly summarizes these ideas when he writes that 'Romantics believed that reforming literary idiom was the first step towards achieving political reform'.[2] This manifested itself in an antipathy towards neo-classical diction and syntax; an idea which was articulated in William Wordsworth's preface to *Lyrical Ballads* (1800). This strand of Romanticism has traditionally been thought of as rejecting elitist literary forms and contrived neo-classical diction in favour of a more accessible and democratic aesthetic.

The emerging visibility of the Irish, Scottish and Welsh contributions to Romanticism in recent years has clear implications for the study of literary language in the period. The ongoing process by which Romanticism is being configured as an archipelagic phenomenon is the latest in a series of challenges that have systematically 'de-centred' traditional constructions of the period. Constructions of the Romantic canon as five or six male English poets have unravelled. The increased scholarly visibility of Irish and Scottish studies and a developing archipelagic consciousness across various academic disciplines have ensured that Romanticism in the British Isles has been reconstructed as a diverse movement with distinct, but interconnected strands in England, Scotland, Ireland and Wales.[3] Significant scholarly studies such as those by Katie Trumpener, Murray Pittock and Fiona Stafford, among others, have established Scotland and Ireland as influential sites of Romantic production.[4]

Recent scholarship on Irish and Scottish writers of the period, most notably concerning Maria Edgeworth and Robert Burns, has shown that Wordsworth was certainly not alone in positing a plainer, more democratic aesthetic. Wordsworth's desire to claim 'the real language of men' for poetry echoes Burns' claim to sing in the 'native language' of himself and his 'rustic compeers'.[5] Edgeworth, too, chose to tell 'a plain unvarnished tale' when she published *Castle Rackrent* in 1800.[6] Indeed, in some senses, the achievement of the Irish and Scottish writers calls into question the extent to which Wordsworth and the other traditionally 'Romantic' writers were truly radical in their linguistic choices. In Susan Manly's study of language, custom and nation, she argues that, of the Romantic period it is the work of Maria Edgeworth that most clearly forges links between politics and language.[7] She argues that, Edgeworth's championing of 'plain language' represents a re-politicization of the idea in response to Wordsworth's neutralization of the import of common language. Furthermore, Wordsworth's 'purged and purified ... real language of men' looks somewhat insipid in the light of recent Burns criticism which has authoritatively established the linguistic hybridity and variety of his poetry. These three major writers certainly seem to suggest an archipelagic impulse to use more accessible or democratic language in literature; their endeavours, however, produced strikingly different results.

Perhaps the most significant difference in the projects of these three writers was the role of dialect in their visions of literary language. Although there was unity across the archipelago in attempts to democratize literary language, there was disunity regarding what this entailed. The role of dialect throws these disunities into sharp relief. The traditional English Romantics, including Wordsworth saw no place for dialect in their democratizing project. For Wordsworth dialect was one of those 'impurities' to be 'purged and purified' from his version of literary language.[8] For a plethora of Scottish writers, on the other hand, most notably Burns, dialect was a crucial strand in a rich linguistic tapestry.[9] Dialect in Irish writing was also fairly widespread. There was a resurgence of writing in Scots in Ulster from the late eighteenth century and an increasing interest in other Irish dialects is evident in the work of Edgeworth and other Irish novelists of the early nineteenth century. This Scottish and Irish interest in the literary potential of dialect is complemented by an understudied English tradition of dialect writing which co-existed with the aesthetics promoted by Wordsworth and the other canonical Romantic poets. Dialect had an important though complex role to play in a neglected archipelagic Romanticism.

Contrasting critical orthodoxies in Scottish and Irish studies have also contributed to radically varying attitudes to work in the respective dialects of the places, particularly Scots and Irish English. For Scottish nationalist critics, Scots has traditionally been seen as central to the national tradition; however, for Irish nationalist critics this role tended to be filled by Irish not Irish English. Whereas Scots is often associated with the projection of a bold, autonomous literary identity, the representation of Irish English has often been seen as riddled with insecurity, and as an incompetent attempt to adopt the language of the colonizer. Contemporary culturally nationalist Scottish critics, Robert Crawford for example, tend to see Scots as part of Scotland's linguistic richness and the source of a creative multiculturalism that generates texts with 'linguistically eclectic energy'.[10] Thus in recent Burns criticism, this iconic Scottish writer has been reconstructed as a poet not confined by the use of dialect, but as an artist who creatively exploits his polylinguistic cultural heritage. Irish post-colonialists, on the other hand, have often cast Irish English not as a source of richness, but as a tongue marred by the legacy of colonialism, and haunted by the vestigial cadences of Irish; the true, lost language of the nation. Seamus Deane, for example, connects the adoption of English in Ireland with the historical trauma of the Famine and opines that Irish English contains a tragic note that is 'audible as silence, the silence of the other language that haunts the English language, sometimes in the shape of its syntax and grammar, or of its idiom and vocabulary, sometimes merely as reference or implication'.[11] Irish English, therefore, had and has a less secure place within the national literary traditions of Scotland and Ireland, and this meant that the inscription of Irish English was often a more fraught and problematic project.

The complex cultural status of dialect in an archipelagic context makes the untangling of politics difficult, particularly in a period when allegiances could be shifting and nebulous.

The new archipelagic consciousness in Romantic studies invites questions regarding the stability of the connection between the Romantic rejection of elitist language and radical politics. In many cases there is certainly a correlation between dialect and radicalism, although this often intersects with the assertion of a national or regional identity. Burns is one central figure whose politics have come under critical scrutiny in recent years. A number of important critics have sought to restore Burns to a radical political tradition and context that has traditionally been obscured.[12] Several influential Burns scholars have argued that Burns' work engaged consistently with wider political and aesthetic debates than traditional narrowly national readings have suggested.[13] A number of scholars working on Ulster writers of the period have shown that writers who used Scots held a range of political opinions and that their engagement with Burns and his political principles could fluctuate.[14] Debates regarding Edgeworth's politics are also re-igniting after years of Irish critics caricaturing her as an Ascendancy colonialist.[15]

This essay makes two major points. First, it suggests that writing in dialect was archipelagic and uncovers some of the connections between writers from three of its constituent nations. In this in seeks to build on the work of critics who have already established connections between writers from different parts of the archipelago. The work of a number of scholars on Ulster writers of the period has been influential in establishing tangible connections between these writers and their Scottish contemporaries and predecessors. This essay seeks to take this further by bringing in a number of English writers who, in many ways, shared the aesthetic, linguistic and political concerns of their Irish and Scottish contemporaries. Indeed, there are tangible biographical connections between some of these writers. This essay will, therefore, focus on the neglected English contribution to dialect writing through a discussion of the aesthetic and political import of the work of the unfashionable English writers Tim Bobbin (John Collier) and Robert Anderson. Second, this essay will discuss the politics of writing in dialect and argue that, whilst complexities abound, the act of writing in dialect almost always correlates to the adoption of oppositional perspectives on politics and society.

A literary exchange that took place in the first decade of the nineteenth century demonstrates the archipelagic connections that existed between writers who used dialect. This exchange took place through a number of poetic epistles in the traditional manner of Scots vernacular writers and Burns in particular. One bard, named Andrew McKenzie, wrote a poem to another, Robert Anderson, entitled 'A Poetical Letter, addressed to Mr R. Anderson, on his long silence'. In this poem McKenzie hypotheses as to the cause of a hiatus in his friend's literary production:

> Has fell 'misfortune's cauld nor-wast,'
> Spent on your head some dreadfu' blast?
> Or clouds o' woe your sky owrecast,
> An' chang'd your joy to mournin'?
> Has poverty's envenom'd dart
> Transpierc'd your independent heart?
> Or snarlin' critics made ye smart?
> Curse on sic spitefu' vermin![16]

A year or so later Anderson wrote to McKenzie to congratulate him on the appearance of a collection of his poems. He addresses McKenzie as 'nature's priest', and celebrates the wholesome 'honied truths' that his poetry contains. In one of several references to Burns he writes:

> For me, while I can think or luik,
> Whare'er I hurkle in a nuik,
> I'll pore wi' pleasure owre yer buik,
> An' bless the time,
> When Rab's advice ye fearfu' tuik,
> To print ilk rhyme.[17]

Carol McGuirk argues convincingly that Burns' epistles function to build a support network around the emerging bard by placing himself and his addressee in opposition to range of antagonistic groups from the literati to the local conservative religious authorities.[18] There is a similar subtext to the exchange between McKenzie and Anderson. The two friends are mutually supportive and cultivate a sense of camaraderie based on their use of non-standard language, principled independence and their common impoverished backgrounds. Furthermore, they are in rhetorical opposition to the hostile and learned critics and the social pretension of those Anderson refers to as 'pamper'd chiels'. There is, therefore, a tangible and oppositional political dimension to this exchange.

It is also significant that the two poets are explicitly linked by their common exemplar, Robert Burns. We can see from Anderson's epistle that Burns' example encouraged them to venture into print. Anderson says that in publishing his poetry McKenzie took 'Rab's advice'. In this case Anderson means that McKenzie followed Burns' example, rather than that he was literally advised by Burns to publish his poetry. The first stanza of McKenzie's quote also includes an intertextual reference to Burns' 'On a Scotch Bard, gone to the West Indies', when he refers to the ravages of 'misfortune's cauld nor-west'.[19] This links his addressee with the proud and independent, but beleaguered bard of Burns' poem and also demonstrates the depth of their familiarity with Burns' work.

These poems and the themes and ideas that they expound are reminiscent of Burns' own epistles, and many aspiring poets used the genre in the wake of the Ayrshire bard's rise to fame. In many ways, therefore, this is a fairly conventional and typical exchange; the fact that it took place not in Scotland, but in Ulster does not detract from this. Andrew McKenzie, who used the pseudonym Gaelus, was bard of Dunover, on the Ards peninsula in County Down, and he produced a successful collection of poetry in 1810.[20] His poetic correspondent was Robert Anderson, from Cumbria in the north-west of England, who was resident in Belfast between 1807 and 1810 as an employee of the Calico printworks in the city. By the time he arrived in Belfast Anderson had produced several collections of poetry including *Ballads in the Cumberland Dialect* (1805). This exchange of epistles, therefore, is emblematic of the archipelagic literary relationships that existed during this period. The Irish bard, McKenzie, hints at a common bond between himself and the English addressee, Anderson, and an integral part of what binds them is their mutual Scottish exemplar, Robert Burns. Anderson also wrote an epistle to Robert Burns just before the Scottish bard's death in 1796.[21] In it he poignantly implores Burns to break his silence and show friends and enemies that he's 'Rabbie still'. These exchanges show that there were a range of linguistic, aesthetic, social and political ties that transcended the national differences between these poets.

This exchange between McKenzie and Anderson was not anomalous, but rather is typical of the literary culture of the British archipelago during the late eighteenth and early nineteenth centuries. The success of Burns' *Poems, Chiefly in the Scottish Dialect* of 1786 engendered an unprecedented upsurge in the publication of verse that used dialect, and indeed there was a corresponding upsurge in the use of dialect in fiction from the first decade of the nineteenth century.[22] The exchange between McKenzie and Anderson demonstrates that this upsurge was not confined by national borders, and although its epicentre was Burns and the south-west of Scotland, it was actually archipelagic in scope with manifestations in Ireland and England. Burns may have been instrumental in generating renewed interest in using dialect in literature, and in popularizing it to greater extent than previously, but in his wake the phenomenon spread and gained momentum so that within a generation a plethora of poets were using it.[23] The heartland of this efflorescent literary phenomenon was a large area in the northern part of the British archipelago. It took firm root in parts of Scotland and in east Ulster and parts of the north of England. Burns' influence, and his vernacular aesthetic, however, spread even beyond the northern heartlands as is evident in the Killeigh poems of Thomas Dermody, originally from County Clare.[24]

It is important to point out, however, that the poets who deployed dialect did not write solely in dialect. This is crucial as it demonstrates, as Murray Pittock and others have contended with regard to Burns, that the decision to use dialect was always taken on the grounds of artistic choice, not linguistic necessity.[25] Poets who used dialect almost universally wrote in standard English as well, with dialect as one dimension of their literary productions. That dialect is borne of artistic choice, not linguistic or educational limitation, is fundamental to an appreciation of the complexity of the voices and personae of these writers. When talking about writing in dialect I am, like Paula Blank, referring to modes of writing that are defined in 'value or status relative to other English dialects'.[26] Writers who compose in Scots, or the regional dialects of Ireland or England, create a literature that works by being different from standard English, but which is nevertheless in constant dialogue with it. It is, as Jeffrey Skoblow argues, in an underestimated account of Burns' poetry, a literary mode that 'both beckons kinship and resists recognition' for many readers.[27] The vernacular aesthetic, although such work often takes the guise of simplicity, produces liminal texts that can have an alienating effect on their readership and disorient by being simultaneously familiar and strange.

Looking at the connections and similarities between writing in dialect from different parts of the archipelago is crucial; it helps to reconfigure these writers into a coherent but neglected literary movement and an important strand of Romanticism, and revises the traditional views of these poets as eccentric, local writers. The most important places outside Scotland for the production of writing in dialect were Ulster and northern England. As in Ulster a tradition of using dialect in the north of England preceded Burns, with Josiah Relph and Tim Bobbin (John Collier) as the most prominent manifestations of this, but Burns' success reinvigorated the tradition with Robert Anderson and his contemporaries John Stagg and Sussanah Blamire producing work in his wake.[28]

The upsurge in Scots writing in Ulster has received an increasing degree of exposure over the last decade or so, re-establishing occluded connections between writers and enhancing the reputation of some neglected poets.[29] Writing in English regional dialects, however, has not been meaningfully connected to Scottish and Irish equivalents. Most of the writing that does mention these texts focuses on the local or national import of the language, rather than looking at the connections and wider context. A similar strand of thinking is evident in the treatment of the English dialect writers. D. M. Horgan, for example, writes of how nineteenth-century editors appropriated the work of Tim Bobbin (John Collier) for 'the celebration of the language, and with it the community, traditions and the collective memory of the people of South Lancashire'.[30] In this way it parallels traditional readings of the Ulster poets, who until recently were often read as having only local interest and scope, which functioned to downplay their aesthetic interest and political import.[31] The wider political and aesthetic concerns of these writers are often subordinated by a restrictive focus on their local significance.

Burns escapes such categorization because of his status as national poet, but this too can be limiting. He can be read as more than a representative of a Scottish national tradition, but rather as the catalyst for a vernacular Romanticism that was archipelagic in scope. Burns' iconic status in Scottish culture and his image as national bard mean that the archipelagic dimension of his influence has been occluded. Clearly the publication of Burns' *Poems, Chiefly in the Scottish Dialect* was an inspirational moment for a generation of vernacular poets from different parts of the archipelago. Burns and his English and Irish contemporaries and predecessors can be more fruitfully understood when re-connected with their archipelagic contexts.

This essay will now turn to the political implications of this corpus of work, and the political motivations of the writers, particularly two of the major English contributors, Tim Bobbin (John Collier) and Robert Anderson. Choosing to write in dialect often contains an oppositional potential; the rejection of linguistic norms often entails a rejection of mainstream political assumptions. This correlation between dialect and oppositional politics underpins what I call 'the vernacular aesthetic'. A text with a vernacular aesthetic, in my definition, is one that uses dialect and accompanies the shift from Standard English with a number of other attitudinal and cultural shifts. The shift from Standard English to dialect often signifies a series of other shifts away from bourgeois norms and cosmopolitan cultural assumptions. This applies to many texts in which a non-standard voice narrates, from *Castle Rackrent* (1800), to *Huckleberry Finn* (1884) and *Trainspotting* (1993). Texts that are narrated in non-standard language often temporarily prioritize groups or individuals usually thought of as peripheral and thus the non-standard language comes to symbolize a non-standard or alternative way of thinking, whilst the non-standard speaker gives voice to a perspective that is outwith the mainstream; as Tom Paulin puts it: 'the springy, irreverent, chanting, quartzy, often tender and intimate, vernacular voice speaks for an alternative community that is mostly powerless and invisible'.[32] It is hardly surprising, therefore, that dialect is often accompanied by a rejection of conventional political thinking and the subversion of familiar political assumptions.

The work of Burns' Scots vernacular predecessor, Allan Ramsay, exemplifies such techniques. His poem 'Lucky Spence's Last Advice', is a fine example of a text that uses a vernacular aesthetic, as Lucky Spence's non-standard language parallels the non-standard morality and values of her community of prostitutes in the Edinburgh underworld. Lucky Spence's dying words are an inversion of the traditional dying words genre, when wholesome values and wisdom are passed on to the listeners by the expiring speaker. Lucky Spence inverts conventional morality, dispensing advice to her young wards on how to solicit and deceive clients. The religious authorities and the laws of the state are decried as troublesome realities that should be side-stepped if possible. Lucky Spence's unconventional moral outlook which says 'My bennison come on good doers, / Who spend their cash on bawds and whores' complements her non-standard mode of expression.[33] Ramsay's poem includes no authorial moral judgment in this poem, but simply includes a frank acknowledgement of a different, marginal perspective articulated in a non-standard voice. Lucky Spence is so uncritically immersed in her own culture and her own values that for her they are the norm, even if they might shock and alienate much of Ramsay's readership. This is the vernacular aesthetic in action.

This distance from standard language and bourgeois and cosmopolitan norms can be configured in a variety of ways. Any deviation from a linguistic standard, and mainstream political views, can be delineated in strongly negative terms, as indicative of illiteracy, ignorance or stupidity. In such instances the inability to command the standard form is stigmatized and the speaker, and consequently any political ideas that they advance, are likely to be subject to ridicule. Commentators on the infamous stage-Irish tradition have long established that dialect could be deployed to suggest the Irishman's bumpkinish lack of sophistication, or even in extreme cases, barbarity. The immensely popular Williamite song 'Lilliburlero' is an example of a piece that deploys such techniques. The song purports to be an excited address from one Irish Catholic to another in the midst of the tumult surrounding the Williamite wars. The song begins 'Ho! brother Teague, dost hear de decree, / *Lilli burlero bullen a la*', which mimics Irish pronunciation of English and parodies the sounds of Irish in a nonsensical refrain.[34] Irish speech in this song denotes stupidity, credulity and brutality as the speaker articulates his murderous predilections, hopes for Catholic ascendancy and faith in ridiculous prophesies. In this instance the non-standard language does reflect a different perspective on the political crisis that became known as the Glorious Revolution, and the way in which it was settled in mainstream British politics. In this instance, however, the alternative perspective is debased and construed as corrupt, foolish and atavistic.

Despite this cautionary note, representations of dialect are by no means uniformly negative. In other instances the distance between dialect and the standard could represent a wholesome distance from degenerate cosmopolitan values, or articulate a refreshing, challenging or subversive viewpoint that defamiliarizes readers' assumptions. Thus in the work of Burns and Tim Bobbin, for example, fashionable, modern trends and finery are ridiculed by the writers' plain-speaking and honest, rustic personae. This is most apparent in Burns' persona of the humble bardie, who audaciously gatecrashes the king's levee in 'A Dream', or admonishes the Scottish ruling classes in 'The Author's Earnest Cry and Prayer'.[35]

Bobbin's *A View of the Lancashire Dialect* (1750) demonstrates the complexity of using dialect in writing. This text relates the 'adventures and misfortunes of a Lancashire clown' in the form of a dialogue, mainly between two characters called Tummus and Meary. It is a disorienting text on several levels, not least due to Bobbin's attempt to phonetically render the dialect of southern Lancashire in the text. But the text is also disorienting in the manner in which it balances the stereotype of the bumpkinish dialect-speaker with political and social critique. In a sense *A View of the Lancashire Dialect* appears to be a text that negatively associates non-standard speech with clownishness and stupidity; the central character Tummus, the 'clown' of the title, narrates a series of escapades and tricks that he falls victim to. As Horgan has convincingly argued, however, it is a more ambiguous and complex text than this suggests as the non-standard language encodes political protest. Horgan argues that it demonstrates 'the voice of popular protest protected by parody and the 'disguise' of the comic and the droll'.[36] He goes on to argue that 'the dialect of the Lancashire clown disarmed, deflecting attention from the voiced protest to the comic voice of the protestor'.[37] This tactic of using disarmingly comic idiom to articulate political protest was deployed by Burns and numerous other writers who used dialect. Certainly the voice of political protest does break through at times in this text. For example, Tummus has cause to critique the legal system after an unscrupulous clerk attempts to extort money from him. At this point Tummus reflects on corruption and implicates the legal hierarchy, in the form of the justices themselves. Tummus complains: 'Had naw this o strung savor of fere cheeoting; ne deawnreet nipping o poor fok. On does theaw think ot tees justices do naw know, when these tikes plene o hundurt wur tricks thin this in oyeer?' Here he accuses the justices of being in collusion with their cheating and corrupt underlings, whose activities impinge particularly on the poor. Meary's response to Tummus' suggestion that the justices should be punished for this corruption is unequivocal. Referring to the justices she says 'th' bigger rascot shou'd ha' th' bigger smacks', after which Tummus pointedly reflects that 'greyt fok oft dun whot te win wi' littleons reet or rank'.[38] In other words the great often treat the poor with disregard. Such political undercurrents are disarmingly insinuated into the texture of *A View of the Lancashire Dialect*.

The political undercurrents of a text such as *A View of the Lancashire Dialect* might have become more apparent during the final quarter of the eighteenth century. The radical challenge ensured that readers were less likely to blindly accept conventional political or linguistic hierarchies and this could alter the readings of a text such as *A View of the Lancashire Dialect*. This is demonstrated by a preface that was added by Bobbin for a later edition. The preface takes the form of a self-reflexive discussion between Collier's author figure, Tim Bobbin, and his personified book. The author tells his book that his money has run out, so the book must go out on another journey. After some complaints the book relents if the author agrees to include some extra poems to the edition, or to 'clap some pleagy rimes, oth' neb o me cap' in the book's words. They then set about composing this additional text:

> *Tim.* Le me see its none so good t' begin o riming, ot i see on – hum – neaw for't.
> Robbing's a Trade that's practis'd by the Great,
> Our ruling men are only thieves of state.
> *Buk.* Howd howd howd the Dickons tak o' – i see whot's topmost; yoan be hong'd or some mischief – on then aw'll be whooup with o' efeath!
> *Tim.* Not e Goddil belike! – dust think so? 'slid bot i hete honging – do thee set ogete then.[39]

This exchange is significant for several reasons. First, it hints at a growing awareness of the dangers of political engagement. Secondly, it perfectly demonstrates Bobbin's tactic of masking barbed political commentary behind his foolish and humble persona and his non-standard language. The non-standard voice is disarming in its naivety, but the controversial critique of the ruling classes has been made. This preface initially appeared in the 1760s, but it would undoubtedly have struck a chord when it was included in the editions brought out in the 1790s.

Burns' political radicalism has received a fair bit of attention over the last decade or so, with the work of Liam McIvanney, Noble and Scott Hogg, Robert Crawford, and others. Equally, for those who are familiar with the Ulster Scots literary tradition, the radicalism of some of its main practitioners is clear. This confluence between dialect and radical politics in the late eighteenth and early nineteenth century is archipelagic, as it exists in the English regions as well as in Scotland and Ulster (even beyond if we include Dermody's Killeigh poems). Robert Anderson is a good example of an English writer in whose work dialect and radical politics converge. He was candid about his radical sympathies even before he published his *Ballads in the Cumberland Dialect* in 1805, which used the dialect of north-west England. He published a collection of poetry in 1798 which rather audaciously included a celebratory sonnet on the radical linguist and philosopher, John Horne Tooke. In this poem Anderson praised the French Revolution and rebuked the British authorities who unsuccessfully prosecuted Tooke in 1794:

> When Gallia's sons shook off despotic pow'r,
> And from their clime fell superstition hurl'd,
> Thou Britain's patriot! Didst proclaim the hour
> When heav'n-born Freedom smil'd upon the world.
> Long shall thy suff'rings tell thy country's shame,
> And long fair Virtue's sons shall venerate thy name.[40]

The politics of this poem is unambiguous and although his Cumberland ballads are less explicitly radical, they are implicitly so in their subversion of linguistic hierarchies and in their prioritization of marginal, dialect voices. The distance from Standard English in these compositions signifies a distance from cultural centres and the niceties of cosmopolitan life. The alternative language signifies the predominance of alternative paradigms and non-standard perspectives within these cultures. 'The Clay Daubin' for example, written in 1804, is a celebration of the raucous culture of the Cumbrian peasantry in tones reminiscent of the Scots 'Christis Kirk' genre.[41] In the opening stanza and a refrain, Anderson's speaker sets up an opposition between the vital, raucous pleasures of the peasant's 'clay biggin' and the sterile grandeur of castles, halls and King George's court:

> We went owre to Deavie's Clay Daubin,
> And faith a rare caper we had,
> Wi' eatin, and drinkin, and dancin,
> And rwoarin, and singin leyke mad
> Wi' crackin, and jwokin, and braggin,
> And fractin, and feightin and aw;
> See glorious fun and diversion
> Was ne'er seen in castle or haw.
> Sing hey for a snug clay biggin,
> And lasses that like a bit spwort;
> Wi' friens and plenty to gi'e them,
> We'll laugh at King Gworge and his cwort.[42]

Throughout the poem and the collection there is prioritization of the language, songs, foods and activities of the peasantry.

This is fairly common in Anderson's Cumbrian dialect verse; the reader certainly gets the sense of a community that is in opposition to mainstream society and which often exists, like Ramsay's Edinburgh underworld, outwith the laws of the state. In 'The Village Gang' Anderson's speaker describes his home town as the antithesis of all civility and politeness.

> Our dogs e'en beyte aw decent fwok,
> Our verra naigs they kick them,
> And if they nobbet ax the way,
> Our lads set on and lick them.[43]

This is a culture in which opposition and belligerence is ingrained. It is a vigorously dystoptian world in which lawlessness, adultery, violence and lying is the norm. It is also full of colourful and vivid, if roguish, unorthodox and at times grotesque characters including Dick the weaver, with his unfaithful wife, the village politician, the local laird's bullying wife, John the village wrestling champion who mangles opponents, the gluttonous blacksmith and the crippled piper's roguish son. These are the people who make up this threatening, though energetic society which is described in the equally threatening yet energetic dialect of Cumbria.

The speaker also critiques the destructive behaviour of the local authority figures, thereby suggesting that they contribute to this destructive culture. They are just as corrupt as the artisans and rustics:

> The doctor he's a parfet pleague,
> And hawf the parish puzzens;
> The lawyer sets fowk by the lugs,
> And cheats them neist by duzzens;
> The parson swears a bonny stick
> Amang our sackless asses;
> The squire's ruin'd scwores and scwores
> O' canny country lasses.[44]

In this stanza the speaker delineates the various corruptions endemic in the representatives of the medical, legal and religious and social authorities. As with Bobbin, the poem might not be explicitly radical, but it does encode a critique of social and political hierarchies from the perspective of the ordinary, dialect-speaking man. The speaker here is a canny commentator who recognizes the shortcomings in his society and the inability or disinclination of the authorities to remedy them.

This essay has argued for a re-evaluation of writing in dialect in the late eighteenth and early nineteenth century. Essentially it is my contention that this re-evaluation should function on two levels. First, the phenomenon should be considered as an archipelagic one to liberate the writers from restrictive readings that emphasize their local import. Further research would undoubtedly bring to light other neglected work in dialect and uncover the literary and political connections between writers from different parts of the archipelago. Underpinning this re-evaluation must be a more considered understanding of the complexity of non-standard texts; these texts often display an acute awareness of linguistic diversity, a self-reflexive playfulness with register and voice, and raise crucial issues pertaining to class and politics. To fully appreciate this requires a re-evaluation of the work of individual writers such as Tim Bobbin and Robert Anderson. Anderson is a good example of a poet whose work and life embodies the archipelagic links discussed in this essay, whilst Bobbin's text typifies the disorienting complexity of good writing in dialect. In both texts the oppositional politics of the writers is encoded in the perspectives of their dialect speakers and in their explicit and implicit critiques of social, linguistic and political hierarchies.

11 'THEAW KON EKSPECT NO MOOAR EAWT OV A PIG THIN A GRUNT': SEARCHING FOR THE RADICAL DIALECT VOICE IN NORTHERN ENGLAND, 1798–1819

Katrina Navickas

This paper examines the radical voice, as expressed in dialect literature and songs published in Lancashire and the West Riding of Yorkshire during the French and Napoleonic Wars.[1] This was a period of tumultuous political, social and economic change in Britain. For the first time, the working classes became involved in forms of overt political action to campaign for parliamentary reform and an extended franchise: political societies, petitions to parliament and mass demonstrations. For the first time also, the north-west of England was at the heart of this political activity. The industrialization and expansion of Pennine towns and villages encouraged a sense of independence among a critical mass of skilled artisans, miners and textile workers. Inspired by events in France, Thomas Paine's *Rights of Man* (1791–2), and a longer heritage of ideas about constitutional reform, inhabitants of Lancashire and the West Riding agitated for suffrage.[2]

The loyalist reaction to working-class radicalism in the 1790s is a perennial topic of debate among historians. The main focus has been William Pitt's government and its so-called 'reign of terror' against nationally-prominent radicals. Royal proclamations and government legislation against the publication of seditious writings fostered an atmosphere of suspicion about expressions of radicalism in public and in print. Such fears were compounded by the arrests of radical writers and activists. This paper by contrast takes a bottom-up approach to the impact of loyalism. Local loyalist elites and their supporters threatened to silence the radical voice too. 'Church-and-King' riots targeted radical printers and 'Jacobin' libraries in 1793–95. Attacks on the *Manchester Herald*, *Sheffield Register* and *Sheffield Iris* amongst other newspapers closed formerly highly fruitful published outlets for radical poetry and song.[3]

This paper considers whether the radical voice was transmuted to other spheres of communication, particularly dialect literature, after these incidents of suppression had fostered an atmosphere where expressing radical views openly was discouraged. The first part examines two significant pieces of radical Lancashire dialect literature in detail: Robert Walker's *Plebeian Politics, or the Principles and Practices of Certain Mole-Eyed Maniacs Vulgarly Called Warrites* (1801), and the ballads and songs of the Wilson family of Manchester.[4] The second part discusses other remnants of political dialect material from this period, principally the ballads in the broadside collection of Manchester Central Library.[5]

The recent cultural history of popular politics and the other contributors to this volume emphasize the integral role of verse and song to the development and dissemination of both radicalism and loyalism.[6] Searching for the radical voice even in Standard English is, however, problematic. Most songs and poetry were sung and read orally rather than in print and were therefore ultimately ephemeral in nature. Even when preserved in the form of the broadside, furthermore, their message was open to myriad interpretations by different audiences. Fear of prosecution or at least a strong beating by local 'Church-and-King' loyalists probably confined such material to dissemination in oral culture alone. Very few radical pamphlets and songs survive in northern England for the turn of the century. This paucity therefore makes *Plebeian Politics* even more significant as a piece of political propaganda.

Though *Plebeian Politics* and the songs of the Wilsons upheld a bold and uncompromising political and social message, they cannot be regarded as representative of a widespread or 'genuine' radical voice. This does not preclude an active oral tradition among radicals, but the paucity of surviving evidence makes it harder for historians to base their entire conclusions on printed literature. Robert Walker employed the phrase 'Theaw kon ekspekt no mooar eawt ov a pig thin a grunt' ('You can expect no more from a pig than a grunt') on the title page of *Plebeian Politics*. The tagline referred to what he regarded to be the inane utterances of his loyalist opponents. However, most of his radical contemporaries did little more than squeal occasionally, and were predominantly silent during this period of political suppression. This paper concludes that we must not overestimate the strength of radicalism expressed in popular song and dialect literature. The radical voice was certainly drowned out by the loyalist and patriotic rounds of 'God Save the King' and 'Roast Beef of Old England' that carolled around the pubs and churches of England during the wars with France.

Plebeian Politics

Robert Walker was born in the village of Audenshaw, Lancashire, in 1728. He worked as a handloom weaver in Rochdale, and died in May 1803. As an autodidact poet and dialect writer, he made a strenuous effort to self-style himself 'Tim Bobbin the Second', that is, the successor to 'Tim Bobbin' or John Collier, the popular Rochdalian dialect writer of the early eighteenth century. His whole family 'held strong Jacobinical opinions', and one of his nephews later became friends with the famous Middleton radical leader and writer Samuel Bamford. In 1795–6, soon after the 'Two Acts' had prohibited radical writings and meetings, Walker composed the comic dialogue *Plebeian Politics*. The radical editor William Cowdroy printed it in installments in his newspapers, the *Chester Chronicle* and *Manchester Gazette*. The series was 'so well received' that it was republished as a pamphlet, which reputedly sold 1480 copies in thirteen weeks.[7] Walker then may have developed contacts with the United Englishmen, the republican cells modelled on the United Irishmen that were formed in Manchester and other northern towns in around the turn of the century. The British government signed peace preliminaries with France in November 1801, and the short-lived Peace of Amiens of 1802 allowed an atmosphere of relief and celebration to calm domestic suspicion of political writings. Walker revised *Plebeian Politics* in response to the new circumstances of 1801, and it was reprinted again in 1812.[8]

The comic dialogue between a proponent and an opponent of particular political tenets was a common device of both radical and loyalist propaganda in this period.[9] *Plebeian Politics* employed this medium to great satirical effect. Walker, in the guise of 'Tum Bobbin', converses with his rambunctious compatriot 'Whistlepig' about various contemporary topics, including the return of peace, their experience of wartime in the 1790s and their predictions for the immediate future. The running theme of the pamphlet is an attack upon the perceived hypocrisy of both national government and local loyalist elites. For example, Tum discusses the royal proclamation of thanksgiving for the signing of the peace preliminaries of late 1801. He compares the description of the war given in the proclamation to that in the more usual proclamations for general fast days that had punctuated the national calendar of patriotic events during the 1790s:

> Boah I tell theh whot Whistle-pig, I're lookink-i'-th' newspaper t'other day, an I fund a Protlamashon for this Thanksgivink dey, and I find, ot tey'n awthurt the'r tone meetyly fro a Protlamashon for a Fast, fot then they kod'n th' war 'just an necessary'. Boah neaw they kone it a 'Bluddy, ekstendot, an ekspensive war': Had'n they kode it *unjust an unnecessary*, sum foak think theyd'n a komn oz nee th' truth.
>
> (But I tell thee what Whistlepig, I was looking in the newspaper the other day, and I found a Proclamation for this Thanksgiving Day, and I find, that they had altered their tone mightily from a Proclamation for a Fast, for then they had called the war 'just and necessary'. But now they call it 'Bloody, extended and expensive war'. Had they called it unjust and unnecessary, some folk think they would have come nearer the truth.)

Walker used this diatribe to argue that the High Church High Anglican loyalists had used religion to support their case for war. Tum pronounces disgust at his local clergy leading militia regiments into their parish church for the thanksgiving service, as sanctioned by the magistrates and government: 'when the'n drunm't an ekorsis't foke o the' Sundy o'er, heaw fort' kill the'r fello kreturs; ods flesh mon! th' kristian religion teaches no sitch wark' ('When they drummed and exercised folk all Sunday how to kill their fellow creatures; God's flesh man! The Christian religion teaches no such work'). The comic rhetoric effectively subverted 'Church-and-King' religious arguments by exploiting clerical complaints about popular disregard for the Sabbath. From the prime minister to the local busybody, no loyalist escaped Walker's wrath. In the final part, Tum declares that a local 'nabob' who illuminated his house for the celebration of the peace is:

> 'Just like th' rest o'th' foos ot han no oppinnions o'the'r own: bod grunt'n afthr eawer nashonal pig-leaders, one dey for war, an another for peeoss' (Just like the rest of the fools who have no opinions of their own, but grunt after our national pig-leaders, one day for war, and another for peace').

Walker concluded: 'Heaw fort' rekonsile sitch kondukt weh consistency, is a paradoks to mee' ('How to reconcile such conduct with consistency is a paradox to me').[10]

Swine form the predominant and heavily knowing leitmotif in *Plebeian Politics*. The title and the theme were most likely a direct homage to Daniel Isaac Eaton's pamphlet, *Politics for the People; Or, A Salmagundy for Swine, or Hog's Wash* (1794), against which Pitt's government had unsuccessfully proceeded three times for seditious libel. The epithet 'Whistlepig' also referenced Edmund Burke's invective against the 'swinish multitude' in his *Reflections on the Revolution in France* (1790) and Thomas Spence's republican riposte to Burke, *Pig's Meat* (1795).[11] Walker mirrored other northern radical poets who also recognized the satirical currency of swine in their work. Joseph Mather of Sheffield (1737–1804) was a prolific composer of radical ballads in the 1780s and early 1790s. He used the swine motif in 'The Norfolk Street Riots', an ironic song about disturbances caused by a Sheffield volunteer regiment refusing to disperse on 4 August 1795.

> Oppression need not fear alarms,
> Since tyranny has got such swarms
> Of gallant heroes bearing arms,
> To butcher-grunting swine.[12]

Yet *Plebeian Politics* did not explicitly aim to explain 'Paineite' or Spencean principles. The pamphlet was not a positive invocation of radical thought but was rather a bitter exposition of the actions and attitudes of loyalists. It was a destructive text, with a virulently anti-corruption and anti-loyalist message. Walker attempted to convince or remind his readers about why and how both local and national government were 'wetherkok, fawnink, krinjink, hypokritical, sykofantine skeawndrils'.[13] Throughout the pamphlet, Walker juxtaposed what he regarded as the major U-turn undertaken by William Pitt's government in 1801 with the similar hypocrisy of local loyalist notables and authorities in the industrializing towns and villages east of Manchester. He sought to expose the hypocrisy of 'Church-and-King' loyalist elites who had ostentatiously celebrated the preliminaries of peace in 1801 despite having refused popular demands for an end to the war expressed in mass petitions to parliament in 1795 and 1800. There is little in his pamphlet that suggests a vision of a revolutionary new order.

Plebeian Politics was very much a reactive text, but it was nevertheless unique in its unpicking of the relationship between local and national loyalism. Walker's observations were also important in describing local radical and loyalist activities, real or fictional, that the more well-known and national radical tracts and poetry overlooked or saw no need to investigate. He employed the comic dialogue in a double-edged way, combining the mode's traditional observations on the peculiarities of everyday life with more sardonic criticism of national events. The pamphlet's criticisms of local Church-and-King loyalists were framed as comedy caricatures punctuated by vignettes of local stories. Walker built upon local knowledge and appealed to the now silent radical minority together with attempting to change the minds of the ambivalent. A particularly moving episode concerned the tale of a factory being inundated during severe flooding in August 1799. A radical man from Stockport built a raft and risked his life to rescue the workers. Walker piled thick criticism upon the local 'Warhawks' because in refusing to help, they could not bring themselves to recognize the humanity of an individual whom they categorized as seditious: 'rook a foos ot wurn brout up e nout boah ignorance, stood'n by, and sed'n, "it wur a theawsunt pittys ot sitch a mon wur a jakobin"' ('a rack of fools who were brought up in nothing but ignorance, stood by and said, "It was a thousand pitys that such a man was a Jacobin"').[14] This incident was not reported in the newspapers or other sources, but the level of detail and feeling behind Walker's story suggests that it probably did occur.

Walker's other aim was to rail against hypocritical attempts by both national and local government to enforce 'soshal order' in their suppression of radicalism. He noted the trials of prominent radical printers John Gale Jones and James Montgomery in Sheffield and 'Church-and-King' attacks on the Manchester printers Matthew Faulkner and Samuel Birch in 1792 and William Cowdroy in 1799: 'Let's look at Gales an Montgomery, at Sheffielt; Faukner an Birch, an Kowdry, at Manchestor; som on 'em put e prison, sum driv'n the'r kuntry, others the'r windows brokk'n an ther property distroid, an o for printink unawnserable truths'.[15] He was equally anxious to criticize the arrests of prominent metropolitan radical leaders Thomas Hardy, John Horne Tooke and John Thelwall in tandem with local loyalists' suppression of the activities of radical circles:

> Hardy, Horne Took, an Thelwell, tri'd for Hee Treeoson, an nout fund agen 'em; beside Gilbert Wakefilt ... an Kneet o' Saddleworth, an a meeny othur foke ot suffert'nt impris'nment, on sum on 'em deeoth, for beeink true lovers o'rashonal liberty; an o this wur dun an suffert for th' sake o' whot Billy and his gang kode'n soshal ordur.
>
> ('Hardy, Horne Tooke and Thelwall, tried for high treason, and nothing found against them, besides Gilbert Wakefield ... and Knight of Saddleworth and many other folk who suffered imprisonment and some of them death for being true lovers of rational liberty; and this was done and suffered for the sake of what William and his gang called social order').[16]

John Knight of Saddleworth was a radical veteran who had been imprisoned in 1794 after a 'Church-and-King' attack on the 'Jacobin library' at Royton near Oldham. After his release, he served on the county executive of the United Englishmen.[17] William Pitt decided to silence what remained of radical opposition in 1798. The outspoken Unitarian minister Gilbert Wakefield of Warrington Dissenting Academy was imprisoned for two years for printing a pamphlet criticizing the government's imposition of the income tax and conduct of the war.[18]

Plebeian Politics propagated the anti-Pitt myth that also featured in much of what remained of radical critique in this period. Radical dinners, for example, toasted the name of William Pitt, but only with reference to his reforming guise of the 1780s. This ironic gesture was often accompanied by a wish for him to return to his former character and leave behind his reputation associated with anti-Jacobin repression and the Two Acts of 1795. The construction of an ideal of the reforming Pitt introduces a counter-part to J. J. Sack's argument about the reinvention of the Tory party in this period. Sack contends that after William Pitt's death, his followers fostered a myth about the political principles and history of their leader to serve their own ends. Pittites stretched the truth far into fiction, creating a picture of anti-Catholicism and anti-reform quite removed from the realities of Pitt's politics. The reconstituted Tory party found the myth useful in their battles against Catholic emancipation and parliamentary reform in the late 1820s.[19] Sack never answers entirely exactly how this false image was made credible and believable. *Plebeian Politics* demonstrates that, when looking from the other side, the radicals had already prepared the groundwork for the new Tories by establishing Pitt's reputation associated with the anti-radical legislation of the 1790s.

Despite his apparent connections with the United Englishmen, Walker's radicalism was reactive rather than republican. Walker did not directly call for universal manhood suffrage or annual parliaments, demands that were common in earlier radical propaganda but had been quietened by government and local loyalists from the mid-1790s.[20] Rather, the pamphlet represented a burst of anti-loyalist energy suited to the brief interlude of peace. The use of dialect and vernacular mode marked an assertion of regional identity and an appeal to the then isolated radical survivors in the locality. 'Theaw kon ekspect no mooar eawt ov a pig thin a grunt' was also a sardonic gibe at local elites, who regarded dialect with disdain. In effect, it proved an effective disguise to express views against an establishment who, out of social and cultural prejudice, refused to understand them.

The Wilsons of Manchester

The Wilsons were a family who kept the radical dialect voice alive in Manchester during the dark days of the Napoleonic wars. It is unlikely that Robert Walker ever crossed their path as he died in 1803. Michael Wilson was the son of a Scottish handloom weaver. He and his sons became infamous locally for expressing their radical principles in some of the many oral ballads they composed. As with many such sources, however, only snippets remain for this period. These fragments were filtered through the lens of the Victorian antiquarian John Harland who collected and transcribed them. In April 1808, striking handloom weavers held mass meetings at St George's Fields in Manchester. The assemblies were put down by cavalry in a foreboding precedent for the 'Peterloo Massacre', the infamous suppression of the mass reform meeting on 16 August 1819. Michael's son responded to the St George's Fields incident by composing a ballad shortly afterwards:

> It was in the year one thousand eight hundred and eight,
> A lot of bold weavers stood in a line straight
> Then coom th' barrack sogers [soldiers] o in a splutter,
> And knock'd the poor weavers right into the gutter.[21]

Harland offered no clues as to where this ballad was sung or circulated, and it is only after the end of the Napoleonic wars that the compositions of the Wilsons appear to have gained local currency. They joined Samuel Bamford and other local poets and writers in a more fruitful literary period that emerged in tandem with the rise of 'mass platform' radicalism. The 'mass platform' involved large open air meetings addressed by Henry 'Orator' Hunt and other prominent speakers; it was accompanied by a carnivalesque culture of processions, of which songs and bands of music were an integral part.[22] Radical alternative words were easily malleable to popular tunes, and such music formed an essential part of the identities of local working-class inhabitants. The reform agitation culminated at the 'Peterloo Massacre' of 1819. Michael Wilson composed a fitting response to the tune of 'God Save the King':

> Chorus: For the gentlemen cavalry,
> Cut 'em down cleverly;
> Real Royal yeomanry!
> Cavalry brave!
> Mr Hunt neaw coom forrard an' spoke a few words,
> When the Peterloo cut-my-throats shaken'd ther swords,
> Aw thowt sure enoof they wur runnin' ther rigs,
> Till aw seed moor nor twenty lay bleedin' like pigs.
> Boh let's ta'e a peep o' these Peterloo chaps,
> 'At ma'es sich a neyse abewt cullers an' caps,
> See what they'n composed on, an' then we may judge,
> For it runs i' mi moind 'ot ther loyalty's fudge.[23]

'The Peterloo Massacre' mixed standard English and dialect to render the song accessible and comprehensive to a wider audience whilst still maintaining a distinctively Mancunian flavour.

Other radical writers were quick to express their anger at Peterloo in song, print and other forms of material propaganda.[24] Yet apart from the Wilsons' efforts, few of the published rejoinders appear to have been in dialect. The radical leader and author Samuel Bamford of Middleton produced a voluminous output of writing, including extensive descriptions of radical activity in Manchester in 1810s and of his trial for involvement at Peterloo. His most famous piece, 'A Song of Slaughter', was written during his incarceration in Ilford Gaol. It was first published by Henry Hunt in his *Letter to Radical Reformers* of July 1820:

> Thou hast made us to inherit
> Strength of body, daring mind;
> Shall we rise, and, in thy spirit,
> Tear away the chains that bind?
> Chains, but forged to degrade us,
> O, the base indignity!
> In the name of God, who made us,
> Let us perish, or be free!

It quickly became the anthem sung at every radical commemoration of Peterloo throughout northern England in the 1820s. The song shunned the gruff and potentially comic tone of dialect in favour of emulating the gravité of Miltonic sentiments.[25] During the 1790s and early 1800s, the use of dialect was not a common feature of radical poetry and song. All the printed versions of the radical songs of Joseph Mather of Sheffield were all in Standard English. These included: the rousing 'Britons Awake!' which called upon local inhabitants not to support the Sheffield address supporting the royal proclamation against seditious writings in 1792; 'True Reformers' about the arrests of Thomas Hardy and Thomas Muir in 1793, and the well-known and popularly sung 'God Save Great

Thomas Paine' of the same year. Notably, Mather composed little after 1795 until his death in 1804.²⁶

Gareth Stedman Jones claims that it was only after the end of the Napoleonic wars that 'confidence in the moral and physical discrimination of a vernacular audience was far more visible'.²⁷ This chronology perhaps should be pulled back until even later than 1819. *Plebeian Politics* and the songs of the Wilsons were the first concerted attempts to connect dialect indelibly with political undertones. In the introduction to his pamphlet, Walker emphasized (in Standard English) that he employed the 'Lancashire idiom' despite it being 'despised by the aristocratic and literary pride of a Burke'. He connected the use of the 'rich vein of forcible expressions' in the Lancashire dialect with independence of thought. Hence he hoped:

> that the county of Lancaster, as well as every other county in England, may yet contain:
> 'Some village Hampden, who with dauntless breast,
> Can bay the little tyrant of his cot;
> Tho' when he sees his country's wrongs redress'd,
> Can rest contented with his humble lot'.²⁸

Perhaps out of a sense of populist idealism, historians and literary critics have attempted to find the 'genuine' voice of working-class opinion in dialect writing. Brian Hollingworth believed in a close connection between the use of dialect in literature and expression of 'the values and insights of working-class communities'. This perception was fostered by Victorian antiquarians.²⁹ Yet dialect literature could never be a completely 'authentic' representation of the voice of the working classes. As soon as any popular song was committed to print, it lost some of its immediate context, and evolved to appeal to the market. Middle-class writers and compilers of broadsides and dialect literature shaped their content, which then circulated back into popular usage to be altered again.

Martha Vicinus has noted that after the death of Robert Burns in 1796 until about 1850, self-educated working-class writers 'lacked sufficient confidence in themselves and their own culture to write seriously in dialect'.³⁰ Perhaps she underestimates the paucity of dialect literature in these years, but it is evident that before the dialect revival of the mid-Victorian period, dialect and speech were scrutinized within the framework of class and respectability. Northern dialect and accent was often regarded as a mark of ill-education and of working-class status. For example, James Adams lamented in his *Appendix to his Pronunciation to the English Language* (1799) that 'education and absence from the country never entirely hide the Lancashire-man'.³¹ Northern authors and poets shied away from the vernacular to demonstrate accomplishment and respectability, and serious radical writers were no different. Self-educated working-class authors of such material were anxious to place dialect literature within the literary canon. Hence they commonly alluded to or emulated the Scottish bard Robert Burns, who was persistently involved as a justification for literary endeavours in the Northern dialects.[32] These tracts were produced by literary men writing in a literary milieu that demanded standardization and conformity. As Vicinus has argued, nineteenth-century dialect literature became so removed from 'folk culture' because it was 'the conscious product of literate individuals who wrote for their own class with encouragement from a wider audience'.[33] Later working-class poets focused on emulating 'nature poetry' and other literary forms that, as E. P. Thompson recognized, 'catch little of the weaver's authentic experience'.[34]

The conscious use of dialect while consciously drawing upon literary influences and structures of writing again problematizes assumptions that dialect was 'genuine'. Although the aim of the original Tim Bobbin and later dialect writers was to recreate the speech rhythms, inflections and narrative methods of the speech of ordinary people, even in the ballads and folk narratives, the widely-used conventions in dialect writing was immediately apparent. By the 1840s, an acknowledged method of annotating dialect speech had been established, which can be seen clearly in the work of Edwin Waugh and Elizabeth Gaskell.[35] Even Tim Bobbin's intention a hundred years earlier was to provide linguistic 'specimens' of interest. In the mid-nineteenth century, Samuel Bamford extensively annotated, corrected and also expurgated the *Tummus and Meary* dialogues.[36] Such dialect tracts were often a source of entertainment out of antiquarian interest for literary types, typified by the inclusion of a glossary of terms. Another problem is the genre itself, the comic dialogue. Dialect writing in this period was knowing, prone to stereotypes, exaggeration and furthermore came to be associated with certain genres and literary modes, particularly comic ones.[37] Tim Bobbin's *Tummus and Meary* quickly became the standard for dialect writing and was imitated to such an extent that later works almost became parodies of themselves.

In this volume, Stephen Dornan argues for the 'radical potential' of dialect writing during the time when potentially 'seditious' writers were being threatened by libel. The republishing of Tim Bobbin the first's works during the 1790s perhaps, as Dornan suggests, could be read as an attempt to seek alternative and hidden channels for political critique. Nevertheless, it is evident that radicals had a bitter-sweet relationship with the comic dialect genre. The relative lack of newly-composed dialect literature in print suggests that a desire for respectability overrode vernacular media. As John Barrell has argued in relation to the paucity of radical caricature, radicals sought to separate themselves from the grotesque comedy of 'vulgar conservatism' by employing classical portraiture.[38] As Maidment points out, it is hard to 'reconcile a belief in a radical self reliant, articulate proletariat with the quietest, domestic and humorous modes of most dialect writing'.[39]

Broadside Ballads

Plebeian Politics essentially failed in its goals. Olivia Smith notes that Daniel Isaac Eaton and John Thelwall found great difficulty in selecting an appropriate mode with which to address the 'swinish multitude'. Their efforts to parody the pig metaphor were only of limited success.[40] Thomas Spence and William Hone's use of the more plebeian chapbook genre seemed to be more promising. However, as Mark Philp and Kevin Gilmartin have suggested, the 'cheap repository tracts' produced by the loyalist Evangelical Hannah More formed the pinnacle of the more successful conservative adoption of the form.[41] *Plebeian Politics* came too late: the loyalists had already got the upper hand in popular literature, if they had ever lost it.

The few radical songs in the Manchester broadside collection are in Standard English, even though they often address local subjects. For example, a 'T. K.' of Ardwick near Manchester composed 'A New Song in praise of Colonel Hanson'.

> He assisted the poor in the time of their need.
> Till he went off to Lancaster town with great speed;
> He stood and the bar, he was tried and got cast
> But we hope that this hero will flourish at last.

Joseph Hanson was a radical manufacturer turned gentleman from Manchester. He was arrested and tried at Lancaster for having addressed the St George's Fields meeting of handloom weavers in 1808 (the same event that inspired the Wilsons to compose their song).[42]

We cannot leave Lancashire dialect literature without analysis of the most widely-known series of broadsides of the time, the 'Jone o'Grinfilt' ballads. These can be categorized as 'industrial folk song', a form that transferred the pastoral folk ballad into the urban context and embraced the commercial forms of the broadside.[43] Originally composed by a local schoolmaster in the mid-1790s, the verses were in a dialect that was deliberately toned down in print, though the print form still retained its essence and evoked its syntax and turn of phrase. John Harland remarked that local Paineite radicals soon issued a parody of the song. However, it 'never became popular and is supposed to be almost wholly forgotten'.[44] This could imply that the more numerous loyalist and patriotic versions were more popular. On the other hand, it could also suggest that the radical ballad was transmitted orally and was therefore less accessible to later antiquarians who collected the print versions. As with many stock characters, 'Jone' was manipulated to be a vehicle for various political messages. A radical version surfaced concerning the Queen Caroline affair in 1820 and he figured as a character in reform propaganda of the 1830s.[45] The second version, 'Jone O'Grinfilt junior', published at the end of the Napoleonic wars, was highlighted by E. P. Thompson in his exposition of the lively but 'socially conservative' popular culture of the weaving districts of the north:

> Aw'm a poor cotton wayver, as mony a one knaws,
> Aw've nowt t'ate i' th' heawse, un' aw've worn eawt my cloas.[46]

This version of 'Jone' was in essence a dialect version of what ballad historians have termed 'work-condition' ballads. Most of these referred in moving but only generic terms to the daily lives of the working classes in order to be as universal (and re-sellable) as possible. Some of the Manchester collection did comment on current economic conditions, for example, 'The Weavers' Garland or the Downfall of Trade', written by John Grimshaw of Gorton after the end of the Napoleonic wars. Other ballads on a similar vein included 'A New Song in Praise of the Weavers' by S. Wood, a Manchester shoemaker, which bemoaned:

> For weaving of late has been eclips'd amain,
> But the sun it will shine on the weavers again.[47]

'Distress of the Poor, a New Song' was another postwar classic that was likely to have been a nationally-circulated text that local printers altered according to the location:

> The spinners of Manchester loudly complain,
> How toilsome their labour, how trifling their gain,
> The hatters, the colliers and weavers also
> Are starving with hunger you very well know.[48]

Previous studies of 'occupational' songs again have suggested such ballads were a medium for voicing the grievances and aspirations of the working class. Yet it is difficult to prove that these were printed versions of songs in oral circulation in the weaving communities. Elbourne has argued that 'even if they began life as occupational songs, once taken up and exploited by a broadside printer, they became commercial products, significantly different in function from the original'.[49] A sense of 'ownership' or close attention to the travails of work could often be transmuted into essentially apolitical forms of entertainment.

Conclusion

Robert Walker, the Wilsons, Joseph Mather and other anonymous or now-forgotten writers and composers certainly felt that they had the power to change minds and politics through the medium of song, poetry and dialogue. We have seen how the lyrics or performance of certain ballads and dialect pamphlets directly or indirectly harboured radical sentiments or ideas of class. However, during the period 1795–1815, these were the exceptions rather than the rule.

Most radicals remained silent. Dialect material did not have the potential to subvert and was itself in abeyance in this period. The predominant form of ballad in the Manchester Central Library collection are patriotic or loyalist: versions of 'God Save the King', odes to Admiral Nelson or songs composed for particular volunteer regiments. This may have been to do with the political proclivities of their original printers or collectors, but it also reflected the fact that mass military mobilization in defence of the nation had become a major feature of life for the ordinary inhabitant during the French and Napoleonic wars. Even though Lancashire and the West Riding were at the heart of popular politics and radicalism in this period, we must not also underestimate the threads of loyalism and conservatism that bound most of the local populations together.

Even the highly popular 'work-condition' ballads, with their tales of poverty caused by the evils of manufacture, did not spur the working classes into action. The main purpose of ballads and dialect literature in the 1790s and 1800s was cathartic rather than inflammatory. As Brian Maidment has commented about the poetry of the Chartists in the 1840s, 'the social aggression in the poem often was sublimated or acted out rather than developed into action beyond the poem. Reading became to some extent a substitute for action, a self-contained political act without further implications'.[50] The legislation against seditious writings and assemblies in 1795, 1817 and 1819 in effect helped to internalize and individualize political thought to some extent by making certain types of recitation politically dangerous. Even to be seen reading such material privately but in public could also risk being classed as potentially seditious. The paucity of radical ballads, especially in dialect, compared with the profusion of patriotic broadsides also suggests that the oral tradition remained the only tradition for radical songs. *Plebeian Politics* gives us a clue in the form of its frontispiece: an illustration of the 'Saddleworth Sheawting Telegraph', in which a message was passed orally from fell to dale to cottage by individuals. An article in the *Bolton Chronicle* of 1831 suggested that oral tradition was still strong in rural areas: 'Sentiment is now propagated amongst the agricultural population, by viva voce communication, from farm to farm – from parish to parish – in their daily or Sunday meetings, in the same manner as before the invention of printing'.[51] In the urban milieu any potentially subversive material was confined to the sharply guarded privacy of the back rooms of pubs or the domestic realm of the working-class home. Radical songs only regained their public voice with the rise of the 'mass platform' after 1815, and even then, a search for respectability and national recognition dissuaded most from using dialect. Hence the radical song or dialect polemic remains lost to the historian dependent upon printed sources: we can only hear its faint echoes in the few antiquarian recollections that we have left.

AFTERWORD: THE LANGUAGES OF RESISTANCE

Katie Trumpener

In 1792, the Belfast Harpers' Society, an association dedicated to the preservation of traditional harp music, held a three-day festival. One Welsh harper and ten Irish harpers (six of them blind) competed against one another in playing the most beautiful parts of the repertoires (which were simultaneously transcribed by nineteen-year-old Edward Bunting, later to edit an influential, multi-volume anthology of Irish traditional music). Festival organizer Henry Joy McCracken had also helped found the United Irishmen Society the year before – and the Harp Festival was timed to overlap in Belfast with a major political convention that drew 6,000 Irish Volunteers and United Irishmen. Framing the harpers' performances were debates on Catholic Emancipation, processions, toasts to the Rights of Man and the fall of the Bastille.

Wolfe Tone attended some of the harp performances, but was not impressed: 'July 11th. All go to the Harpers ... poor enough; ten performers; seven execrable ... No new musical discovery ... July 13th. The Harpers again. Strum, strum and be hanged.'[1]

Yet today the festival is remembered not only as an important ancestor of the modern folk festival, but as a crucial, if transient, conjuncture between cultural and political nationalism. In the festival's wake, indeed, the United Irishmen adopted the harp as their emblem, and the motto 'It is New Strung and Shall be Heard'.[2]

Musicians, scholars, radicals: some 200 years after the Belfast Festival, academics from across the Anglophone world, antiquaries and practicing musicians from various parts of Britain once again gathered in Belfast to hear both scholarly papers and musical performances. In the intervening centuries, both English and history had become established academic disciplines – and now the academics outnumbered the performers many times over. The framework, too, had changed – no longer an attempt to gather Ireland's living antiquities but rather to think about the intersection of song and politics across the British Isles in the era of the Harpers' Festival.

In the interim, too, that period had come to be understood – or at least labeled – using the rubric of Romanticism, a tag which would have been unrecognizable either to Bunting or to his harpers. On the academic side, 'United Islands?' involved a range of efforts to think about the often unquestioning equation between 'Romanticism' as a diffuse literary and lifestyle movement and the late eighteenth- and early nineteenth-centuries' myriad forms of political activity. Some papers recontextualized canonical Romantic poets: Julia Wright described Drennan's intricate relationship to the palimpsest of Irish history, while Luke Gibbons, evoking Thomas Moore, tried to define an Irish romantic sensibility deliberately turned away from the Wordsworthian ideal of inwardness. Leith Davis and Frank Ferguson examined the politics (and gender politics) of the Romantic editorial projects of Charlotte Brooke and Thomas Percy; Nigel Leask and John Barrell reexamined poetic concepts like 'pastoral' within the political framework of the 1790s.

There were also preliminary attempts to define the parameters of radical poetry in this period, and to sound its depths (or shallows). Andrew Carpenter surveyed a vast array of erotic poetry, offered as evidence for a popular libertinism, amounting to a kind of sexual radicalism. In Wales, Ireland and Scotland, conversely, radical sentiment often remained inextricably connected to meditations on tradition and traditional poetic forms. In Wales, as for the Welsh in London, Mary-Ann Constantine demonstrated, radical poetry evoked both bardic and druidic precedents. Vincent Morley analyzed a long-standing vein of Irish Gaelic poetry with an equally long-standing preoccupation with the motif of lament; in light of this tradition, late eighteenth-century poems that might be construed as political protest did not finally appear to be all that deeply affected by – or particularly expressive of – historical developments specific to the Jacobin period. Peter Mackay, conversely, found a clear strand of rights-of-man sentiment in Scots Gaelic poetry. Yet the politics of this poetry, too, remains complex and elusive. For it too remained infused with an older mode of lament inspired by Jacobitism – a utopian political traditionalism not really 'radical' in the sense used in the 1790s. John Barrell's closing remarks evoked the wide range of English radical poetry.

The conference's musical performances, meanwhile, demonstrated the vast generic range of the radical song repertory: ballads, hymns, satires, elegies, anthems, erotic songs, drinking songs, heroic songs, sea songs ... Some of the most memorable songs seemed to *perform* as well as evoke or index political struggle. As the audience realized a few notes in, one Jacobin protest song was being sung to the tune of 'God Save the King.' Now, however, the lyrics pulled in a very different direction than the 'standard' ones. A very familiar – and quintessentially 'loyalist' – tune was being occupied by a new set of words, which essentially inverted or undid the original pairing between song and melody. And the incongruous, subversive juxtaposition moved the audience to smiles, chuckles, even outright laughter.

Even more startlingly was the macaronic song, sung by Dafydd Idris Edwards, which dramatized political tensions in its alternation between Welsh and English (see Appendix below). Edwards prefaced his performance by explaining that until the twentieth century, the Welsh court system was bedeviled by the lack of a shared language, since the judges rarely understood Welsh, while the accused rarely understood English. What his song then recreated performatively was the court's ensuing bedlam, as two monolingual speakers talk past one another – and the attempted intervention of an inept translator makes everything even worse. Yet the auditors of the song, at least, had begun to grasp the complexity of Wales' legal and cultural situation. Exactly who, we might wonder, was the song's intended audience? A small bilingual elite able to get *all* the jokes? Two half-audiences, each fully apprized of one, 'comprehensible' end of the song and mystified, like the song's protagonists, by the other?

This macaronic song provides a good metaphor for the larger 'United Islands?' project. The conference represented a first pooling of sources and knowledge. Those in attendance heard and learned of many things they had never even known existed. As a whole, the conference as a whole imparted a sense of a vast, polylingual, perhaps virtually inexhaustible body of primary sources. Yet we are still a long way from having a full genealogy, map or macro-analysis of these traditions, or even a full sense of their scale. We still do not fully understand the overlaps between poem and song traditions, nor how much thematic overlap – or even overlap of repertoire – there might be between Irish, Scottish, Welsh and English song traditions. And as several participants stressed, we do not yet know enough about the role of women as singers, authors and editors.

Nor do we understand much, so far, about the diasporic dimensions of these radical traditions. Yet the question of diaspora emerged repeatedly both during the conference papers (especially in the work of Kevin Whelan) and during the song performances. One song was set in Australia; another, a Welsh abolition song, was apparently sung on a ship carrying freed slaves to Sierra Leone. In ways still to be specified, then, the radical song repertory seems linked to the question of the overseas Empire.

We have more to learn, too, about possible routes of diffusion within Britain itself. Catriona Kennedy noted appearances of the same poem in Lancashire, Scotland and Wales. How might we track such occurrences on a larger scale? When Bastille Day celebrations were held, in various parts of the Isles, which songs were played (or poems recited) and were there overlaps in repertoire from place to place? It seems clear that 'The Marseillaise', at least, circulated everywhere, in almost every conceivable British Isles language, but we do not yet know much about how it was absorbed. Under what range of circumstances, moreover, were radical songs sung? To answer this question would require much more detective (and archival) work, but there must be traces of many performances of radical song in diaries, letters, memoirs, and novels, in newspaper reports and possibly even police informer records as well.

Such sources might yield a lot of information about what singing practice was actually like, who is singing, what they are singing, how they are singing, and what their songs *meant* to their auditors. From the pioneering mid-twentieth-century work of Zoltan Kodaly and A. L. Lloyd onward, ethnomusicologists have tried to think about the social function and occasion of song – and their questions and paradigms would be helpful in thinking about radical song, as well.[3]

The phenomenon of macaronic song may merit particularly close attention. For as the particular example sung by Dafydd Idris Edwards suggests, the mode permits the whole nexus of language and cultural politics to be quite literally encoded into a song, meeting in a kind of linguistic and cultural showdown. Recent critical work on Richard and Maria Edgeworth's *Essays on Irish Bulls* (1802) might offer a helpful point of comparison. For the Edgeworths' treatise is now generally read as a meditation which redeems apparent acts of parapraxis as emblematic of linguistic and cultural bilingualism – and of unusual windows into the linguistic deep structures and political tensions underlying colonial Ireland.[4] At least in some situations, macaronic song seems to follow a similar logic – and offer a similarly revelatory sense of how political conflict is manifested as form. The resetting of songs, likewise, can constitute a similar political act of political desecration or of blasphemy – enabling political dissonance and divergence to become lodged in the formal structure of the song itself.

As Claire Connolly suggested in her closing remarks, we need to think more about the posterity of this song repertory, what it means for nineteenth-century literary culture and for the lingering culture of sensibility. Many nineteenth-century novels, for instance, use poetic epithets or song verses as their chapter headings. What did it mean for Britain's inhabitants to have an overlapping body of songs, including songs of political critique or defiance, in their heads? What happened when people go to the theatre, or gathered in the pub, and heard certain songs sung again? Or when they read novels and found these songs being evoked and hence reactivated in readers' heads and ears?

Leith Davis' paper positioned itself in relationship to the new, multi-disciplinary interest in performance. Yet despite this performative turn, song remains understudied in universities, for obvious historical and disciplinary reasons. Musicologists, textual analysts, and performers still tend to have mutually exclusive skill sets, very different modes of analysis, and generally considerable suspicion towards the others' modes of analysis (even when, as in the case of musicologists and literary critiques, there are obvious methodological parallels).

The challenge is to approach the song as a kind of pocket *Gesamtkunstwerk*, which habitually meshes melody, words, poetry, voice and performance, often creating a very powerful – and lasting – effect on auditors. In diaries, in poetry and in novels, some auditors remember the singing of songs heard years – or even decades – ago, if the circumstances were right and if the performances were affecting enough.

To be sure, the Welsh song about the breakdown of communications in the courtroom –and the radical song set to the tune of 'God Save the King' – represent the opposite scenario, songs in which everything *does not* come together, in which everything rather falls apart; the levels of song which usually mesh in performance remain mismatched and disjunct. Luke Gibbons' discussion of Moore stressed its appeal to a 'sensorium' – and that is a helpful term to think about song as well. Song has a somatic, subcutaneous effect on its listeners; it creeps into their bodies and nervous systems, moving them to sway or to weep. Music stirs the body – and song hence has a different, potentially deeper and more transformative effect on auditors than words alone would. Song was thus a crucial weapon in the rhetorical arsenal of political radicals – and of their opponents (who on occasion used the singing of traditional religious and political anthems to buttress opposition to change).

Between them, historians and literary historians may be able to reconstruct the world of radical poetry. Radical song is a more elusive, more ephemeral and perhaps more complex object. Its reconstruction truly necessitates a collaborative approach, pooling expertise not only in a range of cultural and linguistic areas but across various disciplines, while bringing together the worlds of academic analysis and of performance.

A further gathering of those who work on poetry and those who work on performance might well explore issues of metrics and prosody. At the 'United Islands?' conference, Terry Moylan mentioned that Ulster singing uses a syllabus style, and Andrew Carpenter mentioned that Irish song uses assonance while English song uses syllabic patterns. Conference discussion of Thomas Moore's 'The Canadian Boat Song', moreover, raised the question as to whether the rippling of surface of the water, under the oarsmen's strokes, was mirrored by a metrical rippling effect on the surface of the song. What is happening, poem for poem or song for song, at a tectonic level? And what happens to nationally-specific metrical traditions when repertoires overlap? Does the macaronic song register the clash of cultures not only as a clash of languages but as a clash of metrics? Does the radical poem challenge metrical as well as political tradition?

A Case for Comparative Literature?

'United Islands?' raises questions that are often within the domain of comparative literature. Yet despite comparative programmes at a range of British universities, this particular discipline has been relatively slow to take root in Britain, for reasons that seem linked, in part, to the same historical factors that have left Britain itself fissured and patently un-united.[5] Elsewhere in Europe – particularly in Central and Southeastern Europe – Comparative Literature took shape not only as one of many nineteenth-century disciplines preoccupied with cultural and philological comparison (that is, alongside linguistics, anthropology, sociology, and the modern language and literature fields) but as a means of making sense of the local, polyglot texture of linguistic and literary life, itself a legacy of the Hapsburg, Russian (and later also Soviet) empires, the nineteenth-century pull of cultural nationalism against the counter-pull of imperial cosmopolitanism.[6]

Britain itself might be understood – and in the eighteenth and nineteenth century, clearly understood itself – as a kind of internal empire, forged from the conquest of Wales, the conquest and occupation of Ireland, and an economically coerced union with Scotland. Like nineteenth-century Central Europe, eighteenth- and nineteenth-century Britain repeatedly confronted armed nationalist uprisings – in the Highlands in 1715 and 1745, in Ireland in 1798 and 1848 – as well as more diffuse, but also more constant subterranean undercurrents of nationalist resentment.

Yet the simultaneous expansion of Britain's overseas empire not only enhanced domestic wealth but also served a ventilation function, becoming a place to transport and exile political prisoners, and a place of emigration and settlement for populations deemed superfluous or economically redundant. Displaced aristocrats, discontented nationalists, frustrated intellectuals often joined these colonial settlements – or, more paradoxically, joined the British army, becoming part of the apparatus of empire.

On the one hand, the comings and goings of settlers, slaves, indentured laborers soldiers, merchants across the empire produced, as a by-product, new cross-cultural encounters and cultural forms, and a new cosmopolitanism within Britain itself. Yet in light of the empire's worldwide reach and its increasingly huge cultural and linguistic diversity, the cultural differences constitutive of Britain itself came to seem smaller and smaller, especially in the view of English academic life. As Robert Crawford has argued, the study of English literature as a university discipline originated at Scottish universities, highly conscious of the divides of culture, tradition and language use still separating Scotland from England. And as Gauri Vishnawatan has established, the introduction of English literature as a constitutive part of the school curriculum took place in colonial schools in British India, representing not only a 'soft' cultural imperialism but a means of offering an emphatically secular curriculum, hence diffusing the Hindu-Muslim religious tensions exacerbated (or even, according to some recent scholars, instigated) by colonial rule and British Orientalists.[7]

Victorian intellectuals were excited by the work both of the Orientalists and comparative philologists like Max Müller – and many sought cosmopolitan perspectives on literature, manifest not only in works like Matthew Arnold's *On the Study of Celtic Literature* (1867) but in the short-lived *Cosmopolis* (1896-8), a multi-lingual journal of ideas and literature, published simultaneously in Paris, Vienna, Amsterdam and St Petersburg as well as in London and New York.[8]

Yet the expansion of the British empire, paradoxically, pushed literary study in Britain *not* so much towards comparative linguistics and literature, as it did in nineteenth-century Central Europe, as towards a monumentalizing conception of *English* letters, understood as a kind of secular (if from some vantage-points, still sectarian) literary glue, a shared literary heritage which could hold together both Britain and its empire. By the early twentieth century, a nominally British, yet actually English-centred and English-dominated literary canon was being studied with increasing assiduousness in British universities and schools. The function of the literary canon, here as everywhere, was to shape and enshrine particular versions of the literary – and hence also the national – past. And despite its often philological emphasis, early university research into 'English' literary history implicitly marginalized the literary pasts of Wales, Scotland and Ireland, *especially* the long traditions, in all three countries, of literature in languages besides English.

Only in the last ten or twenty years has the teaching and disciplinary self-conception of English began to change drastically, mirroring Britain's increasingly conscious sense of itself as a post-colonial and multi-cultural society. For the last forty years, to be sure, the Booker Prize (founded in 1969, as an attempt to create an English-language equivalent of the Prix Goncourt) had regularly drawn literary attention to Anglophone writers; early winners, indeed, included Nadine Gordimer, V. S. Naipaul, Ruth Prawer Jhabvala, Paul Scott, Salman Rushdie, J. M. Coetzee and Keri Hulme. The cultural legacy of empire, and the ongoing process of decolonization, thus retained a high profile in British literary culture, yet only very slowly began inflect the teaching of English literature. (In former settler colonies like Canada, Australia and New Zealand, English departments had long taught regular courses on 'Commonwealth literature', yet until the 1980s, the implicit focus tended to be on 'white writing' and on the difficulties of founding off-shore versions of English literature.)

One turning-point, in retrospect, was *The Field Day Anthology of Irish Writing* (published in three volumes in 1991, with an additional two volumes published in 2002). Conceived in response to the then-ongoing civil war in Northern Ireland, the anthology gathered and juxtaposed writing from Ireland's apparently separate, sectarian and literary traditions. Because of this comparative dimension, the work might be seen as functioning, preemptively, as a kind of literary equivalent of a truth and reconciliation commission. (The anthology did stir intense controversy, yet not primarily for sectarian reasons. Instead, it was heavily criticized for its virtual exclusion of women writers – an omission recently rectified with the belated publication of two further volumes, devoted to Irish Women's Writing and Traditions.)

The last decade, moreover, has seen the establishment of new academic programs for comparative Scottish and Irish studies, particularly the Research Institute of Irish and Scottish Studies at the University of Aberdeen, founded 1999 and the Centre for Irish-Scottish and Comparative Studies at Trinity College, Dublin, also founded 1999. These new centres were created with the help of new government grants (in the United Kingdom from the Art and Humanities Research Council, in Ireland by the Higher Education Authority's Programme for Research in Third-Level Institutions); their work is buttressed academically by a range of conferences as by new publication venues like the *Journal of Irish and Scottish Studies*, and institutionally by new intra-university consortia like the Irish Scottish Academic Initiative (currently involving the University of Aberdeen, the University of Strathclyde, Trinity College Dublin, Queen's University Belfast and the University of Edinburgh). In present-day Britain and Ireland, indeed, the energies for comparative literary study may lie largely in such initiatives, rather than in any wide-scale push for comparative literature departments, at least as traditionally conceived.

Yet it may be useful to consider the disciplinary templates offered not only by area studies but also by comparative literature, as practiced in North America, in parts of continental Europe, in Asia and the Middle East, and in other countries worldwide. There it has functioned, throughout the postwar period, as a discipline or anti-discipline or metadiscipline, a venue for searching, recurrent debates about theory, method, interdisciplinarity and intermediality. Its recurrent discussions of the comparative method have generated a now rather standard repertory of issues: literary relations, mutual influence, parallel genesis, generic conventions. Yet Comparative Literature has also been deeply interested in questions of bilingualism, translation, literary nationalism, communication, and mutual intelligibility, alongside questions of theory, method, interdisciplinary and inter-medial work. Most recently, sparked by general discussions of globalization and ongoing curricular debates over 'world literature' courses, the field has begun examining questions of analytic scales, of literary analogs to world systems theory, and of the relationship between close reading and what Franco Moretti has called 'distant reading', the attempt to gain statistical purchase on whole literary milieus (or publishing industries).[9]

Such methods and methodological discussions are potentially of real utility in thinking about the British Isles as well, the more so given the multilingual nature of the traditions under discussion and comparison. The 1792 Belfast Harpers' Festival inaugurated a new chapter in British ethnomusicology. May the 2008 Belfast United Islands conference help inaugurate a new wing of locally-focused, locally-relevant comparative literature within Britain and Ireland.

Appendix

Hanes y Sesiwn yng Nghymru (The Great Sessions in Wales)
(Tune: Sweet Home / Diferion o Frandi)

A fuoch chi 'rioed mewn Sesiwn yng Nghymru,
Lle mae cyfraeth a ieithoedd yn cael eu cymysgu?
Rhai'n siarad Cymraeg, a'r lleill yn rhai Seisnig,
A nhwythau'r twrneiod yn chware'r ffon ddwyblig.
Efo'u ffol di ral, &c

Bu yno'n ddiweddar ryw helynt mewn treial,
A'r Ustus ar ddodwy wrth wrano'r y ddadal,
Gast o Gadwalad o Ben Ucha'r Nant
A giniawodd ar oen i Siôn Ty'n-y-Pant.

A Siôn aeth i gyfraith trwy lawer o boen,
I wneud i Gadwalad roi tâl am yr oen;
A chownsler o Lundain, dan godi ei glôs,
A gododd i fyny to open the case.

"Gentlemen of the jury:
Cadwallader's dog of the Head of the Nant,
Killed a fat lamb of John Ty'n-y-Pant,
We claim in this court without any dispute,
The value of the lamb, with all cost of suit."

Fe dyngai rhyw Gymro: "Mae'n hysbys i mi
Nad yw Cadwallad yn cadw'r un ci".
Y cownsler a waeddai: "Pray don't be in haste,
If he don't keep a ci well he does keep a gast."

Ond Siôn Robert Roland o Ben Isa'r Dre,
Ddaeth i gyfieithu pob gair yn ei le;
'Rôl sychu ei drwyn i gael edrych yn drefnus,
Ddechreuodd ar osteg i ddysgu'r hen Ustus.

"My lord and Gentlemen of the Jury:
A ci is a dog, and male is a gwrw,
So cow is a buwch and bull is a tarw,
And gast is a bitch – which shaking her cynnffon –
The same sex, my Lord, as your madams in London."

A'r hen Ustus dd'wedau: "It appears to me,
This man lost his lamb between gast and a ci;
The value of verdict we may easily rejoin" –

My Lord, 'twas a cigfran that killed the oen."
"A cigfran!

Against such a name there is no accusation,
It mentions a dog in this declaration,
But what is a cigfran? – I can't make a guess",
"My Lord it's a blackbird who lives upon flesh.

A bird that destroys such an innocent creature,
Of course, he must be of a ravenous nature,
He'll pick out your eyes, my Lord in a crack,
Just like an old lawyer, he's always in black."

Wel, cofiwch i gyd mai gwell yw cytuno,
Rhag ofn y cewch frathiad os ewch i gyfreithio,
A mynd yn y diwedd ar ôl cadw sŵn,
Fel yr aeth yr oen bach rhwng y cigfran a'r cŵn.

Jac Glan-y-gors (John Jones 1766–1821)

Dafydd Edwards, who quite brilliantly sang this song at the symposium, comments as follows: 'According to tradition, John Jones, from Denbighshire, North East Wales, better known as Jac Glan-y-Gors, moved to London in 1789, to escape being press-ganged into the navy. While he was there he got into further trouble by writing, *Seren Tan Gwmwl* ('Star Under a Cloud') in 1795 and *Toriad y Dydd* ('The Dawning of Day') in 1797. These pubications were inspired by Thomas Paine's *Rights of Man* (1791) and got him into trouble with the authorities, causing him to escape back to Wales for a period.

However, he is best known to us today as a writer of witty satirical ballads inspired by his friend, the poet and interlude writer, Twm o'r Nant. One of his subjects was the English judicial system imposed upon Wales, in a language which was foreign to the great majority of Welshmen, by the 1535–1542 Laws in Wales Acts, when Wales was effectively annexed by the English crown. The Acts removed both the ancient Welsh laws of Hywel Dda and the legal legitimacy of the Welsh language. This was a running sore for the people of Wales for centuries, with judicial rights of Welsh Language speakers being largely but not wholly resolved by the Welsh Language Act of 1993. In the 300 years after annexation, of the 300 judges who sat in the Great Sessions of Wales, around 30 were Welsh but few of them spoke the language..

This macaronic song, 'Hanes y Sesiwn yng Nghymru', tells of the utter confusion in a dispute between two farmers over the death of a lamb. They do not speak English, neither the barristers nor the judge speak Welsh, the intervention of a translator makes things worse, and by the end, no one is sure whether the guilty party is a bitch, a dog or a raven. And the moral of the story: sort out your own disputes, and do not trust English justice.

The mutual ill-feeling reflected in this statement is made by a court in 1723 when the crown appealed unsuccessfully for a re-trial following an acquittal in a murder case in Pembrokeshire: 'It was very disappointed to have justice done in Wales by a jury of Welshmen, for they are all related one to another, and would rather acquit a criminal than have the scandal that one of their relations would be hanged; and think to try a man in Wales for murder was like trying a man in Scotland for high treason, these being crimes not much regarded, in those respective places.'

NOTES

Noble, 'Introduction'

1. J. McGann, 'The Third World of Criticism', in M. Levinson, M. Butler, J. McGann and P. Hamilton (eds), *Rethinking Historicism: Critical Readings in Romantic History* (Oxford: Blackwell, 1989), p. 98.
2. For details, see the Acknowledgements section in this volume, also www.qub.ac.uk/unitedislands. To the present volume of edited proceedings, there is a companion volume: J. Kirk, M. Brown and A. Noble (eds), *United Islands? The Cultures of Radicalism in Britain and Ireland*, Political Poetry and Song in the Age of Revolution, vol. 3. (London: Pickering & Chatto, 2013).
3. H. Kearney, *The British Isles: A History of Four Nations* (Cambridge: Cambridge University Press, 1989), p. 6.
4. M. Warner, 'In the Time of Not Yet: Marina Warner on the Imaginary of Edward Said', *London Review of Books*, vol. 32, no. 24 (16 December 2010), p. 17.
5. See K. Trumpener, 'Afterword', in this volume.
6. R. Darnton, *Poetry and the Police: Communication Networks in Eighteenth-Century Paris* (Cambridge, MA: Belknap, 2010), p. 2.
7. Ibid., p. 4. See also www.hup.harvard.edu/features/darpoe [accessed 2 April 2012].
8. *Ça Ira* – 'it'll be fine'.
9. J. Barrell, 'London in the 1790s'. in J. Chandler (ed.), *The Cambridge History of English Romantic Literature* (Cambridge: Cambridge University Press, 2009), pp. 129–58.
10. Darnton, *Poetry and the Police*, p. 79.
11. Ibid., p. 11.
12. R. Darnton, 'Singing in the Streets of 18th-century Paris', *The Guardian*, Review Section. 4 December 2010. See www.guardian.co.uk/books/2010/dec/04/affair-fourteen-robert-darnton [accessed 2 April 2012].
13. *The Letters of Robert Burns*, ed. J. DeLancey Ferguson, 2nd edn ed. G. Ross Roy (Oxford: Clarendon Press), Letter 525, p. 166.
14. Ibid., Letter 528, p. 169.
15. B. Harris, *The Scottish People and the French Revolution* (London: Pickering & Chatto, 2008), pp. 118 and 134.
16. S. Wellington, www.sheena-wellington.co.uk.
17. G. Pentland 'Patriotism, Universalism and the Scottish Conventions, 1792–94', *History*, 89 (2004), pp. 340–60. Public Record Office, Treasury Solicitors Papers TS11/956/3507. William Skirving to Thomas Handy, 25 May 1793, p. 352.

18. The poem is rarely anthologized, but a text is to be found at www.poemhunter.com/poem/for-a-that-and-a-that-2.
19. *To bear the grie*: 'to hold supremacy', 'be pre-eminent'.
20. *And win the day for a' that!*: 'despite the odds'.
21. Th. Koditschek, 'T. B. Macaulay, Whig History and the Romance of Empire: Towards a "Greater Britain"' in T. Brotherstone, A. Clark and K. Whelan (eds), *These Fissured Isles: Ireland, Scotland and British History 1798–1848* (Edinburgh: John Donald Publishers, 2005), pp. 61–82.
22. T. Mayne, 'English, Scots and Irishmen, A Patriot Address to the Inhabitants of the United Kingdom', in B. T. Bennett (ed.), *British War Poetry in the Age of Romanticism: 1793–1815* (New York & London: Garland Publishing Inc., 1976) pp. 311–12.
23. This poem, not published till 1838, is in *The Canongate Burns*, eds. A. Noble and P. Scott Hogg (Edinburgh: Canongate, 2003), pp. 845–51.
24. S. T. Coleridge. This unamended version is in P. Magnuson, *Reading Public Romanticism* (Princeton, NJ: Princeton University Press, 1998), p. 89.
25. See E. Burke, *Empire and Community: Edmund Burke's Writing and Speeches in International Relations*, D. P. Fidler and J. M. Welsh (eds) (Boulder, CO: Westview Press, 1999), Introduction, pp. 18–29.
26. *The Poetical Works of Wordsworth*, ed. T. Hutchinson, (Oxford: Oxford University Press, 1956), pp. 18–19.
27. K. R. Johnston, *The Hidden Wordsworth: Poet, Lover, Rebel, Spy* (New York & London: W.W. Norton & Co., 1998), p. 147.
28. S. T. Coleridge, *Poetical Works*, ed. E. H. Coleridge (Oxford: Oxford University Press, 1967), p. 259.
29. Ibid., p. 258.
30. S. T. Coleridge, *Coleridge's Essays on His Own Times forming a second series of The Friend*, vol. 1. ed. S. Coleridge (London: Wm Pickering, 1850), p. 35.
31. Quoted by G. Vidal, *Inventing a Nation: Washington, Adams, Jefferson* (New Haven, CT: Yale University Press, 2003), p. 46.
32. W. Blake, *The Complete Writings of William Blake*, ed. G. Keynes (Oxford: Oxford University Press, 1966), p. 197.
33. J. McGann, 'The Third World of Criticism', p. 95.
34. L. Colley, 'Little Englander Histories', *London Review of Books*, 32:14 (22 July 2010), p. 13.
35. *The Canongate Burns*, pp. 814–19.
36. T. Paine, 'Letter to the Abbé Raynal', in M. Foot and I. Kramnick (eds), *The Thomas Paine Reader* (Harmondsworth: Penguin Classics, 1987), p. 166.
37. A. W. Wood, 'Kant's *Project for Perpetual Peace*', in P. Cheah and B. Robbins (eds), *Cosmopolitics: Thinking and Feeling Beyond the National* (Minneapolis, MN: The University of Minnesota Press, 1998), pp. 59–76.
38. For Paine, see *The Thomas Paine Reader*, Introduction, 'Paine's Ideology', pp. 19–29. For Kant, see R. B. Louden, *The World We Want; How and Why The Ideals of the Enlightenment Still Elude Us* (Oxford: Oxford University Press, 2007), pp. 55–7.
39. A. Noble 'Burns, Scotland, and the American Revolution', in S. Alker, L. Davis, L. and H.F. Nelson (eds), *Robert Burns and Transatlantic Culture*, (Farnham & Burlington, VT: Ashgate, 2011) pp. 31–51, at pp. 36–8.
40. R. Wells, 'English Society and Revolutionary Politics in the 1790s: The Case for Insurrection', in M. Philp (ed.), *The French Revolution and British Popular Politcs* (Cambridge:

Cambridge University Press, 2004), pp. 188–225. Also R. Wells, *Insurrection: The British Experience 1795–1803* (Gloucester: Alan Sutton Publishing, 1983).
41. S. T. Coleridge, 'Fire, Famine and Slaughter', *Poetical Works*, pp. 238–9.
42. See *The Mad Ox* and his unsigned responsibility for this and other pro-French writings. See 'The Politics of 'Frost at Midnight'', in Magnuson, *Reading Public Romanticism*, pp. 67–94.
43. Ibid., p. 83.
44. Ibid., pp. 83–4.
45. B. K. Bennett, *British War Poetry in the Age of Romanticism*, p. 7.
46. R. Palmer, *The Sound of History: Songs and Social Comment*, (London: Faber & Faber, 1988), p. 252.
47. J. Barrell, *The Spirit of Despotism: Invasions of Privacy in the 1790s* (Oxford: Oxford University Press, 2006), p. 6.
48. K. R. Johnston, *The Hidden Wordsworth*, p. 390.
49. K. R. Johnston, 'Whose History? My Place or Your's? Republican Assumption and Romantic Traditions', in D. Walford Davies (ed.), *Romanticism, History, Historicism: Essays on an Orthodoxy*, Routledge Studies in Romanticism (London: Routledge, 2009), pp. 77–102.
50. P. Hamilton, 'Introduction', in H. Glen and P. Hamilton (eds), *Repossessing the Romantic Past* (Cambridge: Cambridge University Press, 2006), p. 5.
51. M. Butler, 'Repossessing the Past: The Case for an Open Literary History', in M. Levinson, M. Butler, J. McGann and P. Hamilton (eds), *Rethinking Historicism: Critical Readings in Romantic History* (Oxford: Blackwell, 1989), pp. 64–84, at p. 68.
52. Ibid., p. 68.
53. Ibid., pp. 70–1.
54. P. Hamilton, 'Introduction', p. 1.
55. Butler, 'Repossessing the Past', p. 69.
56. *Report of the Secret Committee of the House of Commons, ordered to be Printed on the 15th March 1799*. Published by the Glasgow Constitutional Association (Glasgow: Printed and sold by D. Niven, Bookseller, Trongate, 1799), pp. 1–38.
57. D. Walford Davies and L. Pratt, 'Introduction: Devolving Romanticism', in D. Walford Davies and L. Pratt (eds), *Wales and the Romantic Imagination* (Cardiff: University of Wales Press, 2007), p. 3.

1 Scrivener, 'Reading the English Political Songs of the 1790s'

1. S. Chan, 'On Yankee Stadium Restroom Dispute, the City Settles', *New York Times*, 7 July 2009.
2. *Politics for the People*, vol. I (London: Daniel Isaac Eaton, 1794–5), pp. 377–99.
3. J. Thelwall, *An Appeal to Popular Opinion against Kidnapping and Murder* (London: J. S. Jordan, 1796), p. 48.
4. M. Scrivener, *Poetry and Reform: Periodical Verse from the English Democratic Press 1792–1824* (Detroit: Wayne State University Press, 1992), pp. 94–5.
5. D. Walford Davies, *Presences That Disturb: Models of Romantic Self-Definition in the Culture and Literature of the 1790s* (Cardiff: University of Wales Press, 2002), p. 158.
6. T. Hutchinson (ed.), *The Poems of Percy Bysshe Shelley* (Oxford: Oxford University Press, 1919), p. 570.
7. *Guardian*, 16, 30 March 1713, pp. 64–7.

8. G. Sherburn, *A Literary History of England: The Restoration and Eighteenth Century (1660–1789)*, vol. III (New York: Appleton-Century-Crofts, 1948), p. 733.
9. J. Aikin, *Essays on Song-Writing*, R. H. Evans (ed.), (London: R. H. Evans, 1810), p. 19.
10. Ibid., p. 27.
11. Ibid., p. 97.
12. Ibid., p. 33.
13. Ibid., p. 10.
14. Ibid., pp. 8–11.
15. Ibid., p. vii.
16. J. Thelwall, 'On Song-Writing', *Poetical Recreations of The Champion and His Literary Correspondents* (London: John Thelwall, 1822), p. 163.
17. Ibid., pp. 164–5.
18. T. Wright, *The Political Songs of England, From the Reign of John to that of Edward II*, E. Goldsmid (ed.), (1838; Edinburgh: Unwin, 1884).
19. Scrivener, *Poetry and Reform*, pp. 26–9, and idem, *Seditious Allegories: John Thelwall and Jacobin Writing* (University Park, PA: Pennsylvania State University Press, 2001), pp. 94–127.
20. Scrivener, *Poetry and Reform*, pp. 43–4.
21. 'Jacobin' is a misnomer for all but a small minority of the British radicals whose politics were generally closer to those of the Girondins, the deadly opponents of the Jacobins. The British reformers and radicals were called 'Jacobins' by their loyalist opponents. See my discussion of 'Jacobin' in *Seditious Allegories*, pp. 21–42.
22. An historian to emphasize this conservative, restorative quality of the reform movement is J. Epstein, *Radical Expression: Political Language, Ritual, and Symbol in England, 1790–1850* (Oxford: Oxford University Press, 1995).
23. Scrivener, *Poetry and Reform*, pp. 52–3.
24. Ibid., pp. 95–6.
25. Ibid., pp. 88–90.
26. *Gentleman's Magazine*, 63 (March 1793), p. 261.
27. Both loyalist songs are from B. T. Bennett's *British War Poetry in the Age of Romanticism 1793–1815*, O. Smith (ed.), archived (September 2004) in the Electronic Editions of *Romantic Circles*: www.rc.umd.edu/editions/warpoetry/ [accessed 16 March 2012].

2 Beal, 'Why Should the Landlords Have the Best Songs? Thomas Spence and the Subversion of Popular Song'

1. P. M. Ashraf, *The Life and Times of Thomas Spence* (Newcastle: Frank Graham, 1983), p. 12.
2. T. Spence, *The Important Trial of Thomas Spence* (London: A. Seale for T. Spence, 1803), p. 65.
3. Ashraf, *The Life and Times of Thomas Spence*, p. 19.
4. J. Murray, *Sermons to Asses* (London: J. Johnson, T. Cadell; Newcastle: W. Charnley, 1768).
5. D. B. Murray, 'Glas, John (1695–1773)', *Oxford Dictionary of National Biography* (Oxford: Oxford University Press, 2004), www.oxforddnb.com/view/article/10798 [accessed 5 April 2010].
6. Ashraf, *The Life and Times of Thomas Spence*, p. 11.

7. T. Spence, *The Grand Repository of the English Language* (Newcastle: Thomas Saint, 1775) Sig. A1 recto.
8. R. Robinson, *Thomas Bewick: His Life and Times* (Newcastle: The Author, 1887) p. 34.
9. P. M. Horsley *Eighteenth-Century Newcastle* (Newcastle: Oriel Press, 1971), p. 206.
10. For a full account of this, see J. C. Beal, *English Pronunciation in the Eighteenth Century: Thomas Spence's 'Grand Repository of the English Language' (1775)* (Oxford: Clarendon Press, 1999).
11. Spence, *The Grand Repository*, preface.
12. Spence *The Important Trial of Thomas Spence*, p. 59.
13. *The Newcastle Magazine*, January 1821.
14. H. Dickinson, 'Spence, Thomas (1750–1814)' *Oxford Dictionary of National Biography* (Oxford University Press, 2004), www.oxforddnb.com/view/article/26112 [accessed 31 March 2010].
15. T. Spence, *The Case of Thomas Spence, Bookseller* (London: printed for the author, 1792).
16. D. Bindman *The Shadow of the Guillotine: Britain and the French Revolution* (London: British Museum Publications, 1989), p. 56.
17. T. Spence, *The Restorer of Society to its Natural State* (London: printed for the author, 1801).
18. T. Spence, *Dhĕ Impŏrtănt Triăl ov Tŏmĭs Spĕns* (London: printed for the author, 1803); Spence *The Important Trial of Thomas Spence*.
19. Ashraf, *The Life and Times of Thomas Spence*, p. 84.
20. Handbill of 1801.
21. I. McCalman, *Radical Underworld: Prophets, Revolutionaries and Pornographers in London 1795–1840* (Oxford: Clarendon Press, 1993), p. 1.
22. K. Wilson, *The Sense of the People: Politics, Culture and Imperialism in England 1715–1785* (Cambridge: Cambridge University Press 1995), p. 67.
23. J. Uglow, *Nature's Engraver: a Life of Thomas Bewick* (London: Faber and Faber 2006), p. 118.
24. Ashraf, *The Life and Times of Thomas Spence*, pp. 86–7.
25. McCalman, *Radical Underworld*, p. 18.
26. *Spence's Songs, Part the Second* (London: Seale and Bates, 1811?). McCalman, *Radical Underworld*, informs us that this songbook had previously been dated at 1802 or 1807 but that Malcolm Chase had discovered watermark evidence for this later date. The British Library Catalogue gives the date as [1810?].
27. M. Scrivener, *Seditious Allegories: John Thelwell and Jacobin Writing* (University Park, PA: University of Pennsylvania Press, 2001), p. 97.
28. 'Cracket' here probably means 'cricket'. This makes more sense in context than the Northumbrian/Scots *cracket* meaning 'a low stool'.
29. Uglow, *Nature's Engraver*, p. 147.
30. Ashraf, *The Life and Times of Thomas Spence*, 189.
31. E. Burke, *Reflections on the Revolution in France* (London, 1790).
32. J. Addison and R. Steele, *The Spectator*, issue 70, 21 May 1711.
33. M. Chase 'From Millennium to Anniversary: The Concept of Jubilee in Late Eighteenth- and Nineteenth-Century England', *Past and Present*, 129 (1990), p. 143.
34. Ibid., p. 135.
35. The people in every district or parish in the world have undoubtedly, in strict justice, a right to collect the rents of their common property, and, after paying the taxes for the support of the state, &c. apply the remainder to their own use.

36. C. Mackay, *The Book of English Songs from the Sixteenth to the Nineteenth Century* (London: National Illustrated Library, 1851), p. 174.
37. T. Spence, *Pig's Meat, or Lessons for the Swinish Multitude*, 3 vols (London, 1793–5), vol. 1, pp. 98–9.
38. Ibid., pp. 250–1.
39. Ashraf, *The Life and Times of Thomas Spence*, p. 85.
40. J. Epstein, *In Practice: Studies in the Language and Culture of Popular Politics in Modern Britain* (Stanford: Stanford University Press, 2003), p. 89.
41. J. Barrell, 'Radicalism, Visual Culture, and Spectacle in the 1790s', *Romanticism on the Net*, 46 (2007), p. 10.

3 Constantine and Edwards, '"Bard of Liberty": Iolo Morganwg, Wales and Radical Song'

1. The song appeared, with another one composed by George Dyer for the same occasion, in Thomas Spence's *Pig's Meat: or Lessons for the People*, 3 (1795), pp. 58–9. It is reproduced in Walford Davies, *Presences that Disturb*, p. 144, in an important chapter devoted to Iolo as a model of 'Bardic Jacobinism'. For an account of the acquittal celebrations, see 'Celebration of the Event of the Late Trials for High Treason held at the Crown and Anchor Tavern, London, February 4, 1795', in *Cabinet of Curiosities* (London, 1795) and J. Barrell, *Imagining the King's Death: Figurative Treason, Fantasies of Regicide, 1793–1796* (Oxford: Oxford University Press, 2000), p. 403. For the life and work of Iolo Morganwg (Edward Williams) see G. H. Jenkins (ed.), *A Rattleskull Genius: The Many Faces of Iolo Morganwg* (Cardiff: University of Wales Press, 2005); G. J. Williams, *Iolo Morganwg – y Gyfrol Gyntaf* (Caerdydd: Gwasg Prifysgol Cymru, 1956); and P. Morgan, *Iolo Morganwg* (Cardiff: University of Wales Press, 1975). His radical legacy is discussed in G. H. Jenkins, *Bard of Liberty: The Political Radicalism of Iolo Morganwg* (Cardiff: University of Wales Press, 2012). For other publications from the recent AHRC-funded project see: www.iolomorganwg.cymru.ac.uk.
2. National Library of Wales (hereafter NLW) MS 21401E, p. 33. Iolo's visit to the dissenting preacher William Winterbotham in Newgate is discussed in G. H. Jenkins, *'Perish Kings and Emperors, but let the Bard of Liberty live'* (Aberystwyth: Centre for Advanced Welsh and Celtic Studies, 2006). For Newgate see M. T. Davis, I. McCalman and C. Parolin (eds), *Newgate in Revolution: An Anthology of Radical Prison Literature* (London: Continuum, 2005).
3. J. Mee, '"Images of Truth New Born": Iolo, William Blake and the Literary Radicalism of the 1790s' in Jenkins (ed.), *A Rattleskull Genius*, pp. 173–93.
4. Walford Davies, *Presences that Disturb*, p. 152.
5. This essay offers some preliminary findings from an AHRC-funded research project on Wales and the French Revolution at the University of Wales Centre for Advanced Welsh and Celtic Studies.
6. See F. M. Jones, *Welsh Ballads of the French Revolution* (Cardiff: University of Wales Press, 2012); see also E. W. James, 'Welsh Ballads and American Slavery', *The Welsh Journal of Religious History*, 2 (2007): pp. 59–86.
7. See, for example, G. H. Jenkins, F. M. Jones and D. C. Jones (eds), *The Correspondence of Iolo Morganwg*, 3 vols (Cardiff: University of Wales Press, 2007) [hereafter, *Correspond-*

ence]; M. Löffler, *Welsh Responses to the French Revolution: Press and Public Discourse, 1789–1802* (Cardiff: University of Wales Press, 2012).
8. See R. T. Jenkins and H. Ramage, *A History of the Honourable Society of Cymmrodorion 1751–1951* (London: Cymmrodorion Society, 1951) and, for aspects of the cultural revival in general, P. Morgan, *The Eighteenth-Century Renaissance* (Llandybïe: Christopher Davies, 1981).
9. See e.g. Walford Davies, *Presences that Disturb*, p. 145.
10. This was followed by *The Bardic Museum* (1802); see T. Ellis, *Edward Jones, Bardd y Brenin (1752–1824)* (Caerdydd: Gwasg Prifysgol Cymru, 1957).
11. Llwyd's important but neglected contribution to Welsh literature is currently being researched by Elizabeth Edwards.
12. F. J. Stafford, *The Last of the Race: The Growth of a Myth from Milton to Darwin* (Oxford: Clarendon Press, 1994); for a detailed discussion of Iolo's bardic persona see M.-A. Constantine, *The Truth Against the World: Iolo Morganwg and Romantic Forgery* (Cardiff: University of Wales Press, 2007).
13. For Iolo's much-drafted but never published 'History of the Bards', see C. A. Charnell-White, *Bardic Circles: National, Regional and Personal Identity in the Bardic Vision of Iolo Morganwg* (Cardiff: University of Wales Press, 2007), pp. 26–32, 169–250.
14. *Gentleman's Magazine*, LIX, part 2 (1789): pp. 976–7.
15. W. Owen, *The Heroic Elegies and Other Pieces of Llywarç Hen*, p. xlv. (Iolo was the unacknowledged author of most of the introduction to this collection).
16. For this period see M.-A. Constantine, '"This Wildernessed Business of Publication": The Making of *Poems, Lyric and Pastoral* (1794)' in Jenkins (ed.), *A Rattleskull Genius* (2005), pp. 123–45.
17. For an enlightening discussion of the uses of pastoral in radical periodicals of the 1790s, see J. Barrell, 'Rus in Urbe' in P. Connell and N. Leask (eds), *British Romanticism and Popular Culture in Britain and Ireland* (Cambridge: Cambridge University Press, 2009), pp. 109–27.
18. For Thomson in Wales, see K. McCue '"An individual flowering on a common stem": Melody, Performance, and National Song' in Connell and Leask (eds), *British Romanticism and Popular Culture*, pp. 98–100.
19. D. Huws, 'Iolo Morganwg and Traditional Music' in G. H. Jenkins (ed.), *A Rattleskull Genius* (2005), pp. 333–56; M.-A. Constantine, 'Songs and Stones: Iolo Morganwg (1747–1826), Mason and Bard', *The Eighteenth Century: Theory and Interpretation*, 47 (2006), pp. 233–51.
20. M. G. H. Pittock, *Scottish and Irish Romanticism* (Oxford: Oxford University Press, 2008); for poetic modulations of the language spectrum from English to Scots, see especially the discussions of Allan Ramsay, Robert Fergusson and Robert Burns.
21. For this 'lost' aspect of Iolo's legacy, see M. Löffler, *The Literary and Historical Legacy of Iolo Morganwg, 1826–1926* (Cardiff: University of Wales Press, 2007), pp. 126–9.
22. C. A. Charnell-White, *Detholiad o Emynau Iolo Morganwg* (Aberystwyth: Canolfan Uwchefrydiau Cymreig a Cheltaidd, 2009). For Iolo and Unitarianism see G. Lewis, 'Eighteenth-Century Literary Forgeries, with Special Reference to Iolo Morganwg' (University of Oxford D.Phil dissertation, 1991); D. E. J. Davies, 'Astudiaeth o Feddwl a Chyfraniad Iolo Morganwg fel Rhesymolwr ac Undodwr' (University of Wales Ph.D. dissertation, 1975).
23. For the hymns of Pantycelyn, see E. W. James, '"Blessèd Jubil!: Salvery, Mission and the Millenial Dawn in the Work of William Williams of Pantycelyn' in J. Kirk, M. Brown

and A. Noble (eds), *Cultures of Radicalism in Britain and Ireland* (London: Pickering & Chatto, 2013).
24. For a discussion of some loyalist and radical versions of the song and its performance contexts, see M. T. Davis '"An Evening of Pleasure Rather than Business": Songs, Subversion and Radical Sub-Culture in the 1790s', *Journal for the Study of British Cultures*, 12 (2005), pp. 115–26.
25. E. Williams, *Poems, Lyric and Pastoral*, 2 vols (London: J. Nichols, 1794), ii, pp. 132–5.
26. Ibid., p.133.
27. Different manuscript versions of the song in NLW 13148A give, very clearly, two different dates: 1793 (p. 292) and 1798 (p. 300). There is, however, no mention in the correspondence of 'Breiniau Dyn' before August 1798. See the letter from Thomas Evans (Tomos Glyn Cothi) to Iolo Morganwg, 4 August 1798 in *Correspondence*, ii, p. 96.
28. James, 'Welsh Ballads and Slavery'.
29. R. Thomson, *A Tribute to Liberty: or, A New Collection of Patriotic Songs* (London: Thomson, 1793), p. 5; Thomas Spence included this version in the second volume of *Pig's Meat* (1794), pp. 91–3. The minutes of the LCS for 13 September 1792 note that 'the Delegates of the Divisions No 1, 2 & 9 ... were directed to severely reprimand their respective divisions for a late undue assumption of power in ordering a song to be printed at the expence [sic] & in the name of the Society at large'. See M. Thale (ed.), *Selections from the Papers of the London Corresponding Society 1792–1799* (Cambridge: Cambridge University Press, 1983), p. 20. The question of the song's authorship is too complex to go into here, but it can be noted that the first stanza of Thomson's version also heads a similar poem to the same tune by the American poet, Philip Morin Freneau, in *Poems written between the Years 1768 and 1794* (Monmouth, N.J.: Freneau, 1795), pp. 445–6. His poem appears to have been written *c*. 1792–3.
30. In a letter to his wife Peggy, 19 February 1795, Iolo wrote: 'I was at the Old Baily, an eye and an ear witness to Pitt's perjury on the trial of Horne Tooke and of the evidence that was given by Mr Sheridan at the same time, and by the Duke of Richmond on Hardy's trial, in direct contradiction of what Pitt said'. *Correspondence*, i, pp. 661–2.
31. *The Irish Harp (attun'd to freedom), A Collection of Patriotic Songs; Selected for Paddy's Amusement* (Dublin, 1798), pp. 25–7. For the United Irishmen's deployment of popular song see G.-D. Zimmermann, *Songs of Irish Rebellion: Political Street Ballads and Rebel Songs 1780–1900* (Hatboro, PA: Folklore Associates, 1967), pp. 37–9; K. Whelan, *The Tree of Liberty: Radicalism, Catholicism and the Construction of Irish Identity 1760–1830* (Cork: Cork University Press, 1996), pp. 59–96.
32. Davis, '"An Evening of Pleasure"', p. 122. See M. Löffler, 'The 'Marseillaise' in Wales (via England)' in M.-A. Constantine and D. Johnston (eds, forthcoming) *'Footsteps of Liberty and Revolt': Essays on Wales and the French Revolution* (Cardiff: University of Wales Press).
33. Williams, *Poems*, pp. 134–5.
34. J. Barrell and J. Mee (eds), *Trials for Treason and Sedition*, 6 vols (London: Pickering and Chatto, 2006), iii, p. 403.
35. Ibid., iv, p. 310. For Goddard see Barrell, *Imagining the King's Death*, pp. 495–7, and for the text of 'Plant, Plant the Tree', Ibid., pp. 657–9.
36. See Barrell and Mee (eds), *Trials for Treason and Sedition*, iii, pp. 119 and 420 for examples of this.
37. G. H. Jenkins, '"A Very Horrid Affair": Sedition and Unitarianism in the Age of Revolutions' in R. R. Davies and G. H. Jenkins (eds), *From Medieval to Modern Wales: Historical*

Essays in Honour of Kenneth O. Morgan and Ralph A. Griffiths (Cardiff: University of Wales Press, 2004), pp. 186–7.
38. Evans, known locally as 'Priestley bach' ('Little Priestley') on account of his admiration for Joseph Priestley, tried to establish a radical Welsh-language periodical, *The Miscellaneous Repository, neu y Drysorfa Gymmysgedig*, in 1795.
39. Jenkins, '"A Very Horrid Affair"', p. 176.
40. NLW MS 2137D, f. 7. We are grateful to Marion Löffler for this reference.
41. NLW MS 21401E, f. 10. Original emphasis.
42. A. Liu, 'Preface' in D. Walford Davies (ed.), *Romanticism, History, Historicism: Essays on an Orthodoxy* (London and New York: Routledge, 2009), pp. xxiii–xx, here p. xv. See K. R. Johnston, 'Whose History? My Place or Yours?', p. 99, for a discussion of how the disappeared figures of the 1790s represent 'a central, although largely lost, part of a national cultural – and political – experience.'
43. See Löffler, *Literary and Historical Legacy*.
44. '[T]he cause of truth, justice and humanity, [is] a cause to which I long to be a martyr.' Iolo Morganwg to John Walters, 21 January 1794, *Correspondence*, i, pp. 648–9.
45. Ibid., p. 649.
46. 'Church and King rampant or Satan let loose for a thousand years', NLW 21401E, f. 6. Later in the same manuscript volume (f.29) Iolo has copied out portions of 'Church and King, a song', the source of which he notes as 'Gent. Mag^n 1793 March p. 261'. The stanzas Iolo has copied shows that this song was the 'Church and King' included in the counter-revolutionary song collection *The Anti-Gallican Songster II* (London, 1793).
47. See, for example, 'Y Letani Newydd' ('The New Litany') in *Hen Gerddi Gwleidyddol (1588–1660)* (Caerdydd: Cymdeithas Llên Cymru, 1901), pp. 30–2. We are grateful to Geraint H. Jenkins for this reference.
48. NLW 21401E, f. 3–4. Original emphasis.
49. Ibid., f. 9. Original emphasis.
50. See Barrell and Mee, *Trials for Treason and Sedition*, i, for the trial of Thomas Paine, and ibid., p. 53 for Sir Archibald Macdonald's address, which Iolo has paraphrased in his poem.
51. NLW 21401E, f. 9 Original emphasis.
52. See R. R. Davies, *The Revolt of Owain Glyn Dŵr* (Oxford: Oxford University Press, 1995).
53. NLW 21401E, f. 5.
54. Ibid., f. 11. Original emphasis.
55. We can see Iolo exploring different possibilities and valencies for his paratexts in different manuscript versions of the poem. Version two reads as a set of much more republican signs, in contrast to the quibbling, foolish Burkean nuances of version one: 'Liberty Hall. printed by the assigns of Thomas Paine, and sold by Sawney Mac Muir, at the sign of Algernon Sidney's Head, next door to the Common-sense-Coffee-house, Reason Row, in the year, One thousand seven hundred and nine o clock.' Ibid, f. 12. Original emphasis.
56. T. Spence, 'Examples of Safe Printing' in M. Scrivener (ed.), *Poetry and Reform: Periodical Verse from the English Democratic Press 1792–1824* (Detroit, MI: Wayne State University Press, 1992), p. 68.
57. See Barrell, *Imagining the King's Death*, pp. 108–14 for an account of the 'Chaunticlere' episode.
58. Iolo Morganwg to John Walters, 9 January 1794, *Correspondence*, i, p. 637.
59. Ibid.

4 Sweetnam, 'Canonicity and Radical Evangelism: The Case of Thomas Kelly'

1. For Kelly's biography see G. Carter, 'Kelly, Thomas (1769–1855)', *Oxford Dictionary of National Biography*, Oxford University Press, 2004, www.oxforddnb.com/view/article/46328 [accessed 29 March 2010].
2. Lady Powerscourt features prominently in the biography of John Nelson Darby. See M. Weremchuk, *John Nelson Darby* (Neptune, NJ: Loizeaux, 1992) and M. Field, *John Nelson Darby: Prophetic Pioneer* (Godalming: Highland Books, 2008).
3. See B. W. Gobbett, 'Inevitable Revolution and Methodism in Early Industrial England: Revisiting the Historiography of the Halevy Thesis', *Fides et Historia*, 29 (1997): pp. 28–43; A. D. Gilbert, 'Methodism, Dissent and Political Stability in Early Industrial England', *Journal of Religious History*, 10 (1979): pp. 381–99.
4. Activism, along with Biblicism, crucicentrism, and conversionism are the four emphases that Bebbington identifies as central to evangelicalism. See D. W. Bebbington, *Evangelicalism in Modern Britain: A History from the 1730s to the 1980s* (London: Unwin Hyman, 1989), pp. 2–17.
5. The interaction between evangelicalism and society is investigated in Bebbington, *Evangelicalism*; M. A. Noll, *The Rise of Evangelicalism: The Age of Edwards, Whitefield, and the Wesleys* (Nottingham: Inter-Varsity Press, 2004); D. W. Bebbington, *The Dominance of Evangelicalism: The Age of Spurgeon and Moody* (Nottingham: Inter-Varsity Press, 2005); and J. Wollffe, *The Expansion of Evangelicalism: The Age of Wilberforce, More, Chalmers and Finney* (Nottingham: Inter-Varsity Press, 2007).
6. C. Gribben, *Evangelical Millennialism in the Trans-Atlantic World, 1500–2000* (London: Palgrave Macmillan, 2011).
7. For a discussion of the influence of Trinity College Dublin on the postmillennial formation of Church of Ireland ministers, see G. L. Nebeker, 'John Nelson Darby and Trinity College, Dublin: A Study in Eschatological Contrasts', *Fides et Historia*, 34 (2002): pp. 87–108.
8. An outstandingly comprehensive survey of this context is provided in T. Stunt, 'Trinity College, John Darby and the Powerscourt Milieu', recording available online at http://trinitymillennialismproject.wordpress.com/2010/09/22/%E2%80%9Cthe-future-of-millennial-studies%E2%80%9D/ [accessed 16 March 2012].
9. See M. S. Sweetnam, 'Defining Dispensationalism: A Cultural Studies Perspective', *Journal of Religious History*, 34 (2010): pp. 191–212.
10. For the geo-political implications of dispensationalism, see P. Boyer, *When Time Shall Be No More: Prophecy Belief in Modern American Culture* (Cambridge, MA: Belknap, 1992). An overview of some aspects of its cultural impact is provided in C. Gribben, *Rapture Fiction and Trans-Atlantic Evangelicalism* (Oxford: Oxford University Press, 2009) and Sweetnam, 'Defining Dispensationalism', *passim*. See also E. R. Sandeen, *The Roots of Fundamentalism: British and American Millenarianism 1800–1930* (Chicago: Chicago University Press, 1970); T. P. Weber, *Living in the Shadow of the Second Coming: American Premillenialism, 1875–1925* (Chicago: Chicago University Press, 1979, expanded edition 1987); and G. M. Marsden, *Fundamentalism and American Culture: The Shaping of Twentieth-Century Evangelicalism, 1870–1925* (Oxford: Oxford University Press, 1980).
11. For a discussion of dispensationalism's Irish roots, see M. S. Sweetnam and C. Gribben, 'J. N. Darby and the Irish Origins of Dispensationalism', *Journal of the Evangelical Theo-*

logical Society, 52 (2009): pp. 569–77, and Nebeker, 'John Nelson Darby and Trinity College, Dublin', p. 87.There is no published scholarly biography of J. N. Darby. Three biographies are available: W. G. Turner and E. Cross, *Unknown and Well Known: A Biography of John Nelson Darby* (London: Chapter Two, 1990) is a new edition, with additional material, of a laudatory biography by a contemporary of Darby; Weremchuk, *Darby* and Field, *Darby* are more recent works. See also R. H. Krapohl, 'A Search for Purity: The Controversial Life of John Nelson Darby' (PhD dissertation, Baylor University, 1998). The role of J. N. Darby in the development of dispensationalist has been discussed by a variety of writers. F. R. Coad, *A History of the Brethren Movement*, 2nd edn (Exeter: Paternoster Press, 1976) is a classic study of Darby in relation to the Brethren movement. More recently, T. C. F. Stunt, *From Awakening to Secession: Radical Evangelicals in Switzerland and Britain, 1815–35* (Edinburgh: T. & T. Clark, 2000), has set him in a wider context, with relevance to this chapter. Questions of Darby's influences, with considerable relevance to this article, have been discussed in T. C. F. Stunt, 'Influences in the Early Development of J. N. Darby' in C. Gribben and T. C. F. Stunt (eds), *Prisoners of Hope? Aspects of Evangelical Millennialism in Britain and Ireland, 1800–1880* (Carlisle: Paternoster, 2004), pp. 44–68, and T. C. F. Stunt, 'John Nelson Darby: Contexts and Perceptions' in C. Gribben and A. R. Holmes (eds), *Protestant Millennialism, Evangelicalism and Irish Society, 1790–2005* (Basingstoke: Palgrave Macmillan, 2006), pp. 83–98. J. D. Burnham, *A Story of Conflict: The Controversial Relationship between Benjamin Wills Newton and John Nelson Darby* (Carlisle: Paternoster, 2004) provides further useful material.

12. F. F. Bruce, Review of *The Unbelievable Pre-Trib Origin* in *Evangelical Quarterly*, 47 (1975): p. 58.
13. S. T. Kimbrough, Jr, 'Hymns are Theology', *Theology Today*, 42 (1985): p. 59.
14. R. J. Mouw, 'Introduction', in R. J. Mouw and M. A. Noll (eds), *Wonderful Words of Life: Hymns in American Protestant History and Theology* (Grand Rapids, MI: Eerdmans, 2004), p. xvii.
15. For example, S. Sizer, *Hymns and Social Religion* (Philadelphia, PA: Temple University Press, 1978) and J. H. Hobbs, *'I Sing for I Cannot Be Silent': The Feminization of American Hymnody, 1870–1920* (Pittsburgh, PA: University of Pittsburgh Press, 1997).
16. J. R. Watson, *The English Hymn: A Critical and Historical Study* (Oxford: Oxford University Press, 1999), p. 4.
17. Ibid., p. 5.
18. Mouw, 'Introduction', pp. xiii, xv.
19. S. Marini, 'Hymnody as History: Early Evangelical Hymns and the Recovery of American Popular Religion', *Church History*, 71 (2002): pp. 273–4.
20. D. W. Stowe, *How Sweet the Sound: Music in the Spiritual Lives of Americans*, (Cambridge: Harvard University Press, 2004), p. 3.
21. E. L. Blumhofer, *Her Heart Can See: The Life and Hymns of Fanny J. Crosby* (Grand Rapids, MI: Eerdmans, 2005), p. 263
22. G. Carter, *Anglican Evangelicals: Protestant Secessions from the Via Media, c. 1800–1850* (Oxford: Oxford University Press, 2001), p. 58
23. Carter, 'Kelly, Thomas (1769–1855)', *Oxford Dictionary of National Biography*.
24. Kimbrough, 'Hymns are Theology', p. 66.
25. See D. J. A. Clines, 'Liturgy without Prayerbook', *Christian Brethren Research Fellowship Journal*, 15 (1967): pp. 6–18.
26. T. Kelly, *Hymns on Various Passages of Scripture*, (Dublin: J. and J. Carrick, 1806), p. 30.

27. Ibid., p. 157.
28. Ibid., p. 22.
29. T. Kelly, *Hymns on Various Passages of Scripture*, 7th edn (Dublin: Marcus Moses, 1853), p. 59
30. T. Kelly, *Hymns on Various Passages of Scripture*, 6th edn (Dublin: R.M. Tims, 1826), p. 342.
31. Kelly, *Hymns* (1806), p. 122.
32. Ibid.
33. Ibid.
34. For a far-ranging discussion of this issue see P. R. Wilkinson, *For Zion's Sake: Christian Zionism and the Role of John Nelson Darby* (Carlisle: Paternoster, 2007).
35. Kelly, *Hymns* (1853), p. 290.
36. Ibid., p. 616.
37. Ibid., p. 610.
38. Ibid., p. 612.

5 Davis, 'Charlotte Brooke's *Reliques of Irish Poetry*: Eighteenth-Century "Irish Song" and the Politics of Remediation'

1. J. Leersen, *Mere Irish and Fior-Gael, Studies in the Idea of Irish Nationality, Its Development and Literary Expression Prior to the Nineteenth Century* (Notre Dame, IN: University of Notre Dame Press, 1997), p. 363. C. H. Wilson's *Poems Translated from the Irish Language into the English* appeared in 1782, but it does not seem to have had the same force upon the public as Brooke's translations.
2. See Carolan's 'Monody on the death of his wife' in J. C. Walker, *Historical Memoirs of the Irish Bards. Interspersed with Anecdotes of, and Occasional Observations on the Music of Ireland* (London: T. Payne and Sons, 1786), Appendix 92. Walker notes of this poem: 'For the benefit of the English reader, I shall here give, with the original, an elegant paraphrase of this Monody by a young Lady'.
3. According to Jay Bolter and Richard Grusin 'remediation' is a process whereby one medium 'appropriates the techniques, forms, and social significance of other media and attempts to rival or refashion them in the name of the real'. J. Bolter and R. Grusin, *Remediation: Understanding New Media* (Cambridge, Mass.: MIT Press, 1999), p. 65.
4. Ibid., p. 11.
5. W. H. K. Chun and T. Keenan (eds), *New Media, Old Media: A History and Theory Reader* (New York: Routledge, 2006), p. 3. For an examination of 'media interactions' after 1800 see A. Piper, *Dreaming in Books: The Making of the Bibliographic Imagination in the Romantic Era* (Chicago: University of Chicago Press, 2009), quote at p. 8. For other reflections on media change and media history, see L. Gitelman, *Always Already New: Media, History, and the Data of Culture* (Cambridge, Mass.: MIT Press, 2006) and L. Gitelman and G. B. Pingree, *New Media, 1740–1915* (Cambridge, Mass.: MIT Press, 2003). B. Peters critiques the term; rather than 'new media', he suggests instead the examination of the 'renewable nature of media' in history. B. Peters, 'And Lead us Not into Thinking the New is New: A Bibliographic Case for New Media History', *New Media and Society*, 11 (2009): pp. 13–30.
6. M. McLane, *Balladeering, Minstrelsy and the Making of British Romantic Poetry* (Cambridge: Cambridge University Press, 2008), p. 6. See S. Newman, *Ballad Collection, Lyric,*

and the Canon: The Call of the Popular from the Restoration to the New Criticism (Philadelphia: University of Pennsylvania Press, 2007) and J. Sorensen, 'Orality's Silence: The Other Ballad Revival', *International Journal of Scottish Literature*, 2 (2007), at www.ijsl.stir.ac.uk/issue2/sorensen.htm [accessed 30 June 2009].

7. McLane, *Balladeering*, p. 22.
8. For further discussion of Ireland as colony, see D. Cairns and S. Richards, *Writing Ireland: Colonialism, Nationalism, and Culture* (New York: St Martin's Press, 1988); T. Eagleton, F. Jameson and E. Said (eds), *Nationalism, Colonialism, and Literature* (Minneapolis, MN: University of Minnesota Press, 1990); and L. Gibbons, *Transformations in Irish Culture* (Notre Dame, IN: University of Notre Dame Press, 1996).
9. R. Gillespie, *Reading Ireland: Print, Reading and Social Change in Early Modern Ireland* (New York: Palgrave, 2005), p. 3.
10. T. Barnard, 'Print Culture, 1700–1800' in R. Gillespie and A. Hatfield (eds), *The Irish Book in English, 1550–1800* (Oxford: Oxford University Press, 2005), pp. 34–58.
11. D. Lloyd, *Anomalous States: Irish Writing and the Post-Colonial Moment* (Durham: Duke University Press, 1993).
12. C. Brooke, *Reliques of Irish Poetry: Consisting of Heroic Poems, Odes, Elegies, and Songs, Translated into English Verse: with Notes Explanatory and Historical; and the Originals in the Irish Character. To which is Subjoined an Irish Tale* ([Dublin]: George Bonham, 1789), p. vii.
13. Ibid., p. 239.
14. J. Aikin, *Essays on Song-Writing: With a Collection of such English Songs as are most Eminent for Poetical Merit. To which are Added, some Original Pieces* (London: 1772) and J. Ritson, *A Select Collection of English Songs*, 3 vols (London: 1783). Ritson would go on to edit Scottish songs as well.
15. Although originally printed in 1724, Ramsay's *Tea-Table Miscellany*, along with his *The Gentle Shepherd* (1725), continued to be reprinted throughout the eighteenth century.
16. W. Tytler, Appendix No. VIII: 'A Dissertation on the Scottish Musick' in H. Arnot, *The History of Edinburgh, from the Earliest Accounts to the Present Time* (Edinburgh: William Creech, 1779), pp. 164.
17. For useful perspectives on traditional Irish music, see A. Fleischmann, *Sources of Irish Traditional Music, c.1600–1855*, 2 vols (New York: Garland, 1998) and H. White, *The Keeper's Recital: Music and Cultural History in Ireland, 1770–1970* (Cork: Cork University Press, 1998). See also L. Davis, *Music, Postcolonialism and Gender: The Construction of Irish National Identity, 1724–1874* (Notre Dame, IN: University of Notre Dame Press, 2005).
18. N. Carolan, *The Most Celebrated Irish Tunes: The Publishing of Irish Music in the Eighteenth Century* (Cork: Irish Traditional Music Society of University College Cork, 1990), p. 4. See also P. Holman, review of Barra Boydell and Kerry Houston (eds), *Music, Ireland and the Seventeenth Century, Journal of the Society for Musicology in Ireland*, 5 (2009–10): pp. 73–9; D. Johnson, *Music and Society in Lowland Scotland in the Eighteenth Century* (London: Oxford University Press, 1972).
19. The Neales' collection was heavily influenced by the Italian composer Lorenzo Bocchi, who had moved from Edinburgh to Dublin in 1723 – see P. Holman, 'A Little Light on Lorenzo Bocchi: An Italian in Edinburgh and Dublin' in Rachel Cowgill and Peter Holman (eds), *Music in the British Provinces, 1690–1914* (Aldershot: Ashgate, 2007), pp. 61–86.

20. Burns refers to his use of several 'Irish' airs in his correspondence with George Thomson. In a letter to Thomson in November, 1794, he also suggests the difficulty involved in 'trac[ing] the origin of our [Scottish] airs', given the fact that many of them are heard both in Ireland and Scotland. Quoted in D. Low, *The Songs of Robert Burns* (London: Routledge, 1993), p. 33.
21. See H. Burke, Esq., *The Songs in Jack the Gyant Queller. An Antique History*, 2nd edn (Dublin: George Faulkner, 1749).
22. H. Burke, *Riotous Performances: The Struggle for Hegemony in the Irish Theater, 1714–1784* (Notre Dame, IN: University of Notre Dame Press, 2003), p. 89.
23. D. Dugaw, 'Folklore and John Gay', *Studies in English Literature, 1500–1900*, 31 (1991): pp. 515–33.
24. H. Playford, *Wit and Mirth: Pills to Purge Melancholy* (London: William Pearson, 1707–9). C. M. Simpson writes, 'Begun as a two-volume anthology in 1699–1700, this work grew to five volumes in several editions published up to 1714. Its final six-volume edition of 1719–20 was edited by the well-known dramatist, song writer, and singer Thomas D'Urfey'. C. M. Simpson, *The British Broadside Ballad and its Music* (New Brunswick: Rutgers University Press, 1966), p. xiv.
25. H. Playford, *Songs Compleat, Pleasant and Divertive; Set to Musick by Dr John Blow, Mr Henry Purcell, and Other Excellent Masters* (London: William Pearson, 1719), pp. 244–5.
26. J. O. Bartley notes that a 'marked increase' in the number of Irishmen being represented on stage took place 'at the time of William III's Irish campaign'. J. O. Bartley, 'The Development of a Stock Character I. The Stage Irishman to 1800', *Modern Language Review*, 37 (1942), pp. 438–47.
27. A. Carpenter, 'Introduction' in *Verse in English from Eighteenth-Century Ireland* ed. A. Carpenter (Cork, Ireland: Cork University Press, 1998), p. 7.
28. 'Darby M'Hone's Lamentation. An IRISH SONG' in H. Howard (ed.), *Fun a la Mode, or, Sing, and Be Jolly; An Entire New Collection of Original Songs, Odes, Cantatas, &c. Critical, Comical, and Political* (London: J. Williams, 1763), pp. 47, 45.
29. Ibid., p. 47.
30. 'A New Irish Comic Song' in *Parsley's Lyric Repository, for 1789. Containing a Selection of all the Favorite Songs, Duets, Trios, &c. now Singing at the Theatres-Royal* (London: R. Parsley, 1789), p. 13.
31. 'A Favorite Irish Song' in *The Banquet of Thalia, or the Fashionable Songsters Pocket Memorial. An Elegant Collection of the most Admired Songs from Ancient, & Modern* ([London]: [1788]), p. 123. Subsequent references are to this edition.
32. Ibid., p. 123.
33. C. Dibden, 'Ballad in the Oddities' in *A Collection of Songs, Selected from the Works of Mr Dibdin*, 5 vols (London: [1790]), i, p. 205. See also the Advertisement in *The World*, Issue 908, 3 December 1789.
34. C. Dibden, 'The Irish Drinking Song' (London, 1790).
35. In her study of the changes in aesthetic taste that prepared the way for the fame of Robert Burns, Fiona Stafford remarks, 'The decades immediately preceding the publication of Burns's work [1786] had seen a steady shift in taste from the neoclassical ideals of harmony, order, and rational control to a new aesthetic that placed a higher value on wildness, originality, creative energy, and feeling'. F. Stafford, *Starting Lines in Scottish, Irish and English Poetry from Burns to Heaney* (Oxford: Oxford University Press, 2000), p. 53. See also P. Connell and N. Leask, *Romanticism and Popular Poetry in Britain and*

Ireland (Cambridge: Cambridge University Press, 2009); McLane, *Balladeering*; and K. Trumpener, *Bardic Nationalism: The Romantic Novel and the British Empire* (Princeton, N.J.: Princeton University Press, 1997).
36. *London Public Advertiser and Literary Gazette*, 'Letter', 12 September 1751; *Gentleman's Magazine* 21, 'Letter', 1751, p. 466.
37. T. Percy, *Reliques of Ancient English Poetry. Consisting of old Heroic Ballads, Songs, and other Pieces of our Earlier Poets (Chiefly of the Lyric Kind.)*, 3 vols (London, 1765), i, p. vi.
38. C. O'Conor, *Dissertations on the History of Ireland* (Dublin: 1753); Walker, *Historical Memoirs*. See also S. O'Halloran, *A General History of Ireland*, 2 vols (London: A. Hamilton, 1778); and C. Vallancey, *A Vindication of the Ancient History of Ireland* (Dublin: Luke White, 1786). For further discussion of Walker, see Chapter 2 of Davis, *Music, Postcolonialism and Gender*.
39. Walker, *Historical Memoirs*, p. 26.
40. Ibid., p. 68.
41. Ibid., p. 128.
42. Ibid., p. 128.
43. W. Beauford, 'Caoinan: or some Account of the Antient Irish Lamentations', *The Transactions of the Royal Irish Academy* (Dublin: [1787]–1800), IV: p. 45.
44. Ibid., p. 43. Timothy Taylor suggests how 'eccentric musical techniques' like 'chromaticism, dissonance, avoidance of a tonal center', 'lack of goal orientation' and 'metrical changes and/or ambiguity' became 'devices for representing Others, gendered or racialized' in eighteenth-century opera. T. Taylor, 'Peopling the Stage: Opera, Otherness and New Musical Representations in the Eighteenth Century', *Cultural Critique*, 36 (1997), pp. 55–88, quote at p. 64.
45. Beauford, 'Caoinan', p. 46.
46. Brooke, *Reliques*, p. 237.
47. Ibid., p. 233.
48. Ibid., p. 233.
49. Ibid., p. 234.
50. Ibid., p. 236.
51. Ibid., p. 237.
52. Ibid., p. 238.
53. Ibid., p. 238.
54. As a woman, Brooke was not permitted to become a member of the Royal Irish Academy, which was founded in 1785. She did apply, however, to Bishop Percy for help in her bid to become housekeeper to the Academy, but she was denied the post.
55. Brooke, *Reliques*, p. vii.
56. Ibid., p. iii.
57. Ibid., Advertisement to Poem of Conloch, n.p.
58. Walker, *Historical Memoirs*, p. 158.
59. Brooke, *Reliques*, p. 245.
60. Ibid., p. 260.
61. Ibid., p. 214.
62. Ibid., p. 215.
63. Ibid., p. 18.
64. In his Preface, Walker indicates that he has relied on the help of Theophilus O'Flanagan in order to compensate for his 'confined' knowledge of Gaelic. Walker, *Historical Memoirs*, p. viii.

65. Brooke, *Reliques*, p. 199. The *Reliques* was also the first eighteenth-century publication in Ireland to be printed using a special Gaelic font, a fact which suggests Brooke's concern to do justice to the original Gaelic productions.
66. Brooke, *Reliques*, p. 261.
67. Ibid., p. 251.
68. Ibid., p. 252.
69. Ibid., pp. 248–9.
70. Ibid., p. 233.
71. Ibid., p. 229.
72. Ibid., p. 230.
73. Ibid., p. 232.
74. Ibid., p. 230.
75. Ibid., p. 231.
76. Ibid., p. 233.
77. Ibid., p. vii.
78. Brooke was obviously concerned to avoid the accusations that had been leveled at James Macpherson for his Ossianic poems. But her inclusion of originals for every single poem and song suggests more than a concern to appear more authentic than Macpherson.
79. Brooke, *Reliques*, p. 205.
80. Ibid., p. 206.
81. Ibid., p. 245.

6 Morley, 'Homology, Analogy and the Perception of Irish Radicalism'

1. See *Oxford English Dictionary*, 2nd edn (Oxford: Oxford University Press, 1989), under 'radical'.
2. For an overview, see H. T. Dickinson, *The Politics of the People in Eighteenth-Century Britain* (New York: St Martin's Press, 1994), chapter 7.
3. For an overview of radicalism in Ireland, see J. Smyth, *The Men of No Property: Irish Radicals and Popular Politics in the Late Eighteenth Century* (Dublin: Gill and Macmillan, 1992), chapter 4.
4. V. Morley, *Washington i gCeannas a Ríochta: Cogadh Mheiriceá i Litríocht na Gaeilge* (Dublin: Coiscéim, 2005), p. 88. I have normalized the spelling and punctuation of quotations in Irish.
5. Gaelic 6, MS Boston College, Burns Library, p. 128.
6. Morley, *Washington i gCeannas*, p. 88.
7. Ibid., pp. 88–9.
8. P. Ua Duinnín (ed.), *Eoghan Ruadh Ua Súilleabháin* (Dublin: Connradh na Gaedhilge, 1923), p. 23.
9. P. Ua Duinnín, *Cill Áirne* (Dublin: Connradh na Gaedhilge, 1902), p. 60 and V. Morley, 'The Idea of Britain in Eighteenth-Century Ireland and Scotland', *Studia Hibernica*, 33 (2004–5): p. 122.
10. 23 M 14, MS Royal Irish Academy, p. 221.
11. Ibid., p. 223.
12. Ibid., p. 224.
13. Ibid., pp. 224–5.

14. I have discussed some of these points in V. Morley, 'The Continuity of Disaffection in Eighteenth-Century Ireland', *Eighteenth-Century Ireland*, 22 (2007): pp. 189–205.
15. M 11, MS NUI Maynooth, p. 269.
16. V. Morley, 'Hugh MacCurtin: An Irish Poet in the French Army', *Eighteenth-Century Ireland*, 8 (1993): pp. 49–58.
17. Ú. Nic Éinrí (ed.), *Canfar an Dán: Uilliam English agus a Chairde* (Dingle: An Sagart, 2003), p. 144.
18. R. Ó Foghludha (ed.), *Cois na Bríde: Liam Inglis O.S.A. 1709–1778* (Dublin: Oifig Díolta Foillseacháin Rialtais, 1937). See also, É. Ó Ciardha, 'A Voice from the Jacobite Underground: Liam Inglis' in G. Moran (ed.), *Radical Irish Priests 1660–1970* (Dublin: Four Courts Press, 1998), pp. 16–39. A modern anthology of his verse, edited by Úna Nic Éinrí, appeared in 2003 and set a precedent for the presentation of eighteenth-century Irish verse in that the book was accompanied by a CD containing recordings of twenty of English's songs – including the current example – sung by Pádraig Ó Cearbhaill. Nic Éinrí, *Canfar an Dán*.
19. S. Conway, *War, State, and Society in Mid-Eighteenth-Century Britain and Ireland* (Oxford: Oxford University Press, 2006), p. 258.
20. É. Ó Muirgheasa (ed.), *Dhá Chéad de Cheoltaibh Uladh* (Dublin: Oifig Díolta Foillseacháin Rialtais, 1934), p. 40.
21. The song beginning 'My name is Freedom, new come o'er' is found in *Paddy's Resource, or the Harp of Erin, Attuned to Freedom; Being a Collection of Patriotic Songs Selected for Paddy's Amusement* (Dublin: 'By the printer hereof', no date), pp. 117–18. Internal references indicate that the collection was published some time later then 1798 and may date from the Napoleonic era.
22. R. R. Madden (ed.), *Literary Remains of the United Irishmen of 1798* (Dublin: J. Duffy, 1887), p. 25.
23. Ó Muirgheasa, *Dhá Chéad*, p. 40.
24. D. Ó Muirithe (ed.), *An tAmhrán Macarónach* (Dublin: An Clóchomhar, 1980), p. 111.
25. For a statement of this view, see S. J. Connolly, 'Jacobites, Whiteboys and Republicans: Varieties of Disaffection in Eighteenth-Century Ireland', *Eighteenth-Century Ireland*, 18 (2003): pp. 63–79.
26. L. M. Cullen, *The Hidden Ireland: Reassessment of a Concept* (Mullingar: Lilliput Press, 1988), pp. 10–11, 27–8.
27. Ó Muirithe, *An tAmhrán Macarónach*, p. 111.
28. Ibid., p. 112. 'Gráinne Mhaol bhocht' means 'poor Gráinne Mhaol', a female personification of Ireland.
29. M. Ní Shúilleabháin (ed.), *Amhráin Thomáis Rua* (Maynooth: An Sagart, 1985), p. 57.
30. The text has been edited by Máire Ní Shúilleabháin in her anthology of Tomás Rua's verse and at least one commercial recording is currently available: D. Ní Bhrolcháin, 'Domhnall Ó Conaill' on the *Smaointe* album (Dublin: Gael-Linn, 1990).
31. On the Pastorini phenomenon, see D. McCartney, *The Dawning of Democracy: Ireland 1800–1870* (Dublin: Helicon, 1987), pp. 99–102.
32. P. Ó Fiannachta, 'Eoghan Ó Comhraí: file traidisiúnta' in D. Ó Corráin, L. Breatnach and K. McCone (eds), *Sages, Saints and Storytellers: Celtic Studies in Honour of Professor James Carney* (Maynooth: An Sagart, 1989), p. 287.
33. For Ó Comhraí, see É. de hÓir, *Seán Ó Donnabháin agus Eoghan Ó Comhraí* (Dublin: An Clóchomhar, 1962).

34. N. Buttimer, 'Literature in Irish, 1690–1800: From the Williamite Wars to the Act of Union' in M. Kelleher and P. O'Leary (eds), *The Cambridge History of Irish Literature*, I (Cambridge: Cambridge University Press, 2006), pp. 338–9.
35. See B. Ó Buachalla, 'Seacaibíteachas Thaidhg Uí Neachtain', *Studia Hibernica*, 26 (1991–2): pp. 56–7 and idem, *Aisling Ghéar: Na Stíobhartaigh agus an tAos Leinn 1603–1788* (Dublin: An Clóchomhar, 1996), pp. 292–3.
36. G135, MS National Library of Ireland, p. 89.
37. For an overview of the '*ancien régime*' concept in recent historiography see I. McBride, *Eighteenth-Century Ireland: Isle of Slaves* (Dublin: Gill and Macmillan, 2009), pp. 12–14, 100–3.
38. See D. S. Thomson (ed.), *Alasdair Mac Mhaighstir Alasdair: Selected Poems* (Edinburgh: Scottish Academic Press, 1996) and A. McLeod (ed.), *The Songs of Duncan Ban Macintyre* (Edinburgh: Scottish Gaelic Texts Society, 1952).
39. For Seán Ó Conaill, see V. Morley, 'Views of the Past in Irish Vernacular Literature' in T. Blanning and H. Schulze (eds), *Unity and Diversity in European Culture c. 1800* (Oxford: Oxford University Press, 2006), pp. 171–98.

7 Mackay, 'Lost Manuscripts and Reactionary Rustling: Was there a Radical Scottish Gaelic Poetry between 1770 and 1820?'

1. The terms of the Act are explicit: 'That from and after the first day of August, One thousand, seven hundred and forty-seven, no man or boy within that part of Britain called Scotland, other than such as shall be employed as Officers and Soldiers in His Majesty's Forces, shall, on any pretext whatever, wear or put on the clothes commonly called Highland clothes (that is to say) the Plaid, Philabeg, or little Kilt, Trowse, Shoulder-belts, or any part whatever of what peculiarly belongs to the Highland Garb; and that no tartan or party-coloured plaid of stuff shall be used for Great Coats or upper coats, and if any such person shall presume after the said first day of August, to wear or put on the aforesaid garment or any part of them, every such person so offending....shall be liable to be transported to any of His Majesty's plantations beyond the seas, there to remain for the space of seven years.' 'Abolition and Proscription of the Highland Dress'; Statue 19, George II, Chap. 39, Sec. 17, 1746.
2. C. MacCoinnich, *Òrain Ghaidhealach, agus Bearla air an eadar-theangacha* (Duneadainn: air son an ughdair (Edinburgh: published for the author, 1792), p. 15. 'Chuir sèid ris a'n Ròimh' literally translates as 'breathed on Rome'. The (literal) translations of MacKenzie are my own, with input from Iain S. MacPherson and William Gillies. The verb 'èirigh' – to rise – also appears in the fourth song in the collection, 'Tuirie na Gàilic' (Lament for Gaelic), in an explicitly Jacobite context. Rising is once more related to 'confidence', as Mackenzie describes the plight of the Gaelic language:

'Nan deanadh sibh nise rium èisdeachd,
Dh' innsinn Sgeulachd air a Ghàilic,
Mar fhuair i cuaradh sa milleadh,
Sa gluasad o ionad àrda:
Bha i ri linn *Righ Seumas*,
Gu misneachail treubhach càilear.
Ach fhuair an *Donas* a thol fhèin dhi,
'Nuair a dh'èirich i le *T------h*.

(If you listen to me, | I'll tell you a story about Gaelic, | how it was spoilt and hurt, | in its move from a high place: | It was here in the time of *King James* | Confident, bold and pleasant. | But the Devil took its pleasure on it | When it rose with *T------h*.) MacCoinnich, *Òrain Ghaidhealach*, p. 4. '*T------h*' is 'Tearlach': Charles.
3. MacCoinnich, *Òrain Ghaidhealach*, p. 16. I have been unable to find a suitable translation of 'calanail'; by context it seems associated with pipe music.
4. Ibid., p. 12.
5. Ibid., pp. 12–13.
6. Ibid., p. 11.
7. See Homi Bhabha, *The Location of Culture* (London and New York: Routledge, 1994), p. 162: 'To grasp the ambivalence of hybridity, it must be distinguished from an inversion that would suggest that the originary is, really, only an "effect". Hybridity has no such perspective of depth or truth to provide: it is not a third term that resolves the tensions between two cultures, or the two scenes of the book, in a dialectical play or "recognition". The displacement from symbol to sign creates a crisis for any concept of authority based on a system of recognition: colonial specularity, doubly inscribed, does not produce a mirror where the self apprehends itself; it is always the split screen of the self and its doubling, the hybrid.'
8. D. Meek (ed.), *Caran an t-Saoghal* (Edinburgh: Birlinn, 2003), p. 26.
9. R. Black (ed.), *An Lasair: Anthology of Eighteenth-Century Gaelic Verse* (Edinburgh: Polygon, 2001), 288–91. Black's translation.
10. Ibid., pp. 292–3.
11. Ibid., pp. 286–7.
12. A. Murdoch 'Henry Dundas, Scotland and the Union with Ireland, 1792–1801' in B. Harris (ed.), *Scotland in the Age of the French Revolution* (Edinburgh: Birlinn, 2005), p. 128.
13. Black, *An Lasair*, pp. 286–7. The Disclothing Act was still in effect when this song was written – it was repealed in 1782.
14. Ibid., pp. 288–9.
15. B. Harris, 'Political Protests in the Year of Liberty, 1792' in B. Harris (ed.), *Scotland in the Age of the French Revolution* (Edinburgh: Birlinn, 2005), p. 49.
16. A. Murdoch, *British History 1660–1832: National Identity and Local Culture* (Basingstoke: Macmillan, 1998), pp. 8–9.
17. I. F. Grigor, *Highland Resistance: The Radical Tradition in the Scottish North* (Edinburgh: Mainstream, 2000), p. 27.
18. Ibid., p. 27.
19. D. MacLean, *The Literature of the Scottish Gael* (Edinburgh and London: William Hodge, 1912), p. 35.
20. Ibid., p. 36. MacLean refers to Place's collection in the British Museum, addl. MSS., No. 27816 F.233.
21. MacLean, *Literature of the Scottish Gael*, pp. 36–7.
22. D. Meek (ed.), *Tuath is Tighearna: Tenants and Landlords. An Anthology of Gaelic Poetry of Social and Political Protest from the Clearances to the Land Agitation (1800–1890)* (Edinburgh: Scottish Gaelic Texts Society, 1995), pp. 48, 60. Meek's translation.
23. Ibid., pp. 49, 188. Meek's translation.
24. See, for one example, 'Oran Mhòr MhicLeoid' (The Great Song of MacLeod) by Roderick Morrison, the Blind Harper (An Clàrsair Dall) in A. L. Gillies (ed.), *Songs of Gaelic Scotland* (Edinburgh: Birlinn, 2005), pp. 155–6.

226 Notes to pages 135–42

25. Meek, *Tuath is Tighearna*, p. 52.
26. Ibid., pp. 50, 188.
27. Two Polish men are talking, and one says to the other, 'I wish China would invade.' 'China?' the other replies 'Are you insane? China is a huge country, with a well-equipped army. We'd be decimated'. 'Ah yes, but they would have to come through Russia first'.
28. Meek, *Tuath is Tighearna*, pp. 54, 190. Meek's translation.
29. Gillies, *Songs of Gaelic Scotland*, pp. 267–8.
30. Black, *An Lasair*, p. 372.
31. M. MacLean and T. Dorgan (eds), *An Leabhar Mòr: The Great Book of Gaelic* (Edinburgh: Canongate, 2007), p. 54.
32. Black, *An Lasair*, pp. 78–9. Black's translation.
33. Ibid., pp. 264–7. Black's translation.
34. This is the translation given by Black for 'Oba Nodha', although 'New work' or 'new charm' is also possible. See ibid., p. 374, for a discussion of the term.
35. Ibid., pp. 20–1. Black's translation.

8 Carpenter, 'Virile Vernaculars: Radical Sexuality as Social Subversion in Irish Chapbook Verse, 1780–1820'

1. For a comprehensive overview of printed Irish ballads, see J. Moulden, 'The Printed Ballad in Ireland: A Guide to the Popular Printing of Songs in Ireland 1760–1920' (PhD Dissertation, National University of Ireland, Galway, 2006). This definitive dissertation updates earlier work by E. C. McClintock Dix, N. Ó Ciosáin, J. R. R. Adams, H. Shields and others. Moulden's dissertation is particularly valuable for its extensive Appendixes and Bibliography (pp. 541–1129) which contain full accounts both of notable collections and of individual surviving copies of Irish ballads printed during the period covered by this chapter, as well as lists of all relevant secondary literature.
2. See A. Carpenter, 'Garbling and Jumbling: Printing from Dictation in Eighteenth-Century Limerick' in M. Caball and A. Carpenter (eds), *Oral and Print Cultures in Ireland, 1600–1900* (Dublin: Four Courts Press, 2010), pp. 32–46.
3. The skill of writing Irish was not normally taught in hedge schools. For an exception, see the advertisement in A. McManus, *The Irish Hedge School and Its Books, 1695–1831* (Dublin, 2004), p. 90.
4. S. Whyte (ed.), *The Shamrock: or Hibernian Cresses. A Collection of Poems, Songs, Epigrams etc. ... the Original Production of Ireland* (Dublin, 1772); J. Edkins (ed.), *A Collection of Poems, mostly original, by Several Hands*, 3 vols (Dublin 1789, 1790, 1801). For an assessment of the culture of Irish towns at this time, see T. C. Barnard, 'The Cultures of Eighteenth-Century Irish Towns', *Proceedings of the British Academy*, 108 (2002): pp. 195–222.
5. See E. Rua Ó Súilleabháin, 'Letter to Father Fitzgerald' in A. Carpenter (ed.), *Verse in English from Eighteenth-Century Ireland* (Cork: Cork University Press, 1997), pp. 385–6, and McManus, *The Irish Hedge School*, pp. 89–90. As McManus points out, hedge-schools were not sectarian.
6. See McManus, *The Irish Hedge School*, pp. 91–117 for a good assessment of the learning and pedantry of Irish hedge school masters. See also J. R. R. Adams, 'Swine-Tax and Eat-Him-All-Magee: The Hedge Schools and Popular Education in Ireland' in J. S. Donnelly Jr. and K. A. Miller (eds), *Irish Popular Culture 1650–1850* (Dublin, 1998), pp. 97–117.

7. *The Distressed Rake to which is added, The Gobbio, The Limerick Dandy-O. The New Dhooraling* (Limerick, [1790]).
8. *The Manuel Exercise* [Monaghan, 1790], p. 3.
9. *Paddy O'Rafferty. To which is added, The Black Duck, The Irish Cudgel, Morgan Rattler, Paddy O'Slatery* (Limerick, 1780), p. 8.
10. For 'The Coughing Old Man', see Carpenter, *Verse in English*, pp. 395–6.
11. J. Kelly, 'Regulating Print: The State and the Control of Print in Eighteenth-Century Ireland', *Eighteenth-Century Ireland* 23 (2008): p. 172.
12. Ibid., p. 155.
13. See Zimmermann, *Songs of Irish Rebellion*. For an interesting assessment of the politicization of artisans and labourers in Ireland between 1778 and 1784, see P. Higgins, *A Nation of Politicians: Gender, Patriotism and Political Culture in Late Eighteenth-Century Ireland* (Madison, WI: University of Wisconsin Press, 2010).
14. Zimmermann, *Songs of Irish Rebellion*, p. 101.
15. See J. Moulden, "'James Cleland his Book': The Library of a Small Farming Family in Early Nineteenth-Century County Down' in Caball and Carpenter (eds), *Oral and Print Cultures*, pp. 102–18.
16. Quoted in McManus, *The Irish Hedge School*, p. 102.
17. See G. Ó Crualaoich, 'The Merry Wake' in Donnelly and Miller (eds), *Irish Popular Culture*, pp. 173–200, and D. Ó Giolláin 'The Pattern' in ibid., pp. 201–21.
18. *Stauka an Varaga. To which are added, The Tralee Girl. The Beagles Adventure, The English Slave & Turkish Lady* (Limerick, 1790), p. 4.
19. See for instance 'The Sailor Dear' in Carpenter, *Verse in English*, pp. 393–4.
20. *A Much Admired New Song, Call'd Oonagh's lock. To which are added, 2. Mary Neal's Tragedy. 3. The Bold Sailor. 4. The Weeping Damsel* (Dublin, 1789), p. 4.
21. Microfilm 25 of the Francis Place (1771–1854) collection, British Library. Quoted in J. Wardroper, *Lovers, Rakes and Rogues* (London: Shelfmark Books, 1995), p. 14.
22. J. Swift, 'An Epigram on Scolding' in P. Rogers (ed.), *The Complete Poems of Jonathan Swift* (Harmondsworth: Penguin, 1983), p. 561. What is undermined in these poems is the middle-class view of propriety in language. The middle class does not use such words or describe such behaviour – nor, incidentally, do certain lexicographers of today: the otherwise admirable *Concise Ulster Dictionary* does not include what it terms 'obscenities' because 'they might cause offence'. The editors explain that 'farmyard terms' are retained.
23. See Carpenter, 'Garbling and Jumbling'. There is also evidence that some popular culture was enjoyed by the 'elite' classes; see N. Ó Ciosáin, 'The Irish Rogues' in Donnelly and Miller (eds), *Irish Popular Culture*, pp. 78–96, particularly 78–9.
24. Carpenter, *Verse in English*, p. 339.
25. BL 11622.df.34/7 (Limerick, *c*.1785). The reader's attention is drawn to the use of the *ochtfhoclach*, an *amhrán* metre, in this poem. For an explanation of this phenomenon, see Carpenter, *Verse in English*, pp. 14–16.
26. i.e. 'fates', an example of Hiberno-English pronunciation moving to print through dictation.
27. *frolicker*. Cf. Ir. *smalcaire*, 'a beater', 'a boxer', 'a stout, strong man'.
28. a bag for carrying clothes or workman's tools.
29. *phthisic*: consumption or a wasting disease of the lungs.
30. a purgative drug.
31. Wardroper, *Lovers, Rakes and Rogues*, p. 172.

32. This corrupt line is found in both surviving printings of this song (Monaghan: J. Brown and Limerick: W. Goggin). Such corruptions are common in printings from both these printers, neither of whom seems to have exercised any surveillance over the work of his compositors.
33. BL 11622.df.34/21 (Limerick, c.1785). A diminutive from Ir. *dúr*, 'stiff'.
34. a diminutive from Ir. *dúid*, a stumpy or protuberant part.
35. Patron or 'Pattern' day when large numbers of people would attend masses in honour of the patron saint of a church. Revelry would follow the masses. See Ó Giolláin 'The Pattern'.
36. The finger-pipe of a bagpipe, on which the tune is played.
37. The bass pipe of a bagpipe.
38. i.e. *thrust* – another Hiberno-English pronunciation reflected in spelling.
39. lest.
40. TCD uncatalogued chapbook, *c*. 1795.
41. i.e. *weave* – another example of Hiberno-English pronunciation.
42. A list of such chapbooks can be found in Moulden, 'The Printed Ballad in Ireland', Appendix B.
43. *Freeman's Journal*, 11 May 1784. Quoted in Kelly, 'Regulating Print', p. 154.

9 Wright, 'Thomas Moore and the Problem of Colonial Masculinity in Irish Romanticism'

1. See, e.g., L. Davis, *Music, Postcolonialism, and Gender: The Construction of Irish National Identity, 1724–1874* (Notre Dame: University of Notre Dame Press, 2005), pp. 152–63; D. Saglia, 'Harem Power: Narrative Structure and Sexual Politics in Thomas Moore's *Lalla Rookh*', *Questione Romantica*, 12–13 (2002), pp. 77–88; J. W. Vail, *The Literary Relationship of Lord Byron and Thomas Moore* (Baltimore: Johns Hopkins University Press, 2001), p. 115; S. B. Taylor, 'Irish Odalisques and Other Seductive Figures: Thomas Moore's *Lalla Rookh*' in D. J. O'Quinn (ed.), *The Containment and Re-Deployment of English India* (Romantic Circles Praxis Series, 2000), at www.rc.umd.edu/praxis/containment/taylor/taylor.html [accessed 19 March 2012].
2. T. Moore, *A Selection of Irish Melodies*, No. 3 (Dublin: W. Powers; London: J. Powers), p. 4.
3. See J. Habermas, *Structural Transformation of the Public Sphere: An Inquiry into a Category of Bourgeois Society*, trans. Thomas Burger and Frederick Lawrence (Boston: MIT Press, 1991).
4. T. Moore, *Letter to the Roman Catholics of Dublin* (London: J. Carpenter, 1810).
5. C. Connolly, 'Irish Romanticism, 1800–1830' in M. Kelleher and P. O'Leary (eds), *The Cambridge History of Irish Literature*, 2 vols (Cambridge: Cambridge University Press, 2006), i, pp. 407–48.
6. T. Fulford, *Romanticism and Masculinity: Gender, Politics, and Poetics in the Writings of Burke, Coleridge, Cobbett, Wordsworth, De Quincey and Hazlitt* (New York: Macmillan Palgrave, 1999), p. 12.
7. On Burke's place in an Irish Enlightenment, see L. Gibbons, *Edmund Burke and Ireland: Aesthetic, Politics, and the Colonial Sublime* (Cambridge: Cambridge University Press, 2003).
8. See Fulford, *Romanticism and Masculinity*, p. 9.

9. J. M. Wright, 'Atlantic Exile and the Stateless Citizen in Irish Romanticism', *Wordsworth Circle* 40 (2009), p. 43.
10. Fulford, *Romanticism and Masculinity*, p. 12.
11. A. Sheridan Lefanu, *The Sons of Erin*, 3rd edn (London: Ridgway, 1812); A. O'Keeffe, 'The Irish Officer', *National Characters Exhibited in Forty Geographical Poems, with Plates* (London: Darton, Harvey and Darton, 1818), pp. 23–6.
12. R. Torrens, *The Victim of Intolerance; Or, the Hermit of Killarney: A Catholic Tale*, 4 vols (London, 1814), i, p. 175; hereafter cited parenthetically. Most library catalogues represent this as a three-volume work, but contemporary reviews document a fourth volume that represents the hero becoming a leader in the United Irishmen.
13. Ibid., i, pp. 80–1.
14. Ibid., ii, pp. 1–2.
15. Ibid., iii, p. 218; ibid., ii, p. 47.
16. S. Morgan, *O'Donnel: A National Tale*, 3 vols (London: Henry Colburn, 1814),ii, p. 63; ibid., i, p. 181.
17. Ibid., i, p. 181n.
18. A. Lefanu, *The Outlaw*, in *Tales of a Tourist, Containing The Outlaw and Fashionable Connexions*, 4 vols (London: A. K. Newman and Co., 1823), iii, p. 52.
19. Anon., *The Exile of Ireland! Or, the Wonderful Adventures, and Extraordinary Escapes, of An Irish Rebel Officer* (London: Printed for the author, n.d.), pp. 32–3.
20. The pamphlet is undated and so does not resolve the controversy over the poem's authorship; on the poem, see F. Molloy, 'Thomas Campbell's 'Exile of Erin': English Poem, Irish Reactions' in P. A. Lynch, J. Fischer, and B. Coates (eds), *Back to the Present: Forward to the Past: Irish Writing and History Since 1798*, 2 vols (New York: Rodopi, 2006), i, pp. 43–52.
21. Byron, 'To Thomas Moore' in F. Page (ed.), *Byron: Poetical Works* (Oxford: Oxford University Press, 1984), p. 70.
22. J. Moody, 'Thomas Brown [alias Thomas Moore]: Censorship and Regency Cryptography', *European Romantic Review* 18 (2007): pp. 187–94
23. T. Moore, *The Fudge Family in Paris*, 2nd edn (London: Longman, Hurst, Rees, Orme, and Brown, 1818), pp. vii–viii; Anon., *The Fudger Fudged; Or, The Devil and T***Y M***E* (London: William Wright, 1819).
24. Davis, *Music, Postcolonialism, and Gender*, p. 142.
25. See M. H. Thuente, *The Harp Re-Strung: The United Irishmen and the Rise of Literary Nationalism* (Syracuse: Syracuse University Press, 1994).
26. Moore, *A Selection of Irish Melodies*, No. 1 (Dublin: W. Powers; London: [J.] Powers, undated [c. 1808]).
27. Moore, *A Selection of Irish Melodies*, Nos. 1–2, n.p.
28. Moore, *A Selection of Irish Melodies*, No. 3, n.p.
29. On the dubiousness of the slur, see J. Vail, 'Thomas Moore: After the Battle' in J. M. Wright (ed.), *Companion to Irish Literature* (Oxford: Blackwell, 2010).
30. Fulford, *Romanticism and Masculinity*, p. 12.
31. Torrens, *The Victim of Intolerance*, iii, pp. 112, 113
32. R. Welch, *Irish Poetry from Moore to Yeats* (Totowa, NJ: Barnes and Noble Books, 1980), p. 36. Vail also terms the poem an *apologia* in *Literary Relationship*, p. 186.
33. G. A. Schirmer, *Out of What Began: A History of Irish Poetry in English* (Ithaca: Cornell University Press, 1998), pp. 79–80.

34. T. Moore, 'Oh! Blame Not the Bard' in J. M. Wright (ed.), *Irish Literature, 1750–1900: An Anthology* (Oxford: Blackwell, 2008), ll. 1–8.
35. See Davis, *Music, Postcolonialism and Gender*, pp. 154–5; Welch, *Irish Poetry*, pp. 34–6.
36. Moore, 'Oh! Blame Not the Bard', ll. 13–14.
37. Ibid., l. 17.
38. Ibid., l. 11.
39. Ibid., ll. 29–32.
40. J. E. Adams, *Dandies and Desert Saints: Styles of Victorian Manhood* (Ithaca: Cornell University Press, 1995). Other critics have noted the tensions in Moore's *Melodies* as incoherence. For example, see T. Eagleton, *Crazy John and the Bishop and Other Essays on Irish Culture* (Notre Dame: University of Notre Dame Press/Field Day, 1998), p. 154. For a variant reading which sees the tensions as part of a 'strategy of ambiguity' see Davis, *Music, Postcolonialism, and Gender*, p. 155.
41. Adams, *Dandies and Desert Saints*, p. 2.
42. Ibid.
43. See, for example, D. J. O'Neil, 'The Cult of Self-Sacrifice: The Irish Experience', *Éire-Ireland*, 24 (1989): 89–105.
44. D. Lloyd, *Nationalism and Minor Literature: James Clarence Mangan and the Emergence of Cultural Nationalism* (Berkeley: University of California Press, 1987); M. Howes, *Colonial Crossings: Figures in Irish Literary History* (Dublin: Field Day, 2006). See also, for instance, D. Dwan, *The Great Community: Culture and Nationalism in Ireland* (Dublin: Field Day/NotreDame, 2008).
45. J. Leerssen, *Remembrance and Imagination: Patterns in the Historical and Literary Representation of Ireland in the Nineteenth Century* (Notre Dame: Notre Dame University Press/Field Day, 1997), p. 81.
46. Moore, *Letter to the Roman Catholics of Dublin*.
47. T. Moore, *Memoirs of the Life of the Right Honorable Richard Brinsley Sheridan*, 2 vols, 5th edn (London: Longman, Rees, Orme, Brown and Green, 1827), i, pp. 397–8; ibid., ii, pp. 491–2.
48. Ibid., i, pp. v–vi, v.
49. Ibid., i, p. vi.
50. Thuente, *The Harp Re-Strung*, esp. pp. 179–88.
51. Ibid., p. 189; Wright, *Ireland, India and Nationalism in Nineteenth-Century Literature* (Cambridge: Cambridge University Press, 2007), pp. 92, 102–3.
52. T. Moore, *Travels of an Irish Gentleman in Search of a Religion* (London: Longman, Rees, Orme, Brown, Green, and Longman, 1833), p. 300. T. Moore, *Memoirs of Captain Rock* (1824), E. Nolan and S. Deane (eds) (Dublin: Field Day, 2008).

10 Dornan, 'Radical Politics and Dialect in the British Archipelago'

1. See, for example, J. C. D. Clark, *The Language of Liberty, 1660–1832* (Cambridge: Cambridge University Press, 1994); O. Smith, *The Politics of Language, 1789–1819* (Oxford: Clarendon Press, 1984).
2. R. Marggraf Turley, *The Politics of Language in Romantic Literature* (Basingstoke: Palgrave MacMillan, 2002), p. xv.
3. J. G. A. Pocock, 'British History: A Plea for a New Subject', *Journal of Modern History*, 47 (1975), pp. 601–24, J. Kerrigan, *Archipelagic English* (Oxford: Oxford University Press, 2008).

4. K. Trumpener, *Bardic Nationalism: The Romantic Novel and the British Empire* (Princeton, N.J.: Princeton University Press, 1997); M. Pittock, *Scottish and Irish Romanticism*; F. Stafford, *Starting Lines*. See also G. Carruthers and A. Rawes (eds), *English Romanticism and the Celtic World* (Cambridge: Cambridge University Press, 2003), C. Jones and D. Duff, *Scotland, Ireland and the Romantic Aesthetic* (Lewisburgh, PA: Bucknell University Press, 2007), L. Davis, I. Duncan and J. Sorensen (eds), *Scotland and the Borders of Romanticism* (Cambridge: Cambridge University Press, 2004).
5. *The Canongate Burns*, p.3.
6. M. Edgeworth, *Castle Rackrent* (London: Joseph Johnston, 1800), p.11.
7. See S. Manly, *Language, Custom and Nation in the 1790s* (Aldershot: Ashgrave, 2007).
8. See Davis, Duncan and Sorensen (eds), *Scotland and the Borders of Romanticism*, pp. 1–2 for Wordsworth's opinions on Scots.
9. I am aware that my inclusion of Scots in a discussion of 'dialect' writing is contentious. My use of the term 'dialect' is not intended to question the historical status or future potential of Scots as a language; it is used to describe any literature that departs from Standard English.
10. R. Crawford, *Devolving English Literature*, 2nd edn (Edinburgh: Edinburgh University Press, 2000), p. 129.
11. S. Deane, 'Dumbness and Eloquence: A Note on English as we Write it in Ireland' in C. Carroll and P. King (eds), *Ireland and Postcolonial Theory* (Notre Dame, IN: University of Notre Dame Press, 2003), pp. 227–42.
12. See L. McIlvanney, *Burns the Radical* (Phantassie, East Lothian: Tuckwell Press, 2002); *The Canongate Burns* and R. Crawford, *The Bard: Robert Burns, a Biography* (London: Jonathan Cape, 2009).
13. See, for example, McIlvanney, *Burns the Radical*; C. McGuirk, *Robert Burns and the Sentimental Era* (Athens, GA: University of Georgia Press, 1985); Stafford, *Starting Lines*.
14. McIlvanney, *Burns the Radical*, and F. Ferguson and A. R. Holmes (eds), *Revising Robert Burns and Ulster* (Dublin: Four Courts Press, 2009).
15. See for instance S. Murphy, *Maria Edgeworth and Romance* (Dublin: Four Courts Press, 2004); C. Ó Gallchoir, *Maria Edgeworth: Women, Enlightenment and Nation* (Dublin: University College Dublin Press, 2005) and H. Kaufmann and C. Fauske (eds), *An Uncomfortable Authority: Maria Edgeworth and Her Contexts* (Newark, DE: University of Delaware Press, 2005).
16. A. McKenzie, *Poems and Songs, on Different Subjects* (Belfast: Alexander MacKay, 1810), p. 98.
17. R. Anderson, *The Poetical Works* (Carlisle: B. Scott, 1820), p. 200.
18. McGuirk, *Robert Burns and the Sentimental Era*, pp. 27–44.
19. McKenzie, *Poems and Songs*, p.98.
20. J. Hewitt, *Rhyming Weavers and other Country Poets of Antrim and Down* (Belfast: Blackstaff, 2004).
21. R. Anderson, *Poems on Various Subjects* (Carlisle: J. Mitchell, 1798), pp. 69–78.
22. Most important in this respect was Edgeworth, *Castle Rackrent*.
23. For a selection of these poets, see J. Goodridge (ed.), *English Labouring Class Poets, 1700–1900*, 3 vols (London: Pickering and Chatto, 2005).
24. See R. S. Dornan, 'Thomas Dermody's Archipelagic Poetry', *European Romantic Review*, 21 (2010), pp. 536–43, and idem, 'Robert Burns, Thomas Dermody and the Killeigh Cycle', *Scottish Studies Review*, 6 (2005), pp. 9–21.
25. Pittock, *Scottish and Irish Romanticism*, p. 147.

26. P. Blank, *Broken English: Dialects and Politics of Language in Renaissance Writings* (London: Routledge, 1996), p. 2.
27. J. Skoblow, *Dooble Tongue: Scots, Burns, Contradiction* (Newark, DE: University of Delaware Press, 2001), p. 20.
28. J. Stagg, *Miscellaneous Poems, some of which are in the Cumberland Dialect* (Workington: W. Borrowdale, 1805); S. Blamire, *The Poetical Works* (Edinburgh: John Menzies, 1842).
29. See Hewitt, *Rhyming Weavers*; I. Herbison, 'The Rest is Silence: Some Remarks on the Disappearance of Ulster Scots Poetry' in J. Erskine and G. Lucy (eds), *Cultural Traditions in Northern Ireland: Varieties of Scottishness* (Belfast, Institute of Irish Studies, 1997), pp. 129–45; L. McIlvanney, 'Across the Narrow Sea: The Language, Literature and Politics of the Ulster Scots' in L. McIlvanney and R. Ryan (eds), *Ireland and Scotland: Culture and Society* (Dublin: Four Courts Press, 2005), pp. 203–26; C. Baranuik, 'James Orr: Ulster-Scot and Poet of the 1798 Rebellion', *Scottish Studies Review*, 6 (2005), pp. 22–32; F. Ferguson (ed.), *Ulster-Scots Writing: An Anthology* (Dublin: Four Courts Press, 2008).
30. D. M. Horgan, 'Popular Protest in the Eighteenth Century', *The Review of English Studies*, 48 (1997), p. 327.
31. An example is D. H. Akenson and W. H. Crawford, *Local Poets and Social History: James Orr, Bard of Ballycarry* (Belfast: Public Record Office of Northern Ireland, 1977).
32. T. Paulin (ed.), *The Faber Book of Vernacular Verse* (London: Faber & Faber, 1994), p. x.
33. C. MacLachlan (ed.), *Before Burns: Eighteenth-Century Poetry* (Edinburgh: Canongate Classics, 2002), p. 28.
34. Carpenter, *Verse in English*, p. 37.
35. *The Canongate Burns*, p. 19.
36. Horgan, 'Popular Protest in the Eighteenth Century', p. 310.
37. Ibid., p. 311.
38. T. Bobbin, *The Miscellaneous Works of Tim Bobbin Containing a View of the Lancashire Dialect* (Manchester: J. Slack, 1818), p. 53.
39. Ibid., p. 18.
40. Anderson, *Poems on Various Subjects*.
41. A. MacLaine (ed.), *The Christis Kirk Tradition: Scots Poems of Folk Festivity* (Glasgow: Association for Scottish Literary Studies, 1996).
42. R. Anderson, *Ballads in the Cumberland Dialect* (Carlisle: W. Hodgson, 1805), p. 113.
43. Anderson, *The Poetical Works*, p. 128.
44. Ibid., p. 131.

11 Navickas, '"Theaw Kon Ekspect No Mooar Eawt ov a Pig thin a Grunt": Searching for the Radical Dialect Voice in Northern England, 1798–1819'

1. Acknowledgements to Robert Poole, who provided extra information on Walker and valuable comments on an earlier draft of this paper.
2. E. P. Thompson, *The Making of the English Working Class* (Harmondsworth, Penguin, rev. ed., 1968), p. 710.
3. P. Harling, 'The Law of Libel and the Limits of Repression, 1790–1832', *Historical Journal*, 44:1 (2001), pp. 107–34; K. Navickas, *Loyalism and Radicalism in Lancashire*,

1798–1815 (Oxford: Oxford University Press, 2009), pp. 39–41; B. Harris, *Politics and the Rise of the Press: Britain and France, 1620–1800* (London: Routledge, 1996), p. 32.
4. 'Tim Bobbin the Second' (R. Walker), *Plebeian Politics, or the Principles and Practices of Certain Mole-Eyed Maniacs Vulgarly Called Warrites* (1st ed. 1796; 2nd ed. 24 December 1801; quotations here taken from Manchester: J. Slack, 1818 ed.); J. Harland (ed.), *The Songs of the Wilsons* (London: Whittaker & Co, 1865).
5. BRf 821.04 BA1, ballads, Manchester Central Library.
6. N. Rogers, *Crowds, Culture and Politics in Georgian Britain* (Oxford: Oxford University Press, 1998); Epstein, *Radical Expression*.
7. W. E. A. Axon, *Annals of Manchester* (Manchester: John Heywood, 1886), p. 131; R. W. Procter, *Lancashire Literary Worthies* (Manchester: John Heywood, 1860), pp. 40–9. Thanks to Robert Poole for supplying this information.
8. Further analysis of William Cowdroy and the other surviving Lancashire radicals can be found in Navickas, *Loyalism and Radicalism in Lancashire*, pp. 136–8.
9. I. Haywood, *The Revolution in Popular Literature: Print, Politics and the People, 1790–1860* (Cambridge: Cambridge University Press, 2004), p. 49.
10. Walker, *Plebeian Politics*, pp. 22, 52.
11. D. I. Eaton, *Politics for the People; Or, A Salmagundy for Swine, or Hog's Wash* (London, 1794); E. Burke, *Reflections on the Revolution in France* (London, 1790); T. Spence, *Pig's Meat, or Lessons for the Swinish Multitude*, 3 vols (London, 1793–5).
12. John Wilson (ed.), *The Songs of Joseph Mather* (Sheffield: Pawson and Brailsford, 1862), p. 41.
13. Walker, *Plebeian Politics*, p. 53.
14. Ibid., p. 13. The Oldham diarist William Rowbottom noted 'Upon the whole it was the greatest flood ever remembered in the country'. W. Rowbottom, 'Annals of Oldham', transcript, pp. 99–100, Oldham Local Studies.
15. Walker, *Plebeian Politics*, pp. 27–8. A. Prentice, *Historical Sketches and Personal Recollections of Manchester* (London: A. Gilpin, 1851), p. 419.
16. Walker, *Plebeian Politics*, p. 29.
17. E. Butterworth, *Historical Sketches of Oldham* (Oldham: John Hirst, 1856), p. 173.
18. B. E. Graver, 'Wakefield, Gilbert (1756–1801)', *Oxford Dictionary of National Biography*, Oxford University Press, 2004, www.oxforddnb.com/view/article/28418 [accessed 18 February 2010].
19. J. J. Sack, *From Jacobite to Conservative: Reaction and Orthodoxy in Britain, c.1760–1832* (Cambridge: Cambridge University Press, 1993), p. 88. See also M. Leger-Lomas, 'The Character of Pitt the Younger and Party Politics, 1830–1860', *Historical Journal*, 47 (2004): pp. 641–61.
20. Epstein, *Radical Expression*, p. 20.
21. Harland, *The Songs of the Wilsons*, p. 7.
22. R. Poole, 'The March to Peterloo: Politics and Festivity in Late Georgian England', *Past and Present*, 192 (2006), pp. 109–53.
23. Harland, *The Songs of the Wilsons*, p. 26.
24. See for example MB3p240.989, bronze medal, and 2009,8022.1, earthenware plaque, 1819, British Museum.
25. H. Hunt, *To the Radical Reformers, Male and Female, of England, Ireland, and Scotland* (Chester, 1820), pp. 5–8; J. Gardner, 'The Suppression of Samuel Bamford's Peterloo Poems', *Romanticism*, 13 (2007), pp. 150–2. Gardner argues that Bamford's earlier

234   *Notes to pages 188–95*

poetry was more radical than he later wished to admit. Nevertheless, all the poems were in Standard English.
26. Wilson, *Songs of Joseph Mather*, pp. 37–8.
27. G. Stedman Jones, 'Review: The Politics of Language, 1791–1819 by Olivia Smith', *American Historical Review*, 92 (1987), p. 662.
28. Walker, *Plebeian Politics*, p. 2.
29. B. Hollingworth, *Songs of the People, Lancashire Dialect Poetry of the Industrial Revolution* (Manchester: Manchester University Press, 1977), p. 29.
30. M. Vicinus, *The Industrial Muse, a Study of Nineteenth Century British Working-Class Literature* (London: Croom Helm, 1974), p. 189.
31. K. Wales, *Northern English: A Cultural and Social History* (Cambridge: Cambridge University Press, 2006), pp. 99–100.
32. B. Maidment (ed.), *The Poorhouse Fugitives: Self-Taught Poets and Poetry in Victorian Britain* (Manchester: Manchester University Press, 1987), pp. 355–6; S. Bamford, *Passages in the Life of a Radical* (originally London: MacGibbon & Kee, 1843, reprinted New York: Cosimo, 2005), p. 219.
33. Vicinus, *Industrial Muse*, p. 187.
34. Thompson, *Making of the English Working Class*, p. 324.
35. Maidment, *The Poorhouse Fugitives*, pp. 355–6.
36. Wales, *Northern English*, p. 97.
37. Maidment, *The Poorhouse Fugitives*, p. 356.
38. John Barrell, 'Radicalism, Visual Culture and Spectacle in the 1790s', *Romanticism on the Net*, 46 (May 2007), www.erudit.org/revue/ron/2007/v/n46/016131ar.html#fi14 [accessed 28 March 2012].
39. Ibid., p. 358.
40. O. Smith, *The Politics of Language, 1791–1819* (Oxford: Clarendon Press, 1984), p. 88.
41. M. Philp, 'Vulgar Conservatism, 1792–93', *English Historical Review*, 110 (1995): pp. 42–69; K. Gilmartin, *Writing Against Revolution: Literary Conservatism in Britain, 1790–1832* (Cambridge: Cambridge University Press, 2007), pp. 19–54.
42. K. Navickas, 'The Defence of Manchester and Liverpool in 1803' in M. Philp (ed.), *Resisting Napoleon: The British Response to the Threat of Invasion, 1797–1815* (Aldershot: Ashgate, 2006), p. 70.
43. Elbourne, *Music and Tradition in Industrial Lancashire*, p. 83; Hollingworth, *Songs of the People*, p. 127.
44. J. Harland, *Ballads and Songs of Lancashire: Chiefly Older than the Nineteenth Century* (London: Whittaker & Co, 1865), pp. 216–7.
45. Elbourne, *Music and Tradition in Industrial Lancashire*, p. 227.
46. Thompson, *Making of the English Working Class*, p. 323.
47. 398.8 B1, p. 118, ballads and broadsides, Manchester Central Library.
48. BRf 821.04 BA1, vol. 2, p. 130, ballads, Manchester Central Library.
49. Elbourne, *Music and Tradition in Industrial Lancashire*, pp. 73–4, 86.
50. Maidment, *The Poorhouse Fugitives*, p. 37.
51. Hollingworth, *Songs of the People*, p. 29.

Trumpener, 'Afterword'

1. W. Tone, *Life of Theobald Wolfe Tone*, 2 vols (Washington: Gales and Seaton, 1826), i. p. 155–7.

2. See K. Trumpener, *Bardic Nationalism*, pp. 10–1.
3. A. L. Lloyd, *The Singing Englishman* (London: Workers' Music Association, 1944) and idem, *Folk Song in England* (London: Lawrence and Wishart, 1967); Z. Kodaly, *Folk Music of Hungary*, trans. R. Tempest and C. Jolly (London: Barrie and Jenkins, 1971). On the historical and conceptual overlaps between ethnomusicology and comparative literature, see K. Trumpener, 'World Music, World Literature: A Geopolitical View' in S. Haun (ed.), *Comparative Literature in an Age of Globalization* (Baltimore, MD: Johns Hopkins University Press, 2006), pp. 185–202; and also Trumpener, *Bardic Nationalism*, esp. Introduction and Chapter 2.
4. See for instance S. Kilfeather, 'Strangers at Home: Political Fictions by Women in Eighteenth-Century Ireland' (PhD dissertation, Princeton University, 1989), Chapter 1.
5. The British Comparative Literature Association website (www.swansea.ac.uk/german/bcla/clww.htm) thus lists a number of British programmes and departments in which comparative literature plays a central role. University College London has a Department of Comparative Literature; Goldsmith College, and Warwick have Departments of English and Comparative Literature; York a Department of English and Related Literature; Kent Comparative Literary Studies; Essex a Department of Literature, Wolverhampton European Literature. In addition, East Anglia, Edinburgh, King's College London and Middlesex offer MA courses in Comparative Literature, and Wales Swansea an MA in European Literary and Cultural Studies. Yet as these differences of nomenclature suggest, Comparative Literature has a more decentred disciplinary existence in Britain than in many other parts of Europe and the English-speaking world. According to N. Harrison, 'Life on the Second Floor', *Comparative Literature* 59 (2007): pp. 332–48, the recent growth of comparative literature programs in Britain reflects not only an internationalist and postcolonial agenda but also the gravitational and economic pull of North American academic models (including the wish to attract fee-paying international students).
6. See, for instance, the work of H. Meltzl de Lomnitz, anthologized in D. Damrosch and N. Melas, (eds), *The Text and the World* (Princeton: Princeton University Press, forthcoming) and C. Emerson, 'Answering for Central and Eastern Europe' in Saussy (ed.), *Comparative Literature*, pp. 203–11.
7. R. Crawford, *The Scottish Invention of English Literature* (Cambridge: Cambridge University Press, 1998), G. Vishnawatan, *Masks of Conquest: Literary Study and British Rule in India* (New York: Columbia University Press, 1989). See also A. Mufti, *Enlightenment in the Colony: The Jewish Question and the Crisis of Postcolonial Culture* (Princeton: Princeton University Press, 2007).
8. See T. Agathocleos, *Urban Realism and the Cosmopolitan Imagination in the Nineteenth Century: Visible City, Invisible World* (Cambridge: Cambridge University Press, 2011) and D. Damrosch, *What is World Literature* (Princeton, NJ: Princeton University Press, 2003), Ch. 1.
9. F. Moretti, 'Conjectures on World Literature', *New Left Review* 1 (2000), pp. 54–68. See also idem, *Atlas of the European Novel, 1800–1900* (London: Verso, 1999); idem, 'The Slaughterhouse of Literature', *Modern Language Quarterly*, 61 (2000), pp. 207–27, and idem, *Graphs, Maps, Trees: Abstract Models for a Literary History* (London: Verso, 2005), as well as P. Casanova, *The World Republic of Letters*, trans. M. B. DeBevoise (Cambridge, MA: Harvard University Press, 2004) and N. Melas, *All the Difference in the World: Postcoloniality and the Ends of Comparison* (Stanford, CA: Stanford University Press, 2007).

WORKS CITED

Adams, J. E., *Dandies and Desert Saints: Styles of Victorian Manhood* (Ithaca, NY: Cornell University Press, 1995).

Adams, J. R. R., *The Printed Word and the Common Man: Popular Culture in Ulster 1700–1900* (Belfast: Institute of Irish Studies, 1987).

Agathocleos, T., *Urban Realism and the Cosmopolitan Imagination in the Nineteenth Century: Visible City, Invisible World* (Cambridge: Cambridge University Press, 2011).

Aikin, J., *Essays on Song-writing: With a Collection of such English Songs as are Most Eminent for Poetical Merit. To which are Added, some Original Pieces* (London: 1772).

Aikin, J., *Essays on Song-Writing*, ed. R. H. Evans (London: R. H. Evans, 1810).

Akenson, D. H., and W. H. Crawford, *Local Poets and Social History: James Orr, Bard of Ballycarry* (Belfast: Public Record Office of Northern Ireland, 1977).

Anderson, R., *Poems on Various Subjects* (Carlisle: J. Mitchell, 1798).

—, *Ballads in the Cumberland Dialect* (Carlisle: W. Hodgson, 1805).

—, *The Poetical Works* (Carlisle: B. Scott, 1820).

[Anon.], *The Exile of Ireland! Or, the Wonderful Adventures, and Extraordinary Escapes, of An Irish Rebel Officer* (London, [n.d.]).

—, *The Fudger Fudged; Or, The Devil and T***Y M***E. By the Editor of the New Whig Guide* (London: William Wright, 1819).

Ashraf, P. M., *The Life and Times of Thomas Spence* (Newcastle: Frank Graham, 1983).

Baranuik, C., 'James Orr: Ulster-Scot and Poet of the 1798 Rebellion', *Scottish Studies Review*, 6:1 (2005), pp. 22–32.

Barnard, T., 'Print Culture, 1700–1800', in R. Gillespie and A. Hatfield (eds), *The Irish Book in English, 1550–1800* (Oxford: Oxford University Press, 2005), pp. 34–58.

Barnard, T., 'The Cultures of Eighteenth-Century Irish Towns', *Proceedings of the British Academy*, 108 (2002), pp. 195–222.

Barrell, J., 'Radicalism, Visual Culture and Spectacle in the 1790s', *Romanticism on the Net*, 46 (2007), at <http://www.erudit.org/revue/ron/2007/v/n46/index.html> [accessed 11 February 2012].

Barrell, J., *The Spirit of Despotism: Invasions of Privacy in the 1790s* (Oxford: Oxford University Press, 2006).

—, *Imagining the King's Death: Figurative Treason, Fantasies of Regicide, 1793–1796* (Oxford: Oxford University Press, 2000).

—, 'Rus in Urbe', in N. Leask and P. Connell (eds), *British Romanticism and Popular Culture in Britain and Ireland* (Cambridge: Cambridge University Press, 2009), pp. 109–27.

—, 'London in the 1790s'. in J. Chandler (ed.), *The Cambridge History of English Romantic Literature* (Cambridge: Cambridge University Press, 2009), pp.129–58.

Barrell, J., and J. Mee (eds), *Trials for Treason and Sedition*, 6 vols (London: Pickering and Chatto, 2006).

Bartley, J. O., 'The Development of a Stock Character I. The Stage Irishman to 1800', *Modern Language Review*, 37:4 (1942): pp. 438–47.

Beal, J. C., *English Pronunciation in the Eighteenth Century: Thomas Spence's 'Grand Repository of the English Language' (1775)* (Oxford: Clarendon Press, 1999).

Beauford, W. 'Caoinan: *or some Account* of the Antient Irish Lamentations', *The Transactions of the Royal Irish Academy* (Dublin: [1787]–1800).

Bebbington, D. W., *Evangelicalism in Modern Britain: A History from the 1730s to the 1980s* (London: Unwin Hyman, 1989).

—, *The Dominance of Evangelicalism: The Age of Spurgeon and Moody* (Nottingham: Inter-Varsity Press, 2005).

Bennett, B. T., *British War Poetry in the Age of Romanticism 1793–1815*, ed. O. Smith, archived (September 2004), in the Electronic Editions of *Romantic Circles*: <http://www.rc.umd.edu/editions/warpoetry/>.

Bhabha, H., *The Location of Culture* (London and New York: Routledge, 1994).

Bindman, D., *The Shadow of the Guillotine: Britain and the French Revolution* (London: British Museum Publications, 1989).

Black, R. (ed.), *An Lasair: Anthology of Eighteenth-Century Gaelic Verse* (Edinburgh: Polygon, 2001).

Blake, W., *The Complete Writings of William Blake*, ed. G. Keynes (Oxford: Oxford University Press, 1966).

Blamire, S., *The Poetical Works* (London, 1842).

Blank, P., *Broken English: Dialects and Politics of Language in Renaissance Writings* (London: Routledge, 1996).

Blumhofer, E. L., *Her Heart Can See: The Life and Hymns of Fanny J. Crosby* (Grand Rapids, MI: Eerdmans, 2005).

Bobbin, T., *The Miscellaneous Works of Tim Bobbin Containing a View of the Lancashire Dialect* (Manchester: J. Slack, 1818).

Bolter, J., and R. Grusin, *Remediation: Understanding New Media* (Cambridge, MA: MIT Press, 1999).

Brooke, C., *Reliques of Irish Poetry: Consisting of Heroic Poems, Odes, Elegies, and Songs, translated into English Verse: With Notes Explanatory and Historical; and the Originals in the Irish Character. To which is Subjoined an Irish Tale* ([Dublin]: George Bonham, 1789).

Brooke, H., *The Songs in Jack the Gyant Queller. An Antique History*, 2nd edn (Dublin: George Faulkner, 1749).

—, *Riotous Performances: The Struggle for Hegemony in the Irish Theater, 1714–1784* (Notre Dame, IN: University of Notre Dame Press, 2003).

Bruce, F. F., 'Review of The Unbelievable Pre-Trib Origin', *Evangelical Quarterly*, 47 (January–March 1975).

Burke, E., *Empire and Community: Edmund Burke's Writing and Speeches in International Relations*, ed. D. P. Fidler and J. M. Welsh (Boulder, CO: Westview Press, 1999).

Burns, R., *The Letters of Robert Burns*, ed. J. DeLancey Ferguson, 2nd edn ed. G. Ross Roy, 2 vols (Oxford: Clarendon Press, 1985).

—, *The Canongate Burns*, ed. A. Noble and P. Scott Hogg (Edinburgh: Canongate, 2003).

Burnham, J. D., *A Story of Conflict: The Controversial Relationship between Benjamin Wills Newton and John Nelson Darby* (Carlisle: Paternoster, 2004).

Butler, M., 'Repossessing the Past: The Case for an Open Literary History', in M. Levinson, M. Butler, J. McGann, and P. Hamilton, *Rethinking Historicism: Critical Readings in Romantic History* (Oxford: Blackwell, 1989), pp. 64–84.

Buttimer, N., 'Literature in Irish, 1690–1800: From the Williamite Wars to the Act of Union', in M. Kelleher and P. O'Leary (eds), *The Cambridge History of Irish Literature, Volume One* (Cambridge: Cambridge University Press, 2006), pp. 320–71.

Byron, *Byron: Poetical Works*, ed. F. Page (Oxford: Oxford University Press, 1984).

Caball, M., and A. Carpenter, ed. *Oral and Print Cultures in Ireland 1600–1900* (Dublin: Four Courts Press, 2010).

Cairns, D., and S. Richards, *Writing Ireland: Colonialism, Nationalism, and Culture* (New York: St Martin's Press, 1988).

Carolan, 'Monody on the Death of his Wife', in J. C. Walker, *Historical Memoirs of the Irish Bards. Interspersed with Anecdotes of, and Occasional Observations on the Music of Ireland* (London: 1786), Appendix 92.

Carolan, N., *The Most Celebrated Irish Tunes: The Publishing of Irish Music in the Eighteenth Century* (Cork: Irish Traditional Music Society of University College Cork, 1990).

Carpenter, A., *Verse in English from Eighteenth-Century Ireland* (Cork: Cork University Press, 1998).

Carpenter, A. (ed.), *Verse in English from Eighteenth Century Ireland* (Cork: Cork University Press, 1998).

—, 'Garbling and Jumbling: Printing from Dictation in Eighteenth-Century Limerick', in M. Caball and A. Carpenter (eds), *Oral and Print Cultures in Ireland 1600–1900* (Dublin: Four Courts Press, 2010), pp. 32–46.

Carruthers, G., and A. Rawes (eds), *English Romanticism and the Celtic World* (Cambridge: Cambridge University Press, 2003).

Carter, G., *Anglican Evangelicals: Protestant Secessions from the Via Media, c. 1800– 1850* (Oxford: Oxford University Press, 2001).

Casanova, P., *The World Republic of Letters*, trans. M. B. DeBevoise (Cambridge, MA: Harvard University Press, 2004).

'Celebration of the Event of the Late Trials for High Treason held at the Crown and Anchor Tavern, London, February 4, 1795', in *Cabinet of Curiosities* (London, 1795).

Chan, S., 'On Yankee Stadium Restroom Dispute, the City Settles', *New York Times*, 7 July 2009.

Chun, W. H. K., and T. Keenan (eds), *New Media, Old Media: A History and Theory Reader* (New York: Routledge, 2006).

Charnell-White, C. A., *Bardic Circles: National, Regional and Personal Identity in the Bardic Vision of Iolo Morganwg* (Cardiff: University of Wales Press, 2007).

—, *Detholiad o Emynau Iolo Morganwg* (Aberystwyth: Canolfan Uwchefrydiau Cymreig a Cheltaidd, 2009).

Chase, M., 'From Millennium to Anniversary: The Concept of Jubilee in Late Eighteenth- and Nineteenth-Century England', *Past and Present*, 129 (1990), pp. 132–47.

'Church and King. A Song', *Gentleman's Magazine*, 63 (March 1793), p. 261.

Clark, J. C. D., *The Language of Liberty, 1660–1832* (Cambridge: Cambridge University Press, 1994).

Coad, F. R., *A History of the Brethren Movement*, 2nd edn (Exeter: Paternoster Press, 1976).

Coleridge, S. T., *Poetical Works*, ed. E. H. Coleridge (Oxford: Oxford University Press, 1967).

Colley, L., 'Little Englander Histories', *London Review of Books*, 32:14 (22 July 2010), p. 13.

Connell P., and N. Leask (eds), *Romanticism and Popular Poetry in Britain and Ireland* (Cambridge: Cambridge University Press, 2009).

Connolly, C., 'Irish Romanticism, 1800–1830', in M. Kelleher and P. O'Leary (eds), *The Cambridge History of Irish Literature*, 2 vols (Cambridge: Cambridge University Press, 2006), vol. 1, pp. 407–48.

Connolly, S. J., 'Jacobites, Whiteboys and Republicans: Varieties of Disaffection in Eighteenth-Century Ireland', *Eighteenth-Century Ireland*, 18 (2003), pp. 63–79.

Constantine, M.-A., *The Truth Against the World: Iolo Morganwg and Romantic Forgery* (Cardiff: University of Wales Press, 2007).

—, 'This Wildernessed Business of Publication: The Making of *Poems, Lyric and Pastoral* (1794)', in G. H. Jenkins (ed.), *A Rattleskull Genius*, 123–45.

—, 'Songs and Stones: Iolo Morganwg (1747–1826), Mason and Bard', *Eighteenth Century: Theory and Interpretation*, 47 (2006), pp. 233–51.

Conway, S., *War, State, and Society in Mid-Eighteenth-Century Britain and Ireland* (Oxford: Oxford University Press, 2006).

Crawford, R., *The Scottish Invention of English Literature* (Cambridge: Cambridge University Press, 1998).

—, *Devolving English Literature*, 2nd edn (Edinburgh: Edinburgh University Press, 2000).

—, *The Bard: Robert Burns, a Biography* (London: Jonathan Cape, 2009).

Cullen, L. M., *The Hidden Ireland: Reassessment of a Concept* (Mullingar: Lilliput Press, 1988).

Daly, M., and D. Dickson (eds), *The Origins of Popular Literacy in Ireland: Language Change and Educational Development 1700–1920* (Dublin: Anna Livia, 1990).

Damrosch, D., *What is World Literature?* (Princeton, NJ: Princeton University Press, 2003).

Darnton, R., *Poetry and the Police: Communication Networks in Eighteenth-Century Paris* (Cambridge MA: Belknap, 2010).

Davies, D. E. J., 'Astudiaeth o Feddwl a Chyfraniad Iolo Morganwg fel Rhesymolwr ac Undodwr' (University of Wales Ph.D. dissertation, 1975).

Davies, D. W., *Presences that Disturb: Models of Romantic Identity in the Literature and Culture of the 1790s* (Cardiff: University of Wales Press, 2002).

Davies, R. R., *The Revolt of Owain Glyn Dŵr* (Oxford: Oxford University Press, 1995).

Davis, L., *Music, Postcolonialism and Gender: The Construction of Irish National Identity, 1724–1874* (Notre Dame, IN: University of Notre Dame Press, 2005).

Davis, L., I. Duncan and J. Sorensen (eds), *Scotland and the Borders of Romanticism* (Cambridge: Cambridge University Press, 2004).

Davis, M. T., '"An Evening of Pleasure Rather than Business": Songs, Subversion and Radical Sub-Culture in the 1790s', *Journal for the Study of British Cultures*, 12 (2005), pp. 115–26.

—, I. McCalman, and C. Parolin (eds), *Newgate in Revolution: An Anthology of Radical Prison Literature* (London, New York: Continuum, 2005),

de hÓir, É., *Seán Ó Donnabháin agus Eoghan Ó Comhraí* (Dublin: An Clóchomhar, 1962).

Dibden, C., *A Collection of Songs, Selected from the Works of Mr Dibdin* (London: [1790]).

—, 'The Irish Drinking Song' (London, 1790).

Dickinson, H. T., *The Politics of the People in Eighteenth-Century Britain* (New York: St Martin's Press, 1994).

Dix, E. R. McC., 'Irish Chap Books, Song Books and Ballads', *Irish Book Lover*, 2 (1910–11), pp. 33–5.

Donnelly, J. S. Jr, and K. A. Miller (eds), *Irish Popular Culture 1650–1850* (Dublin: Irish Academic Press, 1998).

Duff, D., and C. Jones (eds), *Scotland, Ireland and the Romantic Aesthetic* (Lewisburg, PA: Bucknell University Press, 2007).

Dugaw, D., 'Folklore and John Gay', *Studies in English Literature, 1500–1900*, 31 (1991), pp. 515–33.

Dwan, D., *The Great Community: Culture and Nationalism in Ireland* (Dublin: Field Day, 2008).

Eagleton, T., F. Jameson and E. Said (eds), *Nationalism, Colonialism, and Literature* (Minneapolis, MN: University of Minnesota Press, 1990).

—, *Crazy John and the Bishop and Other Essays on Irish Culture* (Notre Dame, IN: University of Notre Dame Press & Cork: Field Day, 1998).

Eaton, D. I., *Politics for the People, Volume 1* (London: Daniel Isaac Eaton, 1794–5).

Edgeworth, M., *Castle Rackrent* (London: Joseph Johnston, 1800).

Ellis, T., *Edward Jones, Bardd y Brenin (1752–1824)* (Caerdydd: Gwasg Prifysgol Cymru, 1957).

Emerson, C., 'Answering for Central and Eastern Europe', in H. Saussy (ed.), *Comparative Literature in an Age of Globalization* (Baltimore, MD: Johns Hopkins University Press), pp. 203–11.

Epstein, J., *Radical Expression, Political Language, Ritual, and Symbol in England, 1790–1850* (Oxford: Oxford University Press, 1995).

—, *In Practice: Studies in the Language and Culture of Popular Politics in Modern Britain* (Stanford, CA: Stanford University Press, 2003).

Ferguson, F and A. R. Holmes (eds), *Revising Robert Burns and Ulster* (Dublin: Four Courts Press, 2009).

— (ed.), *Ulster-Scots Writing: An Anthology* (Dublin: Four Courts Press, 2008).

Fleischman, A., *Sources of Irish Traditional Music, c. 1600–1855*, 2 vols (New York: Garland, 1998).

Freneau, P. M., *Poems written between the Years 1768 and 1794* (Monmouth, NJ: Freneau, 1795).

Fulford, T., *Romanticism and Masculinity: Gender, Politics, and Poetics in the Writings of Burke, Coleridge, Cobbett, Wordsworth, De Quincey and Hazlitt* (New York: Macmillan Palgrave, 1999).

'Letter', *Gentleman's Magazine*, 21 (1751), p. 466.

Hen Gerddi Gwleidyddol (1588–1660) (Caerdydd: Cymdeithas Llên Cymru, 1901).

Gibbons, L., *Transformations in Irish Culture* (Notre Dame, IN: University of Notre Dame Press, 1996).

—, *Edmund Burke and Ireland: Aesthetic, Politics, and the Colonial Sublime* (Cambridge: Cambridge University Press, 2003).

Gillespie, R., *Reading Ireland: Print, Reading and Social Change in Early Modern Ireland* (New York: Palgrave, 2005).

Gitelman, L., *Always Already New: Media, History, and the Data of Culture* (Cambridge, MA: MIT Press, 2006).

Gitelman L., and G. B. Pingree, *New Media, 1740–1915* (Cambridge, MA: MIT Press, 2003).

Glen H., and P. Hamilton (eds), *Repossessing the Romantic Past* (Cambridge: Cambridge University Press, 2006).

Goodridge, J. (ed.), *English Labouring Class Poets, 1700–1900*, 3 vols (London: Pickering and Chatto, 2005).

Grigor, I. F., *Highland Resistance: The Radical Tradition in the Scottish North* (Edinburgh: Mainstream, 2000).

Habermas, J., *The Structural Transformation of the Public Sphere: An Inquiry into a Category of Bourgeois Society*, trans. T. Burger and F. Lawrence (Boston, MA: MIT Press, 1991).

Harris, B., 'Political Protests in the Year of Liberty, 1792', in B. Harris (ed.), *Scotland in the Age of the French Revolution* (Edinburgh: Birlinn, 2005), pp. 49–78.

Harris, B. *The Scottish People and the French Revolution* (London: Pickering & Chatto, 2008).

Harrison, N., 'Life on the Second Floor', *Comparative Literature*, 59 (2007), pp. 332–48.

Herbison, I., 'The Rest is Silence: Some Remarks on the Disappearance of Ulster Scots Poetry', in J. Erskine and G. Lucy (eds), *Cultural Traditions in Northern Ireland: Varieties of Scottishness* (Belfast: Institute of Irish Studies, 1997), pp. 129–45.

Higgins, P., *A Nation of Politicians: Gender, Patriotism and Political Culture in Late Eighteenth-Century Ireland* (Madison, WI: University of Wisconsin Press, 2010).

Holloway, J., and J. Black (eds), *Later English Broadside Ballads,* 2 vols (1975; London: Routledge and Kegan Paul, 1979).

Hobbs, J. H., *'I Sing for I Cannot Be Silent': The Feminization of American Hymnody, 1870–1920* (Pittsburgh, PA: University of Pittsburgh Press, 1997).

Holman, P., Review of B. Boydell and K. Houston (eds), *Music, Ireland and the Seventeenth Century, Journal of the Society for Musicology in Ireland,* 5 (2009–10), pp. 73–9.

Holman, P., 'A Little Light on Lorenzo Bocchi: An Italian in Edinburgh and Dublin', in R. Cowgill and P. Holman (eds), *Music in the British Provinces*, 1690–1914 (Aldershot: Ashgate, 2007).

Horgan, D. M., 'Popular Protest in the Eighteenth Century', *Review of English Studies*, 48 (1997): pp. 310–31.

Horsley, P. M., *Eighteenth-Century Newcastle* (Newcastle: Oriel Press, 1971).

Howard, H. (ed.), *Fun a la Mode, or, Sing, and Be Jolly; An Entire New Collection of Original Songs, Odes, Cantatas, &c. Critical, Comical, and Political* (London: J. Williams, 1763).

Howes, M., *Colonial Crossings: Figures in Irish Literary History* (Dublin: Field Day, 2006).

Huws, D., 'Iolo Morganwg and Traditional Music', in G. H. Jenkins (ed.), *Rattleskull Genius*, pp. 333–56.

James, E. W., 'Welsh Ballads and American Slavery', *Welsh Journal of Religious History*, 2 (2007), pp. 59–86.

Jenkins, G. H. (ed.), *A Rattleskull Genius: The Many Faces of Iolo Morganwg* (Cardiff: University of Wales Press, 2005).

—, *'Perish Kings and Emperors, but Let the Bard of Liberty Live'* (Aberystwyth: Centre for Advanced Welsh and Celtic Studies, 2006).

—, *Bard of Liberty: The Political Radicalism of Iolo Morganwg* (Cardiff: University of Wales Press, 2012).

—, F. M. Jones and D. C. Jones (eds), *The Correspondence of Iolo Morganwg*, 3 vols (Cardiff: University of Wales Press, 2007).

—, '"A Very Horrid Affair": Sedition and Unitarianism in the Age of Revolutions', in R. R. Davies and G. H. Jenkins (eds), *From Medieval to Modern Wales: Historical Essays in Honour of Kenneth O. Morgan and Ralph A. Griffiths* (Cardiff: University of Wales Press, 2004), pp. 175–96.

Jenkins, R. T., and H. Ramage, *A History of the Honourable Society of Cymmrodorion 1751–1951* (London: Cymmrodorion Society, 1951).

Johnson, D., *Music and Society in Lowland Scotland in the Eighteenth Century* (London: Oxford University Press, 1972).

Johnston, K. R., *The Hidden Wordsworth: Poet, Lover, Rebel, Spy* (New York and London: W. W. Norton & Co., 1998).

—, 'Usual and Unusual Suspects: John Thelwall, William Godwin and Pitt's Reign of Terror', in S. Poole (ed.), *John Thelwall: Radical Romantic and Acquitted Felon* (London: Pickering and Chatto, 2009), pp. 25–37.

—, 'Whose History? My Place or Yours? Republican Assumptions and Romantic Traditions', in D. W. Davies (ed.), *Romanticism, History, Historicism: Essays on an Orthodoxy* (London and New York: Routledge, 2009), pp. 77–102.

—, Review of Jenkins (ed.), *A Rattleskull Genius*, NBOL–19, <http://www.nbol-19.org/view_doc.php?index=34>

Jones, E., *The Bardic Museum* (London, 1802).

Jones, F. M., *Welsh Ballads of the French Revolution* (Cardiff: University of Wales Press, 2012).

Kaufmann, H., and C. Fauske (eds), *An Uncomfortable Authority: Maria Edgeworth and Her Contexts* (Newark, DE: University of Delaware Press, 2005).

Kearney, H., *The British Isles: A History of Four Nations* (Cambridge: Cambridge University Press, 1989).

Kelly, J., 'Regulating Print: The State and the Control of Print in Eighteenth-Century Ireland', *Eighteenth-Century Ireland*, 23 (2008), pp. 142–74.

Kelly, T., *Hymns on Various Passages of Scripture* (Dublin: J. and J. Carrick, 1806).

—, *Hymns on Various Passages of Scripture*, 6th edn (Dublin: R. M. Tims, 1826).

—, *Hymns on Various Passages of Scripture*, 7th edn (Dublin: Marcus Moses, 1853).

Kerrigan, J., *Archipelagic English* (Oxford: Oxford University Press, 2008).

Kilfeather, S., 'Strangers at Home: Political Fictions by Women in Eighteenth-Century Ireland' (Ph.D. dissertation, Princeton University, 1989).

Kimbrough, Jr, S. T., 'Hymns are Theology', *Theology Today*, 42 (1985), pp. 59–68.

Koch, J. T. (ed.), *Celtic Culture: A Historical Encyclopedia*, 5 vols (Santa Barbara, CA and Oxford: ABC-Clio, 2006).

Kodaly, Z., *Folk Music of Hungary*, trans. R. Tempest and C. Jolly (London: Barrie and Jenkins, 1971).

Koditschek, T. 'T. B. Macaulay, Whig History and the Romance of Empire: Towards a 'Greater Britain'', in T. Brotherstone, A. Clark and K. Whelan (eds), *These Fissured Isles:*

Ireland, Scotland and British History 1798–1848 (Edinburgh: John Donald Publishers, 2005), pp. 61–82.

Krapohl, R. H., 'A Search for Purity: The Controversial Life of John Nelson Darby' (Ph.D. dissertation, Baylor University, 1998).

Lewis, G., 'Eighteenth-Century Literary Forgeries, with Special Reference to Iolo Morganwg' (University of Oxford, DPhil Dissertation, 1991).

Leersen, J., *Mere Irish and Fior-Gael: Studies in the Idea of Irish Nationality, Its Development and Literary Expression Prior to the Nineteenth Century* (Notre Dame, IN: University of Notre Dame Press, 1997).

—, *Remembrance and Imagination: Patterns in the Historical and Literary Representation of Ireland in the Nineteenth Century* (Notre Dame, IN: Notre Dame University Press & Cork: Field Day, 1997).

Lefanu, A., *The Outlaw* in *Tales of a Tourist, Containing the Outlaw and Fashionable Connexions*, 4 vols (London: A. K. Newman, 1823).

—, [Sheridan], *The Sons of Erin: or, Modern Sentiment: A Comedy in Five Acts*. London: Ridgway, 1812.

Liu, A., 'Preface', in D. Walford Davies (ed.), *Romanticism, History, Historicism: Essays on an Orthodoxy (London and New York: Routledge, 2009)*.

Lloyd, A. L., *The Singing Englishman* (London: Workers' Music Association, 1944).

—, *Folk Song in England* (London: Lawrence and Wishart, 1967).

Lloyd, D., *Anomalous States: Irish Writing and the Post-Colonial Moment* (Durham: Duke University Press, 1993).

—, *Nationalism and Minor Literature: James Clarence Mangan and the Emergence of Irish Cultural Nationalism* (Berkeley, CA: University of California Press, 1987).

Löffler, M., *The Literary and Historical Legacy of Iolo Morganwg, 1826–1926* (Cardiff: University of Wales Press, 2007).

—, *Welsh Responses to the French Revolution: Press and Public Discourse* (Cardiff: University of Wales Press, 2012).

—, 'The 'Marseillaise', in Wales (via England)', in M.-A. Constantine and D. Johnston (eds), *"Footsteps of Liberty and Revolt": Essays on Wales and the French Revolution* (Cardiff, University of Wales Press, forthcoming).

London Public Advertiser and Literary Gazette, 'Letter', 12 September 1751.

Louden, R. B., *The World We Want; How and Why The Ideals of the Enlightenment Still Elude Us* (Oxford: Oxford University Press, 2007).

Low, D., *The Songs of Robert Burns* (London: Routledge, 1993).

Madden, R. R. (ed.), *Literary Remains of the United Irishmen of 1798* (Dublin: J. Duffy, 1887).

Magnuson, P. *Reading Public Romanticism* (Princeton, NJ: Princeton University Press, 1998).

Manly, S., *Language, Custom and Nation in the 1790s* (Aldershot: Ashgate, 2007).

Marggraf Turley, R., *The Politics of Language in Romantic Literature* (Basingstoke: Palgrave Macmillan, 2002).

Marini, S., 'Hymnody as History: Early Evangelical Hymns and the Recovery of American Popular Religion', *Church History*, 71 (2002), pp. 273–306.

Mayne, T., 'English, Scots and Irishmen, A Patriot Address to the Inhabitants of the United Kingdom', in B. T. Bennett (ed.), *British War Poetry in the Age of Romanticism: 1793–1815* (New York & London: Garland Publishing Inc., 1976).

MacCoinnich, C., *Òrain Ghaidhealach, agus Bearla air an eadar-theangacha* (Duneadainn: air son an ughdair; Edinburgh: published for the author, 1792).

MacLean, D., *The Literature of the Scottish Gael* (Edinburgh and London: William Hodge, 1912).

MacLean, M., and T. Dorgan (eds), *An Leabhar Mòr: The Great Book of Gaelic* (Edinburgh: Canongate, 2007).

McBride, I., *Eighteenth-Century Ireland: Isle of Slaves* (Dublin: Gill and Macmillan, 2009).

McCalman, I., *Radical Underworld: Prophets, Revolutionaries and Pornographers in London 1795–1840* (Oxford: Clarendon Press, 1993).

McCartney, D., *The Dawning of Democracy: Ireland 1800–1870* (Dublin: Helicon, 1987).

McGann, J. 'The Third World of Criticism', in M. Levinson, M. Butler, J. McGann and P. Hamilton, *Rethinking Historicism: Critical Readings in Romantic History* (Oxford: Blackwell, 1989).

McGuirk, C., *Robert Burns and the Sentimental Era* (Athens, GA: University of Georgia Press, 1985).

McIlvanney, L., *Burns the Radical* (Phantassie, East Lothian: Tuckwell Press, 2002).

—, 'Across the Narrow Sea: The Language, Literature and Politics of the Ulster Scots', in L. McIlvanney and R. Ryan (eds), *Ireland and Scotland: Culture and Society* (Cork: Cork University Press, 2004), pp. 203–26.

McKenzie, A., *Poems and Songs, on Different Subjects* (Belfast: Alexander MacKay, 1810).

MacLachlan, C. (ed.), *Before Burns: Eighteenth Century Poetry* (Edinburgh: Canongate Classics, 2002).

MacLaine, A. (ed.), *The Christis Kirk Tradition: Scots Poems of Folk Festivity* (Glasgow: Association for Scottish Literary Studies, 1996).

McCue, K., '"An Individual Flowering on a Common Stem": Melody, Performance, and National Song', in P. Connell and N. Leask (eds), *British Romanticism and Popular Culture in Britain and Ireland* (Cambridge: Cambridge University Press, 2009), pp. 88–106.

McLane, M., *Balladeering, Minstrelsy and the Making of British Romantic Poetry* (Cambridge: Cambridge University Press, 2008).

McLeod, A. (ed.), *The Songs of Duncan Ban Macintyre* (Edinburgh: Scottish Gaelic Texts Society, 1952).

McManus, A., *The Irish Hedge School and its Books 1695–1831* (Dublin: Four Courts Press, 2004).

Meek, D. (ed.), *Tuath is Tighearna: Tenants and Landlords. An Anthology of Gaelic Poetry of Social and Political Protest from the Clearances to the Land Agitation (1800–1890)* (Edinburgh: Scottish Gaelic Texts Society, 1995).

— (ed.), *Caran an t-Saoghal* (Edinburgh: Birlinn, 2003).

Melas, N., *All the Difference in the World: Postcoloniality and the Ends of Comparison* (Stanford, CA: Stanford University Press, 2007).

Meltzl, H., 'Present Tasks of Comparative Literature (1877)', in D. Damrosch and N. Melas and M. Buthelezi (eds), *The Princeton Sourcebook in Comparative Literature: From the European Enlightenment to the Global Present* (Princeton, NJ: Princeton University Press 2009), pp. 41–9.

Moody, J., 'Thomas Brown [alias Thomas Moore]: Censorship and Regency Cryptography', *European Romantic Review*, 18 (2007), pp. 187–94.

Molloy, F., 'Thomas Campbell's 'Exile of Erin': English Poem, Irish Reactions', in P. A. Lynch, J. Fischer and B. Coates, *Back to the Present: Forward to the Past: Irish Writing and History Since 1798*, 2 vols (New York: Rodopi, 2006), vol. 1, pp.43–52.

Moore, T., *Letter to the Roman Catholics of Dublin* (London: J. Carpenter, 1810).

—, *Life and Death of Lord Edward Fitzgerald*, 2nd edn (London: Longman, Rees, Orme, Brown, and Green, 1831).

—, *Memoirs of the Life of the Right Honorable Richard Brinsley Sheridan*, 2 vols, 5th edn (London: Longman, Rees, Orme, Brown and Green, 1827).

—, 'Oh! Blame Not the Bard', in J. M. Wright (ed.), *Irish Literature, 1750–1900: An Anthology* (Oxford: Blackwell, 2008), pp. 244–5.

—, *Memoirs of Captain Rock* (1824), ed. E. Nolan and S. Deane (Dublin: Field Day, 2008).

—, *The Poetical Works of Thomas Moore, Collected by Himself*, 10 vols (London: Longman, Orme, Brown, Green, & Longmans, 1840–1).

—, *A Selection of Irish Melodies, with Symphonies and Accompaniments by Sir John Stevenson Mus. Doc. and Characteristic Words by Thomas Moore Esq.* nos 1–4. (Dublin: W. Powers; London: [J.] Powers, n.d.).

—, *Travels of an Irish Gentleman in Search of a Religion* (London: Longman, Rees, Orme, Brown, Green, and Longman, 1833).

Moretti, F., *Atlas of the European Novel, 1800–1900* (London: Verso, 1999).

—, 'Conjectures on World Literature', *New Left Review*, 1 (2000), pp. 54–68.

—, 'The Slaughterhouse of Literature', *Modern Language Quarterly*, 61 (2000), pp. 207–27.

—, *Graphs, Maps, Trees: Abstract Models for a Literary History* (London: Verso, 2005).

Morgan, S. (Lady), *O'Donnel: A National Tale*, 3 vols (London: Henry Colburn, 1814).

Morley, V., 'Hugh MacCurtin: An Irish Poet in the French Army', *Eighteenth-Century Ireland*, 8 (1993), pp. 49–58.

—, *Washington i gCeannas a Ríochta: Cogadh Mheiriceá i Litríocht na Gaeilge* (Dublin: Coiscéim, 2005).

—, 'The Idea of Britain in Eighteenth-Century Ireland and Scotland', *Studia Hibernica*, 33 (2004–5), pp. 101–24.

—, 'Views of the Past in Irish Vernacular Literature', in T. Blanning and H. Schulze (eds), *Unity and Diversity in European Culture c. 1800* (Oxford: Oxford University Press, 2006), pp. 171–98.

—, 'The Continuity of Disaffection in Eighteenth-Century Ireland', *Eighteenth-Century Ireland*, 22 (2007), pp. 189–205.

Morrison, R., 'Oran Mhòr MhicLeoid' (The Great Song of MacLeod), in A. L. Gillies (ed.), *Songs of Gaelic Scotland* (Edinburgh: Birlinn, 2005), pp. 155–6.

Moulden, J., 'The Printed Ballad in Ireland: A Guide to the Popular Printing of Songs in Ireland 1760–1920' (Ph.D. dissertation, National University of Ireland, Galway, 2006).

Moylan, T. (ed.), *The Age of Revolution in the Irish Song Tradition 1776 to 1815* (Dublin: The Lilliput Press, 2000).

Murdoch, A., *British History 1660–1832: National Identity and Local Culture* (Basingstoke: Macmillan, 1998).

—, 'Henry Dundas, Scotland and the Union with Ireland, 1792–1801', in B. Harris (ed.), *Scotland in the Age of the French Revolution* (Edinburgh: Birlinn, 2005), pp. 125–39.

Murphy, S., *Maria Edgeworth and Romance* (Dublin: Four Courts Press, 2004).

Mee, J., '"Images of Truth New Born": Iolo, William Blake and the Literary Radicalism of the 1790s', in G. H. Jenkins (ed.), *A Rattleskull Genius*, pp. 173–93.

Morgan, P., *The Eighteenth-Century Renaissance* (Llandybïe: Christopher Davies, 1981).

—, *Iolo Morganwg* (Cardiff: University of Wales Press, 1975).

Mouw, R. J., and M. A. Noll (eds), *Wonderful Words of Life: Hymns in American Protestant History and Theology* (Grand Rapids, MI: Eerdmans, 2004).

Mufti, A., *Enlightenment in the Colony: The Jewish Question and the Crisis of Postcolonial Culture* (Princeton, NJ: Princeton University Press, 2007).

Murray, J., *Sermons to Asses* (London: J. Johnson, T. Cadell; Newcastle: W. Charnley, 1768).

Nebeker, G. L., 'John Nelson Darby and Trinity College, Dublin: A Study in Eschatological Contrasts', *Fides et Historia*, 34 (2002), pp. 87–108.

Newman, S., *Ballad Collection, Lyric, and the Canon: The Call of the Popular from Restoration to New Criticism* (Philadelphia, PA: University of Pennsylvania Press, 2007).

Nic Éinrí, Ú. (ed.), *Canfar an Dán: Uilliam English agus a Chairde* (Dingle: An Sagart, 2003).

Ní Shúilleabháin, M. (ed.), *Amhráin Thomáis Rua* (Maynooth: An Sagart, 1985).

Noble, A., and P. Scott Hogg (eds), *The Canongate Burns* (Edinburgh: Canongate Classics, 2001).

Noble, A., 'Burns, Scotland, and the American Revolution', in S. Alker, L. Davis and H. F. Nelson (eds), *Robert Burns and Transatlantic Culture* (Farnham & Burlington, VT: Ashgate, 2011), pp. 31–51.

Noll, M. A., *The Rise of Evangelicalism: The Age of Edwards, Whitefield and the Wesleys* (Nottingham: Inter-Varsity Press, 2004).

Ó Buachalla, B., 'Seacaibíteachas Thaidhg Uí Neachtain', *Studia Hibernica*, 26 (1991– 2), pp. 31–64.

—, *Aisling Ghéar: Na Stíobhartaigh agus an tAos Leinn 1603–1788* (Dublin: An Clóchomhar, 1996).

Ó Ciardha, É., 'A Voice from the Jacobite Underground: Liam Inglis', in G. Moran (ed.), *Radical Irish Priests 1660–1970* (Dublin: Four Courts Press, 1998), pp. 16–39.

Ó Ciosáin, N., *Print and Popular Culture in Ireland, 1750–1850* (London and New York: Macmillan, 1997).

O'Conor, C., *Dissertations on the History of Ireland* (Dublin: 1753).

Ó Fiannachta, P., 'Eoghan Ó Comhraí: file traidisiúnta', in D. Ó Corráin, L. Breatnach and K. McCone (eds), *Sages, Saints and Storytellers: Celtic Studies in Honour of Professor James Carney* (Maynooth: An Sagart, 1989), pp. 280–306.

Ó Foghludha, R. (ed.), *Cois na Bríde: Liam Inglis O.S.A. 1709–1778* (Dublin: Oifig Díolta Foillseacháin Rialtais, 1937).

Ó Gallchoir, C., *Maria Edgeworth: Women, Enlightenment and Nation* (Dublin: University College Dublin Press, 2005).

O'Halloran, S., *A General History of Ireland,* 2 vols (London: A. Hamilton, 1778).

O'Keeffe, A., *National Characters Exhibited in Forty Geographical Poems, with Plates* (London: Darton, Harvey, and Darton, 1818).

Ó Muirgheasa, É (ed.), *Dhá Chéad de Cheoltaibh Uladh* (Dublin: Oifig Díolta Foillseacháin Rialtais, 1934).

Ó Muirithe, D. (ed.), *An tAmhrán Macarónach* (Dublin: An Clóchomhar, 1980).

O'Neil, D. J., 'The Cult of Self-Sacrifice: The Irish Experience', *Éire-Ireland*, 24 (1989), pp. 89–105.

Owen, W., *The Heroic Elegies and Other Pieces of Llywarç Hen* (London: 1792).

Parsley's Lyric Repository, for 1789. Containing a Selection of all the Favorite Songs, Duets, Trios, &c. now Singing at the Theatres-Royal (London: R. Parsley, 1789).

Oxford English Dictionary, 2nd edn (Oxford: Oxford University Press, 1989).

Paddy's Resource, or the Harp of Erin, Attuned to Freedom; Being a Collection of Patriotic Songs Selected for Paddy's Amusement (Dublin: 'By the printer hereof', [n.d.]).

Paine, T., *The Thomas Paine Reader*, ed. M. Foot and I. Kramnick (Harmondsworth: Penguin Classics, 1987).

Palmer, R., *The Sound of History: Songs and Social Comment* (London: Faber & Faber, 1988).

Paul, R. W., *For Zion's Sake: Christian Zionism and the Role of John Nelson Darby* (Carlisle: Paternoster, 2007).

Paulin, T. (ed.), *The Faber Book of Vernacular Verse* (London: Faber & Faber, 1994).

Pentland G., 'Patriotism, Universalism and the Scottish Conventions, 1792–94', *History*, 89 (2004), pp. 340–60.

Percy, T., *Reliques of Ancient English Poetry. Consisting of Old Heroic Ballads, Songs, and other Pieces of our Earlier Poets (chiefly of the Lyric Kind)* (London, 1765).

Peters, B., 'And Lead us Not into Thinking the New is New: A Bibliographic Case for New Media History', *New Media and Society*, 11 (2009), pp. 13–30.

Philips, A., *Guardian*, 16 (30 March 1713), pp. 64–7.

Piper, A., *Dreaming in Books: The Making of the Bibliographic Imagination in the Romantic Era* (Chicago, IL: University of Chicago Press, 2009).

Pittock, M. G. H., *Scottish and Irish Romanticism* (Oxford: Oxford University Press, 2008).

Playford, H., *Wit and Mirth: Pills to Purge Melancholy* (London: William Pearson, 1707–9).

—, *Songs Compleat, Pleasant and Divertive; Set to Musick by Dr John Blow, Mr Henry Purcell, and Other Excellent Masters* (London: William Pearson, 1719).

Pocock, J. G. A., 'British History: A Plea for a New Subject', *Journal of Modern History*, 47 (1975), pp. 601–21.

Ramsay, A., *Tea-Table Miscellany* (1724).

—, *The Gentle Shepherd* (1725).

Ritson, J., *A Select Collection of English Songs*, 3 vols (London: 1783).

Robinson, R., *Thomas Bewick: His Life and Times* (Newcastle: The Author, 1887).

Saglia, D., 'Harem Power: Narrative Structure and Sexual Politics in Thomas Moore's *Lalla Rookh*', *Questione Romantica*, 12–13 (2002), pp. 77–88.

Scrivener, M., *Poetry and Reform: Periodical Verse from the English Democratic Press 1792–1824* (Detroit, MI: Wayne State University Press, 1992).

—, *Seditious Allegories: John Thelwell and Jacobin Writing* (University Park, PA: University of Pennsylvania Press, 2001).

Shelley, P. B., *The Poems of Percy Bysshe Shelley*, ed. T. Hutchinson (Oxford: Oxford University Press, 1919).

Sherburn, G., *A Literary History of England, Volume 3: The Restoration and Eighteenth Century (1660–1789)* (New York: Appleton-Century-Crofts, 1948).

Shields, H., *Shamrock, Rose and Thistle: Folk Singing in North Derry* (Belfast: The Blackstaff Press, 1981).

Simpson, C. M., *The British Broadside Ballad and its Music* (New Brunswick, NJ: Rutgers University Press, 1966).

Sizer, S., *Hymns and Social Religion* (Philadelphia, PA: Temple University Press, 1978).

Smith, O., *The Politics of Language, 1789–1819* (Oxford: Clarendon Press, 1984).

Skoblow, J. *Dooble Tongue: Scots, Burns, Contradiction* (Newark, DE: University of Delaware Press, 2001).

Smyth, J., *The Men of No Property: Irish Radicals and Popular Politics in the Late Eighteenth Century* (Dublin: Gill and Macmillan, 1992).

Sorensen, J., 'Orality's Silence: The Other Ballad Revival', *International Journal of Scottish Literature*, 2 (2007), at <http://www.ijsl.stir.ac.uk/issue2/sorensen.ht > [accessed 30 June 2009].

Spence, T., *The Grand Repository of the English Language* (Newcastle: Thomas Saint, 1775).

—, *The Real Reading Made Easy* (Newcastle: T. Saint, 1782).

—, *A Supplement to the History of Robinson Crusoe* (Newcastle: T. Saint, 1782).

—, *The Rights of Man in Verse* (Newcastle, 1783).

—, *The Case of Thomas Spence, Bookseller* (London: printed for the author, 1792).

—, *The Coin Collector's Companion* (London: printed for the author, 1795).

—, *The Restorer of Society to its Natural State* (London: printed for the author, 1801).

—, *Dhĕ Impŏrtănt Triăl ov Tŏmĭs Spĕns* (London: printed for the author, 1803).

—, *The Important Trial of Thomas Spence* (London: A. Seale for T. Spence, 1807).

—, *Spence's Songs, Part the Second* (London: Seale and Bates, [1811?]).

—, *Pig's Meat: or Lessons for the People* (London: T. Spence, 1795).

—, 'Examples of Safe Printing', in M. Scrivener (ed.), *Poetry and Reform: Periodical Verse from the English Democratic Press 1792–1824* (Detroit, MI: Wayne State University Press, 1992).

Stafford, F. J., *The Last of the Race: The Growth of a Myth from Milton to Darwin* (Oxford: Clarendon Press, 1994).

—, *Starting Lines in Scottish, Irish and English Poetry from Burns to Heaney* (Oxford: Oxford University Press, 2000).

Stagg, J., *Miscellaneous Poems, some of which are in the Cumberland Dialect* (Workington: W. Borrowdale, 1805).

Stowe, D. W., *How Sweet the Sound: Music in the Spiritual Lives of Americans* (Cambridge, MA: Harvard University Press, 2004).

Stunt, T. C. F., *From Awakening to Secession: Radical Evangelicals in Switzerland and Britain, 1815–35* (Edinburgh: T. & T. Clark, 2000).

—, 'Influences in the Early Development of J. N. Darby', in C. Gribben and T. C. F. Stunt (eds), *Prisoners of Hope? Aspects of Evangelical Millennialism in Britain and Ireland, 1800–1880* (Carlisle: Paternoster, 2004), pp. 44–68.

—, 'John Nelson Darby: Contexts and Perceptions', in C. Gribben and A. R. Holmes (eds), *Protestant Millennialism, Evangelicalism and Irish Society, 1790–2005* (Basingstoke: Palgrave Macmillan, 2006), pp. 83–98.

Sweetnam, M. S., 'Defining Dispensationalism: A Cultural Studies Perspective', *Journal of Religious History*, 34 (2010), pp. 191–212.

— and C. Gribben, 'J. N. Darby and the Irish Origins of Dispensationalism', *Journal of the Evangelical Theological Society*, 52 (2009), pp. 569–77.

Taylor, S. B., 'Irish Odalisques and Other Seductive Figures: Thomas Moore's *Lalla Rookh*', in D. J. O'Quinn (ed.), *The Containment and Re-Deployment of English India* (Romantic

Circles Praxis Series, 2000), available at: <http://www.rc.umd.edu/praxis/containment/taylor/taylor.html>.

Taylor, T., 'Peopling the Stage: Opera, Otherness and New Musical Representations in the Eighteenth Century', *Cultural Critique*, 36 (1997), pp. 55–88.

Thale, M. (ed.), *Selections from the Papers of the London Corresponding Society 1792– 1799* (Cambridge: Cambridge University Press, 1983).

The Banquet of Thalia, or the Fashionable Songsters Pocket Memorial. An Elegant Collection of the Most Admired Songs from Ancient, & Modern ([London, 1788]).

The Irish Harp (attun'd to freedom), a Collection of Patriotic Songs; Selected for Paddy's Amusement (Dublin, 1798).

Thuente, M. H., *The Harp Re-Strung: The United Irishmen and the Rise of Literary Nationalism* (Syracuse, NY: Syracuse University Press, 1994).

Thelwall, J., *An Appeal to Popular Opinion against Kidnapping and Murder* (London: J. S. Jordan, 1796).

—, 'On Song-Writing', *Poetical Recreations of The Champion and His Literary Correspondents* (London: John Thelwall, 1822), pp. 163–5.

Thomson, D. S. (ed.), *Alasdair Mac Mhaighstir Alasdair: Selected Poems* (Edinburgh: Scottish Academic Press, 1996).

Thomson, R., *A Tribute to Liberty* (London: Thomson and Hamilton, 1793).

Tone, W., *Life of Theobald Wolf Tone*, 2 vols (Washington, DC: Gales and Seaton, 1826).

Torrens, R., *The Victim of Intolerance; Or, the Hermit of Killarney: A Catholic Tale*, 4 vols (London: Gale, Curtis, and Fenner, 1814).

Trumpener, K., *Bardic Nationalism: The Romantic Novel and the British Empire* (Princeton, NJ: Princeton University Press, 1997).

—, 'World Music, World Literature: A Geopolitical View', in H. Saussy (ed.), *Comparative Literature in an Age of Globalization* (Baltimore, MD: Johns Hopkins University Press, 2006), pp. 185–202.

Turner, W. G., and E. Cross, *Unknown and Well Known: A Biography of John Nelson Darby* (London: Chapter Two, 1990).

[Tytler, W.], 'A Dissertation on the Scottish Musick', in Hugh Arnot,

The History of Edinburgh, from the Earliest Accounts to the Present Time (Edinburgh: printed for William Creech; and sold by Messrs Robinson & Co, London, 1779), pp. 624–42 [Appendix no. 8, attributed to 'A learned and ingenious friend'].

Ua Duinnín, P. (ed.), *Eoghan Ruadh Ua Súilleabháin* (Dublin: Connradh na Gaedhilge, 1923).

Uglow, J., *Nature's Engraver: A Life of Thomas Bewick* (London: Faber & Faber, 2006).

Vail, J. W., *The Literary Relationship of Lord Byron and Thomas Moore* (Baltimore, MD: Johns Hopkins University Press, 2001).

—, 'Thomas Moore: After the Battle', in J. M. Wright (ed.), *Companion to Irish Literature,* 2 vols (Oxford: Blackwell, 2010), vol. 1, pp. 310–25.

Vallancey, C., *A Vindication of the Ancient History of Ireland* (Dublin: Luke White, 1786).

Vidal, G. *Inventing a Nation: Washington, Adams, Jefferson* (New Haven, CT: Yale University Press, 2003).

Vishnawatan, G., *Masks of Conquest: Literary Study and British Rule in India* (New York: Columbia University Press, 1989).

Walford Davies, D., and L. Pratt (eds), *Wales and the Romantic Imagination* (Cardiff: University of Wales Press, 2007).

Walker, J. C., *Historical Memoirs of the Irish Bards. Interspersed with Anecdotes of, and Occasional Observations on, the Music of Ireland* (London: T. Payne and Sons, 1786).

Warner, M., 'In the Time of Not Yet: Marina Warner on the Imaginary of Edward Said'. *London Review of Books*, 32:24 (16 December 2010).

Watson, J. R., *The English Hymn: A Critical and Historical Study* (Oxford: Oxford University Press, 1999).

Welch, R., *Irish Poetry from Moore to Yeats* (Totowa: Barnes and Noble Books, 1980).

Wells, R. *Insurrection: The British Experience 1795–1803* (Gloucester: Alan Sutton Publishing, 1983).

—, 'English Society and Revolutionary Politics in the 1790s: The Case for Insurrection', in M. Philp (ed.), *The French Revolution and British Popular Politics* (Cambridge: Cambridge University Press, 2004), pp. 188–225.

Weremchuk, M., *John Nelson Darby* (Neptune, NJ: Loizeaux, 1992).

Wheeler, W. G., 'The Spread of Provincial Printing in Ireland up to 1850', *Irish Booklore*, 4 (1978), pp. 7–18.

Whelan, K., *The Tree of Liberty: Radicalism, Catholicism and the Construction of Irish Identity 1760–1830* (Cork: Cork University Press, 1996).

White, H., *The Keeper's Recital: Music and Cultural History in Ireland, 1770–1970* (Cork: Cork University Press).

Williams, E. (Iolo Morganwg), *Poems, Lyric and Pastoral*, 2 vols (London: J. Nichols, 1794).

Williams, G. J., *Iolo Morganwg – y Gyfrol Gyntaf* (Caerdydd: Gwasg Prifysgol Cymru, 1956).

Wilson, C. H., *Poems Translated from the Irish Language into the English* (Dublin: 1782).

Wilson, K., *The Sense of the People: Politics, Culture and Imperialism in England 1715–1785* (Cambridge: Cambridge University Press, 1995).

Wollffe, J., *The Expansion of Evangelicalism: The Age of Wilberforce, More, Chalmers and Finney* (Nottingham: Inter-Varsity Press, 2007).

Wood, A. W., 'Kant's *Project for Perpetual Peace*', in P. Cheah and B. Robbins (eds), *Cosmopolitics: Thinking and Feeling Beyond the National* (Minneapolis, MN: The University of Minnesota Press, 1998).

Wordsworth, W., *The Poetical Works of Wordsworth*, ed. T. Hutchinson (Oxford: Oxford University Press, 1956).

Wright, J. M., 'Atlantic Exile and the Stateless Citizen in Irish Romanticism', *Wordsworth Circle*, 40 (2009), pp. 36–44.

—, *Ireland, India and Nationalism in Nineteenth-Century Literature* (Cambridge: Cambridge University Press, 2007).

—, 'Thomas Moore', in F. Burwick, D. L. Hoeveler, and N. Moore Goslee, *Encyclopedia of Romantic Literature*, 3 vols (Oxford: Wiley-Blackwell, 2012), vol. 2, pp. 873–81.

Wright, T., *The Political Songs of England, From the Reign of John to that of Edward II* (1838), ed. E. Goldsmid (Edinburgh: Unwin, 1884).

Zimmermann, G,-D., *Songs of Irish Rebellion: Political Street Ballads and Rebel Songs 1780–1900* (Dublin: Four Courts Press, 1967).

INDEX

abolition, 6, 67, 197
Act of Union (1800), 153, 155, 156
Adams, James, *Appendix to his Pronunciation to the English language* (1799), 189
Adams, James Eli, 162, 230n40
Addison, Joseph, 57
Aeschylus, 14
Aikin, John, 66
   editor *Monthly Magazine*, 37
   Essays on Song-Writing (1772), 37, 96
   song classification, 38, 39
Aird, James, *Selection of Scotch, English, Irish and Foreign Airs* (1782), 97
Aiseirigh na Seann Chànain Albannaich (MacDonald), 125–6
aisling genre, 29, 119
America, 5, 9, 13, 14, 35–6
America: A Prophecy (Blake), 13–14
America
   'America the Beautiful', 25, 35
   colonists, 110
   evangelicalism, 80
   fundamentalism, 27, 78
   radical diaspora, 31
   revivalism, 81
   Royal Highlanders, 128
   Scottish emigrants, 131
   'Take Me Out to the Ballgame', 35
   Yankee Stadium, 35–6
American War of Independence, 10, 11, 12, 16, 28, 59
Ancient Scottish Songs (Herd), 96, 100
Anderson, Robert, 32, 170
   Ballads in the Cumberland Dialect (1805), 171, 177
   and Burns' example, 171, 173

'The Clay Daubin' (1804), 177
dialect and radical politics, 177
Poems on Various Subjects (1798), 232n21
political commentary, 173, 178
sonnet on Tooke, 177
'The Village Gang', 178
Anglican secessionists, 82–3
anti-Catholic songs, 32, 174–5
anti-imperialism, 6, 14, 15
Anti-Jacobin, and Jacobin poetry, 19–20
Appendix to his Pronunciation to the English language (Adams), 189
Aria di Camera (Wright), 97
Arnold, Matthew, 79
   On the Study of Celtic Literature (1867), 201
Ashraf, P.M.
   effects of Combination Acts, 54
   and radical songs, 56
   on Spence, 51, 52, 55, 61
Austen, Jane, 155

Baillie, Donald (Dòmhnall Bàillidh)
   'Aoir air Pàdraig Sellar' (Satire on Patrick Sellar), 136, 137
   denunciation of the Highland landlords, 136–7
Ballads in the Cumberland Dialect (Anderson), 171, 177
Bamford, Samuel, 183, 187, 233n25, 234n32
   annotation of dialect speech, 190
   ballad 'A Song of Slaughter', 188
Bannockburn (1314), 8
Banquet of Thalia, or the Fashionable Songsters Pocket Memorial (1788), 99
'A Favourite Irish Song', 99, 220n31

Barbauld, Anna, 37
Bard of Dunover *see* McKenzie, Andrew
Bard of Liberty *see* Iolo Morganwg
Bard of Snowdon (Richard Llwyd), 65, 213n11
Bardd y Brenin (Edward Jones), 65, 66, 213n10
   Musical and Poetical Relicks of the Welsh Bards, 65
Barnard, Toby, 96
   'Print Culture 1700-1800', 219n10
Barrell, John, 3, 196, 207n9
   and radical caricature, 190, 234n28
   and Spence's coins, 61
   The Spirit of Despotism, 20–1
Bastille Day, poems and songs, 197–8
bawdy songs, 30, 39, 98, 137–9, 144, 145, 147
   'Dòmhnallan Dubh' (Little Black Donnie), 138
   'Eachainn an Slaoightear' (Hector the Rascal), 138
   'Irish Jigg', 98
   'Merry Muses of Caledonia', 30
   'An Oba Nodha' (The Oobie Noogie), 138–9
   'An Seudagan' (My Handsome Little Tiny Hero), 137–8
   see also chapbook songs
Beal, Joan C., 25, 26, 211n10
Beaufort, William
   in *Transactions of the Royal Irish Academy*, 102-3, 211n43
   notation of 'Caoinan, or Irish Funeral Song', 102
Bebbington, David, and evangelicanism, 78, 216n4–5
Beckett, Samuel, 31
Beggar's Opera (Gay), 97
Beggar's Wedding (Coffey), 97
Belfast Harpers' Festival (1792), 195, 203
Belfast Harpers' Society, 195
Bennett, Betty K., anthology, 20, 208n22, 210n27
Best, Thomas, and Britannia, 44
Bewick, John, and Spence, 56
Bewick, Thomas, 26, 52
   Nature's Engraver: A Life of Thomas Bewick (Uglow), 56

   and Newcastle Philosophical Society, 53
   and Swarley's Club, 55
   Thomas Bewick: His Life and Times (1887), 52
Bhabha, Homi, on colonial hybridity, 29–30, 225n7
Bindman, David, 54, 211n16
Birch, Samuel (printer), 185
Black, Ronald
   An Lasair: Anthology of Eighteenth Century Gaelic Verse, 225n9, 225n13
   and *An Leabhar Liath*, 138
Blake, William 14, 28, 64
   America: A Prophecy (1793), 13–14
Blamire, Sussanah, and dialect, 173, 232n28
Blank, Paula, and dialect, 172, 232n26
Bliss, P.P., 81
Blumhofer, Edith, 81, 217n21
Bobbin, Tim, 32, 170, 178, 179
   and dialect, 172, 173, 190
   influence on Walker, 182–3
   and political commentary, 173, 174–5, 176
   Tummus and Meary, 175–6, 190
   A View of the Lancashire Dialect (1750), 175–6
Bocchi, Lorenzo, 219n19
Bolter, Jay, and remediation, 95, 218n3
Bolton Chronicle, 193
Bonaparte, Napoleon, 8, 120, 122
Booker Prize, 201
Booth, William, use of secular tunes, 56
Boston Chronicle, 59
Boswell, James, 126
Bowles, William Lisle, 32
Brennus, Gallic Chief, 127
British constitution, and Paine, 16–17, 181
British Convention (1793), 6
British National Anthem, 36
   parodies of, 57–8, 59, 67, 69, 70–1, 187–8
Britons (Colley), 22
broadside ballads, 57, 63, 182, 191–3, 220n24
Brooke, Charlotte
   ambivalent political position, 107–8
   bardic poetry, 104–5
   Carolan's songs, 95, 104, 108
   'Cean Dubh Deelish', 107

commentary on Ryan's 'Elegy', 107–8
and Davis' work on *Reliques*, 27, 28, 196
importance of voice, 105
and the Irish drinking song, 103
lack of humour in Irish poetry, 103–4
'The Maid of the Valley', 104, 105, 108
'Poem of Conloch', 104
poem 'Tale of Maon', 107
Reliques of Irish Poetry (1789), 95, 96, 103, 104, 222n65
and remediation of Gaelic song, 28, 95, 96, 105, 107
and Royal Irish Academy, 221n54
'Song by Patrick Linden', 108
'Song for Gracey Nugent', 105, 108
'Thoughts on Irish Song', 95, 96, 105–7
translations of songs, 95, 105–6, *106*, 107, 222n78
Brooke, Henry, Irish tunes in *Jack the Giant Queller*, 97, 220n21
Bruce, F.F., 78–9, 217n12
Bunting, Edward, 195, 196
Bunyan, John, 122
Burke, Edmund, 10, 12, 25, 42, 155, 228n7
allegorical images, 47
and the *Anti-Jacobin*, 19
in Irish nationalist songs, 153
Reflections on the Revolution in France (1790), 184
and Spence's satire, 60–1
and 'swinish multitude', 57, 184
Burke, Helen, on Gaelic Irish tunes, 97
Burns, Robert, 4, 5, 6
and Bannockburn, 8
collector of songs, 30
dialect as artistic choice, 33, 168, 172
and Graham of Fintry, 4–5
influence on Anderson and McKenzie, 170, 171
influence throughout British Isles, 32
influence on working-class authors, 189–90
inspired by Aird and Oswald song collections, 97
and the 'native language', 167–8
poem on Clearances, 30
pro-American poems, 9
rebuttal of his poem by Scott, 6–7, 8
song described as 'The Marseillaise of Humanity', 6
Thelwall on songs of, 40
and Thomson, 5–6, 220n20
use of Irish airs, 220n20
Burns, Robert: works cited
'A Man's a Man for A' That' (1795), 5
'Address to Beelzebub', 30
'The Author's Earnest Cry and Prayer', 175
'A Dream', 175
'Ode for General Washington's Birthday', 15
Poems, Chiefly in the Scottish Dialect (1786), 171, 173
'Scots Wha Hae', 8
'The Tree of Liberty', 9
Butler, Marilyn, 22, 23
Buttimer, Neil, 121, 224n34
Byron, George Gordon, baron, 158, 229n21

'Ça Ira', 3, 4, 8, 36, 48, 71
Caledonian Pocket Companion (Oswald), 97
Cameron, Alan, and the Cameron Highlanders, 136
Campbell, Thomas, 'The Exile of Erin', 157–8, 229n20
Carlyle, Thomas, 162
Carolan, Turlough, 95, 104, 218n2
'Song for Gracey Nugent', 108
'Song for Mabel Kelly', 105
Caroline, queen, 191
Carpenter, Andrew, 30, 98, 196, 199, 220n27, 226n2
Carson, Ciaran, 2
Carter, Grayson, 82, 216n1, 217n22–3
Cartwright, John, 109
Case of Thomas Spence, Bookseller (Spence), 54
Castle Rackrent (Edgeworth), 168, 173
Castlereagh, Robert Stewart, viscount, 9
Catholic church, in Ireland, 145
Catholic Emancipation, 153, 186, 195
Catholic University of Ireland, 121
censorship, 141, 144, 158
High Treason in speech and writing, 20, 54, 212n1
Two Acts (1795), 186
Centre for Irish-Scottish and Comparative Studies, 202

chapbook songs
  'The Boys of Stoneybatter', 146
  'The Coughing Old Man', 143
  'Darby O'Gallagher, or the Answer to Morgan Rattler', 147–8
  'The Gobbio', 143
  'The New Dhooraling', 148–9
  'Oonagh's Lock', 146
  'Shales's Rambles, or the Lurgan Weaver', 149–50
  'Stauka an Varaga', 145
chapbooks, 30, 141
  and bilingual audience, 141
  and dictation, 141, 147
  and double meaning, 142, 143, 149, 150
  and female audience, 148
  in Hiberno-English, 30, 141, 142
  and Irish *amhrán* (song) metres, 142, 150, 227n25
  and Irish-language prosody, 142
  and itinerant singers, 143, 147
  and political comment, 144
  printers of, 141, 144, 146, 147
  purchasers of, 142, 145
  and sexually explicit songs, 143, 144, 145, 146, 147
  subversion of social order, 143–4, 151
  and vernacular poetry, 141
Charnell-White, Cathryn, 67, 213n13, 213n22
Chartism, 32, 40, 68, 193
Chase, Malcolm, on Spence and jubilee, 57–8
Chatterton, Thomas, 66
Chester Chronicle, 183
Chun, Wendy Hui Kyong, history of media, 95, 218n5
Church of England, and fast days, 44
Church of Ireland, and tracts, 144–5
Church-and-King loyalists, 181, 182, 185, 186
Claude (Claude Lorrain), 38
Clearances *see* Highland Clearances
Coetzee, J.M., 201
Coffey, Charles, 97
  Beggar's Wedding (1729), 97
Coin Collector's Companion (Spence), 61
Colection [sic] of the most Celebrated Irish Tunes (Neale), 97, 219n19

Coleridge, Samuel Taylor
  anonymous poems anti-Pitt, 9–10, 17, 18
  on Bowles' poetry, 32
  and British imperial repression, 12, 13
  on Burns' poetry, 32
  and Irish massacres (1798), 11, 12
  and war, 11, 12
Coleridge, Samuel Taylor: works cited
  'Fears in Solitude', 11–12
  'Fire, Famine and Slaughter', 17–18
  'Ode on the Departing Year', 9
Collection of Psalms and Hymns extracted from Various Authors (Kelly), 83
Colley, Linda, 14–15
  Britons, 22
Collier, John *see* Bobbin, Tim
Combination Acts (1799, 1800), 54
Common, Cormac
  and bardic poetry, 104–5
  and Oisin's poems, 105
Comparative Literature, 200, 201, 202, 203, 235n5
  The Field Day Anthology of Irish Writing, 201–2
  Irish Scottish Academic Initiative, 202
  Journal of Irish and Scottish Studies, 202
Connolly, Claire, 155, 198, 228n5
Connolly, S.J., 145, 223n25
Considerations on the Present Disturbances in the Province of Munster ('Trant), 107
Constantine, Mary-Ann
  bardic and druidic precedents, 196
  and Iolo Morganwg, 26
Conway, Stephen, 117, 223n19
Corporation Acts, 109
Corruption and Intolerance (Moore), 159
Cosmopolis (1896-8), multi-lingual journal, 201
Cowdroy, William (printer), 183, 185, 233n8
Cowley, Abraham, 37
Crawford, Robert
  and Burns, 176
  and English literature, 200, 231n10, 235n7
  and Scots dialect, 169
Cromwell, Oliver, 119
Crosby, Fanny, 81, 217n21
Cullen, L.M., the *aisling* genre 119

Culloden (1746), 29
Cumberland dialect, 32, 171–3, 177–9

Darby, John Nelson
  and dispensationalist theology, 90
  and millenarian theology, 27, 78
  and Trinity College Dublin, 85, 216n7–8, 216n11
Darnton, Robert, 3–4, 207n6, 207n10–12
Davis, Leith, 196, 198, 219n17
  on Brooke's *Reliques*, 28
  and Irish Gaelic song, 27, 198
  on Moore, 159
  and remediation, 27–8
Davis, Michael, songs as point of cohesion, 27, 70
Deane, Seamus, 169, 231n11
Defoe, Daniel, *Robinson Crusoe*, 57, 61
Dermody, Thomas, 172, 177, 231n24
dialects
  and archipelagic connections, 170, 171, 172, 178–9
  as artistic choice, 172
  and Burns' influence, 171–2
  English dialects, 31–2
  and English Romantics, 168
  in English writing, 170, 173
  and Irish English, 168–9
  and non-standard speaker, 173–4
  in north of England, 172–3
  and radical politics, 176–7
  in Scottish writing, 168, 169
  and shift from Standard English, 173
  in Ulster, 172, 173, 232n29
  used to portray barbarity, 174–5
  see also Cumberland dialect; Lancashire dialect
Dibden, Charles, and 'Irish Drinking Song', 99, 103, 220n33–4
Dickinson, Harold, *Oxford Dictionary of National Biography*, 53
Dickinson, John, 'The Liberty Song', 59
Dinneen, Patrick (lexicographer), 112
Disclothing Act (1746), 127, 132, 224n1, 225n13
disenfranchised heroes, 31, 155–8, 165
Disney, John, 66, 67
dispensationalism, 78, 90, 92, 216n9–11
Dissenters, 25, 37, 39, 40, 52, 56, 153

  see also Unitarianism
Dissenting Academies, 25, 186
Dissertations on the History of Ireland (O'Conor), 100
Donne, John, 37
Dornan, R. Stephen, 31–2, 231n24
  dialect voices Bobbin and Anderson, 32
  on English dialects, 31
  and 'Lilliburlero', 32
  the radical potential of dialect writing, 190
  and politically comic dialect, 33
  on vernacular modes, 31–2
Drennan, William, 196
  'Wake' (1797), 164
drinking songs, 37, 38, 39
  'Irish Drinking Song' 99, 103
Dublin Library Society, 142
Dugaw, Dianne, and song culture, 98, 99, 220n23
Dùghallach, Ailean *see* MacDougall, Allan
Dundas, Henry, 5, 132, 225n12
Dundas, Robert, 4
Dunlop, Frances, 4
Dyer, George, 66, 67, 212n1

Eaton, Daniel Isaac, 191
  Politics for the People; Or, A Salmagundy for Swine, (1794) 184
  and seditious libel, 75, 184
  The Philanthropist, 44
Edgeworth, Maria, 169
  Castle Rackrent (1800), 168, 173
  and Irish Romanticism, 23, 153, 155
  non-standard voice, 173
  and plain language, 167–8
Edgeworth, Richard and Maria, *Essays on Irish Bulls* (1802), 198
Edkins, Joshua, Irish anthology of poetry, 142, 146
Edwards, Dafydd Idris
  'Hanes y Sesiwn yng Nghymru', 203–4
  and macaronic song, 197, 198, 204
Edwards, Elizabeth, 26, 213n11
Edwards, Thomas ('Twm o'r Nant), 204
Eisenstein, Elizabeth, *The Printing Press as an Agent of Change*, 96
Elbourne, Roger, and occupational songs, 192, 234n43

emigration, 29, 126, 129–32, 145, 200
Emmet, Robert, 164
The English Hymn (Watson), 80, 217n16
English language, vernacular modes, 31–2
English, Scots and Irishmen, A Patriotic Address to the Inhabitants of the United Kingdom (Mayne), 8
English, William, 117
Enlightenment, 3, 43, 155
   and premillennialism, 78
   Radical Enlightenment, 9, 14
   Scottish Enlightenment, 134
Epistles, Odes, and Other Poems (Moore), 159
Epstein, James, 61, 210n22, 212n40
Erdman, David, 24
Essay on the Right and Property of Land (Ogilvie), 25–6
Essays on Irish Bulls (Edgeworth), 198
Essays on Song-Writing (Aikin), 37, 96
ethnomusicology, 198, 203, 235n3
evangelicanism, 77–8, 216n4–5
   in America, 80
   in Ireland, 79, 81, 82, 92
   philo-semitism, 90
   the role of the hymn, 81, 93
   the role of Trinity College Dublin, 85
Evans, Thomas (Tomos Glyn Cothi), 64, 67, 214n27
   and charges of sedition, 71
Evenings in Greece (Moore), 160
exile, 31, 130, 155, 157–8
Exile of Ireland! (pamphlet), 157–8

Farquhar, George, 98
'fast' poetry, 44–5
Faulkner, Matthew (printer), 185
Fenwick, Eliza, *Secresy; Or, the Ruin on the Rock* (1795), 155
Ferguson, Frank, 196, 231n14
The Field Day Anthology of Irish Writing, 201–2
Fitzgerald, Lord Edward, and ballad 'Edward', 164
Flanders Campaign, 112
folksong, 64, 66, 110, 191, 235n3
Fowler, Archbishop Robert, 83
Franklin, Benjamin, 13
Frederick II, king of Prussia, 117

French Republican songs
   'Ça Ira', 3, 4, 8, 36, 48, 71
   'La Carmagnole', 71
   'La Marseillaise', 6, 8, 36, 71, 48, 197, 214n32
French Revolution, 9, 43, 54, 65, 109, 177
   and Burns, 8
   imagery in 'Church and King. A Song', 47–8
   and 'La Marseillaise', 197–8
The Fudge Family (Moore), 158
The Fudger Fudged (Anon), 158
Fulford, Tim, 155, 156, 163, 229n6
Fun a la Mode, or, Sing, and Be Jolly (Howard), 98
Fundamentalist movement, 27, 78

Gaelic language *see* Irish Gaelic; Scottish Gaelic
'Gaelus', pseudonym of Andrew McKenzie, 171
Garrick, David, and 'Heart of Oak', 59
Gaskell, Elizabeth, annotation of dialect speech, 190
Gay, John
   Beggar's Opera (1727), 97
   English words to 'Irish Howl' and 'Irish Trot', 97
Gentleman's Magazine, 65
   'Anti-Gallican', 48–9
   'Church and King. A Song', 45
   and Irish song, 99–100, 101, 103
   'World Turned Upside Down', 57
George II, king, 116
George III, king, 29, 177
   in Irish verse, 117–18
   and reformist 'fast' poems, 44
George IV, king, 120
Gibbons, Luke, 196, 199
Gifford, William, *Anti-Jacobin*, 36
Gillespie, Raymond, 96
Gillray, James, 47
Gilmartin, Kevin, and tracts, 191
Gilroy, Paul, 2, 3
Glasites, 52, 56
Glendower, Owen (Owain Glyndwr), 73, 74
Glorious Revolution, 22
'God Save the King'
   and loyalists, 36, 182
   parodies of, 57–8, 59, 67, 69, 70–1, 187–8

Goddard, Florimand, 71
Godwin, William, 66
   Things as they are; Or, the Adventures of Caleb Williams (1794), 155
Gordimer, Nadine, 201
Graham, Robert, 4
Grand Repository of the English Language (Spence), 52, 53
Gray, Thomas, 65
Grigor, Iain Fraser
   Highland Resistance: The Radical Tradition in the Scottish North, 134
   and *Rights of Man* in Gaelic, 134
Grimshaw, John, 'The Weavers' Garland or the Downfall of Trade', 192
Groves, John, 71
Grusin, Richard, and remediation, 95, 218n3

Habeas Corpus Suspension Act, 20, 54
Habermas, Jürgen, 154, 155
Hamilton, Paul, 22, 23
Hanson, Joseph, 'A New Song in praise of Colonel Hanson', 191
Hardy, Thomas, 186
   Anglo-Scottish radicals, 6
   London Corresponding Society, 6, 134
   and Mather's ballad 'True Reformers', 188
   trial of, 63, 70, 71
Harland, John (antiquarian), 187, 191
Harris, Bob, 4, 133, 207n15, 225n15
Hays, Mary, *Victim of Prejudice* (1799), 155
Hazlitt, William, 9
Heaney, Seamus, 2
hedge schools, 142, 226n3, 226n5–6
Herd, David, *Ancient Scottish Songs* (1769), 96, 100
Hewitt, J., 231n20, 232n29
Hiberno-English, 227n26, 228n38, 228n41
   in chapbooks, 30, 141, 142
   used for comic effect, 98, 99
   see also Irish English
The Hidden Wordsworth (Johnston), 21, 208n27
High Treason, in speech and writing, 20, 54, 212n1
Highland Clearances, 29, 126, 129, 136–7
   'Bliadhna nan Caorach', 129
   effect on poetry, 29–30, 126

Highland dress, 127, 132, 224n1
Highland Regiments, 127–9, 131, 132, 135–6, 224n1
Highland Resistance: The Radical Tradition in the Scottish North (Grigor), 134
Hill, Rowland, 56
Historical Memoirs of the Irish Bards (Walker), 95, 100, 101, 104
Hogg, Patrick Scott, 176, 208n23
Hollingworth, Brian, and use of dialect, 189, 234n29
Hone, William, use of chapbook genre, 191
Horgan, D.M. ,173, 175, 232n30
Horsley, P.M., 52, 211n9
Howard, Henry
   'Darby M'Hone's lamentation. An Irish Song', 98, 220n28
   Fun a la Mode, or, Sing, and Be Jolly (1763), 98
Howes, Marjorie, 162, 230n44
Huckleberry Finn (Twain), 173
Hulme, Keri, 201
Hunt, Henry 'Orator'
   Letter to Radical Reformers, 188
   and mass meetings, 187
Huntingdon, Selina Hastings, countess of, 83
Huws, Daniel, 66, 213n19
hymns, 27, 44, 79–80, 93
   cultural power of, 79, 81
   as ideological *lingua franca*, 81–2
   Kelly's hymns and hymnbooks, 27, 77, 83–92
   role of the evangelical hymn, 81, 93
   and secular tunes, 56
   Welsh language hymns, 26, 67
Hymns by Thomas Kelly: Not before Published (Kelly), 83
Hymns for Social Worship (Kelly), 83
Hymns on Various Passages of Scripture (Kelly), 77, 83, 85

The Important Trial of Thomas Spence (Spence), 51, 53, 54
industrial folk song, 'Jone o'Grinfilt' ballads, 191
Intercepted Letters: Or, the Twopenny Post-Bag (Moore), 158
Iolo Morganwg, 63, 64, 65–6
   and adaptations of 'God Save the King', 70, 71

the 'Bard of Liberty', 26, 63, 64, 72
and Evans' trial, 71
footnotes to 'John Bull's Litany', 74–5
and the Gorsedd, 66
and Jones 'Bardd y Brenin', 65
and Macdonald (Attorney General), 73–4, 75–6
and radical imagery 'Breinian Dyn', 69
and self-censorship, 72
and stanzas from 'Church and King', 215n46
and Tooke's trial, 214n30
and Unitarianism, 26, 67
and Welsh language, 74–5
and Welsh language hymns, 26, 67
Iolo Morganwg: works cited
'Breinian Dyn' (Rights of Man), 26, 27, 68, 214n27
comparison 'Breinian Dyn' and 'A New Song', 69–70
History of the Bards (unfinished), 65
'John Bull's Litany' (unpublished), 71, 72–3, 74–5, 76, 215n55
'Newgate Stanzas', 63
Poems, Lyric and Pastoral (1794), 66, 67, 71
'Trial by Jury', 63, 71, 76, 212n1
'War Song of British Savages' parody, 26, 36, 67
Irish *amhrán* (song) metres, 142, 150, 227n25
Irish English, 168, 169
Irish Gaelic, 2, 27–8, 29, 30, 196
and Brooke, 95, 96, 97, 105, 106, 107
The Irish Harp, and radical songs, 70
Irish language
and chapbooks, 141, 142
Walker's comments, 100–1
Irish language songs
'Cean Dubh Deelish', 107
'The Maid of the Valley', 104, 105, 108
'Song by Patrick Linden', 108
'Song for Gracey Nugent, 105, 108
'Song for Mabel Kelly', 105
Irish Melodies (Moore), 154, 159, 164
Irish radical verse, 27, 110
Mac Cárthaigh verses, 111–12
Mac Cruitín verses, 115–16
Ó Comhraí, Eoghan (Eugene O'Curry), 121

Ó Muirgheasa, Énrí, 117–18
Ó Neachtain, Seán, 121–2
Ó Scannail verses, 112–14
Ó Súilleabháin, Donncha, 118–20
Ó Súilleabháin, Tomás Rua, 120
Irish Rebellion (1798), 1, 11, 12, 157, 200
pamphlet *Exile of Ireland!*, 157–8
Irish Romanticism
the disenfranchised hero, 155–8
and Lady Morgan, 153
and loss of nation-state, 155–6
and Maria Edgeworth, 23, 153, 155
tradition of the 'wild geese', 156
Irish Scottish Academic Initiative, 202
Irish traditional music, 219n17–18

Jac Glan-y-Gors *see* Jones, John
Jack the Giant Queller (Brooke), 97, 220n21
Jacobin poetry, 44
Jacobins, 36–7, 43, 49, 186, 210n21
and anti-Jacobins, 19, 47, 187
and 'God Save the King', 36, 196–7, 198
Jacobitism, 29, 196, 224n2
and Alexander MacDonald, 125–6
and British Imperialism, 126–7
and British militarism, 128, 129, 132
and Irish Jacobitism, 98, 108, 119, 121, 122, 125
James II, king of Scotland, 98
Jebb, John, 109
Jenkins, Geraint H., 71, 212n1–2, 212n7, 213n19, 214n37, 215n47
Jhabvala, Ruth Prawer, 201
Johnson, Joseph (publisher), 37, 66
Johnson, Samuel, 126, 142
Johnston, Kenneth
and anti-Pitt writers, 21–2
and Pitt's government, 21, 71
'Whose History? My Place or Yours?', 21, 209n49
and Wordsworth, 11, 21, 208n27
Jones, Edward (Bardd y Brenin), 65, 66
Musical and Poetical Relicks of the Welsh Bards, 65
Jones, Gareth Stedman, 189
Jones, John Gale (printer), 185
Jones, John (Jac Glan-y-Gors)
Seren Tan Gwmwl ('Star Under a Cloud') (1795), 204
Toriad y Dydd ('The Dawning of Day') (1797), 204

Jones, Owen (Owain Myfyr), 66
Joyce, James, 31

Kant, Immanuel, 17
  Perpetual Peace (1795), 16
Kearney, Hugh, 2, 207n3
Keating, Geoffrey, 122
Keenan, Thomas, 95, 218n5
Kelly, James, 144
Kelly, Thomas, 27, 78, 82
  and Christ's return, 86–7
  eschatology in his hymns, 79
  and hymns, 84, 85, 88
  and influence of Walker, 82–3
  and Kellyites, 83
  and philo-semitism in writings, 90
  prophetic teaching, 84–5, 89
  reward and punishment theme, 87
  theological views, 27, 83, 84, 85–6, 88, 89
  use of Israel as a signifier, 90–1, 92
Kelly, Thomas: works cited
  Collection of Psalms and Hymns extracted from Various Authors (1802), 83
  Hymns by Thomas Kelly: Not before Published, 83
  Hymns for Social Worship, 83
  Hymns on Various Passages of Scripture, 77, 83, 85
  'Israel Encouraged', 90, 91
  'Israel in Exile', 90
  'Israel Forgetful', 90
  'Israel as a type', 90
  'Israel Victorious', 90, 91–2
  'State of joyful hope', 90–1
  'Who is this that comes from Eden', 87–8
  'Zion's King shall reign victorious', 88, 89–90
Kellyites, 27, 83
Kennedy, Catriona, 197
Kidder, Arthur, 55
Kimbrough, S.T., and hymnody, 79–80, 83, 217n13, 217n24
King Lear (Shakespeare), 25
Knight, John, 186
Knox, Vicesimus, 20–1
Kodaly, Zoltan, 198, 235n3

Lalla Rookh: An Oriental Romance (Moore), 159, 160, 164
Lancashire dialect

A View of the Lancashire Dialect (Bobbin), 175–6
  'Jone o'Grinfilt' ballads, 191–2
  Walker, 181, 182, 189
An Lasair: Anthology of Eighteenth Century Gaelic Verse (Black), 225n9, 225n13
Laws in Wales Acts, 204
An Leabhar Liath, 138
Leask, Nigel, 196, 213n17–18
Leavis, F.R., 79
Leavis, Q.D., 79
Leerssen, Joep, 163, 230n45
  on Brooke, 95
  Mere Irish and Fíor-Ghael: Studies in the Idea of Irish Nationality, 95
  on Moore's cultivation of remembrance, 162–3
Lefanu, Alicia Sheridan
  and the disenfranchised hero, 157, 158
  and Moore's 'When He Who Adores Thee', 157
  play *Sons of Erin* (1812), 156, 229n11
  The Outlaw (1823), 157
Legendary Ballads (Moore), 160
Letter to Radical Reformers (Hunt), 188
Letter to the Roman Catholics of Dublin (Moore), 163
'Lilliburlero', 32, 98, 108, 174
Linden, Patrick, 104, 108
Literature of the Scottish Gael (MacLean), 134
Liu, Alan, 71, 215n42
Lloyd, A.L., 198, 235n3
Lloyd, David, and the martyr figure, 162, 164, 219n11, 230n44
Llwyd, Richard (Bard of Snowdon), 65, 213n11
London Corresponding Society, 36, 40, 54, 69, 71
  and Hardy, 6, 134
London Public Advertiser and Literary Gazette, 99–100, 101
London Society for the Promotion of Christianity among the Jews, 90
Louis XV, king of France, 3
Louis XVI, king of France, 47–8, 116
love songs, 37, 38, 39, 100, 108
  'The Maid of the Valley', 104, 105, 108
  'Song by Patrick Linden', 108
  'Song for Gracey Nugent', 105, 108
  'Song for Mabel Kelly', 105, 108

Loves of the Angels: An Eastern Romance (Moore), 159
loyalism, 72, 122, 140, 182, 185
   hyper-loyalism, 1, 5
   propaganda, 20, 36–7, 183, 191
   versus Jacobinism, 36–7
Loyalism and Radicalism in Lancashire (Navickas), 32
loyalist poetry, 8, 9, 20
loyalist songs, 67, 144, 193, 210n27
   anti-democratic ideology, 45
   'Anti-Gallican', 48–9
   'Church and King. A Song', 45–7
   'Church and King. A Song' analysis, 45, 47–8

macaronic song, 118, 119, 197, 198, 199
   'Hanes y Sesiwn yng Nghymru', 203–4
   'Stauka an Varaga', 145
Macaulay, Thomas, 7–8
Macbeth (Shakespeare), 17
McCalman, Iain, 55, 211n21, 211n25–6
Mac Cárthaigh, Ceallachán, 110–11
   restoration of Stuart pretender, 112
   and Volunteer movement, 111–12
MacCodrum, Iain
   celebration of Highland dress, 132
   the creation of sheep runs, 132
   and emigration, 131–2
   and landlords, 129–31, 135, 136
   'Òran do na Fògarraich' (Song to the Exiles), 129
MacCoinnich, Coinneach *see* MacKenzie, Kenneth
MacCoinnich, Seòras *see* MacKenzie, George
McCracken, Henry Joy, 195
Mac Cruitín, Aodh Buí, 115–16
   references to George II, 116–17
   and Régiment de Clare, 116
MacDonald, Alexander (Alasdair Mac Mhaighstir Alasdair), 122, 125–6
   Aiseirigh na Seann Chànain Albannaich (Resurrection of the Old Scottish Language), 125–6
MacDonald, Sir Alexander, 129
Macdonald, Sir Archibald, 73–4, 75
MacDonell, Alexander, 135

MacDougall, Allan (Ailean Dùghallach)
   call for a French invasion, 134–5
   and comparison with MacKenzie, 136
   and Highland Fencible regiments, 135, 137
   'Oran do na Cìobairibh Gallda', 135
McGann, Jerome, 1
   'The Third World of Criticism', 14
McGuirk, Carol, on Burns' epistles, 170–1
MacIntyre, Duncan Ban (Donnchadh Bàn Mac an t-Saoir), 122, 224n38
McIvanney, Liam, 176
Mackay, Peter, 29, 30
   and Scots Gaelic poetry, 29–30, 196
Mackay, Rob Donn, 126
McKenzie, Andrew (Bard of Dunover), 171, 172
   'A Poetical Letter addressed to Mr R. Anderson', 170
   pseudonym 'Gaelus', 171
MacKenzie, George (Seòras MacCoinnich), 'An Oba Nodha', 138–9, 226n34
MacKenzie, John
   and bawdy songs, 137, 138, 139
   'Dòmhnallan Dubh' (Little Black Donnie), 137, 139
   'Eachainn and Slaoightear' (Hector the Rascal), 137, 138
   editor *Sar-Obair nam Bard Gaelach* (1841), 137–8
   'An Oba Nodha' (The Oobie Noogie), 138, 139, 140
   'An Seudagan' (My Handsome Little Tiny Hero), 137, 138
MacKenzie, Kenneth (Coinneach Mac Coinnich)
   imagery in regimental songs, 128–9
   Òrain Ghaidhealach (1792), 127, 224n2
   'Oran do na Chath-Bhuithinn Cheudna', 127–8
   'Oran do'n Chath-Bhuithin Rioghail Ghai'leah air dhoibh teach dhachaidh a America' 128
   songs identifying Scottish Gaels as British, 128, 137
   tune of 'I'll follow the Lad with the White Cockade', 127

McLane, Maureen, and 'mediality', 95–6, 218n6
MacLean, Donald
   Literature of the Scottish Gael, 133–4
   and Paine's *Rights of Man*, 134
McManus, Antonia, 226n3, 226n5–6
MacMurchadha, Diarmait, king of Leinster, 119
MacNeill, Hector, 20
Macpherson, James
   and bards, 65
   Poems of Ossian (1765), 38, 222n78
Madden, R.R., 118, 23n22
Magnuson, Paul, 19, 208n24, 209n42
Maidment, Brian, 190, 193, 234n32
Manchester Central Library, 182
   ballad collection, 192, 193
Manchester Gazette, 183
Manchester Herald, 43, 181
Manly, Susan, 168, 231n7
Marie Antoinette, queen, consort of Louis XVI, 48
Marini, Stephen, 80, 217n19
'The Marseillaise', 6, 8, 36, 48, 71
   circulation, 197–8, 214n32
mass platform radicalism, 187, 193
Mather, Joseph, 192
   'Britons Awake', 188
   'God Save Great Thomas Paine', 188–9
   'The Norfolk Street Riots', 184
   radical ballads, 184
   'True Reformers', 188
Maturin, Charles Robert, *The Milesian Chief: A Romance* (1812), 156
Maurepas, Jean Frédérick Phélypeaux, Comte de, 3
Mayne, John, 8, 20
   English, Scots and Irishmen, A Patriotic Address (1799) 8
Mee, Jon, 64, 212n3, 214n34, 215n50
Meek, Donald, 129, 225n22
   and Highland landlords, 136, 137
Memoirs of Captain Rock (Moore), 164–5
Memoirs of the Life of the Right Honorable Richard Brinsley Sheridan (Moore), 163
Mere Irish and Fíor-Ghael: Studies in the Idea of Irish Nationality (Leerssen), 95
Methodism, 78, 81, 216n3

Metternich, Prince Klemens Wenzel von, 9
The Milesian Chief: A Romance (Maturin), 156
millennialism, 27, 85, 86, 87, 120
   and postmillennialism, 78, 85, 88, 216n7
   and premillennialism, 78, 88–9, 92
Milton, John 13
M.N.M., letter 'To the Inspector', 99–100
Montgomery, James (printer), 185
Monthly Magazine, 37
Moody, Jane, on Moore, 158, 229n22
Moore, Thomas
   and anti-Catholic bias, 159
   anti-Moore satire *Fudger Fudged*, 158
   and aristocratic audiences, 160–1
   and Byron, 158, 229n21
   and classical composers, 160
   and colonial masculinity, 154, 158, 161–2, 165
   and condition of exile, 31
   Davis on, 159
   depiction of women, 153
   images of the warrior-hero, 163
   in Lady Morgan's writing, 157
   in Lefanu's writing, 157
   and Lord Edward Fitzgerald, 164
   and nationalist public leaders, 162–3
   nostalgic commemoration of Irish leaders, 154
   pamphlet on the Veto Controversy, 159
   radical tradition in *Irish Melodies*, 164
   and Sheridan, 163, 164
   use of pseudonyms, 158–9, 229n22
Moore, Thomas: works cited
   'A Canadian Boat-Song', 159, 160, 199
   Corruption and Intolerance (1808), 159
   Epistles, Odes, and Other Poems (1806), 159
   Evenings in Greece, 160
   Fudge Family, The by 'Thomas Brown', 158
   Intercepted Letters: Or, the Twopenny Post-Bag (1813), 158
   Irish Melodies (1808-34), 154, 159, 164
   Lalla Rookh: An Oriental Romance (1817), 159, 160, 164
   Legendary Ballads (1828), 160

Letter to the Roman Catholics of Dublin,
  163
Loves of the Angels: An Eastern Romance
  (1823), 159
Memoirs of Captain Rock, 164–5
Memoirs of the Life of the Right Honorable
  Richard Brinsley Sheridan (1825), 163
National Airs (1818–27), 160
'Oh! Blame Not the Bard' (1810), 161,
  162, 163
Poetical Works (1840), 159
Sacred Songs (1816, 1824), 160
Summer Fête (1831), 160
Travels of an Irish Gentleman in Search of
  a Religion (1833), 159, 164
More, Hannah
  loyalist evangelical tracts, 20, 191
  propaganda pamphlets (1793–97), 36
Moretti, Franco, 202, 236n9
Morgan, Lady Sydney, (*née* Owenson)
  and Irish Romanticism, 153
  and Moore's *Irish Melodies*, 157
  O'Briens and the O'Flahertys: A National
    Tale (1827), 156
  O'Donnel: A National Tale (1814), 156
Morley, Vincent, 28–9, 222n9, 223n14,
  224n39
  and 'aisling' poetry, 29
  anti-Hanoverian sentiment, 29
  the motif of lament, 196
  Washington i gCeannas a Ríochta, 110
Morning Chronicle, 41
Moulden, John, and chapbooks, 145, 226n1,
  227n15, 228n42
Mouw, Richard, and hymnody, 80, 217n14
Moylan, Terry, 199
Muir, Thomas, 188
Müller, Max, 201
Munro, Sir Hector, 133
Murdoch, Alexander
  and emigration, 132
  and Scottish landlords, 133
Murray, D.B., on the Glasites, 52
Murray, Rev. James
  and common land ownership, 25
  and Newcastle Philosophical Society,
    53, 58
  Sermons to Asses, 52, 61
  and Spence family, 25, 52

Naipaul, V.S., 201
Napoleonic Wars, 8, 20, 27, 181, 187, 189,
  193
National Airs (Moore), 160
National Anthems, 25
  'God Save the King', 36
  and parody, 26, 36
  use of 'America the Beautiful', 35
National Eisteddfod, 66
Nature's Engraver: A Life of Thomas Bewick
  (Uglow), 56
Navickas, Katrina, 32–3
  chapbooks of Chartist period, 32
  the dialect of the Wilsons, 33
  Loyalism and Radicalism in Lancashire 32
  on Walker 'Tim Bobbin, the Second', 32
Neale, John and William, *Colection [sic] of*
  the most Celebrated Irish Tunes (1724),
  97, 219n19
Nelson, Horatio Nelson, viscount, 193
New York Times, 35
Newcastle
  Constitutional Club, 52
  Independent Club, 52
  political clubs and debates, 52, 55
Newcastle Chronicle, 53
Newcastle Magazine, 53
Newcastle Philosophical Society (1775),
  52–3, 58
Newman, John Henry Cardinal, 121, 162
Newman, Steve, and 'mediality', 95–6
Ní Mheic Cailéin, Iseabal
  and bawdy songs, 139
  'Éistibh, a Luchd an Tighe-se', 139
Noble, Andrew, 176, 208n39, 214n23
Norton, Caroline, 160

O'Briens and the O'Flahertys: A National
  Tale (Morgan), 156
occupational songs, 187, 192
  'A New Song in Praise of the Weavers',
    192
  'The Weavers' Garland or the Downfall
    of Trade', 192
Ó Comhraí, Eoghan, 121
Ó Conaill, Seán, 122, 224n39
O'Connell, Danie,l 32, 120
O'Conor, Charles, 100, 104
  Dissertations on the History of Ireland
    (1753), 100

O'Curry, Eugene, 121
O'Donnel: A National Tale (Morgan), 156
Ó Fiannachta, Pádraig, 121, 223n32
Ogilvie, William, *Essay on the Right and Property of Land*, 25–6
O'Gorman Mahon, James, 121
O'Halloran, Sylvester, 104
O'Keeffe, Adelaide, poem 'The Irish Officer' (1818), 156
Ó Muirgheasa, Énrí, 117–18
On the Study of Celtic Literature (Arnold), 201
Ó Neachtain, Seán, 121
Open Brethren 78
Òrain Ghaidhealach (MacKenzie), 127, 224n2
Orange Order, 1–2
Orientalists, 201
Orr, William, 164
Ó Scannail, Fínín, 112–14
  contrasted with English radicals, 113, 114–15
  loyalty to Catholicism, 113–14
Ossianic controversy, 126
Ó Súilleabháin, Donncha, 118–20
Ó Súilleabháin, Eoghan Rua, 142, 222n8, 226n5
Ó Súilleabháin, Tomás Rua, 120, 223n30
Oswald, James, *Caledonian Pocket Companion* (1743-64), 97
The Outlaw (Lefanu), 157
Owain Myfyr (Owen Jones), 66
Oxford Dictionary of National Biography (Dickinson), 53
Oxford English Dictionary (1820), 109

Paddy's Resource, 70, 153
Paddy's Resource (Dublin edition), 26, 118, 223n21
Paine, Thomas, 36, 48, 208n36, 208n38
  anti-imperialism, 15–16
  and British constitution, 16–17
  influence on Jones, 204
  in Irish nationalist songs, 153
  and pro-American writings, 9, 13
  and redistribution of wealth, 6
  Rights of Man, 54, 134–5, 181, 204
  Rights of Man Part Two (1792), 74
  trial for seditious libel, 73–4, 215n50
  vision of humanity, 23–4

Parsley, R., 98, 220n30
  'A New Irish Comic Song', 98
Parsley's Lyric Repository for 1789 (Parsley), 98, 220n30
Pastorini, pseudonym of Charles Walmsley, 120, 223n31
patriotic songs
  'Britannia Rules the Waves', 45, 56, 57
  'God Save the King', 36, 56, 57, 59, 70–1, 182, 187
  'Hearts of Oak', 56, 57, 60
Paulin, Tom, 174, 232n32
Peace of Amiens (1802), 32, 183
Penal Laws, 115, 153, 154, 156
Percy, Thomas, 65
  and ballad 'Babes in the Wood', 57
  and ballad 'Chevy Chase', 57
  'Essay on the Ancient Minstrels of England', 37
  Reliques of Ancient English Poetry (1765), 37, 38, 57, 100
  on Welsh bards and rebellion, 37
Peterloo Massacre (1819), 32, 187–8, 233n22, 233n25
The Philanthropist (Eaton), 44
Philips, Ambrose, 37, 38, 40
Philp, Mark, 191, 234n41–2
Pig's Meat (Spence), 57
Pitt, William, 5, 186, 214n30, 233n19
  Pitt's government, 6, 17, 71, 181, 184, 185
Pittock, Murray, 167, 172, 213n20, 231n25
Place, Francis, 134, 146, 147, 148, 227n21
Plato, *The Sophist*, 109, 110
Playford, Henry
  'An Irish Jigg', 98
  'An Irish Wooing,' 98
  Songs Compleat, Pleasant and Divertive (1719), 98, 220n25
  Wit and Mirth: Pills to Purge Melancholy (1707–9), 98, 220n24
Plebeian Politics (Walker), 32, 182, 183, 191
Poems, Chiefly in the Scottish Dialect (Burns), 171, 173
Poems, Lyric and Pastoral (Iolo Morganwg), 66, 67, 71
Poems of Ossian (Macpherson), 38, 222n78
Poems on Various Subjects (Anderson), 231n21

Poetical Works (Moore), 159
Poetry and Reform: Periodical Verse from the English Democratic Press (Scrivener), 24–5, 40
political song, 3, 26, 36, 37, 39, 40, 50
  'Anti-Gallican', 48–9
  'Church and King. A Song', 45–7
  'The Genius of France', 41
Political Songs of England, From the Reign of John to that of Edward II (Wright), 40
Politics for the People; Or, A Salamagundy for Swine (Eaton), 44, 184
Pompadour, Jeanne Antoinette Poisson, marquise de, 3
Poole, Robert, 232n1, 232n7, 233n22
Pope, Alexander, 38
postmillennialism, 78, 85, 88, 216n7
Pound, Ezra, 14
Poussin, Nicolas, 38
Power, James, and Moore's *Irish Melodies*, 159
Powerscourt, Theodosia Wingfield, viscountess, 77, 216n2
premillennialism, 27, 78
  and Kelly's theology, 84, 85, 86, 87, 88–9, 90, 92
Presbyterians, 25, 145
Price, Richard, 9, 13
Priestley, Joseph, 36, 47, 67
printers, attacks on, 181, 185–6
The Printing Press as an Agent of Change (Eisenstein), 96
Prix Goncourt, 201
Property in Land is Every One's Right (Spence), 53
Pughe, William Owen, 66

Queen's University Belfast
  Irish Scottish Academic Initiative, 202
  Seamus Heaney Centre for Poetry, 2
  symposia, 1, 23–4

radical ballads, 184
Radical Enlightenment, 9, 14, 24
radical poets, in Wales, 36, 65, 66, 67, 196
radical politics, and dialect, 176–7
radical voice, 192–3
  broadsides, 182, 191–2
  and dialect, 181–2
  in Lancaster, 191
  in Manchester, 187, 188
  oral tradition, 182, 193
  prohibition, 183
  suppression by loyalists, 182
  and Walker's *Plebeian Politics*, 184–5
radicalism
  citation in *Oxford English Dictionary* (1820), 109
  Irish, 109, 110, 114, 115, 122–3, 154
  Scottish, 169, 176
  Welsh, 70, 72, 74, 75, 76
  working-class dialect, 181, 182, 185, 186, 187, 193
Ramsay, Allan, 40, 174, 146, 178, 213n20
  'Lucky Spence's Last Advice', 174
  Tea-Table Miscellany (1724), 96, 219n15
Raynal, Abbé, 15–16
Reading Ireland: Print, Reading and Social Change in Early Modern Ireland (Gillespie), 96
The Real Reading Made Easy (Spence), 53
Reay, George Mackay, Lord, 126
Reeves, John, 76
Reflections on the Revolution in France (Burke), 184
reform movement, 6, 43, 44
reform songs
  'The Fire of Liberty', 43
  'The Fire of Liberty' analysis, 43–4
  'The Genius of France', 41–2, 43
  'The Genius of France' analysis of, 42–3
  'An Hymn for the Fast, Day, To Be Sung by The Friends of Mankind', 44–5
  'Song' by Thomas Best, 44
Reliques of Ancient English Poetry (Percy), 37, 38, 57, 100
Reliques of Irish Poetry (Brooke), 95, 96, 103, 104, 222n65
Relph, Josiah, 172
remediation, 27, 105, 106, 107, 218n3–5
Repossessing the Romantic Past (Hamilton and Glen), 22
republican songs, 118
  'Ça Ira', 3, 4, 8, 36, 48, 71
  'La Carmagnole', 71

'La Marseillaise', 6, 8, 36, 71, 48, 197, 214n32
'Plant, Plant the Tree', 71
Research Institute of Irish and Scottish Studies, 202
Restorer of Society to its Natural State (Spence), 54
Reynolds, George, patron of Carolan, 108
Reynolds, George Nugent, 'The Exile of Erin', 157–8
Rightboy movement, 107
Rights of Man (Paine), 54, 133–4, 181, 204
Rights of Man Part Two (Paine), 74
Rights of Man in Verse (Spence), 53
Ritson, Joseph, 66, 96, 219n14
    Select Collection of English Songs (1783), 96
Robertson, Ewen, 'Dùthaich MhicAoidh' (Mackay Country), 138
Robinson Crusoe (Defoe), 57, 61
Robinson, Mary, 48
Robinson, Robert, 52
Romantic period, 22, 24, 30–2, 167, 168, 196
    and dialect, 168
    and Irish print culture, 154
    studies, 22, 24, 30
Romanticism, 23, 32, 153, 155, 167–8, 196
    archipelagic scope, 14, 169, 172, 173
Royal Irish Academy, 101, 102, 121, 221n43, 221n54
Royal Jubilee (1809), 57
Rushdie, Salman, 201
Ryan, Edmond (Éamonn An Cnuic), 107–8

Sack, J.J., 186, 233n19
Sacred Songs (Moore), 160
Salvation Army, 56
Samwell, David, 66
Sanky, Ira, 81
Sar-Obair nam Bard Gaelach (MacKenzie), 137–9
Schiller, Friedrich, 40
Schirmer, Gregory, 161, 230n33
Scots language, 66, 168–9, 170, 172–3, 174, 196
    see also Ulster Scots
Scott, Paul, 201

Scott, Sir Walter, 7–8, 20
    America 'There's a bit spot I had forgot', 9
    'For A' That and A' That' (1814), 5, 6–7
Scottish Gaelic, 29, 125–6, 129, 133–4, 137
Scottish Highlands, 122, 126, 133, 134, 135, 139
    emigration, 126, 129–31, 137
    uprisings, 133, 200
Scottish Moderate Enlightenment, 16
Scrivener, Michael, 24, 25, 55–6
    editor *Poetry and Reform: Periodical Verse from the English Democratic Press*, 24–5, 40
    Seditious Allegories, 40
Seamus Heaney Centre for Poetry, 2
Second World War, 22
Secrecy; Or, the Ruin on the Rock (Fenwick), 155
Seditious Allegories (Scrivener), 40
seditious libel, 54, 73, 75, 184, 190
seditious writings, 4, 36, 71, 75, 181, 188, 193
Select Collection of English Songs (Ritson), 96
Selection of Scotch, English, Irish and Foreign Airs (Aird), 97
Sellar, Patrick, 129, 136, 137
Sermons to Asses (Murray), 52, 61
Seven Years War, 117
Shakespeare, William
    King Lear, 25
    Macbeth, 17
Sheffield Iris, 181
Sheffield Register, 181
Shelley, Percy Bysshe, 9, 24, 36
Shenstone, William, 101
Sherburn, George, 37, 210n8
Sheridan, Richard Brinsley, 160, 163, 164
Sheridan, Thomas, 142
Sidney, Algernon, 122
Simpson, C.M., 220n24
Skirving, William, 6, 207n17
Skoblow, Jeffrey, 172, 232n27
Smith, George (Smith of Chichester), 38
Smith, Olivia, 191, 210n27, 231n1, 234n27
Society for Constitutional Information, 109
Society for the Defence of the Bill of Rights, 109
Society of Free Citizens, 110

Society for Promoting Christian Knowledge (SPCK), 29
song classification, 38–40
    Aikin's three groupings, 38
    Anacreon model for drinking songs, 37, 38
    Horace as model for political song, 37, 38
    'Irish song' in the eighteenth century, 96–7
    'Irish' songs in political ballads, 97–8
    political democratic songs, 40–1
    political song in Percy, 37
    political song as subgenre, 37, 40–1, 50
    Sappho model for love songs, 37, 38
    as weapons (parody), 36
Songbook (Spence), 36
Songs Compleat, Pleasant and Divertive (Playford), 98, 220n25
Sons of Erin (Lefanu), 156, 229n11
Sorensen, Janet, and 'mediality', 95, 219n6
Southwark Friends of the People, 41
The Spectator, 57
Spence, Jeremiah, 51–2
Spence, Jeremiah, Jnr, 52
Spence, Thomas, 25, 43, 48, 51–2, 53
    arrest and imprisonment, 54
    and the Combination Acts, 54
    common ownership of land, 25, 26, 52
    'free and easy' meetings, 54–5, 61
    his coin iconography, 61–2
    his songs and their settings, 56, 57
    and London Corresponding Society, 54
    and Newcastle Philosophical Society, 52–3
    and patriotism, 59
    and reformed phonetic spelling, 54
    seditious comments, 75
    and 'Spence's Plan', 53
    use of chapbook genre, 191
Spence, Thomas: works cited
    'Address to all Mankind', 55
    'Burke's Address to the Swinish Multitude', 57, 60–1
    Case of Thomas Spence, Bookseller, 54
    Coin Collector's Companion (1795), 61
    Grand Repository of the English Language, 52, 53
    'Hark how the Trumpet's Sound', 57, 58–9
    The Important Trial of Thomas Spence, 51, 53, 54
    'Jubilee Hymn', 36, 57, 59
    Pig's Meat (periodical), 57
    Property in Land is Every One's Right, 53
    The Real Reading Made Easy (1782), 53
    Restorer of Society to its Natural State, 54
    Rights of Man in Verse (1783), 53
    'Song to be Sung an Hundred Years Hence', 60
    Songbook (propaganda), 36
    Spence's Songs, Part the Second, 55, 211n26
    Supplement to the History of Robinson Crusoe (1782), 53, 57
Spence's Songs, Part the Second (Spence), 55, 211n26
The Spirit of Despotism (Barrell), 20–1
Stafford, Fiona, 167, 220n35, 231n4
Stagg, John, 173, 232n28
Stevenson, Sir John, 159–60
Stowe, David, 80–1, 217n20
Stuart dynasty, 29, 43, 112, 119
Stunt, Timothy, 78, 216n8
suffrage, 33, 181, 187
Summer Fête (Moore), 160
Supplement to the History of Robinson Crusoe (Spence), 53, 57
Sutherland, Elizabeth Leveson-Gower, duchess of, 137
Sutherland, George Leveson-Gower, duke of, 137
Swarley, Richard, 55
Swarley's Club, 55
Sweetnam, Mark S., 27, 216n9–11
Swift, Jonathan, 146–7, 159, 227n22

Taliesin, 6th Century Welsh bard, 65
Taylor, Timothy, 221n44
Tea-Table Miscellany (Ramsay), 96, 219n15
Test Acts, 109
Thelwall, John, 24, 36, 43, 71, 191
    on Burns, 4, 32
    'King Chaunticlere', 75
    'On Song Writing', 39
    trial, 63, 72, 186
    on writing, 39–40

Things as they are; Or, the Adventures of Caleb Williams (Godwin), 155
Thomas Bewick: His Life and Times (Bewick), 52
Thompson, E.P., 190, 192, 232n2
Thomson, George (publisher), 66, 220n20
Thomson, Robert
   'A New Song' in *The Irish Harp*, 70
   parody 'A New Song of 1792', 26, 69
   Tribute to Liberty: or, A New collection of Patriotic Songs, 69, 214n29
Thuente, Mary Helen, 164, 229n26, 230n50
Thumoth, Burke, *Twelve Scotch and Twelve Irish Airs with Variations* (1750), 97
T.K., 'A New song in praise of Colonel Hanson', 191
Tomos Glyn Cothi *see* Evans, Thomas
Tone, Theobald Wolfe, 195, 234n1
Tooke, John Horne, 71, 177, 186
   and treason trial, 63, 71, 214n30
Torrens, Robert
   and the disenfranchised hero, 156–7, 161
   Victim of Intolerance: Or, the Hermit of Killarney, A Catholic Tale (1814), 156, 229n12
Tory party, and Pitt, 186
Trainspotting (Welsh), 173
Transactions of the Royal Irish Academy, 102, 221n43
Trant, Dominick, 107
Travels of an Irish Gentleman in Search of a Religion (Moore), 159, 164
Tribute to Liberty: or, A New collection of Patriotic Songs (Thomson), 69, 214n29
Trinity College Dublin, 77, 142, 202
   and evangelicalism, 82, 85, 216n7–8
Trumpener, Katie, 2, 33, 167, 231n4
Turley, Richard Marggraf, 167, 230n2
Twain, Mark, *Huckleberry Finn*, 173
Twelve Scotch and Twelve Irish Airs with Variations (Thumoth), 97
Twm o'r Nant (Thomas Edwards), 204
Two Acts (1795)
   High Treason Act (1795), 186
   Seditious Meetings Act (1795), 186
Tyrconnel, Richard Talbot, earl of, 98
Tytler, William, 96, 219n16

Uglow, Jenny
   on Bewick, 55, 56
   Nature's Engraver: A Life of Thomas Bewick, 56
Ulster Scots language, 2, 168, 169, 176
Unitarianism, 26, 66, 67, 71, 186, 214n37
United Englishmen, 31, 32, 183, 186–7
United Irishmen, 118
   in Britain, 31, 32, 183
   establishment, 195
   and harp emblem, 116, 195
   in Ireland, 110, 153
   in novels, 157, 229n12
   and songs, 70, 158, 159, 164, 214n31
   and United Englishmen, 31, 32, 183
universalism, 6, 19, 207n17
University of Aberdeen, 26, 202
University of Edinburgh, 202
University of Strathclyde, 202

Vallancey, Charles, 104, 221n38
Vicinus, Martha, and dialect, 189, 190, 234n30
Victim of Intolerance: Or, the Hermit of Killarney, A Catholic Tale (Torrens), 156, 229n12
Victim of Prejudice (Hays), 155
Vidal, Gore, 13, 208n31
A View of the Lancashire Dialect (Bobbin), 175–6
Vishnawatan, Gauri, 200–1, 235n7

Wakefield, Gilbert, 67, 186, 233n18
Walker, John, and Anglicanism, 82–3
Walker, Joseph Cooper, 100, 101, 102, 103, 104, 105
   Historical Memoirs of the Irish Bards (1786), 95, 100, 101, 104
   the Irish language, 100–1, 221n64
   notation 'Provincial Cries' *101*
Walker, Robert, 182–3, 184
   comic dialect, 33
   comic dialogue, 183–4, 189
   defence of Hardy, Tooke and Thelwall, 186
   Navickas on, 32–3
   Plebeian Politics (1801), 32, 182, 191
   Plebeian Politics reprinted (1812), 183
   'Tim Bobbin the Second', 182–3, 233n4

Waller, Edmund, 37
Walmsley, Charles, 120
War of the Austrian Succession, 117
Warner, Marina, 2, 207n4
Warrington Dissenting Academy, 186
Washington i gCeannas a Ríochta (Morley), 110
Waterloo, 20, 115
Watson, J.R.
  The English Hymn, 80, 217n16
  literary value of hymns, 80
Waugh, Edwin, annotation dialect speech, 190
Wellington, Sheena, 5, 207n16
Welsh, Irvine, *Trainspotting*, 173
Welsh ballads, 64, 203–4
Welsh hymns, 26, 67
Welsh language, 204–5
Welsh Language Act (1967), 204
Welsh Societies, 64–5
Wesley, Charles
  hymns and Methodism, 81
  use of secular tunes, 56
West Indies, 10, 11, 49, 171
Whelan, Kevin, 197, 208n21
Whigs ,17, 43, 47, 109, 110
Whyte, Samuel, Irish anthology of poetry, 142, 226n4
Wilkes, John, 109
William the Conqueror, 43
William III, (William of Orange), king, 43
Williamite Wars, 112, 174–5
Williams, Edward *see* Iolo Morganwg
Williams, Margaret (Peggy), 66, 214n30
Williams, William (Pantycelyn), 67
Wilson, Kathleen, on political clubs, 55
Wilson, Michael
  ballad by his son, 187
  ballad 'The Peterloo Massacre', 188
  influence on dialect, 33
  and open air meetings, 187
  radical principles, 33, 187

Wilson family, ballads and songs, 33, 182, 187, 189, 191, 192
Winterbotham, William, 212n2
Wit and Mirth: Pills to Purge Melancholy (Playford), 98, 220n24
Wood, Allen W., 16, 208n37
Wood, S., 'A New Song in Praise of the Weavers', 192
Wordsworth, William, 1, 11, 15, 24, 196
  and dialect, 32, 168
  'Guilt and Sorrow or Incidents upon Salisbury Plain', 10
  memoir by the Female Vagrant, 10
  preface to *Lyrical Ballads* (1800), 38, 167
  The Hidden Wordsworth (Johnston), 21, 208n27
  and 'the real language of men', 167–8
work-condition ballads, 193
World War II, 22
Wright, Daniel
  Aria di Camera (1730), 97
  and Gaelic tunes, 97
Wright, Julia M.
  concept of exile, 31, 229n9
  the 'disenfranchised' hero, 31
  and Drennan, 196
  and Moore's songs, 31
  Romantic scholarship, 30–1
Wright, Thomas (antiquarian) 40
  Political Songs of England, From the Reign of John to that of Edward II (1838), 40
Wyvill, Christopher, 109

Yankee Stadium, 35–6, 209n1
  and 'America the Beautiful', 35–6
  and 'Take Me Out To the Ballgame', 35–6
York, Prince Frederick, duke of, 112
Young Ireland movement, 162, 164
Young, William, 129, 138

Zimmermann, Georges-Denis, 144, 214n31, 227n13–14